12/23

STRAND PRICE
$ 5.00

D1218513

Praise for Award-winning and Best-selling Author
Noah Andre Trudeau

Lincoln's Greatest Journey: Sixteen Days that
Changed the Presidency, March 25 - April 8, 1865

"Trudeau's is a finely-grained study with a rich cast of characters. He weaves together threads of military, political, social, and personal history to create a fascinating chronicle of sixteen unique—and until now largely unexamined—days of Lincoln's presidency."

— Larry Tagg, author of *The Battles that Made Abraham Lincoln*

"*Lincoln's Greatest Journey* presents the gripping story of President Abraham Lincoln's daring and important visit, first to City Point, Virginia, and then on to the Confederate capital in Richmond. After an introductory chapter, Trudeau spends 16 chapters covering 16 days of the Civil War's endgame. The rich detail in this wonderful read, grounded upon many new sources, delicately presents the horror of war, the chaos of war, and the politics of ending a long and bloody civil war. The best of Abraham Lincoln comes through in this insightful new book."

— David Hirsch and Dan Van Haften,
authors of *Abraham Lincoln and the Structure of Reason*

"Trudeau demonstrates great insight by allowing the reader to view this short, but critical, period in Abraham Lincoln's presidency. In this sixteen-day stretch, Lincoln visits City Point to 'participate' in the last days of the Civil War. It is not only relief from the politics and stress of Washington, but a chance for the President to see and meet with his General in Chief, other officers, and especially the troops. It changed the President in a way that was reflected in his evolving policy on how to deal with the Confederates after imminent surrender. His Reconstruction policy was also evolving during this time, and his thoughts on extending some of rights of citizenship to the U.S. Colored troops and their families had become more than an embryo. This is a most worthy addition to the 16,000 volumes written about Lincoln since 1865."

— Frank J. Williams, founding Chair of The Lincoln Forum
and Chair of The Ulysses S. Grant Association and Presidential Library

"Noah Andre Trudeau's *Lincoln's Greatest Journey* is a groundbreaking work that changes our perceptions of this little-known and largely unexplored critical time during the last days of the Lincoln administration. Drawing on a myriad of primary sources and beautifully written in the author's well-known style, Trudeau firmly demonstrates that the final days of the Civil War brought about a transformation in Lincoln and re-energized America's greatest president for the challenges ahead in reconstructing the Union. Unfortunately, his assassination changed the course of American history. This important new work is highly recommended for anyone interested in the end of the Civil War, Lincoln, or Reconstruction."

— Eric J. Wittenberg, author of many Civil War titles including *"The Devil's to Pay!" John Buford at Gettysburg. A History and Walking Tour*, the recipient of the 2014 Gettysburg Civil War Round Table book award

* * *

Bloody Roads South:
The Wilderness to Cold Harbor, May-June 1864
—Winner of the Fletcher Pratt Award—

"A powerful and eloquent narrative. . . . Grant vs. Lee in the Wilderness, at Spotsylvania, and at Cold Harbor has never been told better."

— Stephen W. Sears, award-winning Civil War historian

"Not a formal campaign study, this is a dramatic account told through the eyes of soldiers, civilians and government leaders."

— *Publishers Weekly*

"This popularly written account of the initial months of Grant's decisive Virginia campaign against Lee will find a ready audience among Civil War buffs. Done in the episodic, you-are-there style of such writers as Cornelius Ryan, it rests mainly on a host of published first-hand accounts and regimental histories. Excellent for the general reader and libraries of any size."

— *Library Journal*

The Last Citadel: Petersburg, June 1864 - April 1865

"*The Last Citadel* is most impressive, almost like an account of a newly discovered war. How Trudeau amassed so much fresh material is a wonder. I found the narrative powerful and compelling and the air of authenticity complete. This is the first real Civil War narrative I have read in years."

— Burke Davis (1913-2006), noted Civil War author

"*The Last Citadel* succeeds marvelously at presenting the first full portrait of an immensely important operation, the siege of Petersburg. This is popular history at its finest—grounded in very impressive research, written with literary flair, and filled with new testimony from myriad witnesses whose voices help bring into focus one of the war's most important episodes. *The Last Citadel* merits the attention of anyone seeking to understand the final phase of the war in Virginia."

— Gary W. Gallagher, John L. Nau III Professor in the History of the American Civil War, University of Virginia, and award-winning author

"In the same style as his previous work *Bloody Roads South*, Trudeau provides the reader with an easy-to-understand, month-by-month, topic-by-topic description of one of the lesser-known campaigns of the war. With its easy-to-understand maps, period-artist illustrations, and thought-provoking analysis of the entire military operation, this book will be a must for enthusiasts on all levels of interest."

— Chris Calkins, author of *Battles of Appomattox Station and Appomattox Court House, April 8-9, 1865*

"Trudeau has, with the publication of *The Last Citadel*, enhanced his reputation as a worthy successor to Bruce Catton. Blending his journalistic talents with those of a historian, Trudeau has given us an outstanding overview of the campaign, one that underscores that good history is more exciting and relevant than the best novel."

— Edwin C. Bearss, author of *The Petersburg Campaign: The Eastern Front Battles, June – August 1864* and *The Western Front Battles, September 1864 – April 1865*

"In masterly fashion Trudeau tracks the tactical struggle as Gen. Ulysses S. Grant seeks weak spots in Gen. Robert E. Lee's lines while Lee, forced to spread his smaller army ever more thinly, contests Grant's flanking movements in a series of hard-fought battles. . . . This oft-ignored major campaign of the Civil War receives expert examination here."

— *Publishers Weekly*

"Trudeau salts his narrative with healthy doses of official testimony and soldiers' personal accounts to create a brisk documentary flavor of campfire and war council. [O]ne of the most arresting narratives of any Civil War campaign. This is the stuff of high drama."

— *Library Journal*

Out of the Storm: The End of the Civil War, April-June 1865

"Impressive research and moving prose."

— James I. Robertson, Jr., award-winning author of *Stonewall Jackson*

"In this concluding volume of a trilogy, Trudeau relies on firsthand accounts to tell the compelling story of the Confederacy's death throes. . . . This is a major contribution to the field."

— *Publishers Weekly*

"Trudeau wonderfully concludes his Civil War trilogy by looking beyond Appomattox. It is impossible not to be moved by the graphic descriptions of the sinking of the *Sultana* , the flight of Jefferson Davis, and the last battle of the war in the west. This is a fitting conclusion to a series that masterfully intertwines personal accounts with descriptive narrative. In the words of Lieutenant Colonel Branson upon hearing the last volley: 'That winds up the war.'"

— *Library Journal*

Like Men of War: Black Troops in the Civil War, 1862-1865
Jerry Coffey Memorial Book Prize

"The story of black troops in combat during the Civil War is told comprehensively for the first time, however, in this remarkable history by Trudeau, who takes readers into battle with the U.S. Colored Troops. . . . In an era when standards of manhood were as high as in any other, few whites who saw black troops in action ever again questioned their courage. The legacy was long obscured, but it never disappeared, and its compelling recovery makes this book a major addition to Civil War literature."

— Publishers Weekly

Gettysburg: A Testing of Courage

"Bursting with fresh anecdotes, shrewd analysis, and sterling judgment...."

— Douglas Brinkley, award-winning presidential historian

"Making comprehensive and sophisticated use of a broad spectrum of archival and printed sources, [former] National Public Radio executive producer Trudeau enhances his reputation as a narrative historian of the Civil War with what is to date the best large-scale single-volume treatment of those crucial three days in July 1863, elegantly reconstructing the battle and the campaign from the perspectives of the participants. . . . The operational narratives are remarkable for their clarity."

— Publishers Weekly

"Trudeau skillfully intertwines his narrative with firsthand accounts using letters, diaries, memoirs, and after-action reports from local residents, soldiers, and officers. He unearths many little-known human interest stories and brings to light the trials and tribulations of ordinary people caught in extraordinary circumstances. . . . A monumental work, thoroughly researched and well written, this is the best recent single-volume history of the campaign."

— Library Journal

Southern Storm: Sherman's March to the Sea

"Trudeau, a prize-winning Civil War historian, addresses William T. Sherman's March to the sea in the autumn of 1864. . . . Trudeau praises Sherman's generalship, always better at operational than tactical levels. He presents the inner dynamics of one of the finest armies the U.S. has ever fielded: veteran troops from Massachusetts to Minnesota, under proven officers, consistently able to make the difficult seem routine. And Trudeau acknowledges the often-overlooked contributions of the slaves who provided their liberators invaluable information and labor. The march to the sea was in many ways the day of jubilo, and in Trudeau it has found its Xenophon."

— *Publishers Weekly* (Starred Review)

LINCOLN'S
GREATEST JOURNEY

Sixteen Days that Changed a Presidency
March 24 - April 8, 1865

ALSO BY
NOAH ANDRE TRUDEAU

Gettysburg: A Testing of Courage

Like Men of War: Black Troops in the Civil War, 1862-1865

Out of the Storm: The End of the Civil War, April-June 1865

Bloody Roads South: The Wilderness to Cold Harbor, May-June 1864

The Last Citadel: Petersburg, Virginia, June 1864-April 1865

Southern Storm: Sherman's March to the Sea

Robert E. Lee: Lessons in Leadership

LINCOLN'S
GREATEST JOURNEY

Sixteen Days that Changed a Presidency
March 24 - April 8, 1865

NOAH ANDRE
TRUDEAU

SB

Savas Beatie

California

© 2016 by Noah Andre Trudeau
All maps by author.

All rights reserved. No part of this publication may be reproduced, stored in a retrieval system, or transmitted, in any form or by any means, electronic, mechanical, photocopying, recording, or otherwise, without the prior written permission of the publisher.

First Edition, first printing
ISBN-13: 978-1611213-26-3

Library of Congress Cataloging-in-Publication Data

Names: Trudeau, Noah Andre, 1949- author.
Title: Lincoln's Greatest Journey: Sixteen Days that Changed a Presidency (March 24-April 8, 1865) / by Noah Andre Trudeau.
Description: First edition. | El Dorado Hills, California : California, 2016. | Includes bibliographical references and index.
Identifiers: LCCN 2016017919| ISBN 9781611213263 (hardcover: alk. paper) | ISBN 9781611213270 (e-book)
Subjects: LCSH: Lincoln, Abraham, 1809-1865--Military leadership. | Lincoln, Abraham, 1809-1865--Travel--Virginia--Hopewell. | Virginia--History--Civil War, 1861-1865--Campaigns. | United States--History--Civil War, 1861-1865--Peace. | Civil-military relations--United States--History--19th century. | City Point (Hopewell, Va.)--History, Military--19th century. | Hopewell (Va.)--History, Military--19th century.
Classification: LCC E457.2 .T77 2016 | DDC 973.7092--dc23
LC record available at https://lccn.loc.gov/2016017919

SB

Published by
Savas Beatie LLC
989 Governor Drive, Suite 102
El Dorado Hills, CA 95762

Phone: 916-941-6896
(web) www.savasbeatie.com
(E-mail) sales@savasbeatie.com

Savas Beatie titles are available at special discounts for bulk purchases in the United States by corporations, institutions, and other organizations. For more details, please contact Savas Beatie, P.O. Box 4527, El Dorado Hills, CA 95762, or you may e-mail us at sales@savasbeatie.com, or visit our website at www.savasbeatie.com for additional information.

Proudly published, printed, and warehoused in the United States of America.

Dedicated to Murray Horwitz

– A good friend and Renaissance Man (always with a fine sense of humor).
With deep appreciation for many things over the years, most recently his
unstinting support and sage advice throughout the rough-and-tumble
process of bringing this book to print.

Table of Contents

Table of Contents (continued)

List of Maps

Preface

THE tragic saga of Abraham Lincoln's assassination is profoundly etched in American memory, so much so that a striking story within that story has been all but lost. That inexorable accumulation of small events and ominous portents, building to a point forever frozen in our shared memory, the night of April 14, 1865—a moment that compels our attention as few others. Some 700,000 people annually visit Ford's Theater. New books, films, documentaries, and articles about the president's martyrdom appear just about every year. The image that inevitably dominates this narrative is that of a great man helplessly caught in a fateful vortex, with virtually every aspect of his life in those final weeks viewed through the dark prism of his pending doom. It is a powerful tale, yet one that obscures Lincoln's last and perhaps greatest personal achievement as President of the United States.

For all of his first term and the start of his second, Abraham Lincoln was in a fully reactive mode. "I claim not to have controlled events," he admitted in early 1864, "but confess plainly that events have controlled me." The immense task of prosecuting the war consumed him, and at times it seemed an endless ordeal. It also brought out qualities of leadership that helped define his greatness. Historian Eric Foner, who believes that Lincoln had "grown enormously during the Civil War," identifies some of them as an open-mindedness, a willingness to accept criticism, a firm finger on the people's pulse, and an ability to work with just about anyone to achieve his goals. Lincoln had challenged Congress and the American people at the start of the crisis to "think anew and act anew,"[1] and there's nothing to suggest that he was any less prepared to apply those skills and follow that dictum as the war was ending than he was when it began.

Lincoln's crystal ball was decidedly murky at the beginning of March 1865. As late as his Second Inaugural Address early that month, he was unwilling to predict when the war might end. Some 30 days later everything changed. A new Lincoln emerged, one firmly on a leadership path actively anticipating the postwar era. He was at long last in a position and—equally important—a state of mind to begin to control events. It was a transformation as remarkable as it was unprecedented.

This metamorphosis from a president in time of war to one in time of peace did not—and could not—happen in Washington. It took place in City Point, Virginia, at the headquarters of Lieutenant General Ulysses S. Grant. Lincoln left Washington for what he intended to be a few days away from the Oval Office to rest. Those few stretched into an unprecedented 16, during which the President performed very little of the Chief Executive's business. Instead, he lost himself in the minutiae of a major military campaign, personally witnessed the carnage of combat, came to understand the fears and uncertainties of a defeated society, found a deeper compassion for the aspirations of a long subjugated people, steeled himself to confront the self-inflicted damage and destruction of the war, performed a striking public act of honoring the war's wounded, and, in the end, reset his internal compass to begin to lead the country out of the storm.

This extended period away from Washington demands our attention. Of the 52 days he was out of town during his first term, his longest continuous absence was just eight, and those trips were all business. The prospect of escaping the Executive Mansion to recharge was something many of Lincoln's successors would embrace as absolutely necessary. Dwight D. Eisenhower spent 456 vacation days away from the White House, Lyndon B. Johnson 484, Franklin D. Roosevelt 958, and George W. Bush 1,020. President Lincoln's City Point respite represents his longest time unfettered by the official duties of his office.

It is an inalterable historical fact that the singular trajectory of this new Lincoln ended in his violent death before it had fairly begun. Why, that being the case, does it all matter? It matters because it adds a new piece to the eternally fascinating puzzle that is Abraham Lincoln. It matters because it more fully reveals his determination to lead this nation into a future guided by the principles of "malice toward none . . . charity for all."[2] It matters also because although no one knows precisely what Lincoln would have done in a full second term, his experiences at City Point offer tantalizing clues to some of what might have been. Most important, it signals that the man had changed — and was in the process of changing more — when he returned to Washington after his extended "time out." Such was his greatness, and such is the story told here.

In charting this great Lincoln journey, it is important to pin down details as much as possible. We need to know what he did, when he did it, what he saw, whom he met, what he said, who saw him, what they thought, what they heard. I began my research using the standard template of Lincoln's City Point sojourn; after all, it's a tale that had been told and retold over the years with little variation. I soon realized that the testimonies of the most often cited witnesses to these events were all flawed — some slightly, others substantially. I had to tear down the old edifice and build a wholly new background against which the Lincoln transformation story unfolds. Readers familiar with the basic elements of his activities during this period will note that some celebrated stories have been expunged and the sequence of events is altered in places from the long accepted versions. I have also added new witnesses to Lincoln's visit, many making but brief appearances. Even these little dots, when considered in the aggregate, fill in the picture. Readers interested in the stories behind some of my choices are directed to the "Sources Casebook" at the book's end.

In his immortal Gettysburg speech, Lincoln spoke to the moment and looked to the future. When, 16 months later, he departed Washington for the Virginia front, the nation was still "engaged in a great civil war." He returned from his trip a leader looking ahead to the challenges of bringing the nation its "new birth of freedom." His point of view was forward, not backward, and his purpose was to help the nation reinvent itself, guided by one of his essential principles. As he said: "I hold that while man exists, it is his duty to improve not only his own condition, but to assist in ameliorating mankind; and therefore, without entering upon the details of the question, I will simply say, that I am for those means which will give the greatest good to the greatest number."[3]

The time has come to stop defining Lincoln by the melodramatic manner of his death, and to understand him as a dynamic national leader, hardened and wearied by war, but still capable of personal growth and change. It is my hope that this book is a step in that direction.

THE LINCOLN FAMILY.

Meet the Lincolns: Mary, Robert (in uniform), Tad, and Abraham. LOC

The Grants in early 1865 in front of his headquarters/living quarters cabin at
City Point, Virginia: Ulysses, Jesse, and Julia. LOC

CHAPTER ONE

January - March, 1865

"It was an immense relief to him to be away from Washington."

FOUR years of Civil War had taken a heavy toll of Abraham Lincoln. Friends and colleagues were shocked by the man they now encountered. A Springfield acquaintance visiting in late February 1865, thought that he "looked badly and felt badly—apparently more depressed than I have seen him since he became President," while another at the same time observed that he "appeared to be worn out and almost completely exhausted." "I am very unwell," Lincoln confided to a close acquaintance at this time. A reporter for the Chicago Tribune wrote that many of the president's visitors "were painfully impressed with his gaunt, skeleton-like appearance," while the editor of the New York Tribune described his face as "care-ploughed, tempest-tossed and weatherbeaten." Lincoln was so ill by mid-March that he had to conduct a Cabinet meeting in his bedroom. "I shall never live to see peace," he told Harriet Beecher Stowe at this time, "this war is killing me."[1]

The stresses began with personal matters. His wife, Mary, was continuing to show signs of what later writers would characterize as bipolar disorder: depression, migraines, and obsessive tendencies. Not having the benefit of such a modern analysis, Lincoln feared his wife was going crazy. Atop that were worries about his eldest son, Robert, who was eager to see something of the war in uniform. Father and son were willing, but Mary opposed it. "I am so frightened he may never come back to us," she said. The matter assumed a political dimension when the First Lady was challenged by a New York senator who demanded to know: "Why isn't Robert in the army?"[2] She finally compromised on the arrangement that saw her eldest attached to Lieutenant General Ulysses S. Grant's staff. Though not a field officer, Robert's duties put him in harm's way, and the Lincolns—who had lost a son from illness as recently as 1862—worried about losing another.

Then there were the stresses connected to the Office of the President. Lincoln's reelection once more opened the floodgates for job seekers eager to be rewarded for their efforts on his behalf. He tried to get ahead of the problem by announcing that he would be making very few changes this time around. Still they came, and it seemed to Lincoln that every one "darted at him, and with thumb and finger carried off a portion of his vitality." When he attended a March opera performance in the company of Colonel James Grant Wilson, he explained that he didn't come for the music, "but for the rest. I am being hounded to death by office-seekers, who pursue me early and late, and it is simply to get two or three hours' relief that I am here." He called on a friendly senator from New Hampshire and pleaded, "Can't you and others start a public sentiment in favor of making no changes in offices except for good and sufficient cause? It seems as though the bare thought of going through again what I did the first year here would crush me."[3]

Looming over all of this were the profound stresses of being commander-in-chief in a time of war. Lincoln was not the first American president to govern in wartime, but none of the previous occasions had so pervaded the national fabric as this. No one realized it more than the man whose decisions had sent thousands of young men to their death. Speaking in June 1864, Lincoln explained his perspective in the starkest of terms. "War, at the best, is terrible," he said, "and this war of ours, in its magnitude and in its duration, is one of the most terrible. It has destroyed property, and ruined homes; it has produced a national debt and taxation unprecedented. . . . It has carried mourning to almost every home, until it can almost be said that the 'heavens are hung in black.' Yet it continues."[4]

It speaks to Lincoln's ability to focus on what was important that, despite the distractions, he quietly and patiently pulled strings in early 1865 to assure Congressional approval of the Thirteenth Amendment, abolishing slavery. It further drained him, but he persisted and made full use of the prestige and patronage of the Executive branch to muster the necessary House support. When the vote was called on January 31, 1865, it passed with just three more than the needed two-thirds majority. Lincoln declared it "a great moral victory."[5] In its aftermath, he began thinking more and more about escaping Washington for a while.

Since taking office on March 4, 1861, Abraham Lincoln had been a reluctant and very occasional out-of-town traveler. During his entire first term he had undertaken just 16 trips away from the capital, averaging 3.25 days apiece. These excursions invariably involved either military matters or official appearances. What passed for a rest break were the early summer and late fall weeks (variously from June 1862 to November 1864) that he spent with his family in a house on the grounds of the Soldiers' Home in northeast Washington, an easy three-mile ride from the White House. Even there he was not free from the press of visitors or the need to commute nearly every day to the office to handle necessary matters. With spring military operations in the offing, time away seemed like an unobtainable luxury. Still, he had made no definite decision when an unexpected telegram arrived on March 20, 1865, that made it for him.

Approximately 130 miles south from Washington was City Point, Virginia, known today as Hopewell, just where the Appomattox River entered the James River. Once the clearinghouse for shipping intended for Petersburg (ten river miles distant), since June 1864, it had been the logistical hub for Union forces operating against Richmond and Petersburg. Perched atop a long bluff rising over a busy waterfront and at the point of land thrust between the two rivers was the plantation manor of Dr. Richard Eppes, whose family had occupied the house for more than a century. The current residents had been uprooted when Union troops arrived and the good doctor spent much of the war working as a contract surgeon in a Petersburg Confederate military hospital.

A row of small rustic log cabins (replacing tents in the fall of 1864) stretched out in an orderly line running east of the plantation house. These unassuming habitations represented the command-and-control center for all the armies of the United States. A visitor about this time mused that the "whole place reminds one of a frontier settlement on the skirts of our Indian territories." Near the middle of the line was a two-room structure that doubled as head- and living-quarters for General Grant, who had been general-in-chief for the army's operations since March 1864. Beginning right after January 1, 1865, the cabin was also occupied by Grant's wife, Julia, and their young son, Jesse. Julia described herself as "snugly nestled away" and assured a friend that her general's headquarters "can be as private as a home."[6]

The task of prosecuting the war was Grant's principal, but not his sole, responsibility; even with an abundantly manned War Department in Washington and a modest staff at City Point, the general's days were filled with matters large and small. On the small side, Grant had to intervene in the first three weeks of March for several officers regarding official recognition of their proper ranks, investigate fraud charges laid against an officer at Fortress Monroe, and settle a turf war between the officer commanding in the Baltimore area and the irate railroad president whose trains he was appropriating. A sad personal matter was injected on March 19 when he learned of the death of his oldest sister, Clara, who had passed away thirteen days earlier. His father wrote two letters announcing the fact, the second taking his son to task for his silence. "Your last letter made me feel very badly," Grant told his father.[7]

The list of more significant items requiring his attention that month seemed endless. There were touchy issues regarding the treatment and exchange of prisoners of war, the matter of commodity traders with official Washington passes attempting to move merchandise (mostly tobacco and cotton) between the battle lines, and various military districts needing replacement officers. Important matters to be sure, but they paled in comparison with the decisions Grant had to make every day to keep the prosecution of the war on track.

The essence of Grant's overall plan was to simultaneously press the enemy across the country in as many strategic places as possible, but he found instilling a sense of urgency in distant commanders both a challenge and a frustration. Topping his list of problem people was Major General Edward R. S. Canby, headquartered in New Orleans and charged with capturing the Confederate port of Mobile, Alabama. Grant had wanted it done back in December when Major General William Tecumseh Sherman was beginning his sweep through Georgia, but Canby found reasons to procrastinate. He sidestepped several specific instructions Grant gave him regarding officer appointments and seemed to be spending more time building an infrastructure than organizing an advance. "I am very much dissatisfied with Canby," Grant complained to Secretary of War Edwin M. Stanton on March 14.[8]

Another key officer whose actions fell below Grant's expectations was Major General George H. Thomas. Thomas had delivered a significant victory to the Union in December 1864 at Nashville, but since then he had consistently underperformed, at least in Grant's estimation. Grant did not hesitate to take from Thomas the infantry he needed to support offensives elsewhere. His hope now was that the general would dispatch his ample cavalry in several important raids, but instead of reports of actions accomplished, Grant received a litany of reasons for delay. He vented some of his frustration in a March 16 letter, describing Thomas as "slow beyond excuse."[9] Every dalliance at this critical stage, Grant believed, raised the specter of a long summer of costly operations.

The two shining stars in his constellation were William Tecumseh Sherman and Philip Sheridan. Of the pair, he was closest to Sherman. They shared a biography that included a hardscrabble youth, West Point studies, civilian interludes where failure was a regular visitor, and a feeling that the military life offered the only viable framework for success and recognition. Their personalities, however, were decidedly different. Sherman thought himself more susceptible to doubt than his friend. "I am more likely to change my orders or countermarch my command than he is," explained Sherman. "He uses such information as he has according to his best judgment; he issues his orders and does his level best to carry them out without much reference to what is going on about him and, so far, experience seems to have fully justified him."[10]

Only Sherman could have convinced a skeptical Grant to allow the operation that became known as the "March to the Sea," or that tramping his men overland from Savannah to Virginia was better than waiting for sufficient sea transportation to materialize. Both men grasped the intricacies of modern operational planning, and both had the self-confidence to know when to act and the courage of convictions to act decisively. "To you," Sherman confided to Grant, "I can always unfold my thoughts as one worthy and capable of appreciating the feelings of a soldier and gentleman."[11]

Grant's relationship with Sheridan was different. Grant relied on him to efficiently and effectively accomplish any task given him—just as he trusted Sherman. He knew Sheridan to be a master of the military craft, amply provided with determination, courage, and sheer force of will; unbending in his execution of orders, and ambitious. In many ways he was Sherman without the massive intellectual framework that gave Sherman the confidence to operate independently. Sherman and Grant complemented each other and enhanced each other's skill set; Sheridan always seemed to require an element that Sherman's or Grant's support provided. With their backing he was unstoppable.

Both men had contributed to Grant's anxieties in early March as they disconnected communications in order to carry out their missions. Each was out of contact with higher authorities for days and even weeks as they managed their operations—Sherman somewhere in North Carolina and Sheridan deep in the southern Shenandoah Valley. Grant was reduced to reading Richmond newspapers to glean some evidence of their activities, though the Rebel editors always made it seem as if each had met with disaster. It wasn't until March 12 that he established direct contact with Sheridan, and March 16 with Sherman.

Grant could now finalize his plans to break the Petersburg stalemate and (he hoped) end of the war. He believed that his superior numbers and resources would prevail if he could lever Lee's army out of its entrenchments and transform the situation to a more fluid fight in the open. He had known this since the Petersburg campaign began in June 1864, but now, nearly a year later, everything finally seemed right. He had crafted a battle plan that he believed would get the job done.

Throughout this period Grant's contacts with President Lincoln had been occasional and not always supportive. He complained to Secretary of War Stanton on March 8 that "Rebel prisoners in the North are allowed to take the oath of allegiance and go free," and thought that such a program was wrong. The answer came from Lincoln who admitted that this was happening "in accordance with the rule I proposed." After explaining why he had initiated this policy, Lincoln insisted that "on the whole I believe what I have done in this ways has done good rather than harm." One important constant remained, however, a mutual respect. The same day Lincoln's policy note arrived another went to the White House from Grant recommending the appointment of the son of an army general as a West Point cadet—a request that was promptly honored.[12]

As the days warmed, Grant had been steadily but gently lobbied by his wife to "invite Mr. and Mrs. Lincoln down to visit the army; so many people were coming, and the weather was simply delightful." Julia Grant was motivated by a simple sense of kindness; she had seen several newspaper accounts commenting on the "exhausted appearance of the President" and believed a little time out of the office would do him good. The general wasn't convinced.

"If President Lincoln wishes to come down, he will not wait to be asked," he huffed. "It is not my place to invite him."

"Yes, it is," Julia countered. "You know all that has been said about his interference with army movements, and he will never come for fear of appearing to meddle with army affairs."[13]

Grant still shook his head. Julia now had the happy thought to consult with the one person at City Point who would know for sure. U. S. Grant had received a note from Lincoln not long after the New Year writing "only as a friend" and asking if it would be possible for his 22-year-old son Robert to enter the service as part of Grant's military family "with some nominal rank, I, and not the public, furnishing his necessary means." Grant promptly answered that he would "be most happy to have him in my Military family . . . and I would . . . say give [him] the rank of Captain." He also made it clear that young Lincoln should be paid and treated like any other officer. Robert Todd Lincoln's appointment was finalized on February 11, and he came to City Point shortly after the president's second inauguration. Julia Grant now corralled him, wanting to know "why his father and mother did not come down for a visit."

"I suppose they would, if they were sure they would not be intruding," the young man answered.[14]

Julia promptly renewed the matter with her husband who did something he would never have done as a military man: he capitulated,

CITY POINT, Va., March 20, 1865 — 10 a. m.

His Excellency A. Lincoln,
President of the United States:

Can you not visit City Point for a day or two? I would like very much to see you, and I think the rest would do you good.

Respectfully, yours, &c.
U. S. GRANT,
Lieutenant-General.[15]

That telegram settled Lincoln's thinking about the matter. Although he never explained why he accepted Grant's invitation, there were compelling reasons for him to do so: to make sure that he and Grant were on the same page regarding the military end to the war, to honor the soldiers and sailors for their service and sacrifice, and to clear his mind to confront the multitude of issues that would remain after the fighting stopped. The fact that Lincoln chose to escape Washington by traveling to an active combat area with no urgent matters directing him there speaks to a deeper emotional motivation for his decision. A great and terrible chapter of American history was coming to a close, and the man who decried it as a "mighty scourge of war" needed very much to personally confront the costs, consequences, and future it had bequeathed the country.

He answered Grant's note later the same day:

> Your kind invitation received. Had already thought of going immediately after the next rain. Will go sooner if any reason for it. Mrs. L. and a few others will probably accompany me. Will notify you of exact time, once it shall be fixed upon.[16]

Grant had anticipated a visit by the President alone, but Lincoln's response indicated that a group was involved. It was no problem on Grant's end, but the modification would shortly produce an awkward moment for some eager-to-please naval men.

Lincoln received a follow-up telegram from his eldest son the next day. "Will you visit the army this week?" Robert asked. "We now think of starting to you about One p.m. Thursday," Lincoln replied. "Don't make public."[17] So by March 21 the date and time for the President's departure had been set.

There remained the matter of transportation, which fell to Assistant Secretary of the Navy Gustavus V. Fox, whose manifold duties included organizing V.I.P. water travel. Fox, then on an inspection tour of U.S.N. forces on the James River, had spoken with Grant on the morning of March 20, learned of the invitation extended to Lincoln alone (the President's reply did not arrive until after Fox had departed), and was making plans based on that assumption. He telegraphed Lincoln from Norfolk, promising to be back in Washington the next morning, and offering the services of the very craft he was using, the USS *Bat*, "a regular armed man-of-war and the fastest vessel on the river."[18]

Fox was true to his word and presented himself at the White House on the morning of March 22. With him was the master of the *Bat*, Lieutenant Commander John Sanford Barnes, who was given the honorific rank of "captain" while in charge. The 29-year-old officer was a New Englander whose father was an army brevet major general. Young Barnes became

A late in life image of Captain John S. Barnes, commanding the escort vessel USS *Bat*. He wrote a short, colorful memoir of his time with Lincoln in 1907. *Courtesy of Barnes descendent Susan Hay*

hooked on the smell of sea salt and attended the newly organized Naval Academy at Annapolis, followed by tours of duty on several warships. He returned briefly to the academy as a professor of ethics, studied law, and was looking forward to a civilian career when the war revived his commission. His fine performance during the combined land-sea operations against Fort Fisher in North Carolina led to his assignment commanding the *Bat*, which delivered messages, carried important passengers, and undertook special missions throughout the area patrolled by the North Atlantic Blockading Squadron.

Lincoln was happy to see them. "I'm only a fresh-water sailor and I guess I have to trust to you salt-water folks when afloat," he said by way of starting the conversation. Barnes was proud of his warship. The *Bat* was a steel-hulled, English-built blockade runner about a year old, purchased by the Confederacy and captured by the U.S. Navy on October 10, 1864. At the time of her surrender she was described as a "side-wheel steamer with two masts and two smokestacks." The *Bat* was armed with three cannon and was considered a swift boat. She was rated at 16 knots, but according to her captain "she ran like a deer, sometimes 18 knots per hour."[19]

Barnes and Fox began describing the renovations they planned for the President's trip. The two had spent much of the passage time from Fortress Monroe to Washington deciding how they would modify the *Bat* to convey the President in comfort. As they warmed to their subject it dawned on Lincoln that they had not been told that the travel plan involved more than just him. He interrupted their presentation and, as Barnes recollected, "said that Mrs. Lincoln had decided that she would accompany him to City Point." It was like a dash of cold water. "I was," Barnes later wrote, "in sailor's phrase, taken 'all aback.'"[20] With those words from the President, all the thoughtful planning of the past 12 hours was rendered null and void. Lincoln took them to meet with his wife.

The First Lady greeted them graciously and in her opening small talk mentioned to Barnes a mutual friend, Miss Clara Harris, daughter of New York Senator Ira Harris. Then she got to the point. "I am going with the President to City Point, and I want you to arrange your ship to take me, my maid, and my officer, as well as the President," she said. (Neither Lincoln mentioned that their young son, Thomas, called "Tad", would be coming too, but perhaps that was understood by all.) Fox and Barnes executed a strategic retreat and rejoined Mr. Lincoln who, "in very funny terms . . . translated our difficulties, and Mr. Fox promised the President that he would provide another and more appropriate craft for the transportation of his family."[21]

Assistant Secretary Fox hurried over to the Navy Department, where he learned that the *River Queen*, a commercial passenger steamer previously used by the President, was available, and he instantly arranged for her charter. Barnes returned to the *Bat* to ready the ship to escort the *River Queen*. To make sure they met the President's preferred departure time, Fox instructed the officer in charge of the Navy Yard to have the warship ready to go by noon the next day, March 23.

Captain Barnes afterward recalled his amended mission involving the *River Queen*: "By the orders of the [Navy] Department, I was directed to accompany her, and keep her in convoy, and was placed under the immediate direction of the President and charged with his safe conduct to City Point and return."[22]

The White House was a flurry of activity the next morning. Mary Lincoln supervised the packing, Tad was underfoot, and Abraham Lincoln kept busy clearing paperwork from his desk. He signed and pre-dated a number of minor appointments that would be issued during the coming days. He also remembered to send General Grant confirmation that he was coming—a note he penned in the White House that was then carried to the War Department telegraph office, where it was coded for transmission:

We start to you at One p.m. to-day. May lie over during the dark hours of the night. Very small party of us.[23]

Mary Lincoln also found time to dispatch a note to one of her most intimate confidants, Massachusetts Senator Charles Sumner. An expert in foreign affairs and an outspoken abolitionist (whose sharp tongue sparked a notorious floor rage incident in 1856 when he was nearly beaten to death in the Senate chamber by an enraged South Carolinian), Sumner and Mary engaged in something approaching a political tryst. She welcomed the attentions of such a worldly-wise man, and he enjoyed the access it gave him to the President. Mary had chosen Sumner to be her escort at the second inaugural ball and delighted in sharing confidences with him, as she did now. She informed him of the trip and her hope "that change of air and rest may have a beneficial effect on my good Husband's health."[24] She expected that they would be out of town only a short while and invited Sumner to join her at the opera when they returned, no later than March 29.

It was midday when the Lincoln party bundled into carriages for the short trip to the Sixth Street Wharf where the *River Queen* was waiting. Already on board was the President's personal attendant, Charles Forbes, a convivial Irishman who Lincoln called Charlie. Besides the President, his wife and son, plus an unnamed maid and Forbes, the group was completed by the presence of an army officer personally assigned by Secretary of War Stanton.

Twenty-six-year-old Captain Charles Bingham Penrose was a commissary specialist whose sense of duty was stern enough to get him captured in May 1862 when he remained behind a retreating army to burn extra stores to keep them out of enemy hands. He was exchanged after a short period as a prisoner at Salisbury, North Carolina, and Libby Prison in Richmond, but soon caught typhoid fever, which resulted in his assignment to the Washington home office where Stanton found him. His orders were to remain with the President and his party to see that they were "properly supplied with every accommodation for their comfort and safety," and that their "meals are provided and [there is] suitable attendance."[25] Penrose was to take his directions directly from the President.

A lowering sky lent some urgency to their departure. The temperature was approaching 60 degrees and the clouds thickening with an ugly belt of darkness visible to the west. Moderate breezes were tugging at the President's coattails as the bags and passengers were bundled onto the *River Queen*, where they were greeted by Captain William Bradford, master of the craft. The steamer was not quite a year old, 181 feet long and 28 ½ feet wide at the beam, with two side-wheel paddles and an engine strong enough for

The sidewheeler steamer *River Queen* conveyed the Lincolns
to City Point and shuttled them once there. Mary Lincoln
thought it a most comfortable craft. *Wikimedia Commons*

one observer to call her "very fast and powerful."[26] Lincoln had used her in
early February 1865, when (anchored in Hampton Roads, Virginia) he met
with three Confederate officials in a failed peace conference. The ship was
well appointed and comfortable. The docking lines were cast off about 1:00
p.m. and the *River Queen* nosed into the choppy Potomac.

Grant's invitation had suggested one or two days, but Lincoln had not
settled on any time frame. Mary Lincoln had arranged a tentative opera
outing with Senator Sumner upon their return in six days, suggesting that at
this early stage the President was thinking in terms of a short visit. Yet even
these modest plans were nearly aborted by a violent act of nature.

All that morning a storm front had been building west of the capital as
warm and moist southern air clashed with cooler and dryer northern air. The
arena of conflict became delineated by a skirmish line of thunderstorms that
gradually melded into a dark turbulent squall line that moved purposefully
toward Washington. This was no mere rain event, but a highly volatile mix
of lightning and powerful straight-line winds that had the potential to reach
hurricane force in limited areas. It was more luck than foresight that the
Lincoln party cleared the area before the storm broke with a force that
knocked the war coverage off page one in the next day's newspapers.

Stanton and his wife had hoped to see the President depart but arrived
too late. They prudently sought the nearest shelter as the destructive winds
slammed into the city. The *Daily National Republican* reported on March 25
that the "terrible gale which passed over the city yesterday, blew down signs,
trees and lamp-posts. Awnings were torn off, houses uprooted, and for a

Captain Charles Penrose was assigned by the War Department to accompany Lincoln to City Point. He was present throughout Lincoln's visit, but wrote little regarding his experiences.

Leach, *History of the Penrose Family of Philadelphia*

while a perfect hurricane prevailed." The storm resulted in widespread damage to the Navy Yard, at least two people died across the city because of the storm, and one river boat, the *Medora*, anchored near the Sixth Street dock "was lifted up and capsized."[27] Fortunately those on board were rescued.

It was 1:15 p.m. when the *River Queen* drew abreast of the USS *Bat* off Giesboro Point. The larger (by 49 feet) warship took station just behind the civilian craft as the pair moved south and east with all dispatch, putting as much distance as possible between themselves and the roiling cloud masses charging in from the west. In 45 minutes they were passing Mount Vernon off the starboard side with near gale force wind gusts coming from astern and the temperature down some ten degrees. It is probable that the storm line had arrived in the form of a backward letter C, a formation that would come to be called a bow echo. It was moving southwest to northeast, putting the worst of it in the city and north of it, kicking strong but limited bursts of energy along the Potomac River.

There is no evidence that either the *Bat* or *River Queen* was ever in any distress, though it must have been a stomach churning ride for a while. They had covered some 53 miles by 5:00 p.m. when the Upper Cedar Point Light was logged by the *Bat's* deck officer. The winds had dropped to a fresh breeze, and the outside temperature even nudged up a few degrees. Still, everyone was feeling the effects of the rocking and swaying produced by the storm swells.

Sunset occurred at 6:23 p.m. with twilight lingering another hour. The sun had just dipped below the horizon when the convoy steamed past Blakistone's Island, about 79 miles from Washington. The wind was down

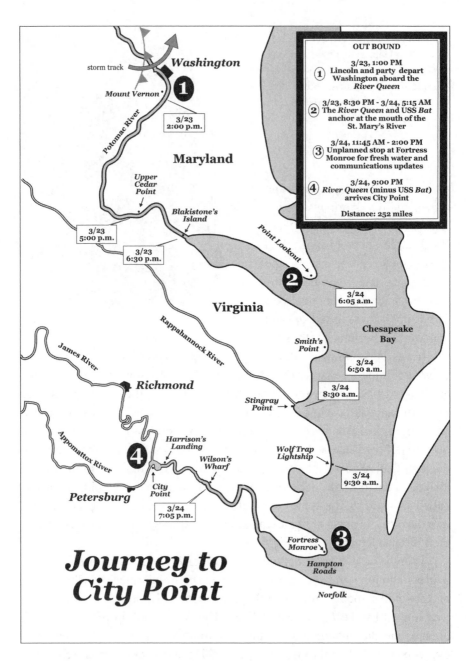

Journey to City Point

(Map labels:)

storm track
Washington
Mount Vernon
1
3/23 2:00 p.m.
Potomac River
Maryland
Upper Cedar Point
Blakistone's Island
3/23 5:00 p.m.
3/23 6:30 p.m.
Point Lookout
2
3/24 6:05 a.m.
Virginia
Rappahannock River
Smith's Point
Chesapeake Bay
3/24 6:50 a.m.
James River
3/24 8:30 a.m.
Richmond
Stingray Point
Appomattox River
Harrison's Landing
4
Wilson's Wharf
Wolf Trap Lightship
3/24 9:30 a.m.
Petersburg
City Point
3/24 7:05 p.m.
Fortress Monroe
3
Hampton Roads
Norfolk

OUT BOUND

3/23, 1:00 PM
① Lincoln and party depart Washington aboard the *River Queen*

3/23, 8:30 PM - 3/24, 5:15 AM
② The *River Queen* and USS *Bat* anchor at the mouth of the St. Mary's River

3/24, 11:45 AM - 2:00 PM
③ Unplanned stop at Fortress Monroe for fresh water and communications updates

3/24, 9:00 PM
④ *River Queen* (minus USS *Bat*) arrives City Point

Distance: 252 miles

to steady breezes and the temperature nudging the low 50s. A later biographer of Tad Lincoln asserted that during the voyage the boy had access to all parts of the *River Queen* and explored it from bow to stern, something an active child would do when it was too stormy to be on deck.

Mary Lincoln later said that during this time her husband "was almost boyish in his mirth and reminded me of his original nature, what I had always remembered of him, in our own home—free from care, surrounded by those he loved so well and by whom he was so idolized."[28]

At 8:00 p.m. the convoy passed a slower guard boat heading to her station at the mouth of the St. Mary's River, and the *Bat's* deck officer exchanged a few words with the other skipper. Thirty minutes later the two steam ships reached the wide river entrance and anchored close together. Nighttime navigation along rivers or close to shore was always tricky, and with no urgency to the journey Captain Bradford prudently decided to hold up until dawn. The Potomac was quite broad here, and any sight of the Virginia shore was lost in the night's cover. Nevertheless, precautions were taken. Arms were issued to the lookouts aboard the *Bat*, who kept vigil while the Lincolns and their companions turned in for the night.

Slightly more than 20 miles west of where the Lincolns were sleeping was the birthplace of Robert E. Lee, who was on the receiving end of plenty of bad news this day. A distressing report had reached the Confederate general's headquarters outside Petersburg from General Joseph E. Johnston, commanding the forces opposing the advances of Sherman's armies in North Carolina. Up until now the distant enemy had been operating in two battle groups; Sherman's pushing northward through the central part of the state, while a second force under Major General John M. Schofield held coastal areas. It had been a part of Johnston's assignment to keep those two from uniting, but the fellow Virginian wrote that he had failed. Not only were the two groups now linked, but Sherman's larger and more potent command had established a secure supply line through Schofield's areas of control. "Sherman's course cannot be hindered by the small force I have," Johnston warned. "I can do no more than annoy him."[29]

Lee also had reports tracking the progress of Sheridan's cavalry, which was approaching the Richmond-Petersburg area after ravaging the Shenandoah Valley. It was capable of anything, from a direct attack on the Confederate capital to a junction with Grant's armies. If the latter, Lee fully expected Grant to deploy this highly mobile force against his overextended right flank, which terminated several miles southwest of Petersburg. He promptly alerted his army commanders north of the James River (Lieutenant General James Longstreet and Major General Fitzhugh Lee) to the danger and ordered them to be ready for anything.

Nearly four years of constant and arduous campaigning had brought Lee —arguably then the South's greatest military leader—to a personal nadir. Following his failure to win a decisive military victory at Gettysburg in 1863, he had dedicated himself and his army to buying time for a political process to win for the Confederate States what he could not produce on the battlefield. A fateful meeting with Confederate President Jefferson Davis in early March 1865 made plain that there was no viable political course to peace—at least none that Davis would endorse. His sole course of action was to make it starkly clear to Southerners that the only choices on the table were to accept unconditional surrender or to continue the struggle for independence. Given such options, Davis believed there would be a rebound in patriotic fervor that would restock his armies with men and stiffen resistance to U.S. incursions. Lee was far less sanguine and anticipated a future that embroiled his army in endless combat against impossible odds with no real hope of influencing events.

Ever the master planner, Lee decided even before his fateful meeting with Davis to develop a military option to break the stalemate at Petersburg long enough to preserve his army. He turned to one of his youngest, newest, and imaginatively boldest corps commanders, 33-year-old Major General John B. Gordon, to devise something to give his army enough running room to escape the earthworks that bound them to the Cockade City as securely as chains pinioned a slave.

Lee summoned Gordon early on a cold morning in early March just before his conference with the Confederate President. "I shall never forget the scene," Gordon wrote. "The General was standing at the fireplace, his head on his arm, leaning on the mantelpiece—the first time I ever saw him looking so thoroughly dejected."[30]

Lee's reluctance to discuss broad military matters with subordinates was legendary, but this early morning he held nothing back from Gordon. He detailed in brutally frank terms the greatly weakened condition of the Confederate army, the sad state of its logistics, the enemy's great strengths, and the dismal overall strategic picture. The situation, as Gordon later admitted, was "infinitely worse than I had dreamed it was." The Georgian quickly got over his shock and proffered some options. One was to negotiate (a non-starter), another was to immediately abandon Petersburg and Richmond (politically impossible), and a third was to hit the enemy hard. Lee asked Gordon to think more about it for the discussion they would have after he returned from Richmond. The subordinate departed with the sense that "the sooner we fight the better, for every day weakens us and strengthens our opponents."[31]

Lee left Petersburg the next day hoping against hope that Jefferson Davis would have some viable political initiatives up his sleeve. He didn't, and so when Lee next spoke to Gordon it was to have him work up a plan of action to strike the enemy. The Georgian threw himself into the task; he and his staff prowled the lines, spoke with officers who knew the ground, and even questioned recent Union deserters. Hours were spent viewing the distant fortifications. Gordon delivered his preliminary report on March 10. Lee listened with great care as the young officer laid it out before him.

The initial target Gordon had selected for a dawn assault was Fort Stedman. The Union bastion was at a point where the opposing earthworks were close—just some 200 yards apart. Besides the strength of the fort itself with its supporting trench network and flanking artillery batteries, the Federal position was guarded by a strong belt of wooden obstructions, and there were additional strong points behind it, making for a real defense in depth. To overcome it, Gordon proposed an audacious and imaginative strike package.

Leading his assault would be an advance party of 50 axmen whose job was to open up passageways through the protective screen. Right behind them would come 100 more soldiers with unloaded rifles and bayonets who were to suppress the enemy's advance picket posts and then, in company with the ax men, swarm into Fort Stedman. Hard on their heels were to be three 100-man squads with instructions to press into the enemy's rear area, spread panic, and capture three small bastions that Gordon's long-distance observation had identified. Behind them would be the bulk of the assault force, slightly more than 17,000 men, a mix of infantry and cavalry.

Once the first wave of infantry had solidified the breakthrough, the "cavalry was to gallop to the [enemy's] rear, capture the fugitives, destroy the pontoons [across the Appomattox River], cut down the telegraph wires, and give me constant information, while the next infantry wave was to move rapidly down Grant's lines, attacking and breaking his division[s] in detail, as they moved out of his trenches." Gordon told Lee that his plan offered a "tremendous possibility . . . [for] the disintegration of the whole left wing of the Federal army, or at least the dealing of such a staggering blow upon it as would disable it temporarily, enabling us to withdraw from Petersburg in safety."[32] Lee agreed to move forward with preparations for the attack, with a final decision scheduled for the night of March 23.

As the clock ticked down, Gordon began carefully and secretly amassing the assault force. The special units had to be designated and instructed in their duties, key officers had to be briefed about their part in the whole, and a few ruses had to be devised. Gordon made it a point to learn the names of the Yankee officers in charge of the sectors to be attacked and told his special infiltration groups to use their names as authority to pass in the dark. Others would take advantage of the Federal policy of paying for deserters' weapons by announcing to the Union pickets that they were coming in with their guns and, once in close, capturing or killing them. Strips of white muslin were distributed among the soldiers detailed in the initial phase to help identify them in the dark as comrades. (Gordon's wife helped prepare them.)

Not long before the Lincoln party was settling in for the night aboard the *River Queen*, John Gordon arrived at Lee's headquarters for the final decision regarding the surprise attack on the Union lines. The Georgia general, who had already taken part in some highly dramatic battlefield conferences, always remembered this one as "the most serious and impressive in my experience." Lee reviewed Gordon's plan one final time and found no flaws. He expressed the hope that casualties could be kept to a minimum. Then, Gordon recalled, with "full recognition by both the commander and myself of the hopelessness of our cause if we waited longer on General Grant's advance, and also of the great hazard in moving against him, the tremendous undertaking was ordered."[33]

Anyone looking at Gordon's battle maps could not have helped but notice that if the "tremendous possibility" was fully realized Confederate units would be poised for a direct strike at the grand prize: the filled-to-bursting Union supply warehouses at City Point.

Even as Gordon's battle orders began filtering into the Confederate chains-of-command, the crew of the *River Queen* and their distinguished guests were stirring. The steamship and her escort, the USS *Bat*, got underway at 5:15 a.m., soon putting the St. Mary's River behind them. A stop at Fortress Monroe (83 miles distant) had not been planned, but two matters necessitated an itinerary change. The President was feeling somewhat queasy, a condition he blamed on the ship's tainted drinking water. He also mentioned to Mary a dream he had had that the White House had been damaged by the recent storm. The First Lady insisted they stop so she could telegraph Washington to learn if the President's vision had been prophetic.

The *Bat's* log keepers charted their progress as the ships steamed southward. At 6:05 a.m. they passed Point Lookout, Maryland; at 6:50 a.m. Smith's Point, Virginia, was logged and the vessels entered the Chesapeake Bay. At 8:30 p.m. Stingray Point, Virginia, was observed; at 9:30 a.m. the Wolf Trap Lightship was spotted; and at 11:45 a.m. the *Bat* came to anchor in Hampton Roads near Fortress Monroe, while the *River Queen* docked at the wharf. The skies were cloudy and the wind breezy, with the temperature approaching 50.

There's no indication that President Lincoln left the ship. It is more likely that Captain Penrose went ashore to see to the water exchange and to visit the telegraph office, where he was handed a message for the President from the Secretary of War. Penrose sent one of his own to his chief indicating that except for the President's slight indisposition, everyone was fine. Mrs. Lincoln also had some business which she seems to have handled herself. She sent a telegram to the Executive Mansion housekeeper demanding to know if everything was "right at the house." She marked her note "answer immediately."[34]

Once back on board the *River Queen* Captain Penrose passed along Stanton's note, which was time dated 8:45 p.m. the previous day. It mentioned just missing the President's departure, described some of the effects of the "furious gale," and reported no news received "from any quarter." Also at this time U. S. Grant was updated on the President's progress, for, according to Captain Barnes, the convoy's stop at Fortress Monroe was "for telegraphic communications with Washington and General Grant."[35]

All this activity consumed perhaps an hour, but the *River Queen* remained tied to the dock as there was a delay in supplying the President with fresh water. The newly appointed post quartermaster, Major William L. James, was livid about his subordinate's failure to quickly resolve the matter and promised the President he would take the man to task. This prompted Lincoln to intercede on behalf of an officer he didn't even know, an act of kindness typical of the man. "I am not at all impatient," Lincoln wrote the quartermaster, "and hope Major James will not reproach himself or deal harshly with the officer having the matter in charge. Doubtless he, too, has met some unexpected difficulty."[36]

The water finally appeared in large, narrow-necked bottles, described by Captain Barnes as "demijohns." It was around 2:00 p.m. when the *River Queen* shoved off from the wharf and, dutifully shadowed by the *Bat*, steamed into the James River. According to another traveler who passed along here about the same time, the lower James "is broad but shallow, with a winding channel and low banks."[37] City Point was 69 miles upstream.

The person most central to Lincoln's visit, Lieutenant General Ulysses S. Grant, spent much of this day preparing his army to move against Petersburg. He had tentatively set March 29 for operations to commence and he sent a long message to Major General George G. Meade (commanding the Army of the Potomac) with instructions for the coming offensive. Days, even weeks, of planning were reflected in the myriad details it addressed, including what to do in the event the enemy suddenly abandoned his lines. No mention was made of any possible Confederate spoiling action.

A key element of Grant's plan depended upon the arrival of Phil Sheridan's cavalry. The horsemen had yet to cross the James and Appomattox rivers, so Grant sent advisories to make certain that commanders north of City Point knew what was happening and what was expected of them when the cavalry forces arrived.

It was probably after 2:00 p.m. when, according to Grant's aide Lieutenant Colonel Horace Porter, "word came that . . . [Lincoln] was on his way up the James aboard the *River Queen*."[38] Only then did the lieutenant general allow himself to review the itinerary his staff had drafted for Mr. Lincoln's visit to the front. No one anticipated that there would be any need to modify the plans for March 25.

The weather was cooperating for the President's journey up the James River, but the *Bat's* engines were balking. Not an hour underway from Fortress Monroe and the warship had to signal the *River Queen* to slow down as she was experiencing problems. Water was foaming in her boilers, squirting a denser fluid into the steam pipes, which reduced the engine's power output. This had happened before, generally when the ship went from salt water to fresh water or vice versa. The fact that Captain Barnes did not order the vessels to halt suggests it was something his engineers could manage, although he reduced the convoy's speed.

The course of the James from its mouth to City Point could be a dangerous stretch of river. The Federal investment of Richmond and

Petersburg was far from airtight, and there were plenty of areas where Confederates could move in and out of the cities without challenge. It had happened before that a small mounted force with a horse battery had slipped past the loose Union patrols to set up an ambush along the banks of the James. It was a rare occurrence so no thought had been given to establishing regular convoys, but the fact that it had happened at all was enough to keep the *Bat's* crew on full alert as the two normally fast vessels chugged slowly up the river.

Lincoln spent a little of the time reading the rest of Stanton's chatty message sent to Fortress Monroe. The Secretary reported that the War Department's solicitor, William Whiting, had tendered his resignation which, barring a dissenting opinion from the President, Stanton was inclined to accept. One of the candidates to replace him, James E. Yeatman, was known to Grant and the Secretary wanted Lincoln to ask about him. Stanton closed his note with a flash of humor that the President must have appreciated: "I would be glad to receive a telegram from you dated at Richmond before you return."[39] What was intended as a joke between colleagues would prove to be prophetic.

It took five hours to cover the fifty miles to Wilson's Wharf, with the *Bat's* deck officer charting the passing at 7:05 p.m. It was here, less than a year ago, that United States Colored Troops (USCT) had resisted Rebel efforts to interdict the Union supply line. It had been a small action as those things went, but the pride felt by those present had been palpable. "That the black men will fight is an established fact," wrote one.[40] Lincoln, whose Emancipation Proclamation had excluded African-Americans from combat roles, had come to realize after a series of such military actions that he might have underestimated the fighting qualities of black soldiers.

Once they drew abreast of Wilson's Wharf the Presidential party was about twenty miles from City Point.

March 24 had proven to be a quiet day along the Federal trench lines east of Petersburg, especially near Fort Sedgwick. Things were so placid, related a member of the 7th Rhode Island, that officers started up a baseball game "on the stumpy slope in rear of the fort." The day's principal activity was to "lie around as convenient, basking in the sunshine and watching fleecy clouds as they float across the ethereal blue."

Like many men and officers of the Union army in front of Petersburg, those in the 7th had been cheered by good news from other fronts and encouraged by what they could see happening behind the enemy lines. They had noticed several fires and the sight of "men running to and fro about them, which suggests the thought that perhaps the rebs are preparing to evacuate Petersburg."[41] No one was expecting any trouble.

The *River Queen* reached City Point around 9:00 p.m. She was unaccompanied at that time, the USS *Bat* having halted six miles below at Harrison's Landing. Captain Barnes likely took advantage of the first opportunity to undertake the boiler adjustments necessary to get the ship back up to full power. The President's craft was directed to the dock used by Grant, forcing the general's headquarters boat, the *Carrie Martin*, to haul off a short distance and anchor.

Waiting for the President and First Lady was their uniformed son, who came aboard to greet his parents and younger brother. There had been emotional distance between oldest son and father during the early years of the presidency, largely because Abraham Lincoln had his hands full and Robert was in that awkward age of self-discovery. The two had become more comfortable with each other by 1864. When Robert graduated from Harvard that year a regretful President couldn't attend the ceremony, but Mary and Tad were there. Robert decided on his own and without any parental pressure to continue his law studies, prompting his father to joke that "you will probably make more money at it than I ever did, but you won't have half the fun."[42]

Captain Lincoln returned ashore after the brief personal visit and escorted General and Mrs. Grant to the dock. "Our gracious President met us at the gangplank, greeted the General most heartily, and, giving me his arm, conducted us to where Mrs. Lincoln was awaiting us," recollected Julia Grant. There would have been pleasantries exchanged and light conversation about their journey. "Now," announced President Lincoln, "I am going to leave you two ladies together while the General and I go for a few moments to my room where we can have a little talk without being interrupted."[43]

This first meeting of current and future First Ladies was not a propitious one, as Mrs. Lincoln lapsed into her imperious persona. According to Mrs. Grant, her first impulse was to sit beside the First Lady as they talked, but the surprised look from Mrs. Lincoln caused her to draw back. "I crowd you, I fear," she said. Mary Lincoln answered that it wasn't the case, but after a few minutes of conversation, Julia Grant eased off the sofa and onto a nearby chair, later saying that it was all a "very awkward mistake on my part."[44]

In decided contrast, the meeting of General Grant and Mr. Lincoln went well. Lincoln mostly listened as the officer filled him in on the current situation and while neither man left any record of what was said, Grant likely recycled comments he had made in recent days. "The weather is now fair," he had explained to a visitor just 24 hours earlier, "the roads are well settled, and the army here is in splendid condition for service." He was confident that they would be "able to wind up matters about Richmond soon."[45]

Lee's demoralized forces were hemorrhaging men and Grant guessed that desertions were costing the Confederate general the equivalent of a regiment every day. "It was a mere question of arithmetic to calculate how long they could hold out while that rate of depletion was going on," he had said. Grant's biggest fear was that Lee would break out to the south to join up with Rebel forces operating in North Carolina under General Joseph E. Johnston. The sooner he could strike at Lee here the better, and Grant believed that the spring campaign he had planned "would close the war."[46]

Grant undoubtedly mentioned the troop review planned for the next day. Lincoln asked for Grant's opinion regarding James E. Yeatman's candidacy for the job of War Department solicitor. Their conversation eased into an incident that had put a strain on their relationship: the unsuccessful Hampton Roads Peace Conference. When three Confederate commissioners appeared unannounced at a Union checkpoint in late January 1865 seeking passage to Washington to confer with Lincoln, Grant had held them at City Point while he conferred with the White House. They purported to be empowered to discuss a peace between the two sides, but Lincoln rightly suspected that his key condition—a reunion of the states—would not be on the agenda. This was confirmed by an administration advance man sent to interview them, but Grant intervened when it appeared the talks would collapse before they began. He spoke with the commissioners, came away convinced that they had negotiating room to maneuver, and urged Lincoln to come.

That was enough for the President, who made the difficult winter passage and at Fortress Monroe joined up with Secretary of State William Seward. The meeting had convened aboard the *River Queen* on February 3, but the talks quickly went nowhere as the Confederate commissioners lacked the authority even to bring up the topic of reunification. Lincoln later paid a political price for making the effort, which he partly deflected by spotlighting Grant's role in promoting it. Now, to ease any tension between them, he told Grant a story about one of the commissioners, the Confederate Vice President Alexander Stephens, a famously thin man, who arrived well bundled against the elements. Lincoln, Grant recalled, asked him if he "had seen that overcoat of Stephens's. I replied that I had. 'Well,' said he, 'did you see him take it off?' I said yes. 'Well,' said he, 'didn't you think it was the biggest shuck and the littlest [corn] ear that ever did you see?'"[47]

A witness watching them return from the meeting (likely Captain Penrose) thought that "Mr. Lincoln appeared particularly happy." Grant now understood that the President "was really most anxious to see the army, and be with it in its final struggle. It was an immense relief to him to be away from Washington."[48]

It must have been approaching 11:00 p.m. when the official welcoming visit ended. It had been a long day for everyone. Grant and his wife took their leave, while the Lincolns retired to their bedrooms. With the ship now a gently rocking platform, no one had any problem falling asleep. A small guard detail watched over the President's boat from the dock area. "We were there seeing nobody disturbed him," recalled one of those sentries.[49]

When the Grants returned to their cabin there were no messages requiring the general's attention and none he had to send. All was quiet along the Union lines at Petersburg.

Many of the forces designated for Major General John B. Gordon's surprise attack were forbidden to approach the front until after dark, in order to maintain operational secrecy. Still, preparations had to begin during the day and more than one soldier began to suspect that there was a battle ahead of them.

A North Carolina infantry captain named Henry A. Chambers grew suspicious when his unit, the 4th North Carolina, and all the other regiments making up Brigadier General Matthew Ransom's division, massed in an open field some nine miles west of Fort Stedman in ranks for a review, or at least that is what they were told. Nothing happened for some time, after which the men were marched back to their camps. Chambers shrugged it off as the left hand not knowing what the right was doing. It didn't occur to him that assembling the men in one place and holding them there for much of the day prevented deserters from bringing word of Lee's buildup to Federal interrogators.

Captain Chambers and his men received orders soon after returning to their camp "to hold ourselves in readiness to move at eight P.M." At this point the officer still didn't know if they were going to attack or retreat. When darkness fell, Chambers realized that Ransom's men weren't the only ones on the move. "No one knew our destination," he reflected. "Many were the conjectures."[50]

It was eerie as the various columns transited Petersburg on their way to the battle site, "the movement of armed bodies through it almost as noiseless and shadowy as the flitting of ghosts, while the strokes of the neighboring clocks sounded on the still night air like the tolling of funeral bells." When the ranks had formed in the 49th North Carolina, the men couldn't help but notice that their commanding officer seemed "scared half to death." Chambers reckoned that either they had to "repel an assault which our Generals felt sure would be made, or we were going ourselves to attack the enemy. On reaching a point near our works we learned that the latter was the business on hand." His observation was seconded by a South Carolina captain who said that they "all agreed on one point, that it meant a fight."[51]

Gordon felt a fierce pride in his tattered warriors as he watched the various combat units file quietly into their staging areas. "They were not mere machine soldiers," he reflected. "They were thoughtful men, with naturally keen perceptions sharpened by long experience in actual war. They well knew that the order [to mass behind Colquitt's Salient] meant more suffering, more fighting, more slaughter; yet, if their conduct and assurances are trustworthy witnesses, these men were prepared for any additional sacrifices."[52]

In all, slightly more than 17,000 men were being concentrated to attack the thin ribbon of Union line fronting Fort Stedman. All the evidence Gordon had seen indicated that the predawn attack would come as a complete surprise to the Yankees.

Chapter Two

Saturday, March 25, 1865

"He typified the very Union itself."

ALL was quiet aboard the *River Queen*. It was approaching 3:30 a.m., March 25, when General Gordon stood atop the breastworks fronting the targeted Union lines with, as he later recalled, "no one at my side except a single private soldier with rifle in hand, who was to fire the signal shot for the head-long rush."[1]

Either crouching expectantly in the trenches behind him or crowded into the deep ravine directly in the rear of the position were the troops selected for the desperate attack—virtually all of Gordon's corps, with two brigades from Bushrod Johnson's division ready for close support, and two brigades from Cadmus Wilcox's division on call. The few units in Gordon's command that were not directly involved in the attack were thinly spread to cover the trenches that had been held by his entire corps. Gordon was also expecting reinforcements from George Pickett's division of Longstreet's corps, then north of the James River.

The men selected for the storming parties waited tensely for the go signal. Louisiana soldiers from Colonel Eugene Waggaman's brigade would pave the way for the rest of Clement Evans's division. "On account of the bravery of your troops, you will be head of column," Evans informed Waggaman, adding, "and charge with unloaded arms." North Carolina axmen were to clear an opening in the Federal barrier of sharpened wooden stakes to make a path for the storming party from James Walker's division. Walker tapped two Virginians to lead the 100-man detachment, officers "personally known to me to be the bravest of the brave, and in whom the men had confidence."[2]

Bryan Grimes's division made up the last of the three attack columns employed in the assault's opening phase. Screening the advance of this command were Georgia sharpshooters under Captain Joseph P. Carson, who was surprised to find his sole surviving brother, Bob, crouched among them. "He did not belong to my command," Carson later explained, "but was serving as courier for General Phil Cook." Captain Carson had no illusions about his prospects of surviving the upcoming action and bluntly told his brother so. "He admitted that he, too, believed that I would be killed, and, for that reason, he was going with me in order to bring back my body. What could I say then? Nothing!"[3]

John Gordon noticed some Confederate obstructions that had not yet been removed. He ordered them cleared away and then froze in horror as the working party's efforts aroused the suspicion of a nearby Yankee picket.

"What are you doing over there, Johnny?" the wary Federal called. "What is that noise? Answer quick or I'll shoot."

Gordon's mind went blank, but the common soldier alongside him kept his wits. "Never mind, Yank," he called. "Lie down and go to sleep. We are just gathering a little corn. You know rations are mighty short over here." The Union guard yelled back his okay. Seconds seemed like hours as the offending obstructions were removed.

"Fire your gun," Gordon ordered the quick-witted soldier. This time, however, the man hesitated, unwilling to return the Union picket's favor with treachery.

"Fire your gun, sir," Gordon repeated.

The solider came to a decision. "Hello, Yank!" he called. "Wake up; we are going to shell the woods. Look out; we are coming." Then, honor satisfied, he fired the signal shot.[4]

Division commander James Walker watched his men disappear into the predawn gloom. "The cool, frosty morning made every sound distinct and clear," he recollected, "and the only sound heard was the tramp! tramp! of the men as they kept step as regularly as if on drill." Private Henry London, in Grimes's Division, never forgot how the storming party "with unloaded muskets and a profound silence, leaped over our breastworks, [and] dashed across the open space in front."[5]

At least one Yankee picket escaped to spread the alarm despite all Gordon's precautions. Standing in the wake of his advancing storming party,

James Walker could hear the frightened man shouting, "The Rebels are coming! The Rebels are coming!"[6]

The combat around Colquitt's Salient began in darkness, so there was no artillery employed on the Rebel side, and the first positions overrun were Federal gun pits, keeping those cannon silenced as well. The tumult was limited to men shouting and hand-guns firing—sounds that did not carry far. No one aboard the *River Queen*—Lincoln, his family, his escorts—heard anything unusual in the morning air, nor was there any alarm at City Point. An easy horseback ride from where the President slept, thousands of men fought hand-to-hand, some to the death.

The opening phase of Gordon's assault unfolded much as designed. The initial objectives were the Union picket posts dotted across the front to alert the main line if trouble was brewing. Most fell without doing their job thanks to a mix of Rebel stealth and subterfuge. Along a section just north of Fort Stedman, North Carolina Lieutenant James Edmondson stage-managed a deadly charade. Chasing behind his leading men he called out: "O boys, come back! Don't go." According to another Tar Heel, "This fooled the enemy in the advance rifle pits into believing it to be a column of deserters, and they allowed the Confederates to approach without firing on them."[7] Not all the Yankees were so gullible, and in some cases the resistance was sharp, but the determined Rebels prevailed and within minutes the picket line had been eliminated along a half-mile stretch of the Union line.

Behind these groups came the men with axes, who frantically chopped and pulled at the Federal obstructions, clearing openings for the storming parties on their heels, determined to take Fort Stedman. The Yankee garrison soldiers kept their cannon loaded for just such a circumstance and managed to fire almost a dozen rounds at the Confederate line. However, many of the enemy poured into the enclosure from the sides, and for several minutes desperate men fought at close range. One of the New York cannoneers caught in the fray later admitted that all "of this was done so quickly and skillfully that the surprise to the Union troops was simply shocking."[8] Fort Stedman passed into Rebel hands; the first important operational goal had been achieved in about 15 minutes.

John B. Gordon's plan next identified two objectives. Even as units of picked men began to infiltrate from Fort Stedman into the Union camps and secondary lines, others moved to secure the outer edges of the Confederate

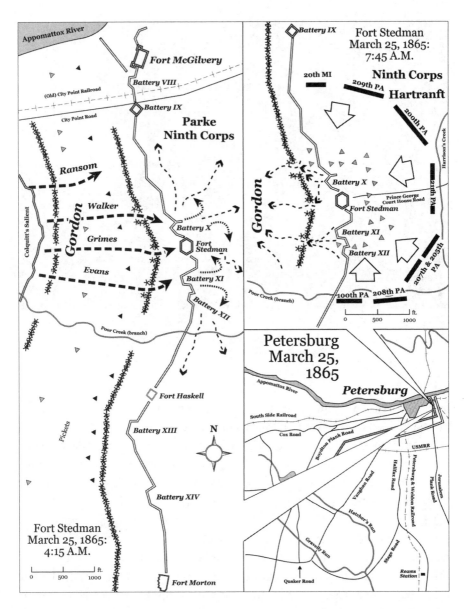

penetration. The Union line at Fort Stedman bowed eastward so that the attackers were actually beyond two powerful artillery positions on either side of the breach: Battery IX to the north and Fort Haskell to the south. Unless both could be quickly neutralized Gordon's men would have enemy cannon firing into them from the flanks and rear. With full dawn just 30 minutes away, determined Rebel units moved to silence those positions. Observing these events unfold, the operation's master planner allowed

The interior of Fort Stedman, photographed about a month after the battle. In the early
hours of March 25 this spot roiled with hand-to-hand combat, not quite ten
miles from where Lincoln slept. LOC

himself a brief moment of satisfaction. "Up to this point," declared Gordon,
"the success had exceeded my most sanguine expectations."[9]

For the next half hour the Confederate assault teams enjoyed deceptively
intoxicating victories. The large encampment of a Massachusetts regiment
posted just north of Fort Stedman was overrun, with many of its occupants
captured or killed in their tents. South of the fort a pair of small Union
batteries were swarmed and knocked out of action. Yet not everything was
going to plan. General Gordon moved forward and established his
headquarters inside Fort Stedman, where he learned that none of the three
infiltration teams had carried out their mission to push deep into the Union
rear areas. The guides who were to direct the special groups never appeared,
leaving them unable to advance in the darkness. It was taking longer than
anticipated for follow-up waves to organize and advance across the
no-man's land, and some of the troops coming from distant portions of the
Confederate line were delayed by breakdowns in the rickety transportation
system. Gordon realized that with full daylight just minutes away his men
were running out of time to eliminate the strong Yankee batteries on either

flank; if they failed in this, they would be caught in a death trap. The time was approaching 6:00 a.m.

According to the staff officer Lieutenant Colonel Horace Porter, it was about 6:00 a.m. when Grant's headquarters "was awakened and was soon all astir by reason of a message from the Petersburg front saying that the enemy had broken through our lines near Fort Stedman and was making a heavy attack." Porter and another aide hurried to Grant's cabin, where they rapped "upon the door of the room occupied by him and Mrs. Grant; and in reply to his questions the dispatch was read loud enough for him to hear it without opening the door. He dressed at once, and as this was a process which never occupied many minutes, he was soon out in front of his quarters."[10] There Grant learned that the telegraph lines to the Fort Stedman front had been cut and that they were relying on couriers for news. Compounding the problems, the army commander George Meade was still at City Point with his wife and equally out of touch with events. Command at the front devolved upon Major General John G. Parke, whose Ninth Corps was fighting for its life.

There was little that Grant or Meade could do for the moment but monitor events as information trickled in. Grant did advise Rear Admiral David D. Porter of the action and requested that the officer send "one or two Gunboats" up the Appomattox River to provide support.[11] He reached out to other commands whose telegraph circuits were uncut, informing them of what was happening. He also marshaled reinforcements and urged officers holding the western lines to probe for any thinning of the enemy forces opposite them. Grant didn't forget about his important guests present at City Point and ordered the units on hand (mostly engineers) to occupy trenches and small forts built to protect the little peninsula from raiding parties. Not enough was known about what was happening to brief President Lincoln at this time.

One element John Gordon's plan did not foresee was the resilience of the Federal troops he attacked. There were moments of confusion and even panic as fierce Rebel soldiers swarmed on them in the darkness, and while the sheer force of the assault tore a hole in the U.S. defenses, there was no contagious collapse of morale among the defending units. Even as Union regiments posted in the rear were forming and advancing toward the maelstrom, others battered from the Rebel blows were improvising defensive positions along the northern and southern shoulders of the penetration. Michigan, Pennsylvania, and Ohio soldiers took station to protect Battery IX north of Fort Stedman, while men from New York, Maryland, Pennsylvania, and Massachusetts plugged the hole east of Fort Haskell to prevent the Rebels from sweeping the line in that direction.

Confederate officers were equally resolute as they reorganized their men, scattered by the night advance and the wild brawls in the enemy trenches, to secure the flanks. Among those assaulting Battery IX was the Tar Heel Henry Chambers. Fully aroused Yankee cannoneers across their front made the Confederates' situation hellish. Chambers remembered that "with shrapnel shell from our right beyond Fort Stedman and minies from the fort near the river on our left, and with shell from the bluffs in our front our position was made, in the opinion of our commanders, untenable." Then Chambers learned that the regimental commander was mortally wounded, "and I, as senior Captain was left in command."[12]

Confederates assaulted Fort Haskell south of Stedman in wave after wave, the troops including all that remained of the storied Stonewall Brigade. Inside the packed Union bastion, "the wounded and sick men [were] loading the muskets, while those with sound arms stood to the parapets and blazed away." A Pennsylvanian in a just-arriving supporting regiment observed that "Fort Haskell was a ring of fire. . . . As daylight approached a slight air movement made a rift in the pall of smoke over Fort Haskell, and we could see Old Glory waving from its ramparts. It looked good, and, oh, how we did cheer!"[13]

The sun was up now and Major General John B. Gordon was beginning to despair. Not only had his men failed to widen the breach, but off to the east he could see a nearly continuous line of Union blue as a dozen or more Yankee regiments formed for a counterattack. "It was impossible for me to make further headway with my isolated corps," Gordon acknowledged and sent a courier to General Lee requesting permission to withdraw. Time passed in excruciating seconds as the fighting raged on the flanks and the Federal battle lines to the east began to advance. Lee finally approved the request around 7:30 a.m. "This was not easily accomplished," Gordon noted, adding that a "consuming fire on both flanks and front during this withdrawal caused a heavy loss to my command."[14]

Captain Henry Chambers watched in astonishment from not a quarter-mile north of Gordon as masses of Confederate soldiers abandoned Fort Stedman and scampered toward the Rebel lines. Then he was told that the order to retire had been given and led his men into no-man's land, now pummeled from end to end by vengeful Yankee cannon. "Good God what a time!" Chambers recollected. "It seemed as if the enemy's artillery opened with redoubled vigor and the minie balls came in showers. Many were wounded and as their unhurt comrades passed them would beg piteously to be carried out. The hearts of many failed them and they did not start at all. Others started but took shelter in the picket trenches and covered ways."[15] Somehow Chambers made it through unscathed, but when he later counted heads he found that nearly half his company was gone.

The Union counterattack began by 7:45 a.m., nearly 4,000 men in all. "The whole field was blue with them," recalled one startled Rebel. "Their lines must have been ten or fifteen deep." They swept forward like an irresistible tidal wave. Among the last to leave Fort Stedman was John B. Gordon, who took advantage of a small ravine to shield him as he withdrew on foot. Not everyone was so lucky. A Louisiana soldier said that "the heroic men who retreated out of that fearful ring of fire and death declare it the most terrific cannonade they ever endured."[16]

Captain Joseph P. Carson of the Georgia sharpshooters was racing to friendly lines when a comrade told him he thought he had seen Carson's brother lying in front of Fort Stedman. The captain and a friend dodged back to find the young courier's body. Bob Carson had joined the fight to be with his brother should he fall, but instead he was the victim. The two men hefted Bob's corpse and waddled into the shot-riddled no-man's land. "Neither my companion nor myself was struck," Joe Carson somberly recollected, "but the body was shot through four times."[17]

One Union observer was appalled at the sight of fleeing Confederates being picked off by the dozens as they re-crossed the deadly no-man's land. "My mind sickens at the memory of it—a real tragedy in war—for the victims had ceased fighting, and were now struggling between imprisonment and death or home." A Wisconsin soldier had a grimmer assessment, noting approvingly that the retreating "rebels were mown down in swaths."[18]

"This last supreme effort to break the hold of General Grant upon Petersburg and Richmond was the expiring struggle of the Confederate giant," reflected John Gordon many years later. "[This] attack was regarded by both General Lee and myself as very hazardous; but it seemed necessary to do more than sit quietly waiting for General Grant to move upon our right, which each day was diminishing our strength by disease and death." Gordon afterward "had very little talk with General Lee after our withdrawal. I recognized that the end was approaching, and, of course, he did."[19]

Lieutenant Colonel Theodore Lyman of General Meade's staff recorded that the first detailed reports regarding the fighting around Fort Stedman didn't come through to City Point until 7:30 a.m. That message and subsequent ones conveyed news that was all positive: the breakthrough had been contained, strong infantry reinforcements were marching to the scene, and there was ample artillery on hand. Finally, at 8:45 a.m. came the word: "General Parke announces the reoccupation of the whole line, capture of many prisoners, and that all is quiet."[20] That note arrived shortly after Captain Robert Lincoln left headquarters to brief his father.

The President was by habit an early riser and there's nothing to suggest that this day was any different. Captain Lincoln came aboard the *River Queen* to find his family at breakfast, along with Captain Penrose. Present as well was Captain Barnes, whose ship (her boiler repaired) had anchored nearby shortly before 6:00 a.m. "Mr. Lincoln ate very little," recollected Barnes, "but was very jolly and pleasant." Everybody listened as Robert passed along the latest news, "that there had been a fight that morning at the front and the action was then going on; that the reports at General Grant's headquarters were meager, but that our troops were successful in repelling an assault upon our lines, and that the proposed review would have to be postponed."[21]

Lincoln promptly wrote out a dispatch for the Secretary of War that conveyed the news. Robert had done such a good job downplaying any danger that his father described it merely as a "little rumpus." He spent more message space answering questions Stanton had raised in his note of March 24. He also passed along what Grant had told him regarding a diplomatic contretemps involving British Foreign Secretary Lord Russell. It was a sign of how far Confederate stock had fallen in the estimation of the English Foreign Office. Angry at the anti-U.S. activities of Southern agents active in Canada, Lord Russell had penned a formal protest, which he had submitted to Union authorities to read before delivering to Richmond. Grant had passed the message through the lines; its contents had circulated throughout the Davis administration, which deftly dodged a response by returning the envelope as undeliverable.

According to Grant's aide Horace Porter: "The President, who was aboard his boat anchored out in the river, soon heard of the attack, and he was kept informed of the events which were taking place by his son Robert, who carried the news to him."[22] This implies a bit of shuttle service on the part of Captain Lincoln. Matters were calm enough at headquarters after 9:00 a.m. that the President was cleared for a visit. The weather outside was cloudy and damp with a slight chill in the air.

Lincoln's tramp to Grant's headquarters (leaving Mary and Tad aboard the *River Queen*) would have been his first foray ashore at City Point since arriving there. His only prior visit had occurred in June 1864, when the transformation of a sleepy backwater into a major military supply hub was just beginning. Eight months later, the City Point complex consisted of some 280 buildings, including warehouses holding a 30-day food reserve and two days of fodder—numbering 9,000,000 meals and 12,000 tons of hay and oats. The half-mile long river front contained two wharves for the quartermaster's department, plus one each for commissary, forage, mail, ordnance, coal, and the railroad. To keep the trains running there was an engine house and a car repair shop.

A delegate of the United States Christian Commission (a religiously oriented soldier service organization) visited the place a week after Lincoln's departure and left a chatty description. He declared it a poor place to build a city, "for while the general surface of the land is level it is cut up by swampy ravines, which run in every direction through it, and on the patches of land between, stands a huge wilderness of tents, stockades, corrals, barracks, hospitals, government, commissary quartermaster, Christian and Sanitary Commission store rooms, military prisons and all things considerably huddled together, without order or arrangement. Its streets, or rather wagon paths, rival in crookedness the secret ways of Cretan Labyrinth of ancient fame."[23]

Another visitor, this one within days of Lincoln's arrival, added more details about what the President would have seen, noting that "shipping and the steamers which cluster about the harbor present a lively scene. . . . A substantial wharf, with long storehouses, line[s] the bank at the foot of the hill, and the military railroad skirts its base. Broad and substantial stairways lead to the top of the hill. . . . All around and about are the huts of the army with their tent-roofs whitening the plain in every direction. Roughly constructed wooden buildings are scattered here and there on the point in which the 'merchants' send their wares and sutlers pocket the spoils, enveloped, at present, in clouds of dust."[24]

A scene sketched by artist-correspondent Alfred Waud showing the United States
Military Railroad in action. Lincoln rode these rails three times while at City Point. LOC

Lincoln followed a fenced walkway, made the climb up the L-shaped
stairway to the top of the bluff and turned right toward the Eppes home,
which housed the quartermaster's headquarters. Just off its south porch was
a 30 by 20 foot log cabin that was tethered to the world by a skein of
insulated cable lines—marking this as the army headquarters telegraph
office. Captain Barnes remembered that there they "learned that the fight at
the front had been quite serious, but at that time was practically over,
resulting in a decided victory for our men. After some discussion, Mr.
Lincoln expressed a great desire to visit the scene of the action, nothing
being known except the general result." According to Barnes, Grant at first
"was rather opposed to the President's proposed trip."[25] But the updates
continued to paint a picture of a battle won and combat ended so that Grant
was hard pressed to maintain his objection, even to the point of letting their
families accompany them.

Orders were issued to the quartermaster's office to assemble a special
train. Word was communicated to George Meade's headquarters at the same
time; the Army of the Potomac commander had departed for the front shortly
before Lincoln came ashore. The President returned to the *River Queen* to
gather his family, while the invitation was extended to Julia Grant. There
was action all along the Union lines, and the railroaders were tasked with
conveying wounded to the rear while bringing men and munitions to the
front. It says much about the capable professionalism of the operation that a

passenger car in place of the typical box and flat cars could be located and staged while this was all happening. Everything was ready after 11:00 a.m.

Mary Lincoln had some unfinished business to attend to before she departed. She still hadn't heard anything from Washington concerning the status of the White House after the powerful storm, so she sent a note addressed to the Executive Mansion doorkeeper Alphonso Dunn demanding a report on conditions there. Like her first message, this one also apparently went unanswered.

When the word came, everyone departed for the no-frills wooden platform that functioned as the City Point Station, located beside the tracks running along the foot of the bluff, a short walk from the wharf used by the *River Queen*. Besides Lincoln, his wife and son, plus General and Mrs. Grant and their son Jesse, there were the two captains (Penrose and Barnes) and two of Grant's aides: Lieutenant Colonels Horace Porter and Adam Badeau, the latter of whom had been assigned to escort the women. There was also a group of officers plus guests, making up what Barnes termed "a large party."[26] Several saddle horses were brought along too, and placed in a special car designed for that purpose. All were in their seats as the train chugged forward about 11:30 a.m.

The United States Military Railroad may have been the oddest operating transportation system in America at that time. It was also one of Grant's secret weapons, keeping his forces along the miles of entrenchments well supplied and serviced, as well as facilitating troop concentrations for offensive moves. When Union operations against Petersburg began in earnest in June 1864 the professionally graded railroad spur running from City Point into the town was quickly blocked by the opposing earthworks. As the Federal trenches slowly extended southward and then westward, U.S. engineers built a branch line running just behind the growing entrenchments that eventually extended nearly 22 miles. Since the official belief was that the siege would soon end, the decision was made to build it quick and dirty. A New York military engineer explained, "when a hill seemed to hinder the onward progress of the construction corps, instead of wasting precious time by grading the aforesaid hill down to a reasonable level in imitation of their brethren of the pick and shovel upon the Northern railroads, the track was laid directly over the hill, thus rendering a trip over the road rather disagreeable when taken under the most favorable circumstances."[27]

The sight of the railroad in action was familiar to Horace Porter, who jokingly described it appearing in the distance "like a fly crawling over a corrugated washboard." It was not unusual for the conductors of overloaded trains to get the passengers off to push it up the steep inclines. A visitor at the time noted that on "each side of the [rail]road is a vast plain, now a desert, destitute of fences or shrubbery, and cut in every direction with the corduroy roads [logs laid on muddy roads for traction] where our teams are hauling wood and supplies to the armies."[28]

The view from the train could also be sobering, as a New Yorker remembered on his journey passing "many deserted mansions, nearly all of which were surrounded with beautiful evergreen trees. No smoke ascended from those old chimneys, and the indefinite something upon every side of those antique structures told of the desolation and ruin which pervades this section of Virginia. Scattered over the entire landscape, so far as the eye could see, were graves without number."[29]

The view was even more sobering on this trip, for as the special train transited the rear area for the Ninth Corps, evidence of the recent combat could be seen. "The serious nature of the fight that day was apparent," Captain Barnes remembered. "The ground about us was covered with dead and wounded men, federals and confederates. The whole army was under arms and moving to the left, where a desultory firing, both musketry and artillery was to be seen and heard."[30]

Lincoln's attention was occupied part of the way by a conversation with Brevet Major General August V. Kautz, commanding some forces north of the James. Kautz happened to be visiting City Point this day and had attached himself to the touring party. "In discussing the probable close of the war," Kautz recalled, "Grant remarked that he thought it would be a great relief to be able to go to bed without any anxiety about the morrow."[31]

The President's special train reached Globe Tavern (also known as Warren Station) between 12:15 and 12:30 p.m., where everyone disembarked. The men mounted horses, and the women traveled in an ambulance that had been modified for passenger use. Grant brought with him his two personal horses, a large chestnut gelding named "Cincinnati," and a smaller black pony named "Jeff Davis." According to one account (likely Penrose again) Lincoln took the latter, creating an unintentionally humorous image of a tall man riding a short horse. "Yet the thought of ridicule was never suggested for this strange man who seemed to dignify and honor everything he touched," observed a nurse at City Point. "He could have ridden bareback without loss of dignity."

Lieutenant Colonel Badeau accompanied Mrs. Lincoln and Mrs. Grant in the ambulance, which he described as "a sort of half-open carriage with two seats besides that for the driver." Badeau chattered away in an effort to distract the ladies from their rough ride and unwittingly ignited a small contretemps. He observed that "all the wives of officers of the army front had been ordered to the rear—a sure sign that active operations were in contemplation." When he added that one exception to this rule was the wife of Major General Charles Griffin, who was able to stay thanks to a "special permit from the President," Mary Lincoln was not amused.[32] Badeau recalled that the First Lady became highly agitated and tried to leave the vehicle to confront her husband over the matter, calming down only when Mrs. Grant intervened. Julia Grant's memoirs do not mention this incident.

According to Meade and Lyman, the Presidential party reached army headquarters at 1:00 p.m. Even as Grant and Meade were conferring, the lieutenant general received a dispatch from Major General Parke describing the battle for Fort Stedman. Grant forwarded this message to the Secretary of War shortly before 1:30 p.m., adding only a brief introductory sentence. The President and Mary had a private moment with George Meade about his recently deceased son. The general wrote his wife that the First Lady "referred in feeling terms to our sad bereavement."[33] Mrs. Lincoln also brought up the matter of Mrs. Griffin's pass and was assured by General Meade that it had come via the Secretary of War's office, an explanation that appeared to mollify her.

As the President stepped outside Meade's headquarters he observed a coffle of Confederate prisoners captured by Parke's Ninth Corps during the final phase of the Fort Stedman affair. Meade appeared with a message in his hand. "I have just now a dispatch from General Parke to show you," he said. Lincoln pointed to the defeated enemy soldiers awaiting transportation to the rear. "Ah," he answered, "there is the best dispatch you can show me from General Parke!"[34]

Lincoln had seen small numbers of captured Rebels before this day, but never so many and so recently taken. According to the observant Lyman, they had "the most matted hair, tangled beards, and slouched hats, and the most astounding carpets, horse-sheets and transmogrified shelter-tents for blankets, that you ever imagined."[35] It was visible evidence of the Confederacy's ongoing implosion.

In that captive crowd was an embittered Georgian, who later recollected passing those in the President's party who "appeared to be delighted to see a lot of dilapidated (but honorable) Southern soldiers who had so recently been engaged in killing off the surplus members of Grant's vast army." Also shuffling past was a Virginia captain who had spent much of the war in the Stonewall Brigade. "It was surprising to us to see Lincoln, Grant & Meade holding a grand review during a fight or directly afterwards," he remembered. "We all agreed our cause was lost to see such a vast army ready to gobble up Lee's skeletons."[36]

Another phase of this day's fighting was unfolding not quite four miles from where Lincoln was standing. It was one measure of the army that Grant had molded over the long Petersburg winter that its senior officers now thought in offensive rather than defensive terms. When informed of the Confederate attack against Fort Stedman on the eastern Union line, commanders along the western portion of the trench system began probing the Rebel positions to determine if Lee had weakened his defenses to reinforce the attack. This sparked hours of moderate-scale combat as Union advances were met by hastily organized Confederate counterattacks, in turn struck by Federal supports coming forward. The battle was over the picket lines—the outposts located hundreds of yards in advance of the main trenches. By day's end the Federals captured some of these positions. The fighting was fitful and often on a small scale, but Lincoln could hear the sounds and understood that men were killing each other within earshot of him.

A full division of the Fifth Corps had been put on alert this morning but not used, and was now on hold just two miles to the south. George Meade instructed it to be readied for a Presidential review. Lincoln dispatched an update to Secretary of War Stanton in Washington just before leaving Meade's headquarters, easy to do now that the lines to City Point had been re-established:

> I am here within five miles of the scene of this morning[']s action. I have nothing to add to what General Meade reports, except that I have seen the prisoners myself, and they look like there might be the number he states 1,600.[37]

Captain Barnes, who had opted to explore areas nearer the day's fighting, remained behind as the President's party departed. Looking toward the main arena of combat the naval officer could see white flags of truce fluttering, and he observed the slow movements of ambulances as the wounded were gently separated from the dead. One of the aid workers handed him a haversack of crackers with a canteen of water, and he went forward to dispense them. "I employed a half hour in going among the wounded lying on the ground," he recalled, "and came across a little red-headed boy in butternut clothes, moaning, and muttering over and over, 'Mother! Mother!' I asked him where he was hurt, when he looked up at me and turned toward me the back of his head, where a bullet had plowed a ghastly furrow, and then with the effort expired."[38] The shaken Barnes tramped back toward the Globe Tavern, his curiosity satisfied.

The Presidential party's route was south from Meade's headquarters. Before reaching the review field they encountered a squad of Pennsylvania boys hurrying to join up with their unit, which was to be part of the ceremony. The soldiers spontaneously decided to get things underway without the rest of their division. They hastily formed a line and presented arms. One recalled that Lincoln "raised his hat and turned to General Meade with some humorous remark as they rode on. It seemed a reversal of things for the head of the nation to pass in review before a couple of stragglers."[39]

The Presidential party turned east onto open and level fields where Brevet Major General Samuel W. Crawford's division was waiting. Its three brigades contained men from Maine, Massachusetts, New York, Pennsylvania, and Wisconsin, estimated by one observer to number 8,000 soldiers.

Philip Cheek, 6th Wisconsin Regiment: "[We] marched down near to the Weldon Railroad and were reviewed by President Lincoln, he riding down the front of our lines, carrying his hat in his right hand. As he came in front of each regiment they presented arms, the drums rolled and the colors saluted. He rode along about fifty paces in front of his escort of generals and their staffs. Lincoln bowed to the troops as he passed in front of each regiment. After his escort passed, each regiment was brought to 'shoulder arms' and then the officers and men cheered him most heartily. We could hear heavy firing in front of the 2nd Corps. Some one remarked that they must be trying to capture the President."[40]

Jeremiah Long, 91st New York Regiment: "[There] was a great stir in our front and a brilliant array of generals and staff officers came along and took up a position to review us. As they ranged themselves in order a civilian figure . . . a tall gaunt man who seemed like a giant, and whose high silk hat was at once remarked, placed himself in the very advance of the gathering.

Beside him on a cavalry charger was a small boy, who seemed crouched up in a heap as if he was hunch backed. Not a man or boy of us but knew instinctively that the man and the boy were President Lincoln and his son Tad, whom we had heard were visiting General Grant at headquarters at City Point."[41]

Jerome A. Watrous, 6th Wisconsin Regiment: "It was nearly 5 o'clock when they arrived at the right of the corps. Word was sent down the line . . . telling regimental commanders that if their men want to cheer to cheer. It

was freedom the corps heartily welcomed. Cheering? I never before heard such cheering. Each regiment gave three times three cheers and a tiger, and then threw their caps in the air. The President was kept busy lifting his hat and bowing. He rode so close to the lines that we could see his smile and hear his 'Thank you, my brave boys.'"[42]

It was a sight that could leave no President unmoved. In his four plus years as commander-in-chief Lincoln had reviewed troops on at least 40 separate occasions, but there was something different this time. Before it had been a necessary act of his office, now it was something approaching a

A newspaper sketch of President Lincoln reviewing troops at Petersburg that accompanied syndicated articles about his visit.
Orleans Republican [Albion, New York], *February 9, 1910*

communion of purpose between the President and his boys. "It was a most agreeable as well as encouraging spectacle," wrote *New York Herald* reporter Leonard A. Hendrick, ". . . particularly because his presence on such an occasion showed that in the present crisis, when no one could tell what fierce onslaught of battle any moment might bring forth, he was not afraid to show himself among them, and willing to share their dangers here, as often, far away, he had shared, the joys of their triumphs." Another correspondent on hand wrote that all "was pomp and pageantry and playfulness."[43]

Even as the review of Crawford's division was winding down, a low throaty crescendo of cannon fire and musketry signaled that the fight for the picket lines was far from over. The Presidential party turned west to the Halifax Road at Meade's suggestion, intersecting it near Fort Dushane. The position was garrisoned by members of the 138th Pennsylvania (Sixth Corps), one of whom was struck by the sight of Lincoln's passing. "We were all out along the road and we gave him 3 cheers and he took (off) his hat and smiled," the soldier wrote. "He looks very thin . . . I assure you I hollered as loud as I could. . . . The old fellow took [off] his hat to every set of callers that passed him."[44]

Lincoln's presence among them was a gesture not lost on the soldiers. "I remember now as keenly as I felt then that Lincoln seemed to me to be the very personification of the Union cause," recollected Jeremiah Long. "That he typified the very Union itself; and his form and features as he sat there, the sound of the distant firing coming to our ears, and the troops marching steadily in its direction, imprinted themselves indelibly on my memory." Pennsylvanian Jason Butler declared that "Abraham Lincoln is the greatest man that ever lived in my estimation." "The unrestrained hearty cheers greatly pleased him," added Jerome A. Watrous. "Dear 'Old Abe,' I wonder if he realized how deeply he was loved by the men he had called to serve their country."[45]

The Presidential party traveled north as far as Fort Wadsworth, where a corner of the fort's parapet offered a relatively unobstructed view of the battle lines slightly more than two miles to the northwest. A Canadian doctor working under army contract who had been viewing the front and was standing nearby wrote in a letter the next day that "General Mead[e] told the President he could not give him a very good show, on account of the little battle in the morning, to which he replied, 'He would gladly dispense with the show if he would take 1,800 prisoners each day.'"[46]

Lincoln's interest in the distant combat was intense. "The President carried a map with him, which he took out of his pocket and examined several times," observed Horace Porter. "He had the exact location of the troops marked on it, and he exhibited a singularly accurate knowledge of the various positions." A Sixth Corps soldier waiting nearby for the word to advance glanced at Fort Wadsworth and spotted his commander-in-chief. "With a spyglass viewing the front he could be easily distinguished, from where we stood, by his tall form, which towered above the others. His tall hat was also conspicuous." An artilleryman posted in the fort never forgot "that sad and careworn face when the President, bending over to reach the hand of his little son, pointed out to him the scene before them."[47]

The men under observation belonged to the Sixth Corps, who had battled over this ground throughout the morning only to be knocked on their heels by even more determined counterattacks launched by the South Carolina troops opposing them. That would have been the finish of things a few month's earlier, but Grant's army wasn't ready to call it quits. The troops Lincoln saw in action may have been Connecticut boys belonging to the 2nd Heavy Artillery (fighting as infantry) who, advancing with "yells that would have shamed a tribe of Indians," momentarily cleared a section of Rebel rifle pits only to find that their enthusiasm had led them into a pocket with Confederates on three sides. The men eventually fell back a short distance and dug in, actions being duplicated all along the western front. When he came to write his diary entry of the President's visit, Meade's aide Lyman summed it up, "A review, a pleasure party and a battle all in one day."[48]

According to Captain Barnes, who had rejoined the group, "Mr. Lincoln was quiet and observant, making few comments, and listened to explanations in a cool, collected manner, betraying no excitement, but his whole face showing sympathetic feeling for the suffering about him." Sunset was approaching when the President and his guests headed back to the special train waiting to carry them to City Point. "As they left the fort," a Wisconsin chaplain wrote the next day, "three times three hearty cheers were given for them by the crowd who had gathered to see them."[49]

Once aboard, Barnes took a few moments to relate his encounter with the dying Rebel boy. "Mr. Lincoln . . . remarked that he had seen enough of the horrors of war," the naval officer recollected, "that he hoped this was the beginning of the end, and that there would be no more bloodshed or ruin of homes."[50] With the military trains busily engaged in servicing the fighting lines, it was a slow journey back to City Point. Once there, Mrs. Lincoln, Tad, and probably Captain Penrose, returned to the *River Queen*, while Lincoln plus Captain Barnes and Grant's men clambered up the bluff to army headquarters.

Grant disappeared to send a short update to War Secretary Stanton. As Horace Porter remembered the moment, Lincoln "sat for a while by the camp-fire; and as the smoke curled about his head during certain shiftings of the wind, and he brushed it away from time to time by waving his right hand in front of his face, he [talked] . . . in a most interesting manner about public affairs, and illustrating the subjects mentioned with his incomparable anecdotes."[51] The President seemed especially focused on England, and observed that through their passivity in 1862 and 1863, English leaders had allowed the Confederates to secure several commerce raiders whose activities would ultimately be charged against British accounts.

General Grant rejoined the group while Lincoln was discoursing and during a thoughtful pause asked, "Mr. President did you at any time doubt the final success of the cause?" Lincoln answered without hesitation, "Never for a moment." As Horace Porter observed, "Mr. Lincoln leaned forward in his camp-chair and enforced his words by a vigorous gesture of his right hand." The talk went back to England before dinner was announced. At this point according to Captain Barnes "Mr. Lincoln, overcome by the excitement and events of the day, desired to rest on the [River] Queen with his family, and, declining the invitation to take supper at General Grant's headquarters, saw no one again that evening."[52]

Grant still had office work to do and during the next 45 minutes or so he sent off a number of messages: two updates to Stanton; a thanks to Admiral Porter for dispatching the requested gunboats; a pat on the back to George Meade for the army's successes this day; and notes to Army of the James commander Major General Edward O. C. Ord and to Phil Sheridan confirming the routing for the cavalrymen arriving from the Shenandoah Valley.

The March 25 fighting throughout Lincoln's first full day at City Point cost the Army of the Potomac 2,080 casualties: 161 killed, 1,201 wounded, and the rest missing. Hardest hit was the Ninth Corps which, in retaking Fort Stedman and the flanking Federal trenches, suffered 911 killed, wounded, or missing. According to the most reasonable accounting, the Fort Stedman operation alone cost Lee 2,681 men, nearly 2,000 of whom were prisoners. The fight for the picket lines along the western front added roughly 1,600 more. Summing it up for his wife, George Meade declared that the "day turned out to be a very successful one, we punishing the enemy severely."[53]

The President ended his day still in the "flying visit" mode. Scheduled for Day Two were more army reviews and an up-close look at the navy. What he didn't know, and could not have anticipated, was that an incident involving Mary Lincoln would cast an ominous shadow over his visit to the front.

CHAPTER THREE

Sunday, March 26, 1865

"How grateful I feel to be with the boys."

P RESIDENT Lincoln's morning reading included two telegrams sent the previous evening from Washington by War Secretary Stanton. One involved planning for an important symbolic occasion: the ceremonial re-raising of the U.S. flag over Fort Sumter in Charleston Harbor. While the event did not warrant Lincoln's personal participation, he was taking an active role in choosing speakers and determining the program. Stanton wanted Lincoln's approval to have the prominent Congregationalist clergyman Henry Ward Beecher deliver the keynote address. He also desired that the area's occupation commander, Major General Quincy A. Gillmore, handle all military arrangements, and he had designated the officer who had surrendered the fort in 1861—then Major, now Brigadier General Robert Anderson—to raise the flag once more.

Lincoln's reply addressed Stanton's Sumter ceremony choices, picked up some loose ends from messages exchanged on Sunday, and noted that he had "no later war news than went to you last-night." Stanton's second message showed that his sense of humor hadn't abandoned him in these stressful times. After mentioning nothing fresh to report on his end, he observed about the Fort Stedman affair that the "rebel rooster looks a little worse, as he could not hold the fence." The self-designated worrywart asked the Chief Executive to be careful, reminding him of President William

Henry Harrison's "advice to his men at [the battle of] Tippecanoe, that they 'can see as well a little farther off.'"[1]

There was additional reading matter thanks to General Grant, who had thoughtfully copied the President on messages he had sent the previous evening. Lincoln was going over these when a knock on the door signaled the arrival of Captain Barnes. "I found him quite recovered from the fatigue and excitement of the day before," the naval officer recalled; "reports from the front were wholly reassuring, our troops back in their original positions, with some material advantages gained along the lines. The President, while lamenting the great loss of life and the sufferings of the wounded, expressed the greatest confidence that the war was drawing to an end. He read me several dispatches from Mr. Stanton, expressing anxiety as to his exposing himself, and drawing contrasts between the duty of a 'general' and a 'president'; also several dispatches from the front sent him by General Grant. He was greatly pleased to hear that General Sheridan had reached the bank of the river at Harrison's Landing, and that his cavalry would that day cross and join General Grant's army."[2]

Even as the two were chatting, General Grant was having a fateful meeting with the one man he considered absolutely indispensable for his coming military strike against Lee's Petersburg lines. Major General Philip H. Sheridan had hurried down this morning from his cavalry's camp to settle a matter that had been gnawing at him since he'd received Grant's orders assigning him and his men to Sherman's command upon his return to City Point. Sheridan hated the idea and he was greeted on his arrival by Grant's chief-of-staff, Brigadier General John A. Rawlins, who quickly made it clear that he was a kindred spirit. Rawlins checked to see that Grant was available and waved his friend in.

"How are you?" Grant asked as Sheridan entered. The cavalryman noted that the lieutenant general's tone "gave assurance of welcome, although his manner was otherwise impassive." Knowing something of his commander's ways, Sheridan launched into a terse summary of his just-completed campaign, which Grant fully approved. Now it was Grant's turn to restate his intentions for Sheridan to pass with his command through City Point bound for North Carolina. He even shared a portion of his instructions to Sherman that referenced the matter. All this was too much for the fiery cavalry commander, who threw propriety to the wind. In what he later termed an "emphatic manner," Sheridan began to offer my objections. . . . These were, that it would be bad policy to send me down to the Carolinas with a part of

Grant with his chief-of-staff, Brigadier General John A. Rawlins (left), and his aide, Lieutenant Colonel Horace Porter (right), in front of Grant's City Point cabin. LOC

the Army of the Potomac, to come back to crush Lee after the destruction of General Johnston's army; such a course would give rise to the charge that his own forces around Petersburg were not equal to the task, and would seriously affect public opinion in the North; that in fact my cavalry belonged to the Army of the Potomac, which army was able unaided to destroy Lee, and I could not but oppose any dispersion of its strength."[3]

Grant calmly informed Sheridan "that the portion of my instructions from which I so strongly dissented was intended as a 'blind' to cover any check the army in its general move to the left might meet with, and prevent that element in the North which held that the war could be ended only through negotiation, from charging defeat." Grant insisted that it was his intention "to close the war right here, with this movement, and that he should go no farther." Sheridan's dark face brightened noticeably. "I am glad to hear it and we can do it," he said. "The fact that my cavalry was not to ultimately join Sherman was a great relief to me," he admitted, "and after expressing the utmost confidence in the plans unfolded for closing the war by directing every effort to the annihilation of Lee's army, I left him."[4]

President Lincoln and Captain Barnes had climbed up the bluff from the *River Queen* while this critical discussion was occurring. The day was clear and pleasant, with temperatures on the cool side. Lincoln stopped first at the military telegraph office next to the Eppes House. There he found several of Grant's staff officers, Lieutenant Colonel Porter among them. According to the aide, Lincoln "pulled out of his pocket a telegram which he had received from the Secretary of War, and his face assumed a broad smile as he said: 'Well, the serious Stanton is actually becoming facetious. Just listen to what he says in his dispatch,'" and proceeded to read aloud Stanton's 8 p.m. note from yesterday. A good laugh was had by all and Lincoln handed over his thoughts concerning the Fort Sumter rededication for transmission to Secretary Stanton.

It was likely here and now that Lincoln first encountered a small litter of kittens whose mother could not be found. The President picked them up, took them on his lap and stroked their soft fur. Several times during his numerous visits to the telegraph office he would find them wandering about, and often, according to accounts, he "would wipe their eyes tenderly with his handkerchief, stroke their smooth coats, and listen to them purring their gratitude."[5] Members of the staff working the communications center made sure that the little creatures were fed.

Sheridan was gone by the time Lincoln emerged from the telegraph office and headed for Grant's cabin. Captain Barnes, still running escort duties, was anxious to learn the day's agenda. He was informed that the President would take a river excursion "to see Sheridan's troops crossing the river [and] . . . review the naval flotilla,"[6] then inspect General Ord's Army of the James.

It was agreed that the *River Queen* would be used, prompting a flurry of activity. Grant sent Admiral Porter a message, alerting him that Lincoln "will start up the river about 11 o'clock this morning." Instructions went to Captain Bradford to prepare to depart and to Mary Lincoln to get ready for company that would include Mrs. Grant. Grant called in Horace Porter to inform him that he would team up with Adam Badeau to escort the ladies. The general also invited Sheridan along. According to Captain Barnes, "Horses and ambulances for the ladies were placed on the *River Queen*,"[7] and Grant made it clear that, having learned his lesson from the previous day, the President would ride the larger "Cincinnati" this time.

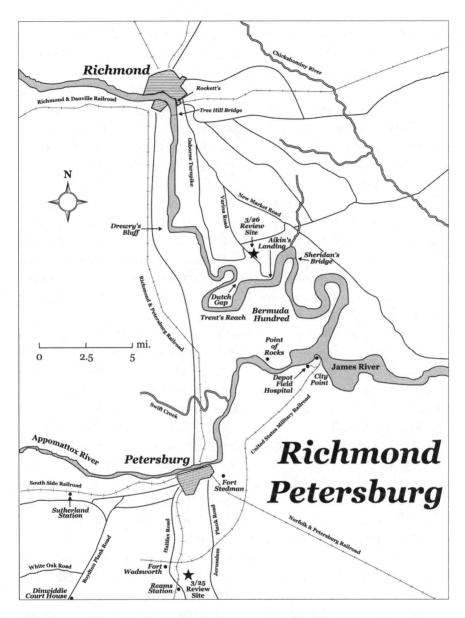

The notation in the USS *Bat's* log indicates that the *River Queen* departed at 11:30 a.m. Both Lieutenant Colonel Porter and General Sheridan thought that the President's mood at the outset was darkly subdued. Porter termed it "gloomy," while Sheridan characterized it as "not very cheerful." Given the President's generally convivial mood throughout the morning, it would seem that something aboard the *River Queen* triggered the emotional backslide. A postwar society news piece on Mrs. Grant says that at this time she sent the President a "handsome bouquet," and when Mrs. Lincoln saw it she "became furiously angry, and a lively scene ensued."[8]

Although rated a fast ship, the *River Queen* was moving slowly as she steamed up the James River channel, still an active combat zone. Lincoln eventually regained his morning's composure, even joking to the bantam cavalry commander: "General Sheridan, when this peculiar war began I thought a cavalryman should be at least six feet four high; but I have changed my mind—five feet four will do in a pinch."[9]

After about 90 minutes the *River Queen* reached the pontoon bridge just below Deep Bottom that was being used by Sheridan's horsemen to cross to the south side of the James. "The scene was a lively one, and the President enjoyed it hugely," observed Captain Barnes. A medical man viewing the crossing from the riverbank declared: "It was a glorious sight. These fellows are war-worn & weary, dusty & shabby—but brave, tried & true men are they all."[10]

Horace Porter noted that Lincoln "manifested considerable interest in watching the troopers, and addressed a number of questions to their commander." According to Sheridan, the President "spoke to me of the impending operations and asked many questions, laying stress upon the one, 'What would be the result when the army moved out to the left, if the enemy should come down and capture City Point?' the question being prompted, doubtless, by the bold assault on our lines and capture of Fort Steadman [sic] two days before by General Gordon. I answered that I did not think it at all probable that General Lee would undertake such a desperate measure to relieve the strait he was in; that . . . [the] successful check to Gordon had ended, I thought, attacks of such a character; and in any event General Grant would give Lee all he could attend to on the left."[11]

A gap was opened in the bridge allowing the *River Queen* to pass. The deck officer aboard Admiral Porter's flagship, the USS *Malvern*, then anchored near Aiken's Landing, logged the time as 1:40 p.m. when they arrived. In his entry, he managed to add young Jesse Grant to the Lincoln family, noting that "President Abraham Lincoln, Lady & two sons, General U.S. Grant & Lady & Major General Ord & Lady were received on board under a salute of 21 guns."[12]

While a band played "Hail to the Chief," a large U.S. flag was unfurled on cue. The President and guests were greeted on the *Malvern* by Admiral Porter, who spared no expense to entertain the commander-in-chief. Upon entering the main cabin the guests found a lavish luncheon awaiting them. "How the Admiral could have gotten up such a repast on so short a notice was a source of wonder and surprise to Mr. Lincoln," noted Captain Barnes, "as it was to everyone who enjoyed it. It was the cause of funny comments and remarks by the President, contrasting army and naval life, as was witnessed by the laughter among the group immediately about him, of which he was the moving spirit."[13]

Admiral Porter was no stranger to the President, having made it a point to drop by the White House whenever his duties took him to Washington, so the naval officer brought to this moment a deep understanding of his inner spirit and personality. "To me he was one of the most interesting men I ever met," Porter later wrote. ". . . I saw more to admire in this man, more to reverence, than I had believed possible; he had a load to bear that few men could carry, yet he traveled on with it, foot-sore and weary, but without complaint; rather; on the contrary, cheering those who would faint on the roadside."[14]

Lincoln willingly agreed to Admiral Porter's request that he review some of the warships on active station in the James River. At 2:30 p.m. the President with members of his party went aboard a tug that brought them near Trent's Reach, the navy's front line on the James. Not a mile ahead and out of sight around a bend were ample means of destruction: sunken obstructions, torpedoes (mines), and an impressive cannon array. Several nervous army officers commented that they were being observed by enemy artillery spotters. Admiral Porter made light of it all.

"Oh, no!" he laughed. "There is no danger. We are perfectly safe. These Southern fellows are all too gallant. They would not fire on a boat with women in it. These ladies' bonnets will protect us. We can turn and go back in safety."[15]

With most of the party remaining aboard the tug, Lincoln transferred to the admiral's barge to be rowed down river past some of the armed might of the United States Navy. One of the first ships he encountered was the powerful double-turreted monitor USS *Onondaga*. A sailor aboard the vessel recalled that the "crew were drawn up on the port-side, rigged and equipped with Sharp's rifles, and on his passing presented arms, which Father Abraham acknowledged and passed on." A second double-turreted monitor, USS *Monadnock*, offered a similar turnout, noting in its deck log, "Call all the divisions and formed a line on quarter deck and saluted the President with present arms as he was passing." The same order was given

One of the James River Squadron's premier warships, the monitor *Onondaga*. Her
assembled crew presented arms as Lincoln passed them in Admiral Porter's barge. LOC

aboard the single-turreted monitor, USS *Mahopac*, one of whose sailors
observed that Lincoln "arose in the stern of the launch and returned the
salute." Also a witness to the moment was the USS *Casco*, whose "company
mustered with small arms and saluted as he passed." Perhaps the most
impressive ship honoring Lincoln was the iron casemated warship USS
Atlanta, captured from the Confederates in 1863 and now flying the Stars
and Stripes. Captain Barnes never forgot the image of Lincoln "waving his
high hat in reply [to the naval salutes], as happy as a school boy."[16]

It was 3:30 p.m. when the admiral's barge and following vessels steered
past the USS *Malvern* to Aiken's Landing, where horses and vehicles were
waiting to take them to the army review. Most of the men transferred to
horseback, even Captain Barnes, who was loaned a mount by Lieutenant
Colonel Porter. The women took to the carriages and ambulances, Mrs.
Lincoln and Mrs. Grant sharing one with their escorts Badeau and Porter.
The fair skies overhead didn't show it, but a storm was about to break.

The excursion thus far had been all to Mary Lincoln's liking. The respect
shown her and her husband, the joyous accolades given him by the troops
and sailors, the respectful treatment she received all fulfilled her sense of
what was right and proper for America's First Lady. But her elegant facade
began to unravel once they arrived at Aiken's Landing. There was little

appealing about this place. It was an entry point for supplies intended for the forces operating against Richmond, and both the land and facilities had seen hard use. Whatever might have been colorful or attractive about the area—the grass and trees, the buildings—had long ago been ground down into a muddy brownish tinge that splashed across wharves and shacks, and obliterated anything cheerful that once grew there.

As soon as the procession began to move it became clear to Mary that the mounted men were not going to pace themselves with the ladies. What she didn't know was that Mr. Lincoln had been informed that the soldiers had been standing in formation since the morning. The President had come to the front determined to pay his respects and was adamant that the troops not be kept waiting any longer than necessary. So while the vehicles moved with difficulty along the rutted supply road that alternated sections of slippery mud with others of uneven corduroy, Mr. Lincoln and those with him soon disappeared in the distance. Mary was no longer at the center of attention and it began to disturb her.

The rough ride did not help matters. "Some additional springs had been put under [the carriage] . . . and cross-seats arranged so as to make it ride more easily than the ordinary army ambulance," recollected Porter, "but the improved springs only served to toss the occupants higher in the air when the wheels struck a particularly aggravating obstacle." Mary Lincoln insisted after a short while that the pace be picked up, an order that Porter passed along with great reluctance. "We were still on a corduroyed portion of the road, and when the horses trotted the mud flew in all directions, and a sudden jolt lifted the party clear off the seats, jammed the ladies' hats against the top of the wagon, and bumped their heads as well."[17] A furious Mrs. Lincoln demanded she be allowed to walk. It took all the patient argument that Porter and Julia Grant could muster to persuade her that attempting to plod through the hub-deep mud would be even worse. The First Lady reluctantly agreed, but her rising anger was palpable. The ambulance lurched on.

Accompanying Mrs. Lincoln's party was the wife of the commander of the Army of the James, Mary Ord, whom Captain Barnes—reminiscing with rose colored glasses—remembered as "a remarkably handsome woman, and a most accomplished equestrienne." (An Irish housekeeper who encountered Mrs. Ord in postwar Richmond offered a different opinion, describing her as "an unladylike vulgar woman."[18])

Mrs. Ord was supposed to share the ride with Mrs. Lincoln, but finding that the vehicle was full, she changed over to a saddled horse and rode at the rear of the column. During the halt, when the First Lady attempted to continue on foot, Mrs. Ord passed to the head of the line, something that greatly upset Mary Lincoln, who jumped to the conclusion that the lady was trying to catch up with the President. "What does the woman mean," she hissed, "by riding by the side of the President? and ahead of me? Does she suppose that he wants her by the side of him?" Julia Grant tried to assure Mary Lincoln that Mrs. Ord had no ulterior motives, but the First Lady would have none of it and pressed Mrs. Grant to tell what she knew about Mrs. Ord. Having been told yesterday that Mrs. Charles Griffin was an exception to the rule banning females from the army camps, she wondered why this woman was also allowed to be there. Julia tried to put her off with a little humor. "General Grant is much opposed to their being present," she said, "but when I wanted to come I wrote him a nice, coaxing letter, and permission was always granted."[19]

Her light touch seemed to convince Mary that Julia Grant was herself conniving with Mrs. Ord's behavior. "I suppose you think you'll get to the White House yourself, don't you?" she said. Julia Grant calmly answered that she was satisfied with her current situation; indeed, that it was far more than she had ever expected to attain. "Oh!" Mrs. Lincoln answered, "you had better take it if you can get it. 'Tis very nice."[20] The atmosphere in the vehicle lapsed into an awkward silence.

The faster-moving horsemen were approaching the Army of the James review site, in fields off to their right roughly parallel to the Varina Road. Portions of three divisions were present in lines: one from the Twenty-Fifth Corps on the southern end and two from the Twenty-Fourth corps continuing it northward. The plan had been to meet first with the Twenty-Fifth Corps commander Major General Godfrey Weitzel, but the lateness of the hour forced a change in the program with Lincoln and company turning off early to ride directly for the troops. A reporter present recorded the scramble as "the cavalcade collected at [Weitzel's] headquarters were dashing across the country to join the Presidential party."[21]

The Twenty-Fifth Corps was both an object of pride for the nation's few black newspapers, but also evidence of a failed experiment. At the beginning of the Eastern campaigns of 1864, black divisions had been mixed with white ones in the two participating armies, the Army of the Potomac and the Army of the James. However, by the end of that calendar year conservative forces within the army had successfully lobbied Grant to consolidate all the African-American infantry regiments into a single corps (the Twenty-Fifth) placed within the Army of the James, balancing it with an all-white corps (the Twenty-Fourth). Limited integration had fallen before a military version of separate but equal.

Still, there was no denying that most, if not all, the black soldiers lined up in the fields along the Varina Road believed they were part of something larger than themselves. "I hope that the day is not far distant when we shall see the colored man enjoying the same rights and privileges as those of the white man in this country," said one member of the 43rd USCT. "We are fighting as hard to restore the Union as the white man is." God, noted another in the regiment, has "worked wonders through the agency of this rebellion. He has struck the chains of bondage from nearly half a million of our race, and given new strength and vigor to the doctrine of Universal Freedom and Equal Rights."[22]

The tall, lanky man in black riding toward them this March day was considered by some of these soldiers to be the Lord's instrument. It was God, declared one of them, speaking through Lincoln who "saw fit to remove the only dark spot (slavery) from one of the most glorious flags the sun ever shone upon." Thomas Morris Chester, the only accredited African-American reporter covering this front, thought that the dressed ranks of black soldiers was a "grand sight, and must have been a source of considerable satisfaction to his Excellency." A white colleague concurred, proclaiming that Lincoln "must certainly have felt profoundly gratified at the fine appearance and thorough drill of the large body of men drawn up before him." Present in body as well as spirit was Sergeant John C. Brock of the 43rd USCT who declared that "we all looked upon him with that holy awe and reverence which was due him who was the nation's pride, as well as the bondsman's savior."[23]

Lincoln had long harbored doubts about blacks serving as soldiers. "If I were to arm them," he had told a delegation of anti-slavery clerics in the fall of 1862, "I fear that in a few weeks the arms would be in the hands of the rebels." Even the changing circumstances that moved the President to issue the Emancipation Proclamation and authorize black recruitment did not fully answer the question, since he initially limited their service to "garrison forts, positions, stations, and other places." Only after a number of brave African-American regiments proved with their lives their willingness to defend the United States did Lincoln come to accept and even embrace these soldiers as a "great . . . force for restoring the Union." A white officer in the ranks, watching the President review the proud files of black soldiers this

March day, observed that his "rugged face was illuminated by a smile the like of which for benignity I have never seen."[24]

Lincoln and company continued northward where portions of two divisions of the all-white Twenty-Fourth Corps were waiting. He was greeted by what one soldier termed "well nigh miraculous cheering." It was at this time that the vehicles carrying the First Lady and other guests reached the reviewing area. Who should Mary Lincoln and Julia Grant first observe but Mrs. Ord riding "quite near the President and General Grant." Mrs. Grant hoped to calm the roiling waters by asking Mrs. Ord to move closer to the carriage. When she arrived Julia Grant presented her to Mrs. Lincoln, "who received [Mrs. Ord] most graciously."[25]

While the account by Adam Badeau has Mrs. Lincoln giving Mrs. Ord a tongue-lashing, that of Lieutenant Colonel Porter, who was also present, is more in line with Mrs. Grant's. "Mrs. Grant enjoyed the day with great zest," he wrote, "but Mrs. Lincoln had suffered so much from the fatigue and annoyances of her overland trip that she was not in a mood to derive much pleasure from the occasion." Captain Barnes says that he accompanied Mrs. Ord to the First Lady's carriage and felt that things were not entirely right. "Our reception was not cordial; it was evident that some unpleasantness had occurred," he recalled years later. "Porter and Badeau looked unhappy, and Mrs. Grant silent and embarrassed. It was a painful situation from which the only escape was to retire."[26] Even as this soap opera was running, Lincoln commenced reviewing the all-white Twenty-Fourth Corps.

A Maine man in the ranks recalled, "It was an impressive scene, none the less so that it was not a show review, one held near a large city for the admiration of crowds of citizens, but was held in a great wood-surrounded field, and was witnessed only by the President and Mrs. Lincoln and their brilliant escort of officers." "Our tall President with his 'stove-pipe' hat was conspicuous, especially on horseback," added a New Yorker. An Ohio officer present noted that the "troops marched finely."[27]

Contrary to the negative accounts of Mrs. Lincoln's behavior, she seemed at times to enjoy herself. "Every one was cheerful and happy," a New York soldier observed. "During a part of the review several persons were introduced to Mrs. Lincoln, who appeared to hold from her wagon a reception en passant. Mr. Lincoln was silent, thoughtful, heavy; Mrs. Lincoln, courteous, gracious, pleasant."[28]

Another interested observer was General Grant's son, Jesse, who remembered that the "bands were playing and many of the staff horses, seasoned troopers though they were, were prancing. Father's horse, in particular, danced along with arching neck and curving body. But the horse President Lincoln rode walked calmly, almost as though conscious that his burden must be carried with anxious care, while the President sat stiffly erect, the reins hanging slack from his hands."[29]

It was clear to some observers that this had been a long day for the President. "I can never forget that care-worn face we beheld as he rode in our front, hat in hand, while our bands were playing 'Hail to the Chief.' Neither can I forget the cheers that rose from the boys in blue as he passed each command," remembered one. The *New York Herald's* man on the scene seconded that opinion and added one of his own, writing that after the review was over "the President and his friends instantly rode to the James [River] and embarked for City Point. The remark was common . . . that the President looked enfeebled and thin, and it was not clear to my mind that General Grant was in the best of health." It was at some point during these events that Lincoln told Grant, "How grateful I feel to be with the boys and see what is being done at Richmond!"[30]

In the category of "too much of a good thing," a reporter present thought that the glittering array of officers on hand "swelled the suite of the Commander-in-chief to proportions beyond the primitive ideas of republican simplicity." It was perhaps inevitable that someone on hand would have missed out, and in this case it was the Army of the James artillery. The gunners assembled as ordered at 11:30 a.m. and waited and waited. The men, explained a cannoneer, "were hungry and cold, but the thought that their beloved President would soon be on the field kept them from harsh thoughts and silenced the tongue of the grumbler. A shout arose that the President was coming. Every man tried to look even more soldierly; his heart was in his mouth, for each felt an emotion hard to describe. They saw the cavalcade in the distance, but to their great dismay it headed off across the hill and at dark the batteries were dismissed."[31]

Major General Ord rode up to the First Lady's carriage to announce that he had been given the honor of escorting them back to Aiken's Landing. He made it a point to introduce "a great many of the officers as they passed our carriage." This tired Mrs. Lincoln even more, and her mood was not improved when Mrs. Ord rode past. "Seeing Mrs. Lincoln was much fatigued," recalled Julia Grant, "I requested the General not to present any more of the gallant fellows who dashed past, all eager to catch a glimpse of the wife of their beloved and honored President."[32] Captain Barnes decided to forego the river return, so rode his borrowed horse down to City Point.

This day's Presidential review was not the most significant story north of the James. The plan crafted by General Grant to break Confederate control of Richmond and Petersburg was underway with an important part assigned to the Army of the James. Many of the troops Lincoln had just reviewed would be on the march within the next 24 hours heading south, as Grant took a calculated risk. He needed about 20,000 extra soldiers to take over portions of the Petersburg earthworks in order to free up as many Army of the Potomac men for offensive action. Grant was confident the Confederates guarding Richmond were in no condition to undertake a serious action of their own, so his orders reduced the Union force opposing them from more than 32,000 to fewer than 12,000.

Grant also wanted the officer running the Army of the James to take charge of the mobile contingent, so Major General Ord would be marching south as well. The capable Ord had supervised a stealthy withdrawal of these troops from their front line duties in recent days, and had staged them outside enemy cannon range preparatory to their movement to Petersburg. For many of those who had cheered Lincoln today, the next would bring final preparations and a night of hard marching. Grant realized that in the past General Lee had shown an uncanny ability to seize momentary advantages, but this time he believed the Rebels would have a lot more to occupy their attention, especially once Sheridan's cavalry began operating.

The deck officer aboard the USS *Bat* logged the *River Queen* returning at 8:15 p.m. Horace Porter found the journey back made enjoyable when Lincoln launched into one of his stories:

> In speaking of a prominent general, and the failure of the numerous attempts on the President's part to make the officer's services useful to the country, and the necessity finally of relieving him from all command, he said: "I was not more successful than the blacksmith in our town, in my boyhood days, when he tried to put to a useful purpose a big piece of wrought-iron that was in the shop. He heated it, put it on the anvil, and said: 'I'm going to make a sledge-hammer out of you.' After a while he stopped hammering it, looked at it, and remarked: 'Guess I've drawed you out a little too fine for a sledge-hammer; reckon I'd better make a clevis of you.' He stuck it in the fire, blew the bellows, got up a good heat, then began shaping the iron again on the anvil. Pretty soon he stopped, sized it up with his eye, and said: 'Guess I've drawed you out too thin for a clevis; suppose I better make a clevis-bolt of you.' He put it in the fire, bore down still harder on the bellows, drew

out the iron, and went to work at it once more on the anvil. In a few minutes he stopped, took a look, and exclaimed: 'Well, now I've got you down a leetle too thin even to make a clevis-bolt out of you.' Then he rammed it in the fire again, threw his whole weight on the bellows, got up a white heat on the iron, jerked it out, carried it in the tongs to the water-barrel, held it over the barrel, and cried: 'I've tried to make a sledge-hammer of you, and failed ; I've tried to make a clevis of you, and failed; I've tried to make a clevis-bolt of you, and failed; now, darn you, I 'm going to make a fizzle of you'; and with that he soused it in the water and let it fizz.[33]

Darkness had fallen when the *River Queen* returned to City Point, but there was more to come—a dinner followed by a dance that lasted until midnight with the music provided by a military band. Grant and Lincoln remained noticeably apart from the general festivities, huddled together and conversing in the after part of the boat. The general departed a little before 10:00 p.m.

What did Grant and Lincoln discuss? Most likely it would have been an overview of Grant's plans, still without much specificity. Horace Porter says that "General Grant now confided to the President his determination to move against Lee as soon as the roads were dry enough, and to make what he intended should be the final campaign." The essence of Grant's comments would have echoed his general orders issued three days earlier, in which he said, "the Armies operating against Richmond will be moved, by our left, for the double purpose of turning the enemy out of his present position around Petersburg, and to insure the success of the Cavalry under General Sheridan, which will start at the same time, in its efforts to reach and destroy the South Side and Danville railroad."[34] Any questions Lincoln asked would have been to allow him to understand the overall shape of the operation.

The President may have used the occasion to emphasize again the need to finish the fighting here and now. "It was President Lincoln's aim to end the whole business there," Grant recalled in later years. He continued:

He was most anxious about the result. He desired to avoid another year's fighting, fearing the country would break down financially under the terrible strain on its resources. . . . The entire expense of the government had reached the enormous cost of four millions of dollars a day. It was to put an end to this expense that Lee's capture was necessary. It was, in fact, the end and aim of all our Richmond campaign—the destruction of Lee, and not merely the defeat of his army.[35]

Adam Badeau insists that on this occasion Mary Lincoln publicly argued with her husband over the behavior of General Ord's wife, and even questioned Ord's command fitness. His account has no support from Horace Porter or Mrs. Grant. Yet it was clear the First Lady felt disrespected by the free-spirited Mrs. Ord. After the guests departed Mrs. Lincoln insisted that Captain Barnes be summoned to account for his part in what happened this afternoon. The President, at the end of an extremely long day, did as she wished and the naval officer appeared only to find himself in the middle of a squabbling couple. "Of course I could not umpire such a question," he wrote years later, "and could only state why Mrs. Ord and myself found ourselves in the reviewing column, and how immediately we withdrew from it upon the appearance of the ambulance with Mrs. Lincoln and Mrs. Grant. . . . I extricated myself as well as I could, but with difficulty, and asked permission to retire, the President bidding me good night sadly and gently."[36]

The lights burned late as well at Grant's headquarters, where a series of messages were dispatched beginning at 10:00 p.m. Two of his key corps commanders for the upcoming campaign were still on "temporary" appointments, and Grant requested that the Secretary of War make them official. Additionally, he took time to find a spot in the upcoming campaign for "an excellent officer" who had been on sick leave but was ready for a new assignment.[37] Most important, he made some minor changes to his instructions for the coming operation as suggested by George Meade. Grant was also trying to get a handle on how much damage had been done yesterday to Lee's army. A little after 11:00 p.m. he wired Meade for more details, which came within ten minutes. Meade's answer made it clear that Robert E. Lee had paid a high price for his failed March 25 efforts to upset or delay the accumulation of forces that Grant was now actively bringing against him. Grant intended to use every advantage at his disposal to ensure that the coming battle for Petersburg would be the last.

With this day's events, General Grant reached the end of the mental time limit he had put on the President's visit. Starting March 27, the tempo of events at Petersburg would move rapidly to a climax that would either hasten the end of the war or prolong it. No U.S. general about to undertake a major campaign would choose to have his commander-in-chief perched and watching from just miles away, but Grant and Lincoln were of one mind. Both were determined, as the President reminded his general, "to end the whole business there."

For his part, Lincoln was still on his quick-turnaround schedule with a day or so to go before he intended returning to Washington (if Mary was to make her March 29 opera date). An unexpected visitor would change those plans.

Chapter Four

Monday, March 27, 1865

"You are joking, General."

ADMIRAL David Porter would write often in his later years of his time with Lincoln at City Point, strongly implying they were constant companions. Yet the USS *Malvern* logbook entries for this day indicate he was aboard his flagship, anchored near Aiken's Landing, for the entire morning and much of the afternoon. His full schedule included a meeting with a civilian engineer and inventor named George W. Beardslee. The New Yorker was known in military circles for his development early in the war of a portable military telegraph that, unfortunately, worked better in the laboratory than in the field. This time Beardslee brought Porter a new design for torpedoes (mines) that promised to be easier and safer to assemble as well as more resistant to water seepage. That was enough for the admiral, who issued a circular to his commanders instructing them to give the scientist "all assistance in carrying out his wishes and in making such experiments as he may desire."[1] Porter left the ship for two hours in the afternoon. A corresponding entry in the logbook for the USS *Monadnock* indicates that he passed upriver toward the navy's front line, possibly engaged with the talented Mr. Beardslee.

Ten miles downriver at City Point, Lieutenant General Ulysses S. Grant was also managing multiple tasks on a critical day for his upcoming offensive, and finding it increasingly hard to make time for the President. Now that Sheridan had transferred his cavalry to the southern side of the James, it was up to Major General Ord to march his three infantry divisions (two white, one black) south from outside Richmond to Petersburg, where he was to take over a section of the trenches currently held by the Army of the Potomac. Ord's men had long been restricted to static warfare and their commander believed that if he pushed them too hard the straggling would be severe. Keeping to a more moderate pace guaranteed they would arrive with formations intact, but it also meant that some would cross the Appomattox military bridge in daylight and be visible to the enemy. Having them reach their destination ready to fight was more important to Grant than a stealthy passage, so he instructed Ord to proceed accordingly and coordinated with George Meade regarding their placement.

Also crossing Grant's desk this day were more specifics regarding losses suffered in the Fort Stedman attack (information he forwarded to Stanton and Lincoln) and a conundrum regarding the shipment of Rebel prisoners scheduled for exchange. Grant instructed the officer in charge to process those already on hand and then to suspend the proceedings. If Grant's plan went as he hoped, the Confederates would soon have more on their minds than exchanging prisoners. He also had to adjudicate an army dispute with a legally authorized Louisiana cotton trader and provide Stanton with a short version of General Sherman's latest report.

Grant had expected Lincoln would be gone by this time, so he might be excused for not paying full attention to his chief. Captain Barnes was of the opinion that "General Grant was not particularly desirous of Mr. Lincoln's presence at City Point, and it was, in fact, a somewhat embarrassing factor during those trying days. However that may have been, General Grant never for a moment manifested any impatience, but gave to the President every possible consideration."[2]

With both Grant and Porter tied up in the morning, Lincoln still managed to have a busy agenda with items not directly related to the pressing military matters. The President's first visitor aboard the *River Queen* this morning wasn't Captain Barnes, but two U.S. Treasury officials he knew: General Agent William P. Mellen and Special Agent Hanson A. Risley. The pair was deeply involved in one of the greyest of grey areas—Northern commercial trade with "loyal" Southern civilians. For both political and economic reasons, the Lincoln administration pursued a low-key policy of issuing some limited import licenses for Southern commodities such as cotton and tobacco. There were rules in place meant to prevent hard currency from going into Rebel coffers, in addition there were other safeguards regarding who could engage in the trade and the guarantees they had to provide. All

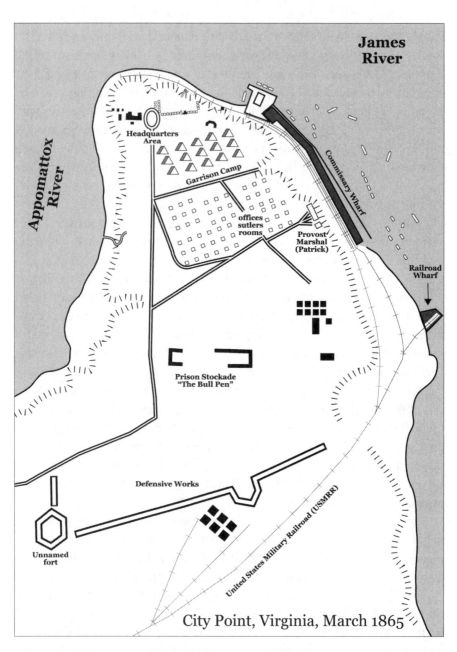

James River

Headquarters Area

Garrison Camp

Appomattox River

offices
sutlers
rooms

Commissary Wharf

Provost Marshal (Patrick)

Railroad Wharf

Prison Stockade
"The Bull Pen"

Defensive Works

Unnamed fort

United States Military Railroad (USMRR)

City Point, Virginia, March 1865

these regulations were regularly bent, twisted, and broken by those charged
with implementing the policy. Agent Risley, for instance, viewed himself as
facilitating these activities, not policing them, and though called to account
for a number of irregularities by a Congressional committee, he was not
censured.

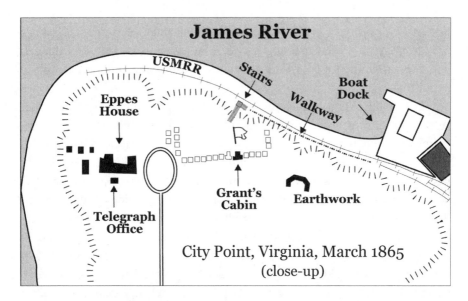

James River

Eppes House

USMRR

Stairs

Walkway

Boat Dock

Grant's Cabin

Earthwork

Telegraph Office

City Point, Virginia, March 1865
(close-up)

Risley and Hanson were on hand when Captain Barnes made his usual morning call on the President, finding him with Tad, who "was about, demonstrative as usual, clinging to his father and caressed affectionately by him."[3] Lincoln had been reviewing the revised casualty list for the March 25 fighting that Grant had sent over. The captain was undoubtedly introduced to the two Treasury men (whom he did not recall when reconstructing this day in later years). Barnes diplomatically asked after Mrs. Lincoln and was told that yesterday's events had been a bit much for her and that she was resting in her cabin. The President chatted for a few minutes before announcing that he was off to see Grant and invited everyone to join him. The four men went out to a day that was bright and fair.

The imminent offensive meant that City Point was humming with activity. Barnes observed "the river crowded with gunboats, monitors, transports, and colliers; the quartermaster's docks lined with vessels of every description unloading stores and munitions for the Grand Army; large storehouses filled to repletion covered the docks and approaches; innumerable teams were going and coming to and from the front every hour of the day and night."

Once atop the bluff, Lincoln and the others headed for Grant's cabin where there was always a crowd during daylight hours. "There was no formality," continued Barnes. "The news of the day was discussed, and dispatches were read or referred to in general conversation. All seemed confident that Petersburg must soon fall, and with it, Richmond."[4] Captain

Robert Lincoln likely would have been in that bluecoated crowd, and it's easy to imagine a brief greeting between father and son. Barnes remained with the staff while Lincoln, Grant, and the Treasury men found a quiet place to talk.

Risley described the conversation in a letter published in 1885. According to him Lincoln asked the two to explain to Grant the Treasury policy on the matter of trading with Southerners. The lieutenant general was not a friendly audience as he generally opposed such activities, especially when military operations were commencing. "The conversation was conducted with earnestness and some warmth on both sides," remembered Risley. In the end nothing changed as Grant "firmly adhered to his determination to suppress the traffic." As the meeting broke up, Lincoln confided to Risley that there were "military movements immediately pending which would render unnecessary all concern about the matter."[5] Risley and Mellen headed back to Washington, while Lincoln and Grant joined the crowd near the general's cabin. Several members of the group took advantage of the moment to introduce themselves to the President.

One was a minister named John Heyl Vincent, who later wrote that he "called on President Lincoln at Grant's headquarters. . . .Took with me Mr. [Charles] Coffin of *The Boston Journal* (the correspondent "Carlton" who writes so much & well). General Grant introduced me to President Lincoln & we had a pleasant interview." The presence of a man of the cloth and the fact that yesterday, Sunday, Lincoln had carried on business as usual, moved their interview into a religious realm and the President remarked "'that he supposed it was wrong—it being Sunday—but that it was war-time now, & that we get ourselves into it.' Grant told him he had not attended church more than three or four times since he got into the war and that then he was followed during the service by some 'orderly' with rattling spurs, bearing dispatches that required his immediate answer. He said that when he was in Galena he used to hear me preach regularly. He said he thought he never missed a morning service while I was there."[6]

The reporter Coffin spoke up to tell Lincoln about his recent visits to Charleston and Savannah.

"Indeed! Well, I am right glad to see you," the President said. "How do the people like being back in the Union again?"

"I think that some of them are reconciled to it," Coffin answered, "if we may draw conclusions from the action of one planter, who, while I was there, came down the Savannah River with his whole family—wife, children, negro woman and her children, of whom he was the father—and with his crop of cotton, which, of course, he was anxious to sell."

"Oh yes; I see," Lincoln said with a faint smile; "patriarchal times once more—Abraham, Sarah, Hagar, Isaac, and Ishmael, all in one boat." He chuckled a moment, and added, "I reckon they'll accept the situation, now that they can sell their cotton."[7]

Somebody (perhaps one of Grant's staff officers wishing to get the President out from underfoot without making him feel he was in the way) suggested that Lincoln and his family might enjoy visiting a nearby site identified by high sandstone cliffs called Point of Rocks. It was about four miles west of City Point on the north bank of the Appomattox River. A small army hospital was there, plus there were some nice views of the surrounding area and points of interest. While Lincoln headed back to the *River Queen* to alert his wife and son, Captain Barnes retired to the *Bat* satisfied that he had discharged his escort duties for the day.

Barnes had been aboard his ship for only a short while when Captain Robert Lincoln arrived to tell him that the President wished the navy captain to accompany the party going to Point of Rocks. Barnes had hoped to avoid any further interactions with Mrs. Lincoln, but the wish of the commander-in-chief, he told Robert, was the same as an order, so he returned to the *River Queen* with great misgivings. Barnes's instincts proved correct; Mrs. Lincoln was looking for someone to blame for the indignities she believed had been heaped upon her during the past few days, and the lowly naval officer headed her list, along with Mrs. Grant.

Soon after they got underway Barnes observed a heated exchange between Mary Lincoln and Julia Grant. "I . . . saw that it was exciting;" Barnes recollected in later years, "Mrs. Lincoln talking excitedly; Mrs. Grant gradually but in a low, gentle voice and quiet dignified manner, becoming for her, emphatic." Once again Julia's preference for informality clashed with the First Lady's insistence on protocol. According to what Julia afterward told Barnes, Mrs. Lincoln promised "that if Mrs. Grant ever came to Washington she would learn what etiquette demanded. Mrs. Grant . . . replied that if Mrs. Lincoln was the wife of the President, she was the wife of the General in Command of the armies of the United States . . . and that she would sit down anywhere if she thought it more agreeable than to stand in any one's presence. Whereupon Mrs. Lincoln asserted that she had observed Mrs. Grant and me 'laughing at her,' and directed her to say to me that she desired me to leave the boat and never come near her again."[8]

A view of the General Hospital of Point of Rocks, which Mary Lincoln
toured during their visit to this spot. LOC

That was enough for Captain Barnes. As soon as the *River Queen*
docked he borrowed a horse to make his way back to City Point. Mrs. Grant
remained on the ship while the Lincolns went ashore.

Upon arriving at Point of Rocks the First Family was given a tour by Dr.
Moses Greeley Parker. There was a "fine old farm house" owned by the
Strachan family that now quartered Federal surgeons, and near it was the
hospital building that had been constructed from materials taken from a
nearby church. (The hospital had a fairly constant patient population, Parker
said, of "one thousand, never less, and oftener 1,200 and 1,300."[9]) Lincoln
chose not to enter the wards, leaving that to Mrs. Lincoln, who visited some
of the patients along with several officers' wives. (Captain Robert Lincoln
and Tad likely accompanied their mother, while Captain Penrose kept
company with Mrs. Grant aboard the *River Queen*.)

The President, observed Dr. Parker, "seemed anxious and careworn. He
was very kind and genial in his manner, and was carelessly dressed, wearing
a tall hat, making his tall figure look even taller than any of our officers. He
moved easily and whenever he sat down he would cross his legs, throwing
one knee over the other, and then one leg would hang down nearly parallel
with the other, making this position of his graceful, easy and natural."[10]

While the First Lady visited the sick and injured, Lincoln walked out to
the stone bluff, sat under a sturdy oak (said to be where Pocahontas rescued

A view of the Appomattox River from Point of Rocks, taken in the approximate area where Lincoln contemplated the scene. LOC

Captain John Smith) and stared thoughtfully at the Union lines across the river. (An observer present at the beginning of the Petersburg siege described this spot as having a "most delightful view.") "Obviously he was thinking of something we knew not of," surmised the good doctor.[11]

Lincoln wandered back to the hospital area in time for a lunch with his family served by Private Byron Thompson. "I well remember that we got up a fine dinner for them," recalled the soldier. "By this time hundreds of convalescent soldiers came out to see the President and his wife," noted Dr. Parker. "When they cheered him, President Lincoln simply raised his hat, bowed and returned to the boat," which conveyed them back to City Point.[12]

Lincoln refrained from tramping up the bluff to visit Grant and instead turned his attention to a telegraphic missive from War Secretary Stanton finalizing the ceremonial plans for restoring the U.S. flag over Fort Sumter. Everything looked fine except for the date Stanton had chosen for the event—April 14. It bothered Lincoln enough that around 3:00 p.m. he sent Robert off to the telegraph office with a short note to the Secretary of War. In it he argued that Sumter had surrendered on April 13. "Look up the old Almanac & other data and see if I am not right," he wrote.[13]

Even as the Lincolns were lunching at Point of Rocks, General Grant received a message he had been anticipating. Sent at 12:30 p.m. from Old Point Comfort, Virginia (near Fortress Monroe), it confirmed that William Tecumseh Sherman was on the final leg of his journey to City Point. Sherman requested that Grant have a number of specific maps ready for their discussion and that he summon Admiral Porter, if possible. Grant was familiar with the travel time from Fortress Monroe and estimated Sherman would arrive around 6:00 p.m. He promptly informed Admiral Porter aboard the USS *Malvern*, knowing full well that Sherman's great friend would not miss the opportunity to visit with him.

Among Grant's guests this afternoon was Major General Mortimer D. Leggett, a western officer of his acquaintance posted with Sherman and on his way back to North Carolina following a medical leave. Grant and Leggett were conversing when another visitor arrived, the recently appointed provost marshal general, Brevet Major General Marsena R. Patrick. After wrapping up their business about 4:00 p.m. Grant asked the pair if they would like to join him to meet the President, an invitation they eagerly accepted. "[We] spent half an hour or three quarters, with the President," Patrick wrote this night in his diary. "He was very happy and talked very freely about many persons in high position; as freely as I would talk of them in my own family—Grant and I bore our full share in the conversation—As we were coming out he thanked us for calling upon him—Grant said that Sherman would be there at Six o'clock, which appeared to astonish him greatly."[14]

According to the reporter Charles Coffin (who likely got the story from Patrick), the dialogue following Grant's announcement went like this:

Lincoln: "You are joking, General."

Grant: "No, he will be here in an hour."[15]

It was Sherman who had asked for this meeting with Grant, not the other way around. Sherman and his men had just completed marching from Savannah, Georgia, through the heart of South Carolina and much of the same of North Carolina. It had been, to say the least, a demanding campaign, starting with South Carolina.

Heavy rains swelled minor rivers that had to be crossed and turned the landscape into thicketed lakes. Soldiers learned how to corduroy roads that were themselves under water, and campsites were often made in trees. Just as he had done on his march to the sea, Sherman cut his supply lines, necessitating his men bring along more than 3,000 wagons and ambulances since marshlands offered little in the way of sustenance. One weary Yankee wrote that he was "stuck in the swamps, in the sand knee deep, cold as a dog, sick as the dickens on poor rations."[16] Confederate opposition, while disorganized and inconsistent, added to the men's miseries but never stopped their forward movement.

Sherman's columns reached higher ground by early February and the real business of the campaign began. The general had made it clear at the outset that kid gloves were off when it came to South Carolina—the state that many believed had started the Civil War. "I almost tremble at her fate," he declared, "but feel that she deserves all that seems in store for her." Everything linked to the Confederacy was destined for destruction, along with anything nearby or along the way. Even a veteran officer from civilized New England agreed that "this terrible example is needed in this country as a warning to those men in all time to come who may cherish rebellious thoughts."[17] The stately city of Columbia became the symbol for Sherman's way of war when a fire, which each side accused the other of starting, roared out of control, consuming 450 buildings.

The North Carolina border was crossed in early March and Sherman ordered the kid gloves back on. "It should not be assumed," read one official order, "that the inhabitants are enemies to our Government."[18] This toned down but did not eliminate the widespread scouring of the countryside for supplies and the destruction of Confederate property. Rebels attempted to organize resistance, and there were planned (or semi-planned) strikes at Sherman's columns at Averasboro (March 16) and Bentonville (March 19-21), which merely delayed his schedule but did not change his itinerary. Soon after reaching Goldsboro, Sherman linked with other Union forces based along the North Carolina coast that reconnected his army to its supply line. Once again his audacity and logistical acumen had been crowned with success.

Sherman always insisted that his march through the Carolinas "was an important factor in the final result, the overwhelming victory at Appomattox, and the glorious triumph of the Union cause." Yet he also knew that, for all their high drama, his advances through the South did not of themselves deliver the victory. It was something he recognized even as he had begun the "March to the Sea." He insisted in his *Memoirs* that he and his men understood that their ultimate goal was to participate in the final battles that would take place in Virginia. "Indeed," he wrote, "the general sentiment was that we were marching for Richmond, and that there we should end the war." With the Carolinas campaign now essentially complete, Sherman looked to accomplish an even more important ambition, which he described as "the greater object of uniting my army with that of General Grant before Richmond."[19]

Sherman needed a face-to-face meeting with Grant to work out the details of his part in the war's end game. The two were great friends and mutually supportive, though Sherman was not above counting on that friendship to have his way in certain matters. It was Grant's great trust in Sherman that set the stage for the unprecedented movements from Atlanta to Savannah and from Savannah to Goldsboro. Now Sherman wanted to get into the fight against Robert E. Lee's army.

Grant seemed to be thinking along the same lines, having initially tried to ship Sherman's men directly from Savannah to Virginia only to be frustrated by a lack of sufficient tonnage to transport such a force. He had also hinted that Sherman could count on the services of Major General Philip Sheridan's cavalry, which was just finishing cleansing the Shenandoah Valley of Rebel supporters. Sherman was convinced that a short visit with Grant would seal the deal to have his men participate in the final campaign against Lee's army. He advised Grant on March 23 that as soon as the logistical connections to the coast were established to feed his armies, he "might run up to see you for a day or two."[20]

It took 48 hours to accomplish this and on March 25 Sherman was off to Morehead City to connect with transportation to take him to City Point. One officer overheard Sherman joke that Grant had been stuck "so long behind fortifications that he had got fossilized, and he was going to stir him up." A *New York Herald* reporter who was in New Berne when Sherman transited through heard him tell a group of curious soldiers that he was "going up to see Grant for five minutes and have it all chalked out for me and then come back and pitch in. I only want to see him for five minutes and won't be gone but two or three days."[21] Sherman went aboard the steamer *Russia* early on March 26, which weighed anchor and set course for Grant's headquarters.

He believed this would be his last, best chance to be in on the kill.

It was approaching 6:30 p.m. when Sherman's boat reached City Point, a fact announced by a ten-gun salute from Porter's flagship, which had dropped down from Aiken's Landing. Sherman wasted no time coming ashore, where he was met by several members of Grant's staff along with Admiral Porter. *New York Herald* reporter Sylvanus Cadwallader was close enough to note that the verbal welcomes were followed by "hearty greetings and handshakings, as officers of his acquaintance gather around, glad to meet under such favorable auspices a comrade whose name will henceforth adorn one of the brightest pages of history."[22]

Porter was singled out by Sherman for special public praise regarding his part in the capture of Fort Fisher and Wilmington, North Carolina. A correspondent present summarized the general's comments regarding Porter's role, "He said it was a grand affair, and exercised a most favorable influence on his plans in the Carolinas." Other questions came fast, and Cadwallader only caught the fragments of Sherman's answers: "But I whipped 'em too." "My boys chased 'em everywhere." "No trouble at all." Added the reporter, "The latter sentences uttered in his quick, nervous manner, sound so peculiarly Shermanish that all were smiling at his eagerness."[23]

General Grant had eased himself into the admiring crowd and even managed a joke of his own, concerning regular announcements in Southern newspapers proclaiming Sherman's defeat. "Ah, but you see, Sherman, we've heard the other side of the story," Grant remarked, adding, "How d'you do, Sherman!"

"How are you, Grant!" Sherman answered. According to a bystander, "Grant took both of Sherman's hands in his own, and shook them heartily." Sherman at once got down to business. "I want an hour's talk with you," he said. "Certainly, certainly," Grant replied. With that, wrote another reporter, the pair "walked off together, both smoking, and as cordial to each other as two school boys."[24]

Sherman was confident that his friend would agree to delay the advance upon Lee until he could personally participate, but Grant had other plans. "Sherman was anxious that I should wait where I was until he could come up, and make a sure thing of it," Grant remembered, "but I had determined to move as soon as the roads and weather would admit of my doing so. I had been tied down somewhat in the matter of fixing any time at my pleasure for starting, until Sheridan . . . should arrive, as both his presence and that of his cavalry were necessary to the execution of the plans which I had in mind."

Sheridan was here, the wheels were turning, and Sherman's appeal never had a chance. Grant did allow that if he hadn't run Lee's army to ground by the time Sherman was ready to move in about two weeks then his friend and subordinate would have his chance. Grant proceeded to explain his plans to Sherman and the part he expected him to play. Sherman's remembrance of this entire conversation was that "we talked over matters very fully."[25]

Grant then mentioned his other important guest. "I 'm sorry to break up this entertaining conversation," he said, "but the President is aboard the *River Queen*, and I know he will be anxious to see you. Suppose we go and pay him a visit before dinner." Sherman answered "All right," and they headed for the *River Queen*.

Grant left no account of the meeting but Sherman did. The President, he wrote, "remembered me perfectly, and at once engaged in a most interesting conversation. He was full of curiosity about the many incidents of our great march, which had reached him officially and through the newspapers, and seemed to enjoy very much the more ludicrous parts—about the 'bummers [foragers],' and their devices to collect food and forage when the outside world supposed us to be starving." The general referred to the bummers as "a regular institution" and, as he would do again later this evening, expanded his commentary into a story shared with him by one of Schofield's officers at Goldsboro. "He said Schofield's army was maintaining a telegraph line to keep up communication with the sea-coast, and that one of my men, who was . . . far in advance of my army, was seen up a telegraph-pole hacking away at the wires with a hatchet. The officer yelled out to him: 'What are you doing there? You're destroying one of our own telegraph-lines.' The man cast an indignant look at his questioner, and said, as he continued his work of destruction: 'I'm one o'Billy Sherman's bummers; and the last thing he said to us when we started out on this hunt was; 'Be sure and cut all the telegraph-wires you come across, and don't go to foolin' away time askin' who they belong to.'"[26]

Lincoln injected a serious element into the conversation when he expressed his anxiety that something might happen to Sherman's army while he was away from it. "I explained to him that that army was snug and comfortable, in good camps, at Goldsboro'," Sherman answered; "that it would require some days to collect forage and food for another march; and that [Major] General Schofield was fully competent to command it in my absence. Having made a good, long, social visit, we took our leave and returned to General Grant's quarters."[27]

The two army officers agreed to return the next morning for a more formal conference with the commander-in-chief. The President had always planned to talk over matters with Grant before departing, but Sherman's arrival was an unexpected bonus. Very likely before they departed Sherman got his good friend Admiral Porter added to the select guest list.

Once back among his friends Sherman held court while dinner was passed around. Grant's aide Horace Porter was quite overwhelmed as Sherman "gave a most graphic description of the stirring events of his march through Georgia. The story was the more charming from the fact that it was related without the manifestation of the slightest egotism. His field of operations had covered more than half of the entire theater of war; his orders always spoke with the true bluntness of the soldier; he had fought from valley depths to mountain heights, and marched from inland rivers to the sea. Never were listeners more enthusiastic; never was a speaker more eloquent. . . . At times he became humorous, and in a nervous, offhand, rattling manner recounted a number of amusing incidents of the famous march."[28]

Army provost marshal Patrick thought that Sherman looked "remarkably well, better than he did when he was about Washington in 1861." He was, Patrick continued in his diary, "so full of fun and cracking jokes, especially with Admiral Porter—Porter, Grant, [Gen. George L.] Hartsuff & some one or two Naval Captains were there." The admiral gleaned from some of what Sherman said that he had not been happy with his slow passage from North Carolina in the steamboat *Russia* and decided to provide "him the naval steamer Bat to take him back again to his post a vessel that could make sixteen knots an hour."[29]

Captain Barnes was summoned. His apprehensions about spending more personal time with Mrs. Lincoln were relieved as he received verbal orders "temporarily detaching me from service with Mr. Lincoln, and directing me to take General Sherman and his staff back to Newbern, or such other place as he might designate, with all possible speed. Then I was to return at once and resume my duties with Mr. Lincoln."[30] Barnes hurried off to ready his ship for Sherman's departure, scheduled for the next day.

The Sherman social wound down around 10:00 p.m. as the guests dispersed, leaving just Sherman, Grant, Mrs. Grant and a few aides. Julia asked the generals if they had inquired after Mrs. Lincoln when they were aboard the *River Queen*.

"Oh," replied her husband, "we went rather on a business errand, and I did not ask for Mrs. Lincoln."

"And I didn't even know she was aboard," added Sherman.

Mrs. Grant shook her head. "Well, you are a pretty pair!" she exclaimed. "I do not see how you could have been so neglectful."

"Well, Julia," said Grant, "we are going to pay another visit in the morning, and we'll take good care then to make amends for our conduct to-day."[31] Perhaps hoping to change the subject, Sherman began to banter with Ulysses and Julia about her access to military secrets. To test her knowledge, he began to call out place names which she was to identify. Geography happened to be one of Julia's strengths and in the spirit of the moment she gave back carefully concocted wrong answers.

One slight mystery that evening was the absence of Sheridan, whose presence had been specifically requested by Grant. The matter was solved close to midnight when the cavalry commander appeared, sputtering over the delays he had had to endure when the military railroad train he was taking jumped the track (not an uncommon experience), forcing him to cool his heels for hours. His mood wasn't helped by his worries that Sherman somehow would change Grant's mind about the detested orders for his troopers to go into North Carolina. (The reporter Coffin observed him preparing for the meeting, "He walks backward and forward, smoking, looking upon the ground, up to the sky, into vacancy, thinking how to do it."[32]) Then it was time to have it out with Sherman.

Sheridan recalled that as soon as he entered the cabin Sherman began to explain how he planned to link up with the cavalry officer's force. "I made no comments on the projects for moving his own troops, but as soon as opportunity offered, dissented emphatically from the proposition to have me join the Army of the Tennessee, repeating in substance what I had previously expressed to General Grant. My uneasiness made me somewhat too earnest, I fear, but General Grant soon mollified me, and smoothed matters over by practically repeating what he had told me in regard to this point at the close of our interview the day before, so I pursued the subject no further."[33]

It was late before everyone was talked out. Sheridan left for the Eppes house and the hospitable lodgings of the army quartermaster, Brevet Major General Rufus Ingalls, while Sherman was given space in one of Grant's cabins. Just a few miles west of this domestic tableau long columns of armed men were in motion as the divisions selected from the Army of the James were tramping south to play their part in Grant's grand plan. This night march, wrote a Maine soldier, "was a forced one, and was made over roads that were in a terrible condition." Such was the effort that most diarists were hard put to record more than navigational points. Notations kept by Private Richard Treat in the 148th New York were typical. "We came to Deep Bottom;" he wrote, "then crossed to Jones's Landing; we traveled all night; we got to Broad Landing in the morning and crossed the pontoons."[34]

Had the weary soldier stopped to ask, someone might have pointed out the sandstone cliffs overlooking the pontoon crossing, Point of Rocks, where earlier this day a president had sat and gazed at a fair sky knowing that a terrible storm was building just below the horizon.

CHAPTER FIVE

Tuesday, March 28, 1865

"You have never found fault with me."

EVEN as the President slept aboard the *River Queen*, Major General William Tecumseh Sherman decided to make another run at having Sheridan's command attached to his. He made his move well before the camp was stirring, catching Sheridan still in bed. The cavalryman recalled that Sherman "came to me and renewed the subject of my joining him, but when he saw that I was unalterably opposed to it the conversation turned into other channels, and after we had chatted awhile he withdrew."[1]

One officer who had missed the March 27 Sherman party was the Army of the Potomac's commander, Major General George G. Meade, whom Grant had allowed the privilege of visiting this morning. So, with aide Lieutenant Colonel Theodore S. Lyman, he caught an early military railroad train for City Point, arriving just as Sherman was retreating from Sheridan's bunk space in the Eppes House. Members of the headquarters staff were beginning to stir when Meade and Lyman spotted him. Lyman remembered Sherman as "a very remarkable-looking man. . . . He is tall, spare, and sinewy, with a very long neck, and a big head at the end of the same. . . . He is a very homely man, with a regular nest of wrinkles in his face, which play and twist as he eagerly talks on each subject; but his expression is pleasant and kindly. But he believes in hard war. I heard him say: 'Columbia! pretty much all burned; and burned good!' There too was 'little Phil Sheridan,' scarce five feet high, with his sun-browned face and sailor air. I saw

Sherman, Grant, Meade, and Sheridan, all together. A thing to speak of in after years!"[2]

Generals Meade and Sherman disappeared into the cabin of Grant's staff officer, Lieutenant Colonel Theodore S. Bowers. The assistant adjutant-general maintained an impressive map collection and Sherman needed a few visual aids to supplement his narrative. They were seen working at it by Grant's chief telegrapher, who remembered that Sherman "was pointing out on a map which hung on the rear 'flap' of the tent his route from Atlanta to Savannah. . . . Gen. Meade, the hero of Gettysburg, stood beside him, following his finger as it traced the line of march. A few feet away and watching intently the demonstration, but making no comment, was Sheridan."[3]

City Point was bustling this day. "The most ceaseless activity is every where in the quarter-master & ordnance departments," a reporter for the *New York Times* wrote. "A million cartridges in addition were sent out yesterday, and Sheridan's dismounted men were being remounted all yesterday and during the whole night, with fresh horses that came pouring in by boat-loads from Washington." A *New York World* reporter was even more emphatic. "It is no longer a secret that the armies before Richmond are preparing for a move," he jotted. "Baggage has been sent to the rear, and the army is stripping for the fight—perhaps the last great one on Virginia soil."[4]

Grant, on the eve of unleashing a major military operation, seems to have frittered away this morning, seduced by Sherman's dominating presence. George Meade wasn't the only officer who had missed last evening's gathering, and Sherman entertained them all. In his *Memoirs* he noted that this day "all the principal officers of the army and navy called to see me." He did find time to lobby Grant on approving a minor restructuring of his forces in North Carolina, a proposal that Grant promptly telegraphed to the War Department with the request for a quick positive response. (It still took 24 hours to process, the Secretary of War blaming "an oversight in my office" for the tardy reply.[5])

Lincoln, a few hundred yards away aboard the *River Queen*, likely spent the morning catching up on the national news. Each day would see recent issues arrive at City Point from the *New York Herald, Washington Chronicle, Philadelphia Inquirer, Baltimore American, New York Tribune, New York Times, New York World*, and a host of smaller papers. Lincoln may have escaped Washington, but he still needed to monitor the nation's mood. Also this morning, he would have enjoyed a chuckle over Stanton's reply to his note about the correct day that Fort Sumter fell. While agreeing with the President's sequence of events, the War Secretary pointed out that the formal surrender ceremony actually happened during the afternoon of April 14, but assured Lincoln that he would defer to his wishes.

Lincoln wrote out a response that allowed Stanton to choose either date (he picked April 14). He also passed along Sherman's reaction to the pending Yeatman appointment. Sherman pronounced him "almost the best man in the country for anything he will undertake."[6] This would prove to be the only communication that the President sent or received this day.

The sun was approaching the midday position when Admiral Porter made his appearance at City Point. That was Grant's cue. According to his aide Horace Porter, the lieutenant general explained "that the President was expecting them aboard his boat, and the two generals and the admiral started for the *River Queen*. No one accompanied them."[7] The weather was about perfect, warm and pleasant. The *River Queen* happened to be moored in the channel, necessitating that the officers catch a tug ride. Lincoln greeted them as they disembarked and led them to the upper saloon, which Sherman referred to as the after-cabin. The two army men immediately corrected their *faux pas* of yesterday by inquiring after Mrs. Lincoln and were told that she was well but not receiving visitors.

The informal nature of this gathering was reinforced by the sparse furnishings that awaited them. An artist named George Healy later created a painting of this scene based in part on a description Sherman provided him. "We did not sit to a table nor do I recall having any maps or papers," he told the painter, "we merely sat at ease in such chairs as happened to be there."[8] No one else was present and no transcript was kept of what they discussed. With yesterday's get-together having taken care of Sherman's campaign stories, and Lincoln aware that the general was returning to North Carolina as soon as they were done, the men quickly got down to business.

Protocol dictated that Grant would speak first. He provided the President with an update regarding the movements of Sheridan's troopers and Ord's infantry, and he pointed out that some of the cavalry assigned to Sheridan was marching past City Point even as they met. Lincoln, who liked to follow the unfolding of a military operation on maps, undoubtedly asked a few questions so he would know roughly where the various commands were positioned. Grant's only worry, as recalled by Sherman, was that Lee would get wind of what was taking place and withdraw his army before the blow could fall. Beyond that, the lieutenant general did not reveal much. "I would

Except for George H. Thomas (who was very much on Grant's mind), everyone pictured encountered Lincoln at some point during his visit to City Point. *LOC*

have let him know what I contemplated doing," Grant later admitted, "only while I felt a strong conviction that the move was going to be successful, yet it might not prove so; and then I would have only added another to the many disappointments he had been suffering for the past three years."[9]

Sherman chimed in next with a breezy assessment of his position in North Carolina and made light of his opponent's capability to do more than annoy him. When Lincoln again expressed a concern about his absence from his armies at this critical time, the major general reassured him that his second-in-command could manage, and besides, he was returning that very day. Admiral Porter, quite outclassed by the three heavyweights in the room, simply affirmed that the Navy was ready to do its part. He recalled that throughout these briefings "the number of shrewd questions propounded by Mr. Lincoln was remarkable, and some of them were found difficult to answer. His topographical knowledge . . . as well as other military matters he was not supposed to be familiar with, surprised those who listened to him."[10] Then it was time for the commander-in-chief to take the floor.

"He stated his views in regard to what he desired;" remembered Porter, "he felt sure, as did every one at that council, that the end of the war was near at hand." According to General Grant, "Mr. Lincoln asked if it would not be possible to end the matter without a pitched battle, with the attendant losses and suffering; but was informed that that was a matter not within the control of our commanders, and must rest necessarily with the enemy." The prospect of further casualties pained the President, especially with the end in sight. In a letter written in 1872, Sherman vividly recalled Lincoln's exclamations: "Must more blood be shed? Cannot this last bloody battle be avoided?" On another occasion Sherman recalled the President adding: "We have had so much of it."[11] The two generals repeated that it was all up to the Confederates.

Lincoln wanted to talk in a non-specific way about how surrendering soldiers should be treated. Here he parsed his words very carefully. There was a clear distinction in his way of thinking between individuals who laid down their arms and the corporate entities (national and state governments) that had organized and prosecuted the rebellion. The latter would be a matter for him and Congress, but the former would be the responsibility of the field officers who subdued them. Sherman wrote in his *Memoirs* that all Lincoln expected from his generals "was to defeat the opposing armies, and to get the men composing the Confederate armies back to their homes, at work on their farms and in their shops."[12]

Admiral Porter enthusiastically seconded Sherman's version. "Let them surrender and go home," he quoted Lincoln, "they will not take up arms again. Let them all go, officers and all, let them have their horses to plow with, and, if you like, their guns to shoot crows with. Treat them liberally. We want these people to return to their allegiance and submit to the laws. Therefore, I say, give them the most liberal and honorable terms." Just months after this discussion, Sherman affirmed to a Congressional committee that no particulars were discussed, "it was simply a matter of general conversation—nothing specific and definite."[13]

The President was closely observed by his officers throughout the discussions. Sherman remembered that when "at rest or listening, his legs and arms seemed to hang almost lifeless, and his face was careworn and haggard; but the moment he began to talk his face lightened up, his tall form, as it were, unfolded, and he was the very impersonation of good humor and fellowship."[14]

Sherman wanted some clarification regarding Southern leaders, specifically Jefferson Davis. He had come to feel that these men bore the heaviest weight of responsibility for the conflict. They had been blessed with "intellect, wealth, power and experience" yet they "chose war." Sherman felt little mercy toward these men and would personally favor their drinking "the cup of poisoned venom to its bitterest dregs."[15]

Lincoln's response was to tell one of his stories. "A man once had taken the total-abstinence pledge," he began. "When visiting a friend, he was invited to take a drink, but declined, on the score of his pledge; when his friend suggested lemonade, which was accepted. In preparing the lemonade, the friend pointed to the brandy-bottle, and said the lemonade would be more palatable if he were to pour in a little brandy; when his guest said, if he could do so 'unbeknown' to him, he would not object."

Sherman understood this to mean that Mr. Lincoln preferred Davis to escape, "unbeknown" to him.[16]

The meeting lasted not quite 90 minutes. There were handshakes all around as the officers rose to leave. Although he had said the least of all those present, Ulysses S. Grant was the most profoundly influenced by what was discussed. Speaking afterward to Horace Porter, the lieutenant general praised the President's "tenacity of purpose," which he felt was all that "could be desired in a great statesman. His quickness of perception often astonishes me. Long before the statement of a complicated question is finished his mind will grasp the main points, and he will seem to comprehend the whole subject better than the person who is stating it."[17]

"I know, when I left him, that I was more than ever impressed by his kindly nature," Sherman reflected, "his deep and earnest sympathy with the afflictions of the whole people, resulting from the war, and by the march of hostile armies through the South; and that his earnest desire seemed to be to end the war speedily, without more bloodshed or devastation, and to restore all the men of both sections to their homes."[18]

Lincoln managed a private moment with his major general as they began to depart.

"Sherman," he said, "do you know why I took a shine to Grant and you?"

"I don't know, Mr. Lincoln," the officer replied. "You have been extremely kind to me, Mr. Lincoln, far more than my deserts."

"Well," the President continued, "you have never found fault with me."[19]

Grant may have had his plans all in order, but the enemy was not just waiting for something to happen. The Union troop movements had been observed, and from his headquarters at Edge Hill, two miles west of Petersburg, General Robert E. Lee took countermeasures. He had already begun to concentrate as much of his cavalry as he deemed prudent in the threatened sector, but cavalry alone could not hold back strong infantry columns, so Lee reviewed his deployments and instructed Major General George Pickett to shift his division from the north side of the Appomattox River to the south, in order to bolster Petersburg's threatened defenses.

In a classic case of bad timing, Lee's daughter Agnes was completing plans to come down from Richmond for a visit, so he wrote her a note apprising her of the circumstances. "It would be very dreadful if you should be caught in a battle when the road would have to be used for military purposes & you cut off," he said. "I think it necessary to inform you that you may be prepared."[20]

Back at City Point, U.S. Grant was anxious to confirm Sherman's proposed reorganization of his forces but nothing had arrived from Washington by the time the lieutenant general returned to headquarters. The gaggle of officers who had come to greet Sherman had dispersed, Meade and Sheridan had both returned to their commands and most of the other visitors had drifted away. Admiral Porter wished his great friend well and departed, returning to the flagship at 1:30 p.m. Grant, his wife, and Sherman would have enjoyed a few moments together and the two officers likely reviewed their respective plans for the coming days. Once he had fully resupplied his forces, Sherman would move against the Confederate force confronting him, commanded by General Joseph E. Johnston. It would be left to Grant—and Grant alone—to tackle Robert E. Lee.

It was a little before 2:00 p.m. when word came that the USS *Bat* was ready to go. Sharing the ride, besides Sherman and his aide, Major James A. McCoy, were Major General Mortimer D. Leggett, Brevet Brigadier General Daniel C. McCallum (superintendent of military railroads), and interestingly, Brevet Brigadier General George H. Sharpe, who directed Grant's intelligence-gathering operations. Sharpe would go over a variety of security matters with Sherman before disembarking at Fortress Monroe. What thoughts Captain Barnes may have had as the *River Queen* (and Mrs. Lincoln) faded in the distance at 3:15 p.m. are not recorded.

Grant immediately threw himself into the task of running the armies of the United States. Telegrams went to the army's chief-of-staff Major General Henry Halleck (clearing up some confusion regarding Sheridan's command responsibilities); to Major General George Meade (clarifying who now commanded the City Point garrison and helping him locate extra telegraph operators to keep the elements of the Army of the Potomac in contact with headquarters once the operation began); and to Major General Godfrey Weitzel (seeking the latest intelligence on the Rebel units still posted north of the Appomattox River).

The most important were the instructions he provided to Major General Sheridan regarding his part in the upcoming operation. Just so there would be no misunderstanding, Grant officially repeated something he had told the cavalryman. "It is not the intention to attack the enemy in his intrenched position but to force him out if possible," Grant wrote. "Should he come out and attack us, or get himself where he can be attacked, move in with your entire force, in your own way, and with the full reliance that the army will engage or follow the enemy as circumstances will dictate."[21]

Among the rank and file beyond City Point, Lincoln's conference with Grant, Sherman and Porter had not gone unnoticed. "A great battle is expected in a few days," scribbled soldier diarist Calvin Berry, "something desperate will be done soon."[22]

There is no further accounting of Lincoln's activities this day, or any evidence that he came ashore. However, one immediate result of his meeting with Grant, Sherman, and Porter was a rethinking of his travel plans. The prospect of being close at hand when Grant engaged Lee's army suddenly became very meaningful to him. He was now reconsidering his original timetable for a "flying visit" in order to remain at City Point until Lee's army had been defeated. As he would soon explain, he could not leave now without seeing nearer to the end of General Grant's present movement.

CHAPTER SIX

Wednesday, March 29, 1865

"Your success is my success."

GENERAL Grant's offensive operations began in earnest this day, even as Lincoln was sleeping. Not long after midnight the camps of the three divisions of the U.S. Fifth Corps, Major General Gouverneur K. Warren commanding, located near the southern end of the Union Petersburg line at Hatcher's Run, began stirring. The plan was for them to depart without attracting attention. Musicians were instructed to play reveille "not at the hour of march, but as sounded under ordinary circumstances." The soldiers were cautioned to leave camp "as quietly as possible," and they were to take great care to ensure that "nothing in the camps is set on fire."[1] The columns began moving at 3:00 a.m. Their route would take them south across Hatcher's Run at a point called Monk's Neck Bridge, before heading westward to the intersection of the Vaughan and Quaker roads.

Grant's opening gambit was twofold. On Day One his infantry would extend the existing Union entrenched lines southward so that the left-most units would be within easy marching distance of Dinwiddie Court House, which was about 15 miles southwest of Petersburg. Sheridan's cavalry would simultaneously swing even farther south before turning west and camping for the night around Dinwiddie. On Day Two, with the infantry ready to provide support, Sheridan would push northward, fighting anything the Rebels threw in his path, or, if he found the way clear, he was to cut Lee's supply lines. Should the enemy fail to react and Sheridan completed his program of destruction, he still had the option of turning south to unite with Sherman, though he bridled at such a prospect.

The entrenched Union lines at Petersburg extended some 16 miles: southward from the Appomattox River, east of the town, then swinging westerly and southwesterly as far as Hatcher's Run. The last two miles or so were held by the Second Corps, commanded by Major General Andrew A. Humphreys, with the Fifth Corps bivouacked behind them. Even as Warren's men were tramping south, units from the Army of the James led by Major General E. O. C. Ord were beginning the tricky process of replacing Humphreys's soldiers on the firing line. Warren's movement to take up a line below Hatcher's Run parallel to the Boydton Plank Road would result in a gap between his right flank and the end of the Union entrenchments; Humphreys was sending his soldiers to fill that void so there would be no vulnerable openings for the anticipated Confederate counterattack.

Moving as well was the Army of the Potomac's headquarters, which packed up and set off at 7:15 a.m. Major General George G. Meade's hyper-observant staff officer, Lieutenant Colonel Theodore Lyman, indulged himself in a moment of whimsy, bidding adieu to the now former camp. "It was like to the ruins of Carthage to behold those chimneys, which, since October last, have been our comfort at Headquarters, now left lonely and desolate, deprived of their tents, which seemed to weep, as they were ruthlessly torn down and thrown into wagons." The beauty of the day inspired some purple prose from a New York chaplain under Warren's command, who remarked that "gentle zephyrs breathed through the woods, which had begun to blush with vernal beauty, and the tender grass was beginning to greet us with its verdant freshness, and all things, that silent spring morning, seemed to conspire to make the march of our august column to its terrible work grand in the highest degree."[2]

Also stirring this morning were the 9,000 or so cavalrymen that Major General Philip Sheridan was leading into harm's way. They had encamped near Hancock Station, close to the Jerusalem Plank Road, after crossing the James and Appomattox Rivers several days earlier. There they had rested and refitted, keeping the supply-bearing trains busy, while comrades without horses waited at City Point for remounts. Now as the bugles sounded the men gathered their kits and their wits. Each trooper carried five days' rations, 30 pounds of forage, and 40 rounds of ammunition. Word had been passed not to plan on returning to this campground, so the men expected they would find a fight before too long.

Sheridan's cavalrymen were to march south and west about 11 miles—past the site of the August 1864 battle of Reams' Station—then turn west a dozen more miles to reach the object of this day's movement: Dinwiddie Court House. Twenty-five miles in a day was well within cavalry range, given decent conditions, but the Virginia roadways they were using were anything but decent.

"Whoever has traveled the highways of Dinwiddie County, Virginia, in the melting days of spring, has probably recollections of black soil appearing here and there, islands in ponds of black water fringed with green; whoever has left the highways for a short-cut will remember how his horse broke through the upper crust and found apparently nothing below but space," mused one of Sheridan's cavalrymen. A New Yorker described the route they followed as "miry from the winter frosts and rains," while a Rhode Island trooper could only refer to them as "horrible roads." A Massachusetts man claimed to have seen a horse and rider get stuck in the muddy bed of a stream, "and with every struggle [they] sank deeper and deeper into the slime till nothing but his [horse's] ears were visible, and his rider was barely rescued from being buried alive." Matters were even worse for the supply train and its escort, which trundled along after thousands of hooves had wholly churned the ground. A West Virginia cavalryman swore that in places the wagons "had literally to be carried through the deep mud and quicksand of that region."[3]

There was never a doubt that Phil Sheridan would keep his columns moving. There was a revealing moment at the very start of the day's march. Back in the spring of 1864 Sheridan had commanded all the cavalry assigned to the Army of the Potomac. When Grant needed a troubleshooter that autumn to subdue an enemy threat in the Shenandoah Valley, he had sent Sheridan, who took two of his three divisions with him. The one left behind had served under a capable officer who had recently resigned, leaving the men with an unknown quantity at their head and the prospect of a tough campaign in the offing. Spirits and morale were low.

All that changed when a familiar headquarters flag appeared along their column.

"In a few moments we saw 'Little Phil' himself, and his staff, and . . . his cavalry fresh from their glorious victories in the Shenandoah Valley," recalled one of the left-behinds. "The cheers we sent up told us no uncertain story, and with those cheers went out all the distrust, all the melancholy forebodings with which we had been tormented. Then we were ready to go anywhere or to fight anything. We were new men in a moment. What might be in store for us we knew not, nor really cared, for we were with Sheridan; once more were a portion of his glorious cavalry, and we felt that with him at our head we were safe."[4]

That was one reason Grant absolutely needed Sheridan with him on this campaign. Within 24 hours the lieutenant general would personally experience another.

Lincoln would have known of Grant's impending departure for the front so he likely spent the early morning waiting for word that his army chief was ready to go. When it arrived (one imagines that the messenger was Captain Robert Lincoln who also visited with his mother), the President wasted no time hustling ashore. He had spent too much of his tenure as commander-in-chief urging reluctant subordinates to act, and he certainly was not going to be the cause now for any delay. The morning weather was fine, with no indication that a meteorological storm was simmering along with the military one.

Grant had made arrangements the day before regarding Julia's safety. "I have . . . decided that you and Mrs. [John A.] Rawlins had better remain on the dispatch boat for the present, and if all my plans turn out as I hope and expect they will, I will then return with you to Washington," he told her. "But," he continued, "if Lee should escape me—and I am desperately afraid he will move now before I am ready—and make his way to the mountains, there is no telling when this war will end, and in that case you would have to go back home alone."[5]

Horses for the staff were being loaded aboard the special train held for Grant's use. It would appear that Lincoln made it up the bluff to army headquarters while there was still time to spare. "We had the satisfaction of hearing one good story from him before parting," remembered Horace Porter:

> General Grant was telling him about the numerous ingenious and impracticable suggestions that were made to him almost daily as to the best way of destroying the enemy, and said: 'The last plan proposed was to supply our men with bayonets just a foot longer than those of the enemy, and then charge them. When they met, our bayonets would go clear through the enemy, while theirs would not reach far enough to touch our men, and the war would be ended.'

Mr. Lincoln laughed, and remarked: 'Well, there is a good deal of terror in cold steel. I had a chance to test it once myself. When I was a young man, I was walking along a back street in Louisville one night about twelve o'clock, when a very tough-looking citizen sprang out of an alleyway, reached up to the back of his neck, pulled out a bowie-knife that seemed to my stimulated imagination about three feet long, and planted himself square across my path. For two or three minutes he flourished his weapon in front of my face, appearing to try to see just how near he could come to cutting my nose off without quite doing it. He could see in the moonlight that I was taking a good deal of interest in the proceeding, and finally he yelled out, as he steadied the knife close to my throat: 'Stranger, kin you lend me five dollars on that?' I never reached in my pocket and got out money so fast in all my life. I handed him a bank-note, and said: "There's ten, neighbor; now put up your scythe.'[6]

Then they learned that the animal loading was completed and that the track was clear. Ulysses and Julia enjoyed a final embrace, he "kissing her repeatedly as she stood at the front door of his quarters," observed Lieutenant Colonel Porter. "She bore the parting bravely, although her pale face and sorrowful look told of the sadness that was in her heart." As Julia later reflected, "I knew, or thought I knew, my General would return to me."[7] The group of officers and the President now ambled their way down the hill to the platform near the wharf, where the special train was waiting for their journey.

A merchant standing nearby named James A. Skilton was a witness. "Grant walked back and forth alone and thoughtfully, near the head of the train," he recalled. "Mr. Lincoln stood in the midst of a little group near the rear steps of the single passenger car, chatting with all in his characteristic way." Horace Porter, a member of that clique, recollected that as the "party mounted the car the President went through a cordial hand-shaking with each one, speaking many words of cheer and good wishes." Skilton heard the President tell one officer (identified in another source as Brigadier General John A. Rawlins): "Good luck to you, General. Your luck is my luck," as well as the answer, "Yes, Mr. President, and everybody's luck."[8]

"Suddenly," continued Skilton, "Gen. Grant, having received some message, turned, walked briskly toward the President, took his hand and simply said: 'Good-bye, Mr. President,'" and climbed aboard. "As the train was about to start we all raised our hats respectfully," added Horace Porter. "The salute was returned by the President, and he said in a voice broken by

A news magazine montage of some of the USMRR stations that figured in Lincoln's visit: City Point (center) and (clockwise from 4 o'clock position) Patrick, Warren (Globe Tavern), Meade, and Hancock stations.
Harper's Weekly, December 24, 1864

an emotion he could ill conceal: 'Good-by, gentlemen. God bless you all! Remember, your success is my success.'"[9]

The reports coming into General Robert E. Lee's headquarters were consistent enough that at midmorning he signaled the War Department in Richmond that the enemy was moving against his right flank.

While Lee may not have known the enemy's ultimate objective, the growing accumulation of Union forces near Burgess Mill could not be ignored. He thinned out a section of his line east of Hatcher's Run and sent those troops to bolster the threatened sector. He also accelerated the gathering of a mixed cavalry/infantry force to operate beyond the line of entrenchments by directing the three infantry brigades of Major General George Pickett's division (just arrived from north of the Appomattox River) to move to Sutherland's Station on the Southside Railroad, ten miles west of Petersburg. (Later in the day he would order the cavalry that had come to Petersburg from the north side to mass at that same point.)

Somehow he found the time to pen a quick note to his daughter, Agnes. "I have just heard of your arrival in Petersburg," Lee said. "I am too sorry I cannot go in to see you, but I must go to the right. The enemy in strong force is operating in that direction. I do not yet know to what extent or when I can visit you."[10]

Seven miles southwest from where Lee was absorbing data and making decisions, the officer in charge of the Burgess Mill sector was making some of his own. Lieutenant General Richard Anderson alerted his subordinate, Major General Bushrod R. Johnson, to be ready for the approaching enemy and to oppose any advance. Anderson, like Lee, subscribed to the philosophy that a strong offense was the best defense.

The departure of Grant and most of his staff instantly transformed City Point into a backwater. With the navy on hold until something developed, Admiral Porter was also footloose, so he proposed a little diversion that the President accepted. According to the *Malvern* log, it was 10:00 a.m. when Porter and Lincoln "proceeded up the Appomattox River in the [admiral's] barge in tow of a tug." No mention is made of the presence of Tad Lincoln, but given the relaxed nature of this trip it is reasonable to assume he was aboard. This may account for one of those Admiral Porter reminiscences that otherwise appears in an ambiguous context. "While these [army] movements were taking place the President, myself, and Tad were making excursions up and down the James River in my barge," wrote Porter. "We would make fast to a tug with a long line, and let her tow us. If this is not the luxury of locomotion, I don't know what is, and it certainly seemed very grateful to the President then. He said he should always look upon this time as the real holiday of his administration. He seemed almost to forget that he had any public cares."[11]

The *Malvern* log indicates that Lincoln and Porter spent an hour and ten minutes up the Appomattox River, followed by a 25-minute roundtrip to Bermuda Hundred. There is no evidence that Lincoln landed at any point, nor any witnesses to what he did. The Appomattox River cruise would have brought him as far as the pontoon bridge below Point of Rocks and possibly a view of the logistical tail of the Army of the James cavalry operating with Sheridan. The party could not have continued much past the pontoon bridge, since that would have brought them within range of Rebel cannon.

Grant had asked the Admiral to station some gunboats in the Appomattox River near the pontoon bridge just in case the enemy made an effort to get in rear of the Federal lines on Bermuda Hundred. Porter likely mixed a little business with pleasure by checking on those warships. Lincoln was probably clearing his thoughts. With his face-to-face meeting with his generals over and the military operations underway, the commander-in-chief was merely a bystander who needed to adjust to his new role as observer. Lincoln and Porter returned to the *River Queen* by 11:35 a.m.

The Washington rumor mill began churning this day with a story that would prompt much speculation. Without any formal announcement to the press, Secretary of State William H. Seward, his daughter Fanny (accompanied by a female friend), plus the English and Spanish ministers were rowed out in small boats from the landing near Anacostia Bridge and boarded the steam revenue cutter *Northerner*, bound for Fortress Monroe. No other information was released. Within 24 hours newspapers around the country would ponder the implications of this unscheduled foray, recalling only too vividly that in early February Seward had quietly traveled to Fortress Monroe to join Lincoln in a meeting with Confederate commissioners about negotiating a peace. Suddenly, the presence of Grant and Sherman together with the President with the addition of the Secretary of State suggested to some that the biggest story of the war was about to break.

Grant's operation aimed at breaking Lee's hold on Petersburg continued to unfold, though not quite as scripted. The head of the Fifth Corps column reached the intersection of the Vaughan and Quaker roads around midday. According to the plan, the men were to halt here while contact was made with the Second Corps, which was then extending the Federal line southward. However, the Second Corps was running behind schedule. If Major General Warren pushed westward another two miles as ordered and began entrenching along the Boydton Plank Road, his corps would be isolated with its flanks open, a tempting target for Rebel troops poised behind nearby earthworks. It took a couple of messages between Warren and Meade to clarify that Warren had a new mission to send a strong force up the Quaker Road to join hands with the Second Corps.

He chose Brevet Major General Charles Griffin's division for the job, and those troops set off about 1:00 p.m. It was not easy going; there was a bridge out, and sections of the road had been choked with felled trees. A thin line of Confederates barred passage at the ruined bridge. Leading the way for Griffin's command was a two-regiment brigade led by Brigadier General Joshua L. Chamberlain, an officer who had found glory at Little Round Top near Gettysburg in July 1863. He quickly organized an advance across the waist-deep stream. "This led to a hand-to-hand encounter," he wrote. "The attack was impetuous; the musketry hot."[12] The task given the Rebel soldiers was just to delay, so they fell back toward their earthworks.

Southern reinforcements were on the way, for little more than a mile north of where Chamberlain was crossing Gravelly Run, Bushrod Johnson received authority from Anderson to drive the enemy back. Johnson commanded four brigades charged with holding the extreme right end of the Confederate line at Petersburg. The standard Robert E. Lee playbook called for prompt responses to threats with all available assets, even if that meant dangerously minimizing any reserve. So Johnson ordered out three of his brigades to meet the Yankee advance. Taking the lead were a trio of Virginia regiments, which soon encountered and drove back Union skirmishers. Upon reaching an open area near the Lewis farm, the Virginians halted until their comrades arrived.

General Chamberlain advanced his skirmishers after opening the way across Gravelly Run before moving the rest of his 2,000 men forward as far as the Lewis farm, which represented the largest clearing in the neighborhood. Spotting the enemy in some force at the opposite end of a broad field, he ordered his two regiments to dig in until the rest of Griffin's division could join them.

It was while Grant and his staff were traveling to the front that, as Horace Porter recalled, the general "sat down near the end of the [railroad] car, drew from his pocket the flint and slow-match that he always carried, struck a light, and was soon wreathed in the smoke of the inevitable cigar. I took a seat near him, with several other officers of the staff, and he at once began to talk over his plans. Referring to Mr. Lincoln, he said: 'The President is one of the few visitors I have had who have not attempted to extract from me a knowledge of my movements, although he is the only one who has a right to know them. He intends to remain at City Point for the present, and he will be the most anxious man in the country to hear from us, his heart is so wrapped up in our success; but I think we can send him some good news in a day or two.' I never knew the general to be more sanguine of victory than in starting out on this campaign."[13]

Grant had allotted himself a critical role in the upcoming operation. His plan involved three separate commands, each reporting directly to him. The largest was George Meade's Army of the Potomac, followed by the elements from Ord's Army of the James, and finally Sheridan's cavalry. As long as these units operated within their own spheres, little coordination was required; but sooner or later circumstances would dictate that some be shuffled from one chain-of-command to another. It would be up to Grant to initiate those temporary transfers as well as monitoring the fortunes of each element of his plan. Combat actions that meshed together such disparate units were notoriously difficult to manage, but for Grant's plan to succeed he would have to do just that.

It took a little less than an hour for the military railroad train to reach the next to last stop on the line, Humphreys Station, where men and horses disembarked and headed overland. The location of army headquarters would be governed by events in subsequent days, but on this first one its position was known and advance preparations had been made. That included being hooked into the field telegraph network, which, as the *Philadelphia Inquirer* reporter Edward Crapsey crowed, meant that the Lieutenant General "can talk to-night with [Secretary of War] Stanton in Washington . . . with all parts of our immense line, as well as the North. The army telegraph is an institution that has been brought to practical perfection. Put up faster than infantry can march, an operator riding with a corps commander, the General

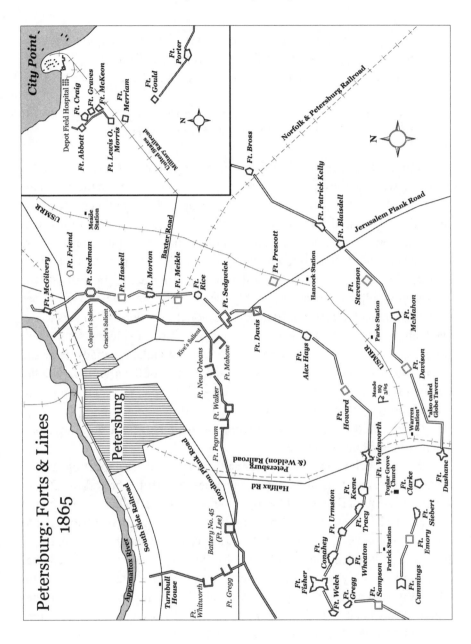

Petersburg: Forts & Lines
1865

can, during a brief halt for rest, communicate with his chief and send any intelligence he may have acquired and receive orders from him."[14]

One of the first notes Grant sent was to the President:

> Just arrived here 11.12 a.m. Nothing heard of from the front yet—No firing—I start [for the front] in a few minutes. Sheridan got off at 3 this morning.[15]

Admiral Porter returned to the *Malvern* at 1:30 p.m. (after presumably lunching with the President on the *River Queen*), there to spend the rest of his day. Lincoln's subsequent actions are not recorded by any witness. Not long after the Admiral departed, a courier likely brought over Grant's first message from his field headquarters. Knowing that communication was now established, and well used to hanging out in the War Department telegraph office in Washington to monitor the news during active operations, the President would have been irresistibly drawn to the place next to the Eppes house. Grant had left behind Lieutenant Colonel Theodore S. Bowers to run the facility. Bowers would have welcomed Lincoln, most likely setting him up in his personal cabin, which was well stocked with area maps. Here the commander-in-chief may well have passed the rest of the afternoon and the evening following events as described in a series of messages that went to or passed through the central station manned by Bowers.

There would soon be news to report, as matters were heating up along Grant's lines of advance.

The help Brigadier General Joshua Chamberlain was expecting arrived at the Lewis Farm area in the form of another of Griffin's brigades—Brevet Brigadier General Edgar M. Gregory's—that closed in on his left. Prompted by Brevet Major General Griffin himself, the combined force advanced into the woods ahead, where the enemy was waiting. Chamberlain sent in a reinforced skirmish line, followed by his two regiments in combat formation. Gregory pursued a parallel course. The time was about 3:30 p.m. This provoked a violent response from the Virginians inside the tree line, who laid down a heavy fire. Chamberlain's line was staggered but, he later reported, the men "advanced . . . with great steadiness and drove the enemy from their position and far into the woods." However, the Rebel commander Bushrod Johnson had committed three of his four brigades to the task, and the two yet unengaged now laced the Federal line with what Chamberlain called "a withering fire;" even a reporter on hand made mention of the "vehemence of their musketry."[16] Adding a touch of the bizarre to the combat tableaux was the looming presence of a huge pile of sawdust produced by a now defunct sawmill.

Slightly more than 24 hours earlier a U.S. president, two of his generals, and an admiral may have sketched a framework for allowing the armies of the Confederacy to disband, but the infantrymen from Virginia, North Carolina, South Carolina, and Alabama clearly weren't yet on the same page. Private A. M. Rice, one of Chamberlain's New Yorkers, hunched against the torrent of fire, and later termed this a "fierce engagement."[17] The two Yankee regiments (approximately 2,000 men, each unit in the field for less than a year) held on. Chamberlain's line of battle bent and twisted, but did not break, and more help was at hand as Regular Army cannoneers pushed up four guns and began hammering the Rebel positions. Still, the deadly pressure was unrelenting and the outcome in doubt until portions of a third Federal brigade deployed on the scene to add to the cacophony. Anderson promptly pulled his men back to the Boydton Plank Road.

The late afternoon fight was over. The blood-spilling that Lincoln had hoped to avoid had begun. "The struggle was terrible," recalled Private Rice. Federal losses in this small-scale engagement were 381 for Warren's corps and an estimated 371 for Anderson's. "Nearly all the wounds received were severe as it was at close range and the rebels shot to kill," attested Rice.[18] Among the Union wounded was General Chamberlain, who had been punched in the chest and briefly incapacitated by a bullet that had first passed through his horse. Chamberlain would retain command of his brigade for the rest of the current campaign.

Most of Grant's objectives for the day had been realized. The rest of Warren's corps reached the Boydton Plank Road without serious challenge, and a link was established between the Fifth and Second corps. A few miles to the south, Sheridan's cavalrymen (except for those herding supply wagons) took possession of Dinwiddie Court House and picketed the area.

With all the information on hand, Grant made an important modification to his initial plan. Up to this point Sheridan had been given the option of swinging farther westward to go after Lee's supply lines. Now, with his forces closed up on the enemy's lines and engaged, Grant was no longer satisfied with simply maneuvering. In a message sent to Sheridan, he declared: "I now feel like ending the mat[ter] if it is possible to do so. . . . I do not want you therefore to cut loose and go after th[e] enemy's [supply] roads at present. In the morning push round the enemy if you can and get on to his right rear. . . . We will act together as one Army here unt[ill] it is seen what can be done with the enemy."[19]

Grant sent Lincoln a second message that added but little to the first. His third message to the President this day came into the City Point telegraph office at 5:10 p.m.:

> The enemy attacked Griffin Div 5 AC near where the Quaker road intersects the Boydtown [sic] road about 4 P.M. The enemy were repulsed leaving about 60 prisoners in our hands. There was some loss of life on both sides.[20]

Lincoln consulted his maps, thought about matters, had some dinner, and after waiting three hours transmitted his first response:

> Your three despatches received. From what direction did the enemy come that attacked Griffin? How do things look now?[21]

Grant's reply was time stamped 9:00 p.m.:

> Griffin was attacked near where the Quaker road intersects the Boydtown [sic] Plank—at 5:50 P.M. Warren reports the fighting pretty severe but the enemy repulsed leaving one hundred prisoners in our hands. Warren advanced to attack at the hour named but found the enemy gone. He thinks inside of his main works. Warren's Pickets on his left along Boydtown Plank road reported the enemys cavalry moving rapidly Northward & they thought, Sheridan after them. Sheridan was in Dinwiddie this P.M.[22]

This would be their final exchange for March 29. Lincoln was curious how matters stood north of the James and sent a note a little after 8:00 p.m. to Major General Godfrey Weitzel asking what he had observed this day. Weitzel had seen little other than some cavalry riding south. A follow-up note that arrived after midnight reported no change.

There were other official messages coming into City Point addressed to Lieutenant Colonel Bowers that Lincoln would have examined. Some were administrative housekeeping; others reported more details regarding the position of the Union forces. All painted a picture of an army that had shrugged off a minor attack and was pausing for the night with no imminent threats. One non-army message addressed to the President was sent from Washington at 8:30 p.m. by the Secretary of War, Edwin M. Stanton. The

Secretary assured him that there was nothing happening in Washington that required his being there and offered the observation that Lincoln's continued presence at the front would be "gratifying to officers and soldiers, while relieving you from torment."[23]

There was some unexpected excitement for the President after dark as this day's actions provoked a brief but lively artillery duel along the Petersburg lines not far from City Point. The Confederates opened the ball to prevent any Federal advances in the sector and to give Grant something else to worry about. For a New York chaplain posted at the Point of Rocks hospital it "seemed as if two contending thunder storms had met." Veteran reporter Charles Coffin declared that it "surpassed all other firing I ever witnessed at night, in beauty and grandeur. . . . The air was filled with fiery arches, crossing each other at all angles—some from the north, east, south and west—passing and repassing, meeting midway and cut across by lines of fire streaming from the rifled cannon sending swiftly revolving balls point blank into the rebel works."[24]

One account closer to where the President was sitting came from a member of the 15th New York Engineers, posted at City Point and ordered into one of its battlements, Fort McKeon. Private Darwin C. Pavey wrote his hometown newspaper describing "the most sublime but awful sight of an artillery duel. The constant flashes of the guns, followed by the reports, seemed to impress upon the minds of beholders a most intense feeling of awe. Words are wholly inadequate to convey a true idea . . . of this artillery fight, and when I state that the discharges of the guns were nearly as rapid as the snapping of each fire-cracker, (only significantly louder) when a pack is ignited."[25]

President Lincoln mentioned the hubbub in a telegram sent the next day to the Secretary of War:

Last night at 10:15 . . . a furious cannonade, soon joined in by a heavy musketry-fire, opened near Petersburg and lasted about two hours. The sound was very distinct here, as also were the flashes of the guns upon the clouds. It seemed to me a great battle, but the older hands here scarcely noticed it.[26]

Lincoln probably returned to the *River Queen* around midnight and surely took note of the heightened level of security. He would have walked back to his floating quarters more rapidly this time because it was raining. A soldier in the field described the precipitation crescendo as "first a Scotch mist, then unsteady showers, and then a pour, as if the equinox, hurrying through the elements, had kicked over the water-buckets." Civil War armies in the field had just one way to deal with a major rain event; hunker down and hope it would soon pass. The commander-in-chief had seen enough operations imperiled by such conditions that he would have been philosophical about it, perhaps recalling a biblical quotation he had previously used that some "seemed to think, in defiance of Scripture, that heaven sent its rain only on the just, and not on the unjust."[27]

CHAPTER SEVEN

Thursday, March 30, 1865

"I dislike to leave without seeing nearer to the end."

An important item widely reported in the news was the presence of Secretary of State Seward at Fortress Monroe this day. Located at the southern tip of the Virginia Peninsula, it was a strategically positioned military base as well as a critical junction in the East Coast communication network. The military telegraph office there was virtually hard-wired to the War Department in Washington and in direct contact with New York and Philadelphia via a cable switch in Wilmington, Delaware. Ships bringing messages about U.S. military operations as far south as Florida and the Gulf of Mexico dropped them off at Fortress Monroe for rapid transmission northward. In similar fashion, newspaper correspondents often transmitted through Fortress Monroe when time was of the essence. So, although there hadn't been any military action in the area of note since 1862, several of the larger papers maintained bureaus there to facilitate the passage of breaking news. These men also reported what they were hearing and seeing to their editors in the North, who considered their information valuable intelligence.

Word of the arrival of the steam revenue cutter *Northerner* bearing the Secretary of State, his daughter, and a few guests, spread quickly. William Seward spoke to no one on shore, nor was he seen by any of the newsmen, but his presence fueled speculation. Enough so that the editorial writer for the *New York Sun* mused in a piece to run the next day, that at a time "when affairs of State require such close attention as they now do, when the several departments are crowded with business, it would certainly seem strange that both the President and the Secretary of State should absent themselves from the Capital at the same time, without some important cause. But so far, the reports are all vague and unsatisfactory. Nothing authentic has appeared to indicate that a peace conference is in progress, and it is . . . a subject that is . . . completely enveloped in mystery."[1]

With Grant and most of his staff gone to the war front, President Lincoln briefly felt some guilt over his decision to remain at City Point. In a message he would send this evening to the Secretary of War, he admitted that it was natural to feel that he "ought to be at home." But the promise of the long awaited victory and Grant's calm assurance that he would prevail pulled Lincoln in the other direction. "I dislike to leave without seeing nearer to the end of General Grant's present movement," he continued. "He has now been out since yesterday morning, and although he has not been diverted from his programme, no considerable effect has yet been produced, so far as we know here."[2] Lincoln would stay put.

The President began this day having breakfast aboard the *River Queen* with his son, Tad, and perhaps Mary as well, followed by a reading of the most current newspapers available: March 28 editions for those from New York, Philadelphia, Washington, and Boston. Most of their Petersburg coverage still concerned the March 25 fighting, but the President would have read through them for any details missed in his briefings. There would have been a few Rebel papers too, though of an older vintage because of the circuitous route they took through the picket lines. These would have been less useful for facts and more valuable for attitude and insights into the mood of the South.

At some point, perhaps as late as after lunch, Lincoln may have buttressed himself against the rain, gone on shore, and walked up the bluff (probably leaving Tad behind) to join the skeleton crew handling Grant's headquarters operations. Lieutenant Colonel Bowers would have summaries for him, and there would be military telegraphic traffic to examine. Had Grant sent anything this morning to his attention a courier would have brought it over, but the President was certain that there would be some developments before the day ended.

"Heavy rains had made every movement difficult," reported a Pennsylvanian in the Fifth Corps. "In many places artillery and wagon trains sank hub-deep in the mud and sand." The precipitation, added a Second

Grant's cabin (left), and the Eppes House (right). Lincoln would spend much time at
the telegraph office, which is not visible on the left side of Eppes House, and the
cabin of Lieutenant Colonel Bowers, which is the closest to house. LOC

Corps New Jersey soldier, "fell so unceasingly that the bottom dropped out
of the roads. The fields and woods were a quagmire. MUD, in capital letters,
reigned supreme." A Pennsylvania officer avowed that the saturated soil
"presented little more support to wheels or hoofs than would snow." The
rank and file of one New York regiment had at first welcomed the new
campaign as a break in the monotony, and many were so convinced that it
would be of a short duration that they had discarded their heavy overcoats
and blankets. Posted to a marshy area in the downpour, the soldiers,
recollected one of them, "minus overcoats and blankets, and with no chance
to boil coffee or cook their pork, probably wished themselves back in the
trenches near Petersburg."[3]

''It has rained nearly all day and it's horrid," observed a Wisconsin
soldier, "but it does not stop the fighting." Miles of corduroy were installed,
men with picks and shovels built slimy earthworks and battery positions,
patrols slithered across squishy fields to locate the enemy's line. One

Pennsylvania regiment moved through the area where Chamberlain's men had battled not 24 hours earlier. "In the field there were dark patches of blood on the ground, here and there, which the rain had not yet washed out," a soldier recalled. "Guns that had dropped from the hands of wounded or slain, knapsacks, haversacks, accouterments stripped from mangled men ere they were borne from the field, lay scattered on the ground over which we passed."[4]

"The rain extinguished most of the fires and those that did burn were soon made targets for the enemy's fire, which spilled the coffee and knocked over the cooks," grumbled a Pennsylvanian. Artillerymen on both sides found ways to keep their guns firing. The chaplain-historian for a New York regiment recorded one fatal result. "At four o'clock a solid shot came, careering on its deadly mission at a lower range than the rest, and striking in the midst of Company F, instantly killed Jamain Kimball, Henry Davis, and Frank Emery, mangling them fearfully, and wounded Frederick Ulmer and Henry McDonald. Ulmer, poor fellow nobly endured amputation of one leg near the thigh, while the other ankle was badly mutilated. How pale he looked when, after the operation of amputation and dressing was over, he left the field-hospital for City Point! His spirit was soon after called home to a better world." An Ohio soldier summed things up when he wrote in his diary, "Today has been a day of war in the elements, and the fierce passions of men."[5]

Lieutenant General Ulysses S. Grant's abrupt decision to forego the sweeping maneuvers he had originally envisaged and instead to try to quickly end the matter, changed everything and exponentially upped the pressure on him. Instead of merely supporting Sheridan's flanking movement, Grant needed to energize his commanders all along the Petersburg front to probe for weaknesses and perhaps even to attack. For a period of time in the early evening, he instructed the commanders of his Sixth and Ninth corps to prepare for a morning assault against Lee's lines, but a note from Meade that no changes had been observed in the Rebel defenses, and communications confusion thanks to the weather playing havoc with the hastily laid transmission lines, resulted in Grant's cancelling the order.

There was also the need to fine tune the deployments of the Second and Fifth corps as they moved to confront the Confederate positions at Burgess Mill and along the White Oak Road. General Warren (Fifth Corps) was something of a worrier, and with his men posted at the very end of the line he did have more worries than anyone else, save Sheridan. His concerns via Meade were loud enough that for a while Grant alerted Sheridan that he might have to watch out for Warren's open left flank, instead of that infantry assisting the cavalry in its mission.

The combination of pitiless weather plus the steady barrage of nagging problems it created were enough to give Grant pause, and for him to seriously consider putting everything on hold. By late afternoon Sheridan had pushed his outposts up close to the White Oak Road, a position that Grant told him was vitally important to maintain. Yet Grant's next message to his cavalry chief seemed to come from a different person, suggesting that Sheridan pull back and surrender the initiative. From where the feisty "Little Phil" was sitting, it looked as if his boss was losing his nerve.

General Robert E. Lee had undertaken an uncomfortable ride in the rain from his headquarters to the outpost at Sutherland Station, lying outside his entrenched lines, in order to assure himself that his special force was coming together. There he learned that the cavalry he had assigned to the task was still arriving, but that the infantry under Major General George E. Pickett was as close as Burgess Mill. Pointing to the map, he made clear to the ranking officers present the importance of the road intersection just to their south known as Five Forks. Two prongs of that multiple crossroads represented the east-west running White Oak Road, which also fronted the extreme right of Lee's entrenched Petersburg lines, just five miles eastward. If the Federals took control of this junction they could get behind those lines and unravel the entire defensive scheme. On the offensive side (Lee's preferred position) Confederate control of that point provided a jumping off place for an attack against the Yankee cavalry gathering at Dinwiddie Court House.

The mission Lee gave his officers was simple: maintain control over Five Forks and drive the enemy cavalry away from Dinwiddie Court House. The briefing over, he returned along the sloppy roads to his headquarters. Lee had taken immense risks to block Grant's effort to roll up his right flank; he had thinned his existing Petersburg defensive forces well past any point of prudence and pulled troops away from his Richmond defenses. Everything now rested with the composite force he had organized to counter Grant's cavalry. On this occasion Robert E. Lee was playing a weak hand and he knew it. According to a staff officer riding with the general, "Don't think he was in good humor."[6]

Soon after reaching the army telegraph office at City Point, President Lincoln asked Lieutenant Colonel Bowers to prod Major General Godfrey Weitzel for a Richmond front update. Weitzel reported no change in the enemy's dispositions and indicated that he had just forwarded "to-day's Richmond papers to you."[7] Later this evening, in a message time-stamped 10:00 p.m., Weitzel added a note from his interrogation of recent deserters indicating that the enemy still seemed unaware of the departure of Major General Ord and half the Federal troops that had been manning the Richmond siege lines. (To be fair, Weitzel himself was clueless regarding the units Lee had pulled out of the Richmond defenses to bolster his threatened right flank.)

Lincoln likely entertained Brevet Brigadier General Charles H. T. Collis and his wife, Septima, this afternoon. General Collis, a Medal of Honor recipient for bravery at Fredericksburg in 1862, commanded a special brigade not attached to any corps but reporting directly to army headquarters. His base of operations was City Point, where he and his wife were well known and popular. Mrs. Collis had met the President in 1862, and her husband was familiar to Lincoln. According to her memoirs, it was a "few days" before April 1 when they called on the President.

Septima, a South Carolina belle who forever juggled her sympathies for the South with her duties to her husband, was flattered that Lincoln remembered their previous encounter. They chatted about nothing in particular, before the general asked the commander-in-chief how long he planned to remain with the army. "Well," Septima remembered Lincoln saying, "I am like the western pioneer who built a log cabin. When he commenced he didn't know how much timber he would need, and when he had finished, he didn't care how much he had used up. So you see I came down among you without any definite plans, and when I go home I shan't regret a moment I have spent with you."[8] A few more polite words between them and the couple departed.

Grant's only messages to the President this day (there were two) came just after 2:00 p.m. The first opened with a revision of the casualty figures for yesterday's combat actions, then Grant summarized the army's movements, thoughtfully referring the President to some of the maps he knew that Bowers had in his cabin.

The second note was really an addendum to the first, containing a further revision of the casualty tabulations. Grant conveyed a guardedly positive mood. At approximately 3:30 p.m., Admiral Porter likely checked in with

Lincoln. He later recalled that the "President used to sit there [in Bowers's cabin] nearly all day receiving telegrams, and I sat there with him. 'Here,' he said once, taking out his little chart, 'they are at this point, and Sheridan is just starting off up this road. That will bring about a crisis.'"

Turning from Bowers's maps, Lincoln added, "Now let us go to dinner; I'd like to peck a little." Porter was back aboard his flagship by 5:15 p.m.

There was no formal security detail assigned to Lincoln, and the President walked between the *River Queen* and City Point alone or in the company of whomever he happened to be with at the time. According to a just-elected visiting U.S. Senator from Oregon, he "seemed to be moving about and going from place to place without any apparent apprehension of danger."[9]

Except for Weitzel's follow-up there would be no additional notes addressed to Lincoln from any source this day. There were several later messages sent by Grant to Lieutenant Colonel Bowers, which one can presume were shared with the President. Both painted a picture of tough slogging, with nothing to suggest the crisis of self-confidence Grant was feeling as the horrible conditions undermined his plans. It was in this context that Lincoln composed his message to the Secretary of War, which was dispatched at 7:30 p.m. It was probably around midnight when the President walked back to the wharf and the *River Queen*. The rain had stopped. A good sign.

Along the battle front, the rain had finally begun to sputter out after dark, leaving everyone and everything soggy. Several of Grant's staff officers were standing outside the general's tent when one of them noticed approaching riders. Grant had already worried this day about the exposure of his headquarters to Rebel raiding parties, so the armed men closing on them were given a sharp scrutiny. Lieutenant Colonel Horace Porter allowed himself to exhale when he realized that the lead horseman was Phil Sheridan, "with a staff-officer and an escort of about a dozen cavalrymen. . . . He was riding his white pacer named 'Breckinridge,' a horse which had been captured from General Breckinridge in the valley of Virginia. But instead of striking a pacing gait now, it was at every step driving its legs knee-deep into the quicksand with the regularity of a pile-driver."[10]

The mud-splattered Sheridan reached the headquarters tent, dismounted, and chatted with the staff officers while word was brought to Grant that he had a visitor. Another Grant aide, Lieutenant Colonel Adam

Badeau, found the cavalryman to be "full of pluck, anxious for his orders, certain that the enemy would be beaten if an attack was made. His splendid talk roused every flagging spirit, and converted every man who dreamed of counseling return. The officers, who felt the influence of his magnetic manner and stirring words, and knew how apt Grant was to be affected by the temper of his subordinates, believing that those who expect success are almost certain to succeed; aware, too, how especially he appreciated the soldierly instinct as well as the judgment of Sheridan, urged the cavalry leader to repeat to the chief what he had said to them."

Sheridan was summoned and entered the tent. As he recalled, Grant was listening to his chief-of-staff Brigadier General John Rawlins make the case for pulling everything back until the weather cleared and the roads dried. Not happy with where that discussion was going, Sheridan said that he needed to warm himself by the fire and went out again. He encountered his friend, Quartermaster Ingalls, who invited him into his tent and out of the elements. That is where Grant found him. The lieutenant general explained that he was apprehensive enough about current conditions that he was considering suspending operations. "I at once begged him not to do so," Sheridan recollected, "telling him that my cavalry was already on the move in spite of the difficulties, and that although a suspension of operations would not be fatal, yet it would give rise to the very charge of disaster to which he had referred at City Point, and, moreover, that we would surely be ridiculed." Then, with the kind of emphatic language that had won over the staff officers, Sheridan declared: "I can drive in the whole cavalry force of the enemy with ease, and if an infantry force is added to my command, I can strike out for Lee's right, and either crush it or force him to so weaken his intrenched lines that our troops in front of them can break through and march into Petersburg. . . . I tell you, I'm ready to strike out to-morrow and go to smashing things."[11]

It was just the tonic that Grant needed. Whatever doubts he had suffered were banished in that instant. "We will go on," he said. Waiting with the group outside Ingalls's tent, Horace Porter guessed that about 20 minutes passed before "they came out, and Sheridan mounted his horse, waved us a good-by with his hand, and rode off to Dinwiddie." When Grant had based his timing for this operation on the presence of Sheridan, he had expected that the cavalryman's single-minded purpose and relentless drive would help inspire the Army of the Potomac commanders to carry out their parts of the scheme. He had never imagined that "Little Phil" would do the same for him.

Grant had found time during this stressful day to pen a short note to his wife, ending it with a sentiment that Lincoln would have understood: "This weather is bad for us but it is Consoling to know that it rains on the enemy as well."[12]

CHAPTER EIGHT

Friday, March 31, 1865

"General Grant telegraphed me as follows."

ULYSSES S. Grant personally assessed the weather conditions at sunrise and concluded that he should scale back this day's operations. Following a break in the overnight precipitation, a fresh line of showers swept across the region this morning, dumping more water onto the already saturated landscape. He informed Major General Meade at 7:40 a.m. that "the troops will remain substantially as they now are."[1] As things turned out, Grant seriously underestimated Confederate General Robert E. Lee's determination to drive off the interlopers.

Sheridan (whose connection to army headquarters was via couriers) reported from Dinwiddie Court House that the enemy had spent the night digging in at the Five Forks intersection, some five miles to the northwest. He was certain that, properly supported by infantry, he could knock out any Rebel blocking force, and he put his dibs in for the Sixth Corps, which had fought alongside him in the Shenandoah Valley. (Grant would have to turn down his request, since that corps occupied a critical stretch of trenches in the middle of the Union line.) At the same time the cavalry officer stiffened the units he had blocking roads leading in from the west, as well as those watching Rebel activity along the White Oak Road. His experience had taught him not to take unnecessary risks and it was good that he took these actions.

The morning rains did not deter his opposite number from arranging his forces around Five Forks for a sharp strike against Sheridan's troopers. Virginia Major General George E. Pickett had worked out his plan by the time the early showers began to lift. He would march all his infantry plus two cavalry brigades west and south in order to bring them against the western side of the Yankee line, which paralleled a rain-swollen creek called Chamberlain's Bed. To complete the destruction he would drive this line eastward, at the same time pushing the remaining Union cavalry south from Five Forks. He knew that Robert E. Lee expected nothing less.

Farther north from Dinwiddie, along the Boydton Plank Road, just below the Confederate trenches representing Lee's right flank, the Union Fifth Corps intended to complete its mission of extending Federal control far enough to the west to inhibit Rebel use of the White Oak Road. The east-west lane represented the most direct route for sending troops to oppose Sheridan's movement, so by bringing it under cannon fire the Federals would deny Lee that option.

Major General Gouverneur K. Warren's men spent the early morning hours consolidating their positions. Two divisions of Major General Andrew A. Humphreys's Second Corps had finally taken over some earthworks on Warren's right, freeing up Griffin's First Division to mass as a reserve near corps headquarters. To make space for Griffin, Warren advanced Brigadier General Samuel W. Crawford's Third Division into the fields northwest of the plank road. Posted northwest of Crawford was Warren's Second Division, Brigadier General Romeyn B. Ayres commanding. Ayres's pickets had been posted just 500 yards from the White Oak Road late yesterday, and the officer intended to move up his entire command to solidify that position. While there was no intention to assault fortified lines, Ayres had been alerted to interdict any unguarded sections of the road.

Warren assumed that the Confederates would remain quiet since it was believed they had pulled troops from here to reinforce units opposing Sheridan. Lee had done this to some extent, but he had also shifted men down from other sectors to strengthen the Burgess Mill section. He had five brigades at his disposal this morning and was present in person. When scouts reported that a Yankee division (Ayres) advancing toward the White Oak Road had its left flank in the air (i.e., unsupported), Lee promptly committed four of these brigades to break up the enemy formation. The Confederate general knew better than anyone that his only chance to sustain himself at Petersburg was to decisively disrupt any attempts to compromise his right

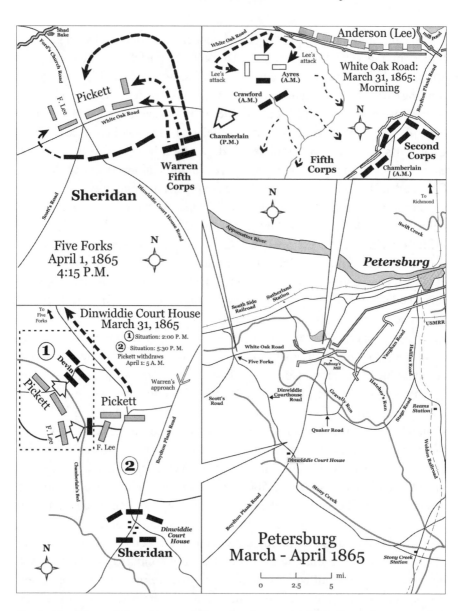

flank. To this end, he was gambling that he could foil efforts here, trusting that the enemy would refrain from testing his formidably constructed but woefully undermanned defensive lines closer to the city.

Secretary of State William H. Seward paid a call on the Chief Executive aboard the *River Queen* this morning around nine o'clock. No one who was there recorded any details of the visit. Seward never spoke of it directly and

Lincoln only mentioned it once. There were no special or urgent matters before the Secretary requiring the President's opinion, and while the Lincoln-Seward relationship was now mutually respectful (it hadn't always been so), there was no warm friendship between them that would have allowed Seward to just casually drop in. Nor would this have been a courtesy call on Mrs. Lincoln, since she had tried several times to persuade her husband to dump Seward from his Cabinet. So why had he come?

He had most likely followed the newspaper rumors about the President quietly brokering a peace deal and felt the need to investigate. The two had been up this road once before, in February, when they met the trio of Confederate commissioners aboard the *River Queen*, then anchored in Hampton Roads. Lincoln and Seward had presented a united front on that occasion, with neither willing to consider any arrangement that did not fully restore the Union. The Confederates across the table were barred by Jefferson Davis's instructions from floating such a prospect, even if just to see how high the bidding would go with other concessions. As a result, the conversation had rambled aimlessly and nothing was accomplished. Still, Seward came away feeling that under certain circumstances Lincoln would be willing to give back more than he thought prudent to entice Southern states to reenter the Union. This hastily arranged visit was meant to set his mind at ease. His cover story was that he, his daughter, and some guests were on a short excursion to tour points of interest.

Lincoln was probably polite but guarded. He would have correctly indicated that he had had no talks with any Rebel officials, nor were any planned. His discussions with Grant and Sherman had been on purely military matters, and he had not returned to Washington because, as he had cabled Secretary of War Stanton just yesterday, he did not want to leave "without seeing nearer to the end of General Grant's present movement."[2] As he often did on such occasions, Lincoln would have shared the most recent dispatches from the front. And that would have been it. Seward remained only a short while, departing as unobtrusively as he had arrived to continue his outing. In the end he got what he came for—satisfaction that Lincoln had no hidden agenda and that his continuing presence at the war front had nothing to do with any scheme to end the conflict by negotiation.

Seward's only reference to this affair would come a few days hence, as the capital celebrated news of the fall of Petersburg and Richmond. Speaking to one of the happy crowds, Seward said, "I started to go to the front, the other day, and when I got to City Point they told me it was out to Hatcher's

Run, and when I got out there, I was told it wasn't there, but somewhere else; and when I got back [to Washington] I am told by the Secretary [of War] that it is at Petersburg; but before I can realize that, I am told again that it is at Richmond, and west of that. Now I leave you to judge, what I ought to think of such a Secretary of War as that."[3]

Even as Lincoln and Stanton were having a meeting that would briefly consume plenty of media attention but where nothing happened, much was happening along the battle lines.

It was just past 10:00 a.m. when the leading elements of Brevet Major General Romeyn Ayres's division sighted the White Oak Road, which appeared to be only lightly held. Before the Federal soldiers could claim the prize, however, the first of the four brigades that Lee had released for action struck hard from an unexpected direction. "We drove through the woods. . . ," recollected an officer in McGowan's South Carolina Brigade, "and swinging round the right of the [enemy] brigade so as to enfilade the Federal line, poured such volleys of musketry along their ranks as speedily sent them flying."[4] At the same time the two other Rebel brigades hit the center and opposite flank of the suddenly imperiled Federals.

Catastrophe engulfed all of Ayres's men within minutes, one of whom remembered that the "left of the division was flanked and hopelessly turned. The right was stubbornly resisting, but giving way before the overpowering force that was crowding down upon it. . . . Wounded men were limping past. We could see the smoke through the trees, and the men slowly yielding, fighting as they came. . . . The line, broken and shattered, went back past us, and we met the enemy with the rapid fire of our repeating rifles. We brought them to a stand in our front. If fresh troops could have been thrown in on our left, the disaster could have been retrieved at this point, and the rebel charge hurled back; but our flanks were exposed, and we were many times outnumbered, and in danger of being surrounded. There was nothing left but to get out of that the best we could."[5]

The thousands of Federal soldiers trying to get out of that the best they could tumbled into the division following behind them—Crawford's—and within a short time it too was coming apart. As the *New York World's* reporter George Alfred Townsend tactfully explained to his readers: "Crawford's men do not seem to have retrieved the character of their predecessors, but made a feint to go in, and, falling by dozens beneath the murderous fire, gave up the ground." Sylvanus Cadwallader of the *New York*

Herald was less diplomatic, terming it "irreparable confusion." A Confederate soldier in the mix recalled chasing the Yankees "on the run, yelling, shooting and killing all that we could."[6]

What had begun as a routine tidying up of the Fifth Corps lines now looked to be a major setback for Grant's efforts to eject Lee from Petersburg.

It wasn't long after Seward departed and the morning rain ended that Abraham Lincoln made his way off the *River Queen* and up the muddy bluff to army headquarters at City Point. He was greeted as he entered the telegraph office by Captain Samuel H. Beckwith, the man assigned by Grant to serve as his personal communications specialist. The 25-year-old enjoyed a special relationship with Grant as his cipher operator, a position he had held since September 1863. It was Beckwith's responsibility to handle all of Grant's sensitive telegraphic communications, and to that end he was the sole person on the general's staff entrusted with the all-important code book.

Many military messages were transmitted in code since it was a relatively simple matter for the enemy to tap into a telegraph line to read the passing transmissions. There existed a special War Department bureau to train, oversee, and manage the operators charged with coding and decoding these messages. These men became something of an elite force, proud of their special skills and fiercely insular when it came to sharing their secrets with outsiders. Once, when Grant found himself in the field needing to transmit important orders without Beckwith at his side, he commanded the telegrapher to share the codes with his chief-of-staff. This proved a lose-lose situation for the young specialist, since standing War Department regulations prohibited an operator from releasing them to unauthorized personnel. Beckwith obeyed Grant's order and was promptly sacked by the War Department. Grant personally intervened to reinstate his cipher operator, which bound them even closer in their careers.

It took a mind that delighted in puzzles to be a top cipher operator, and Beckwith was one of the best. There were multiple layers to the Union code system. To begin, there was a small glossary of commonly used words, proper names, and military phrases that would be represented in messages by arbitrarily assigned alternatives. In one edition of the glossary, for instance, the city of Washington appeared as "Nimrod" and Major General George B. McClellan was "Egypt." Once these substitutions had been made, the entire message would then be coded by a system that would change all the letters in a manner that depended upon a specific key word. And, to further confuse

The young military telegrapher Samuel Beckwith (seated, right) was assigned to assist Lincoln while he was at City Point. The President's all-consuming interest in the progress of Grant's campaign kept Beckwith "pretty busy with my official labors." LOC

interlopers, short lines would be padded out with nonsense words. "It was no child's play to reduce to intelligible English the weird jumble of meaningless words that made up a message," Beckwith wrote after the war. "The utmost care was required in the solution of the puzzle and patience was an indispensable virtue."[7]

In Grant's present military operation there were a number of authorized telegraph operators available (though not as many as he would have liked), enough so that the general decided he could loan out Beckwith to the President while he was at City Point. The general considered the young telegrapher to be "one of the best of men . . . competent and industrious."[8] Whether Beckwith remained behind when the rest of headquarters moved on March 29, or if he returned to City Point sometime thereafter is unclear from his memoirs. Starting this day, Lincoln would assume a special role that was possibly suggested to him by someone who understood better than most the communicative power of the telegraphic medium: Samuel H. Beckwith.

"I was kept pretty busy with my official labors," he recollected, "for Mr. Lincoln was exceedingly anxious to secure information about everything of importance that was going on. Occasionally I would find him poring over a map of the State of Virginia and diligently tracing the positions of the armies."[9] It was well that Lincoln did so, for this day, despite Grant's expectations to the contrary, would see Union infantry and cavalry engaged in major combat.

The success of General Robert E. Lee's counterstroke depended on the bold determination of his men to fight and a cascade failure of nerve on the Union side. The former he could still rely on, but the latter was more reminiscent of 1862 than 1865. Warned by the sounds of battle and the sight of untidy clumps of blue-clad fugitives, General Warren's only unengaged division, Brigadier General Charles Griffin's, was positioned behind earthworks and mentally prepared for trouble well before the first Rebels appeared. Griffin's position was bolstered by several Union batteries which had come forward to assist. Further help came from off the northern end of Griffin's line where two Second Corps divisions were also engaging the enemy.

The hitherto unstoppable Rebel wave rolled into Griffin's field of fire and recoiled. The combat subsided into a snarly exchange of musketry and cannon fire, and the advantage started to shift. Both Ayres and Crawford were able to regroup, and the steady Union pressure began to drive fissures into the Confederate deployments, which were badly shuffled after advancing so far so fast. Warren had organized a counterattack by midafternoon with Griffin's division in the lead (Chamberlain's brigade in front). It pressed forward, driving the Rebels back toward their White Oak entrenchments. Portions of Chamberlain's brigade were actually across a section of the White Oak Road, blocking it as the firing sputtered out. By late afternoon it was clear that Lee's gamble had not been worth the cost. The

Fifth Corps had taken a beating, shaken it off, and regained all the ground it had ceded earlier in the day, plus a little more. Confederate losses were estimated at 800 and the Union casualties were counted at 1,865 with 177 of them killed.

While Rebel success along the White Oak Road had been fleeting, a few miles to the south the other component of Lee's counter-plan was on the verge of wrecking the one absolutely indispensable element in Grant's operation.

Brevet Major General Marsena Patrick dropped by Lieutenant Colonel Bowers's City Point cabin a little after 3:00 p.m., where he saw Lincoln sitting with Admiral Porter, who had been there about 60 minutes. The three chatted for half an hour about nothing in particular, at least nothing recalled by either of the officers. Patrick had left, but Porter was still present when Beckwith came in with Grant's first message of the day addressed to the President. "Whenever a message arrived directed to the President an orderly brought it to me, if it was in cipher, and I translated it as quickly as possible," recollected Beckwith. "This done I took it myself to Lincoln, always saluting as I presented it and awaiting orders."[10] It was time stamped as sent at 12:50 p.m., though it wasn't marked received until 4:00 p.m.

Grant reported that there had been "much hard fighting this morning." The general pulled no punches as he explained that the enemy's initial attack had driven back the Fifth Corps lines "well towards the Boydton plank road." Then he added, in typical Grant fashion, "We are now about to take the offensive at that point and I hope will more than recover the lost ground." Finally, there was an admission that the "heavy rains and horrid roads have prevented the execution of my designs, or attempting them, up to this time." No answer was required to this message and Lincoln sent none, though he fully understood what the fighting meant. "The results of a battle pained him as much as if he was receiving the wounds himself, for I have often heard him express himself in pained accents while talking over some of the scenes of the war;" recalled Admiral Porter, "he was not the man to assume a character for feelings he did not possess; he was as guileless in some respects as a child."[11]

Just as the Rebel tide was ebbing along the White Oak and Boydton Plank roads, combat was roaring to life northwest of Dinwiddie Court House. Two roads crossed Chamberlain's Bed coming from the west, and

Confederates attacked along both. It was cavalry against cavalry over the southern ford, and infantry plus cavalry versus cavalry on the northern one. While the Federal troopers to the south held against their mounted opponents, the heavy weight of four infantry brigades and one cavalry division overwhelmed the single U.S. cavalry brigade tasked with maintaining that blocking position.

Times had changed for the Union cavalry, which, in the early years of the war, had not been known for having staying power in a slugfest. This day the troopers fought furiously for every bit of ground they were forced to yield, even as Sheridan sent word back to Custer's division to stop protecting his wagon train and come forward. For a while it seemed as if George Pickett's scheme to shatter the Federal cavalry was succeeding and Sheridan prepared for a last stand. He selected a defensive line about three-quarters of a mile north of Dinwiddie Court House and began to plug his units into the position as fast as they came tumbling back or up from the rear. Troopers who were cut off had to make wide detours to get to the final position, but they did so. To further slow the advancing Rebel infantry, Sheridan targeted their flanks with small unit strikes that forced them to halt and deploy.

It was a race: could the Confederates reorganize for the final push before Sheridan had all his men set to receive them? Sheridan's luck was holding, and there was even an opportunity for a morale-raising ride among the men. A Massachusetts trooper never forgot how the general and his aides "dashed at a gallop with flying colors and clanging sabres along the front of battle between the skirmish line which our brigade was slowly drawing in and the rail barricade which Custer's men were putting up; and with waving hats and resounding hurrahs they cheered us again and again, while the band played 'Hail, Columbia,' all together raising our spirits to the highest enthusiasm, and making us almost unmindful of the air thick with the missives of death."[12]

Everything was ready as the powerful lines of Southern infantry tramped forward in the failing light. "It was really magnificent to see them, as they came, a double line, the men standing shoulder to shoulder; on they come over the open field as tho' on parade," noted an Ohio sergeant. Sheridan's line managed to hold as darkness closed down the combat, but it had been a close call. Federal cavalry counted 354 killed, wounded, or missing, while the Rebel loss was estimated at 360 cavalry and 400 infantry. One of Sheridan's brigadiers wrote, "The close of this day put an end to one of the hardest and severest actions that the cavalry had ever been engaged in, and that tested to the fullest extent the skill and resources of the commander and the courage and endurance of the troops."[13] The usually indomitable "Little Phil" was so shaken that his first reports to Grant promised only to hold as long as possible and identified the routes he would take in his retreat.

Grant's second message of the day addressed to Lincoln was handed to the President at around 7:00 p.m. It reported Warren's successful counterattack and promised to forward one of four Rebel battle flags captured in that fighting. Then the line went silent. What Lincoln didn't know was that Grant had decided to relocate his headquarters closer to the front, near the large sawdust pile representing what once had been Dabney's Mill. The transfer of operations wasn't without glitches, as Grant's telegraph operators either got lost or were misdirected for a while, causing the lieutenant general much annoyance and a temporary communications blackout.

By this point in the conflict the War Department had worked out a system for releasing battle bulletins to the press, a process that was less than a year old. Before that time the government found itself in the unexpected position of having to do damage control when irresponsible or malicious individuals released misleading news reports or actual counterfeits. Perhaps the most notorious incident came in mid-May 1864 when a purported Presidential proclamation calling for a peremptory draft of 400,000 more troops was released and immediately picked up by two New York newspapers. The declaration was soon determined to be bogus (an effort to manipulate the price of gold), but in the aftermath Secretary Stanton decided to release occasional summaries of military engagements using dispatches sent to him from the field in order to establish an official outlet for war information.

Under this new system, the commanding general would write a short version of events with public readership in mind that he would transmit to the War Department in Washington. After a quick review (and perhaps slight editing) the bulletin would be forwarded to Philadelphia and New York for wider dissemination. The former was addressed to the department commander, Major General George Cadwalader; the latter to his counterpart, Major General John Adams Dix, though the New York bulletins were automatically passed through the Associated Press. From there they spread across the country via telegraph. The reports appeared in communities large and small within one to three days of release.

Newspapers across the country quickly embraced this source for officially verified war information. The editors of the *Philadelphia Inquirer* considered it "giving the news to the people." The *New York Times* editorial writers praised the War Department bulletins as "facts without fringe, circumstance without imagery." Their counterparts at the *New York Herald* believed that these news releases "were a check upon the wild rumors which agitate the money market when no official intelligence is vouchsafed."[14]

These messages would occasionally be prefaced by a short note over the Secretary of War's signature, but on this day President Lincoln began to edit and annotate some of the Petersburg battle summaries he forwarded to Washington. No explanation was ever offered why he began to do so, but it is possible that someone at headquarters listening to the President explain what was going on suggested that the nation might benefit from his insights. The model was already there, so substituting Lincoln for Stanton was an easy matter. The first in what would prove to be a series of Lincoln-annotated war bulletins hit the wire some 90 minutes after Grant's second message reached City Point (Lincoln's emendations have been highlighted):

City Point,

March 31, 1865 8:30 p.m.

Hon. Edwin M. Stanton,

Secretary of War:

At 12:30 p.m. to-day General Grant telegraphed me as follows:

There has been much hard fighting this morning. The enemy drove our left from near Dabney's house back well toward the Boydton plank road. We are now to take the offensive at that point, and I hope will more than recover the lost ground.

Later he telegraphed again as follows:

Our troops, after being driven back on the Boydton plank road, turned and drove the enemy in turn and took the White Oak road, which we now have. This gives us the ground occupied by the enemy this morning. I will send you a rebel flag captured by our troops in driving the enemy back. There have been four flags captured to-day.

Judging by the two points from which General Grant telegraphs, I infer that he moved his headquarters about one mile since he sent the first of the two dispatches.[15]

Lincoln's impulsive act was a hit. News editors were quick to banner these releases as an "Official Dispatch from President Lincoln," or "A War Bulletin from the President," or "The President to the People."

"People who never believed in him before, began to think that his was just the face to keep guard over the news today," proclaimed one editorial writer, "and they involuntarily cheered for the Rail Splitter, *alias* the Confederacy Splitter." Lincoln, noted another observer, "regarded himself as a public servant no less when he issued that immortal paper, the proclamation of emancipation, than when he sat at City Point, sending telegraphic dispatches to the country, announcing the progress of Gen. Grant's army." With its tongue firmly in its editorial cheek, the *New York Herald* quickly offered the Chief Executive a correspondent's job in the next war, "at a salary of one hundred dollars a week, his rations and a fresh horse every six months."[16]

Sheridan's battle updates—still hand-carried—were slow in reaching Lieutenant General Grant at his new headquarters. Those composed while the combat was still raging and Sheridan's men were hanging on by the skin of their teeth were the first to arrive, alerting Grant that the key piece of his operational plan was in deep trouble. Quickly sustaining Sheridan jumped to the top priority in Grant's thinking, though his rapid response to the crisis was inhibited by the stovepipe command structure he was using. Sheridan reported directly to him. Major General George Meade reported directly to him. The cavalry officer desperately needed infantry which would have to come from Meade, but Meade took his cues from Grant, not Sheridan, so there was an unavoidable extra step in communications that increased the response time and potential misunderstandings.

It was a little after dark when Grant's aide, Lieutenant Colonel Horace Porter, returned from the mission given him to report on Sheridan's situation. He arrived at Dinwiddie Court House not long after the battle lines had stabilized and the worst of the combat ended for the day. With the specter of a looming defeat lifted from his shoulders, Sheridan had regained his equipoise and had made the mental shift from defense to offense. Referring to the Rebel infantry and cavalry that had attacked him, Sheridan informed Porter that the enemy "is in more danger than I am. If I am cut off from the Army of the Potomac, it is cut off from Lee's army, and not a man in it ought ever be allowed to get back to Lee. We at last have drawn the enemy's infantry out of its fortifications, and this is our chance to attack it."[17]

This was the message that Grant was waiting to hear. It was time to act with speed and decisiveness. The Union infantry closest to Sheridan also happened to be the only corps not spread along the trenches: Major General Gouverneur K. Warren's Fifth Corps. Grant promptly telegraphed Meade to have Warren relinquish his advance position near the White Oak Road (giving up all the ground the men had fought so hard to reclaim this afternoon) and to immediately send a division to help Sheridan. Subsequent instructions further refined a new plan calling for the other two divisions to target the rear of the enemy formation confronting Sheridan at Dinwiddie Court House. If everything happened fast enough, the Rebels would be caught between them in a pincer movement and crushed.

Things did not happen quickly this dark night, however. In passing the message along to Warren, Meade specified the division to send as Griffin's, probably because it was the only one that had not been badly shaken in the day's fighting. This proved to be the first in a series of miscues that would complicate Warren's response. Griffin's men, whose counterattack had finally carried the day, were actually the farthest from the Boydton Plank Road of Warren's three divisions. If speed was of the essence then Ayres's division would have been the best choice since it was already on the thoroughfare. It took an exchange of messages (and valuable time) between Meade and Warren to straighten out the matter and order Ayres on his way. There would be more misunderstandings and more delays as Warren struggled to reorient an entire corps onto a muddy single-lane road at night to conform to a plan that was constantly evolving.

Grant could not comprehend the reasons for things not progressing faster. His anxiety to both support Sheridan and salvage his plan to turn Lee's flank came to the fore as he made assurances to his cavalry chief that help would be on hand within a few hours, a time estimate he made without consulting anyone. He was operating solely on the basis of a map, and not from any knowledge of the ground or the condition of the troops taking part. Combat has a way of degrading organizational efficiency, and Warren's three divisions had been in some hard fighting this day. The stage was being set for a decision that would stain Grant's reputation and ruin the military career of a fellow officer.

Abraham Lincoln wasn't forgotten as Grant worked to organize a counterstroke. From army headquarters near Dabney's Mill, the Lieutenant General advised the President at 9:30 p.m.:

> Sheridan has had hard fighting to-day. I can only communicate with him by Courier. At dark he was hotly engaged near Dinwiddie. I am very anxious to hear the result. Will let you know when I do hear. All else is apparently favorable at this time and I hope will prove so also. Infantry has been sent down the Boydton road to his assistance.[18]

Grant's third message would prove to be the last addressed to Lincoln this day, though the President had no way of knowing that would be the case. Likely he held his position until well after midnight before it seemed apparent to all that nothing more was going to happen until daylight. Then, with an admonition to Beckwith to contact him if there was any fresh information, a concerned President picked his way back down the bluff and onto the *River Queen*.

Chapter Nine

Saturday, April 1, 1865

"Having no great deal to do here."

E**VEN** as the President slept aboard the *River Queen*, thousands of men were moving in the darkness not 25 miles away, and critical decisions were being made that would determine the fates of Petersburg and Richmond. Lieutenant General Grant, anxious to reinforce Sheridan to maintain the offensive, had ordered Major General Gouverneur K. Warren's Fifth Corps soldiers to essentially drop what they were doing and hustle down the Boydton Plank Road to Dinwiddie Court House.

Grant had promised Sheridan that Warren's men would be on hand by midnight, and the cavalryman planned accordingly. Midnight came and went. While Warren struggled with a washed-out bridge across swollen Gravelly Run and the multiple delays involved in marching soldiers at night, Sheridan fumed. Meade continued to prod his subordinate to hurry but never informed Grant of the problems vexing Warren. At 5:00 a.m. first contact was made between infantry and cavalry, but not until 9:00 a.m. did Warren learn that once the forces joined he was to operate under Sheridan's authority.

To round out a night of thoroughly botched cues and opportunities, daylight on April 1 also revealed that the enemy was pulling back. Warren's approach had been tracked by Rebel scouts, who alerted Major General George E. Pickett. It didn't take a military mastermind to realize that the Federals were approaching the left and rear of the Confederate position, and if nothing was done Pickett's force would be caught between two fires. So, with orders issued while it was still dark and the movement commencing as soon as it was light enough to see, Pickett's men began retracing their steps to Five Forks.

At City Point this morning, Brevet Major General Marsena Patrick dropped by the tent of Lieutenant Colonel Bowers a little after 10:00 a.m. to find the President there. Lincoln was completing arrangements for his wife's passage back to Washington on the army steamer *Monohassett*, scheduled to depart at noon. Mrs. Lincoln later spun the story that she and her husband were still worried about his dream of White House storm damage to explain her return, but with the Secretary of War in regular contact with the President plus Seward's recent visit, something of that magnitude would have been mentioned. More likely she wanted to return to familiar turf and a circle of friends who paid her the respect she felt was her due. The rough-and-ready conditions at City Point and the egalitarian intimacy of Mrs. Grant and her friends were not to her liking, and she was cut off from social outlets so important to her. Whether she or her husband suggested she return, the end result was a berth on the *Monohassett*.

The President had completed his business when he encountered Carl Schurz. The Prussian-born intellectual had worked vigorously for Lincoln's 1860 presidential campaign and had been rewarded, first with a posting to the Spanish legation, then by an appointment as brigadier general of volunteers—despite his having no formal military training. Known and respected in loyal German communities throughout the United States, Schurz had performed well enough in action to be promoted to major general and was currently on assignment for the War Department. He was an activist when it came to the cause of emancipation and a popular orator in multiple languages.

Schurz had wrapped up the War Department business that brought him to City Point and was waiting for a dispatch boat to return to Washington. Sensing the opportunity to provide his wife with intelligent companionship, Lincoln asked Schurz what vessel he intended to take to the city. "I answered, the government tug, on which I had come," Schurz recollected. "'Oh,' said he, 'you can do better than that. Mrs. Lincoln is here, and will start back for Washington in an hour or two. She has a comfortable steamboat to carry her, on which there will be plenty of room for both of you, if you keep the peace. You can accompany her, if you like.' Mrs. Lincoln joining in the invitation, I accepted."[1]

Lincoln checked in with his telegrapher Beckwith and was handed a long note from Grant summarizing recent activities. The general revisited the changing fortunes of the Fifth Corps near the White Oak Road, Sheridan's hard fought action around Dinwiddie Court House, and the dispatch of the Fifth Corps to support the embattled cavalry. "I have not yet heard the result," Lincoln's man added. There was also mention of a picket-line fight along the section of trenches held by the Twenty-fourth Corps. Beckwith brought a follow-up message just before midday in which Grant corrected some details in his previous note, griping that the "quicksand of this section exceeded anything I have ever seen," but adding no new information.[2]

The *Monohassett* weighed anchor at noon and nosed her way downstream, destination Washington. Aboard were Mrs. Lincoln, Carl Schurz, Mrs. Lincoln's maid, and Charles Forbes. Captain Penrose remained behind, as did Tad Lincoln.

The President next sent Edwin Stanton a note summarizing what he had heard from Grant and made a personal request: "Mrs. L. has started home; and I will thank you to see that our coachman is at the Arsenal wharf at Eight (8) o'clock to-morrow morning, there wait until she arrives."[3]

Just to be sure that nothing went wrong when Mrs. Lincoln docked, he sent a second note on the matter, this addressed to the White House doorkeeper, Alphonso Dunn, advising him of her estimated time of arrival and directing that the carriage be waiting for her "without fail."[4]

Twenty-three miles southwest from where Lincoln was sorting out his domestic affairs, Major General Philip Sheridan was in a foul mood. He had been assured by Grant that the first Fifth Corps units would reach him just after midnight, but dawn arrived with no sign of the infantry. To make matters worse, the enemy force that had beaten up on his cavalry yesterday, and that he had hoped to catch today outside its earthworks, was getting away. There was little Sheridan could do but shadow their movement, and he ordered his patrols to dog the retiring Confederates. The only bright spot was a literal one: the rain storms had passed and the day promised to be very pleasant.

It was Griffin's division, with Joshua Chamberlain's brigade leading the procession, which made the first formal contact. It was a little before 7:00 a.m. when the brigadier met up with the cavalry chief.

"I report to you, General, with the head of Griffin's Division," Chamberlain announced. If he was expecting a welcome of some sort he was disappointed.

"Why did you not come before?" Sheridan snapped. "Where is Warren?" Told he was at the rear of the column, Sheridan turned sarcastic. "That is where I expected to find him. What is he doing there?"[5] No answer Chamberlain could provide assuaged the cavalry officer's temper. But the anger passed and Sheridan was soon all business. There was nothing that could be done until the enemy had been tracked to his new lair, so he instructed the arriving Fifth Corps units to mass north of Dinwiddie Court House while his horsemen shadowed the Rebels to determine where they would make their stand.

Confederate Major General George E. Pickett had notified General Robert E. Lee once his retrograde movement was underway. It appears that Pickett's intention was to withdraw some five miles to a strong defensive position behind Hatcher's Run, but that would have meant abandoning Five Forks—a move that would compromise Lee's earthworks lining the Boydton Plank Road. Back came Lee's response which, for the gentlemanly general, was blistering. "Hold Five Forks at all hazards," the message began. "Regret exceedingly your forced withdrawal, and your inability to hold the advantage you gained [on March 31]."[6] Pickett dutifully ordered his men to expand and improve the entrenchments they had hastily built yesterday along the White Oak Road centered on Five Forks. If the enemy continued to press, they would fight there.

At about the time that Mrs. Lincoln's transport was moving off from City Point, Phil Sheridan received a special messenger from Ulysses S. Grant conveying a command decision that would add a controversial element to the events later this day. The verbal instructions were brought by Lieutenant Colonel Orville Babcock of Grant's staff, who later recollected them as: "Tell General Sheridan that if, in his judgment, the Fifth Corps would do better under one of the division commanders, he is authorized to relieve General Warren and order him to report [to me]."[7]

Lincoln's conversations with Grant in the past days had never wandered far from the need to end the war as soon as possible. "The end and aim of all our Richmond campaign [was] the destruction of Lee," Grant said later, "and not merely the defeat of his army."[8] He believed that to accomplish this he needed officers with Sheridan's drive and determination, or at least those who would dutifully obey orders without fussing about them. Anything less increased the chances that the wily Robert E. Lee would extend the war into the summer, further draining the nation of its blood and treasure.

Gouverneur K. Warren was the last of the four corps commanders who had marched with the Army of the Potomac in May 1864 when Grant began his grapple with Lee. One had been killed in action, a second relieved for a bungled attack, and a third reassigned for medical reasons. Only Warren remained, and in the marches and battles that Grant had presided over his opinion of the officer had grown more and more jaundiced. Now, with so much in the balance, the lieutenant general felt compelled to take the extraordinary step of pre-approving Warren's relief.

It was a decision that afterwards Grant was loath to discuss with anyone. Not until 15 years had passed, and his friend Sheridan was defending his reputation in an official inquiry into Warren's performance on this day, did Grant explain himself. "It had been determined to strike a blow," he said, "and I meant that it should be a final blow to the rebel army. I thought of the consequences if the movement should fail, and I intended to give Sheridan to understand that nothing should be allowed to stand in the way of success, so that, if necessary, he should not hesitate to remove any officer." He continued, "I wanted my orders promptly obeyed, and generally had them. Where officers undertook to think for themselves, and consider whether the officer issuing the instructions fully understood the circumstances, it tended to failure and delay."[9]

The stage was set for the climactic battle of the Petersburg campaign and, some have argued, the Civil War itself.

It was just past midday when Lieutenant Colonel Bowers handed the President a note he wanted Lincoln to see. Grant believed that the Secretary of War was visiting City Point and asked Bowers to pay his respects for him. Lincoln took up a military telegraph note pad and penned an answer. He explained that the Secretary of *State* had been visiting, but that he "started back to Washington this morning." The President added, "I have your two despatches of this morning and am anxious to hear from Sheridan."[10]

There was nothing further from Grant for the rest of the afternoon. The weather was pleasant and fair, so it is not improbable that the President would have stretched his legs a bit and walked around City Point, perhaps even riding on horseback. It was an agreeable relaxation for the President, but for those he encountered it was a moment etched in memory for the rest of their lives. According to a Massachusetts officer on duty at City Point,

Lincoln "was very sociable with the private soldier." A 17-year-old in the 5th New York named John Salsburg saw the President passing around this time, something that in his later life the private "remembered very well." Another City Point sighting was recollected by James Lunnon, employed as a teamster. "I saw him," Lunnon insisted in later years, "why, his hands were as long as two of mine—he was tall and stooped with the weight of a distressed nation that saddened his great heart—yes, I saw him—and loved him."[11]

A short hike from headquarters would have put the President in sight of the military railroad, congested with a steady procession of trains hauling wounded to the large Depot Field Hospital located just southwest of City Point. A member of the Sanitary Commission working at the facility recalled, "One result of Sheridan's getting busy was to keep us busy at the hospital. I hardly slept on the nights of March 31 and April 1 and 2, as there was almost constant stream of wounded from the front."[12]

Lincoln's feeling toward his soldiers was expressed in something he had said just a year earlier. "This extraordinary war in which we are engaged falls heavily upon all classes of people, but most heavily upon the soldier. For it has been said, all that a man hath will he give for his life; and while all contribute of their substance the soldier puts his life at stake, and often yields it up to his country's cause. The highest merit, then, is due to the soldier."[13]

Sheridan's cavalry had closed up by midday on the line of earthworks the enemy had erected running along the north side of the White Oak Road (with a short stretch south of the lane). The Five Forks intersection was located roughly in the middle. From a distance of perhaps 2,500 feet the troopers scouted the Rebel position and reported their findings to Sheridan, who immediately made plans to attack it, using his men and the Fifth Corps infantry now attached to his command. At about 1:00 p.m., orders were delivered to three divisions resting near Dinwiddie Court House to come forward, and there was a meeting of Sheridan and Warren to finalize details.

The cavalry chief wanted to attack with shock and awe. While his dismounted horsemen engaged the enemy all along their front, Warren's tightly bunched divisions (two side by side, one trailing as a reserve) were to engulf the enemy's left flank—the easternmost end of the mile-and-three-quarter entrenched line. As soon as the infantry had swarmed the flank, the troopers would press ahead to prevent the Rebels from shifting forces to counter the blow. If all parts of the plan clicked, most if not all of the force Lee had detached to secure his flank would be destroyed.

It was no simple matter to march 12,000 infantrymen along a single dirt road and put them into combat formation close enough to the enemy's works to minimize the length of the charge but not so near as to alert the enemy to what was happening. Warren accomplished the task thoroughly and methodically. Sheridan champed at the bit, worried that the Rebels would pull another disappearing act before the blow could be landed. He also fretted that his troopers would fire off all their ammunition by the time the infantry got going. Already alerted by Grant to expect Warren to fumble, Sheridan felt that every passing minute was a priceless gift to the Confederacy.

Unknown to him, and certainly not a part of the plan, the leadership on the receiving end of this attack was itself making decisions that would benefit the Federals. The relatively quiet afternoon helped convince Major General George E. Pickett that nothing of significance was going to happen this day. His men were well dug in and prepared. Grant's order pulling back the Fifth Corps last night had cleared the White Oak Road and allowed Southern cavalry patrols to reopen communication between Lee's lines and Pickett's command, so Pickett also felt the confidence of being in touch with the general. Such was the Rebel commander's reputation that Pickett convinced himself that if the Yankees were cooking up something Lee would know about it and take steps to meet it.

All of which filled several of the senior commanders with a false sense of security. When a cavalry officer in reserve about a mile north of the position invited his commander and Pickett to a shad bake in the early afternoon, both accepted and rode off. Pickett neglected to designate an acting commander during his absence, nor did he tell anyone where he was going. The result was that Confederate units holding the line at Five Forks would fight the coming battle independently rather than as a single entity.

Warren had everything in place by 4:00 p.m. Sheridan then unleashed Phase One: a cavalry thrust against the section of the White Oak Road linking Five Forks with Lee's main position four miles to the east. In a short, sharp fight, the Yankee troopers scattered the Rebel patrols and re-blocked the road, not only protecting the flank and rear of the advancing Union infantry, but also breaking Pickett's communications with Lee.

Warren's three divisions began tramping forward as Phase Two. One unanticipated problem arose and it was a dilly. In their reconnaissance of the

Rebel position, Sheridan's cavalrymen had misjudged the location of its eastern flank, placing it a good three-quarters of a mile farther east than it actually was. So when Warren's leading division charged across the White Oak Road girded to grapple with the enemy, the Union soldiers instead encountered empty space.

Since the road itself was not especially prominent and the men were all keyed up in their advance, the right-most of the first two divisions (Major General Crawford's) kept pushing northward expecting to engage the enemy. Only because the Confederates manning their eastern flank opened fire on the distant columns, did the other Union division commander (Major General Ayres) halt his advance, reorient his men roughly 90 degrees to their left, and resume the attack. The officer in charge of the reserve division (Major General Griffin) alertly followed suit to come in against the enemy position alongside Ayres's men (to their right). Nevertheless, the attack planned so carefully by Sheridan was in a matter of minutes a shambles.

Even as Major General Warren rode forward to redirect Crawford's errant division, the other two units piled into the entrenched Confederates. The Rebels were no amateurs, and their first volley staggered the attacking formation. With a warrior's instinct for knowing the point of crisis, Sheridan rode among the infantrymen, his red and white swallow-tailed guidon marking him for all to see. "Go at 'em with a will!" he shouted. "See the sons of bitches run! Give them hell, boys!" A reporter familiar with the man wrote on this occasion, "Probably no living soldier is so terrible in battle as Sheridan. With the first smell of powder he becomes a brilliant, blazing meteor, and a pillar of fire to guide his own hosts."[14]

Energized by Sheridan's exhortations and with their two division-front overlapping the enemy's short, refused flank, the Yankee soldiers began to chew their way west, routing the Confederates unit by unit. With no one in overall command, each Rebel brigade and battery fought on its own until overcome by superior numbers and forced to surrender or flee. Further helping the Union cause, Major General Warren finally corralled Crawford's wandering division, swung it west and then south to bring it down against the Five Forks intersection even as the Federal wave rolled in from the east. Proving that this day Pickett's luck was all bad, the area where the general was enjoying his fish fry was in an acoustic shadow that nullified the sounds of combat (musketry and cannon), though it was less than a mile off. It wasn't until he saw a pair of couriers heading toward Five Forks captured by Yankee infantry did he realize what had happened.

Artist-correspondent Alfred Waud's sketch of the Fifth Corps assaulting the vulnerable flank of Pickett's Five Forks position. The corps emblem was the Maltese Cross, visible on a flag in the center. LOC

All Pickett could do by the time he reached the fighting was cobble together a scratch line to keep an open path of retreat, while the remnants of his men caught in the blue onslaught fought for their lives. Back along the Five Forks line, triumphant Federals were claiming cannon, grabbing flags, and herding prisoners. The Battle of Five Forks proved to be one of those rarities in Civil War combat: a complete and comprehensive victory. Confederate losses approached 3,000, with 545 of those killed or wounded and the rest captured. Total Union casualties were 830, broken down into 196 cavalry and 634 infantry.

There was a celebrity casualty of a sort as the last-ditch fighting still sputtered. At a point just north of the Five Forks intersection, Major General Warren encountered one of Sheridan's staff officers, who handed him a message informing him that he had been relieved of command. Phil Sheridan had delivered Grant the game-changing victory he had been seeking and at the same time had rid the lieutenant general of an unreliable (in his mind at least) corps commander.

When a distraught Warren finally found Sheridan he asked him to reconsider his decision. "Reconsider?" Sheridan answered. "Hell! I don't reconsider my determination."[15] Warren would dedicate the rest of his life (he died in 1882) to restoring the reputation he lost this day.

Daylight was fading as the Federals mopped up at Five Forks. Lieutenant Colonel Horace Porter gathered all the available information and began working his way to army headquarters with word of the great victory.

It was party time aboard the USS *Malvern*, anchored near City Point. At 8:15 p.m. the deck officer dutifully recorded in the ship's log that "the 114th Regt P.V. Band came on board and serenaded Admiral Porter & Lady." A member of the ensemble remembered that present were "a great many ladies, including the Admiral's wife, and the band did its best to entertain the select company with its choicest music, and from the Admiral down to the colored waiters all seemed delighted."[16]

President Lincoln at the telegraph office on the bluff had received an update three hours earlier from Grant that enclosed a message the general had received from his aide Horace Porter, then posted at Sheridan's headquarters. Porter (who time dated his communication 2:00 p.m.) reported on the advance of Sheridan's cavalry and the preliminary movements of the Fifth Corps. He mentioned the capture of a Confederate barricade "at the five forks" (though the point in question was only briefly held). Porter avowed that the Union soldiers were "in excellent spirits and anxious to go in," while the Rebels were "pretty much demoralized."[17]

Lincoln promptly put his summary of the message on the wire north, sending it to both Secretary of War Stanton (in Washington) and Secretary of State Seward (at Fortress Monroe). The latter was likely a courtesy since protocol dictated that battle bulletins were released to the press through the Secretary of War.

Despatch just received, showing that Sheridan, aided by Warren, had at 2 P.M. pushed the enemy back so as to retake the five forks, and bring his own Head Quarters up to J. Boss[e]au's [house]. The five forks were barricaded by the enemy, and carried by [Brigadier General Thomas C.] Devin's Division of Cavalry. This part of the enemy seem to now be trying to work along the White Oak Road, to join the main force in front of Grant, while Sheridan & Warren are pressing them as closely as possible.[18]

(The President's analysis was off the mark this time, as there was no effort by Pickett to rejoin Lee's main body near the Boydton Plank Road.)

When this dispatch appeared in the press it carried a preface from Secretary Stanton (dated 11:00 p.m., April 1) that read: "The following letter from the President, received to-night, shows the desperate struggle between our forces and the enemy continues undecided, although the advantage appears to be on our side."[19]

Lincoln addressed a second note to Grant right after sending his war update, offering his congratulations on what had been accomplished thus far (this was before the Five Forks victory was known) and adding a modestly self-deprecating excuse for funneling his messages to the War Department (and from them to the press):

> Yours showing Sheridan's success of to-day is just received, & highly appreciated. Having no great deal to do here, I am still sending the substance of your despatches to the Secretary of War.[20]

A visitor from the front appeared at Bowers's cabin not long after Lincoln sent this message. It was the *New York Herald's* chief correspondent, Sylvanus Cadwallader, carrying with him the flag that Grant had promised yesterday to deliver. Arriving "between sundown and dark" the reporter passed the standard to the President, which he carefully unfurled and held in his hands. "Here is something material—something I can see, feel, and understand," Lincoln said. "This means victory. This is victory."[21]

The President brought the *Herald* man into Bowers's space, where all the maps with their marked troop positions were spread about, and had him correct anything he knew to be faulty. In the course of their time together the reporter conveyed the substance of the story he had just filed and which would appear in the newspaper in two days' time. Cadwallader felt certain that now that the Federal infantry and cavalry had linked up, the enemy force would be entirely cut off from Petersburg. Lincoln reacted to the analysis and "manifested the joy of a schoolboy," the *Herald* reporter noted.[22] After completing his briefing, Cadwallader went off to grab a few hours sleep before returning to army headquarters.

It would appear that Lincoln reboarded the *River Queen* by 7:30 p.m., perhaps intending to join the Porter party on the *Malvern* but deciding he was too tired to do so. There is no evidence that Lincoln was present when Lieutenant Colonel Bowers received two Grant updates. The first (time dated 7:45 p.m.) said only that Sheridan's cavalry and the Fifth Corps "evidently had a big fight this evening." The second (9:30 p.m.) recorded the bare bones of Sheridan's great victory.[23]

It had been a surreal journey for Lieutenant Colonel Horace Porter, sent to monitor events at Sheridan's headquarters and now returning to Grant's with news of the Five Forks victory. "The roads in many places were corduroyed with captured muskets," he recollected; "ammunition-trains and ambulances were still struggling forward; teamsters, prisoners, stragglers, and wounded were choking the roadway; . . . cheers were resounding on all sides and everybody was riotous over the victory."[24] When Porter finally reached Grant's headquarters and spotted the commander, impulse got the better of him and he began shouting the news even before he dismounted.

Military formalities were forgotten as Porter ran over to his chief and began joyously pounding him on his back as he blurted out the story. Grant finally got his aide calmed down enough to provide details of what had happened a few hours earlier at Five Forks. Satisfied with the information, Grant took up his manifold writer, which allowed him to instantly make multiple copies of a dispatch, and carefully wrote out a message, which he promptly handed to another orderly for transmission to the various corps headquarters. Returning to the group of celebrants, Grant announced ("as coolly as if remarking upon the state of the weather"), "I have ordered a general assault along the lines." Porter put the time at 9:00 p.m.[25]

The enemy was reeling. The pressure had to be maintained all along the trench lines. For the moment the burden would be carried by the Union artillery, whose orders from Grant were to open fire at once. Cannoneers were roused from slumber and hurried into firing positions all along the earthworks held by Major General John G. Parke's Ninth Corps and Major General Horatio Wright's Sixth Corps. Nearly 150 Federal cannon pointed toward the enemy in the darkness as the artillerymen readied their equipment, waiting for the signal to unleash the dogs of war.

At the extensive Depot Field Hospital, just southwest of City Point and a few miles to the rear of the Union lines, the U.S. Sanitary Commission agent Homer Anderson took a break from tending to patients. Another train of wounded was due soon, and Anderson needed fresh air. Years later he recalled the time as being a little after midnight, but a consensus of military reports puts it closer to 10:00 p.m., when all hell broke loose. "As I walked toward my own tent my face was toward Petersburg," Anderson remembered, "and I just chanced to see a skyrocket shoot heavenward off toward the right of Petersburg. Knowing it must be a signal, I stopped and watched for developments. Almost immediately there was a blaze of light all

This sketch (penned by Alfred Waud earlier in the campaign), suggests the activity and violence of the bombardment mostly heard by Lincoln late on April 1. LOC

along our lines that confronted Petersburg, and the flash was followed by a terrific roar of cannon that came to us like reverberating thunder. After the first volley the firing became irregular, but was kept up without cessation. After a while I saw two other rockets still further to the right, and the firing opened all along the lines toward Richmond."[26]

Even veteran soldiers were awestruck by the raw power of the massed Union artillery. Never "was such firing heard on this side of the Atlantic," a Buckeye in the Sixth Corps avowed. "Those miles and miles of huge engines of war seemed fairly to leap into the air, the very earth beneath quaking and trembling at each discharge of those war monsters which sent shot and shell into the enemy's camp so rapidly that there was a constant flash as of lightning in intense darkness."

"The cannonading" added a comrade, ". . . t'was terrific. It literally shook the ground. It resembled fearful peals of thunder, . . . [and at] intervals the musketry would peal forth and almost drown the cannon." According to a Ninth Corps soldier, the "air was filled with screaming and screeching shells flying in every direction." A nearby Pennsylvanian described it as "like an earthquake twenty miles long with perpetual volcanic eruptions," while a naval officer aboard the USS *Sassacus* found it a "tremendous but grand sight this continuous flash flash." A number of Admiral Porter's warships added their bit to the cacophony with what a reporter called "a very heavy fire upon some of the rebel batteries on the James" which was "maintained for quite an hour."[27]

The not-so-distant rumble kept the President awake. "Almost all night he walked up and down the deck," reported a witness aboard the *River Queen*, "pausing now and then to listen or to look out into the darkness to see if he could see anything." Not long after midnight there was the sound of music forming a counterpoint to the thunder as the band of the 114th Pennsylvania, just back from Admiral Porter's party, was mustered to play "a few patriotic airs" with the "drums putting in their parts with unusual vigor."[28] It was sometime after 1:00 a.m., April 2, before the firing noticeably diminished and then halted altogether.

Lieutenant Colonel Bowers had learned around midnight from Lieutenant Colonel Ely S. Parker, a fellow aide at Grant's headquarters, that orders had been issued for an all-out infantry attack at dawn. Bowers took a copy of the message along with the victory signal sent at 9:30 p.m. out to the *River Queen*, handing them over to Captain Penrose. "I hesitated about arousing the President," Penrose recollected. But when Bowers explained what the messages contained, the aide "knocked at Mr. Lincoln's door and, with an apology, gave him the dispatches."

"I can see him now," Penrose continued, "as he stood there in his night shirt that reached barely to his knees and left exposed his long, thin legs that were thickly covered with black hair. He held a candle in one hand, and, while I was reading the dispatches, with the other kept reaching down and scratching his legs. He was mightily pleased with the victory, and putting his hand on my shoulder he said, 'Captain, I should never have forgiven you if you hadn't waked me up to hear such good news.'"[29]

Delighted with the Five Forks victory, yet also knowing that a grand, if unavoidable, battle was in the offing, it is unlikely that President Lincoln slept much if at all for the rest of this night.

CHAPTER TEN

Sunday, April 2, 1865

"The country can never repay these men."

PRESIDENT Lincoln wasn't the only one having trouble sleeping on the night of April 1-2. Grant's order for a general assault had special significance for the soldiers in the Sixth and Ninth corps. With the Second and Fifth corps in action at the extreme end of the Rebel line and the Twenty-fourth tasked with holding a stretch of trenches, the main blows would be landed by the Sixth and Ninth. This meant doing something that for much of the Petersburg Campaign had been considered suicidal—frontally attacking defended earthworks.

Everyone knew the story of the 1st Maine Heavy Artillery Regiment (fighting as infantry) on June 18, 1864. The 900-strong unit had been sent across open ground against entrenched Rebel positions near what became Fort Stedman. This was the regiment's baptism of fire and no one wavered, even though hardened veterans crouching nearby yelled at them as they advanced, "Lie down, you damn fools, you can't take them forts!"[1] Confederate rifles and cannon turned the field into a slaughter pen and when it was over the 1st Maine Heavy had lost 632 killed or wounded—the highest loss by a regiment in a single unit engagement—and the Stars-and-Bars still waved over the target. From then on it was dogma that manned earthworks were not to be attacked. Yet now, for Grant's plan to succeed, the soldiers in the Sixth and Ninth corps had to ignore conventional wisdom and do the very thing that gave them nightmares.

Grant knew that Robert E. Lee could not manufacture soldiers. The threat that the Federals had mounted against Lee's extreme right flank had been met by his pulling men out of the entrenched lines and shifting them to the point of danger.

So, even though he had no solid intelligence on how much of this had occurred, all of Grant's experiences, training, and intuition told him that it was significant. He now directed his Sixth and Ninth corps commanders to hurl their men against some of the most carefully constructed and sited enemy positions in North America. If Grant was right, his troops would break through and Lee might well be destroyed; if he was wrong, he knew that President Lincoln would be appalled at the results.

Both corps commanders had carefully examined their fronts over the past weeks, scouting for weak points they felt could be exploited, and each believed they had found them. Major General John G. Parke's Ninth Corps held the Union line from the Appomattox River to just south of Petersburg, a distance of some seven miles. The opposing trenches were especially close in the area where an important pre-war thoroughfare—the north-south running Jerusalem Plank Road—transited through both sides. Parke felt that a dawn attack along this road offered the best chance for a breakthrough.

Major General Horatio G. Wright's Sixth Corps picked up the coverage where the Ninth Corps ended and followed the earthworks west and then south. Thanks to the picket lines captured on March 25, Wright believed that it would be possible to stage his attackers so close to the Rebel positions that the enemy would have little, if any, time to react. One of his brigadiers had spotted an area where a ravine actually penetrated the enemy's entrenchments. This route had long been blocked by a tangle of trees and a couple of batteries set to cover it. However, during the past winter fuel-starved Confederates had hauled most of the trees away to burn, and Wright believed that there had been a significant thinning of the covering forces, enough that would make it possible for a strong and determined assault to succeed.

The men selected for the attack eased into their positions well before dawn, and no one needed to be told what lay ahead of them. "Forebodings of the coming contest were borne in the anxious faces of officers and soldiers," one of the Ninth Corps men reflected, "and even the sighing breezes seemed freighted with them. There was a memory, to the old 9th Corps, of the bloody days of the 18th of June . . . and when on Saturday night . . . [we] were called into line, with the intention of charging upon the rebel fortifications, each man, though he took his place bravely, could not forget the bloody day of yore. It was as severe a test of courage as was ever made to mortal man."

A common phrase of conversation in the Sixth Corps was, "Well, good-by, boys, that means death."[2]

The closeness of the opposing lines in the Ninth Corps area meant that the storming troops had to be staged behind the Federal main line. However, because of the gains made by the Sixth Corps on March 25, Major General Wright opted for a more risky deployment. The attacking force—some 14,000 strong—would assemble in the no-man's land outside the main Union line of resistance and just short of the most advanced picket line. If the Confederates got wind of what was happening, their cannon and musketry would rip into the masses of men with terrible effect. So the soldiers divested themselves of anything that could make noise, and most carried rifles that were loaded but uncapped to avoid accidental discharges.

For a quiet movement of this size the men needed to take their time; the first troops began filing into the no-man's land even as the artillery exchange was at its height, around 10:00 p.m., April 1. Since it was a gun-versus-gun fight, the great majority of the shells passed well overhead. It took several hours for the designated troops to reach their jump-off positions, and even after the cannonade had ended and the process was nearing completion, rifle firing erupted along the picket lines that for a while made it seem as if Wright's risky bet had been called. Incredibly, most of the Yankees huddling within range took the pummeling in silence, even though an occasional musket ball or shrapnel found a living target. The firing eventually ended on both sides, leaving the Sixth Corps bloodied but poised for the advance and unobserved by the enemy.

Everyone now waited for dawn.

Evidence suggests that Lincoln was up by dawn, soon left the *River Queen* (which City Point soldiers were now calling the "President's Flagship"), and was at the telegraph office early, on a day that started cloudy but promised to be clear and warm. He was shortly shown a message time-stamped 6:40 a.m. from Grant to Bowers. It reported the attacks made by Wright and Parke; it also noted advances by Sheridan's cavalry, the Second and Fifth Corps; and mentioned that even the troops from Ord's Army of the James were engaged. The usually taciturn lieutenant general allowed himself what passed for optimism when he concluded: "All now looks highly favorable."[3]

Lincoln took this latest and incorporated it into a note he wrote out for transmission to his wife in Washington at 7:45 a.m. with a copy to the Secretary of War. It provided an overview of military events and a personal bit of information:

> Robert yesterday wrote a little cheerful note to Capt. Penrose, which is all I have heard from him since you left.[4]

Somebody instructed the telegraphers that when they copied Stanton to be sure to omit the last personal bit. So the newspapers got the war news only in a release with a Stanton lead-in timed April 2, 11:00 a.m.: "The following telegram from the President, dated at 8:30 this morning, gives the latest intelligence from the front, where a furious battle was raging with continued success to the Union arms."[5]

From the time Lincoln first arrived at the telegraph office to the transmission of his official message to the country, the situation all along Petersburg's embattled lines had undergone dramatic and profound change.

Ninth Corps commander Major General John G. Parke staged a noisy diversion farther north, where his lines touched the Appomattox River, as a prelude to the main attack northward along the Jerusalem Plank Road. The cannon began firing at 4:00 a.m. and was a grand show. Thirty minutes later the troops massed just behind Parke's fortifications across the Jerusalem Plank Road received the order to advance. "Go in, boys," an officer shouted. "It's your last chance for a fight." An overcast sky made this an especially dark morning, and the men struggled to stay on course. "Nothing could be distinguished beyond a few paces in front," one of the infantrymen claimed.[6]

The attacking masses were detected just as they reached the first Confederate strong points; pre-plotted reactive cannon fire and musketry erupted from the bastions and took its bloody toll of the leading ranks. One who survived later recalled that he "could hear the thud as it hit men, their cries of agony, curses and cheers, and by the flash of bursting mortar shells could see men falling all about in the rear."[7] All the subterfuge had done its job, for despite the heavy losses, the dark masses of Yankee soldiers swarmed the outer line of Rebel works and captured a number of powerful batteries. At 6:50 a.m. Parke messaged Army of Potomac headquarters with an inventory of the captures but also noted that the Confederates still held the works in the rear. This proved a tragic forecast of the day's combat here as

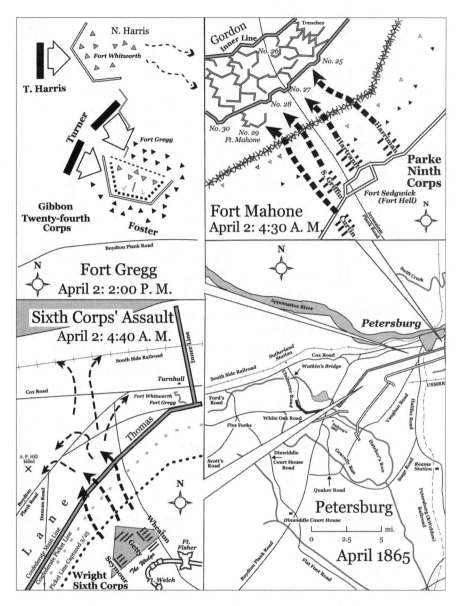

the Rebels clung to those positions throughout the day with scant regard for casualties. There was even a series of counterattacks which began boiling forward around 11:00 a.m.

Along the Sixth Corps front, the morning darkness and a heavy ground fog also caused a delay in Major General Wright's attack plan. It was not until 4:40 a.m. that a signal gun was fired to launch the Federals toward the looming enemy earthworks a few hundred yards away. Officers rushed among the prone ranks to get the men moving; many were stiff from lying on the damp ground for hours, and more than one was awakened by the rude prod of a boot. The soldiers had gone to ground in formation, so as quickly as they could stand the lines began to advance. They had covered some 200 yards without words, the only sound being the passage of 14,000 men across an uneven field in the dawn twilight. The Rebel pickets did their job to the extent of spotting the advancing horde, wildly firing their muskets, and scampering back to their main lines. This shattered the mood, and the men of the Sixth Corps gave what one of them described as a "full, deep, mighty cheer. . . . It swept away all lingering fears and doubts from every manly breast like mists before the whirlwind."[8]

While the mass formation employed and the determined advance of the Sixth Corps might project an image of a huge human wave engulfing the Confederate positions, the reality was quite different. There was no way to create openings in the thick belts of entanglements (mostly abatis—chopped trees with interwoven branches) except by individual men making paths with axes or bare hands. In the cold calculus of combat this bought time for parapets to be manned and cannon to be fired more than once at established target areas. In the past this had resulted in a bloody repulse for the attackers, but this time things were different.

Lee's thinning of his lines to support his right flank meant that where there might have been hundreds of rifles now there were only one or two dozen. The loss of the original picket lines on March 25 had denied the Rebels the invaluable minutes of target shooting at the advancing formations, and the masses of blue were hard against the main line of resistance in a matter of just a couple of minutes. There was something different on the Federal side too, a pervading sense that this was *it*—the grand final attack that all had known was coming. And while not every one of the 14,000 was a hero this day, enough were that they turned their advantages into a breakthrough.

No soldier better exemplified this do-or-die spirit than Captain Charles G. Gould of the 5th Vermont, one of the units tasked with exploiting the ravine that pierced the enemy lines. Racing ahead of his regiment with a small squad, Gould piled into a Rebel battery posted to blast the ravine's length. An enemy rifleman had him dead to rights, but his musket misfired; a second, however, thrust at the young officer with a bayonet that sliced into Gould's mouth, under his lip and out the lower part of his jaw. The terribly wounded Vermont man instinctively rammed his sword into his attacker, killing him, but in doing so, exposed himself to a third enemy, who laid open his skull with a sword blow. As he reeled back in red agony, another defender stabbed him from behind with a bayonet that just missed his spine.

Gould collapsed against the earthworks, but the next hands laid on him were friendly ones that hauled him over to the other side. Somehow the Vermont officer staggered to his feet and lurched back the way he had come to urge the troops still advancing to take the battery. He accomplished this even while seeking help, and by the time someone assisted Gould to the nearest aide station, the Rebel position was in Union hands. The young man would recover from his multiple wounds, write about what happened to him, and in 1890 receive the Medal of Honor for his actions.[9]

Lee's soldiers briefly held at some points, but at others the line was quickly breached. While some Union squads moved up and down the line remorselessly flushing out the defenders, others pressed into the enemy rear, a few making it as far as the Southside Railroad. Writing of the Rebels, a reporter on the scene exclaimed: "Oh, the wild haste they made, from the conquering Yankees in their rear."[10] A critical segment of Lee's defensive lines had been ripped open, and all bets were off as to whether the vaunted Army of Northern Virginia would survive this day. The time was just past 5:30 a.m.

Major General Wright wired news of the breakthrough to Army of Potomac headquarters, which passed the information along to Grant, who forwarded it to City Point, where President Lincoln eagerly consumed every word.

As each new message arrived at City Point, Lincoln would have consulted his maps to get a feel for the rhythm of events, wanting to understand the great scheme of things as the enemy defenses unraveled before his eyes.

At 8:45 a.m. Grant provided Lieutenant Colonel Bowers with a reasonably detailed update. He recorded Wright's breakthrough and the advances of Humphreys (Second Corps) and Ord (Twenty-fourth Corps). He reaffirmed that Sheridan was in motion as well from his starting position well in the rear of the enemy. All this, Grant concluded was "bringing our troops rapidly to a focus with a portion of the rebels in the center." An untimed follow-up note added that Parke's Ninth Corps had scored some success (but no breakthrough) and that while Grant wasn't certain exactly where Sheridan was located he had "an abiding faith that he is in the right place and at the right time."[11]

Lincoln felt that the information he had at this point warranted another bulletin to the country so at 11:00 a.m. he sent his summary to the Secretary of War, who promptly put it on the national wires.

> Dispatches frequently coming in. All going finely. Parke, Wright, and Ord, extending from the Appomattox to Hatcher's Run, have all broken through the enemy's entrenched lines, taking some forts, guns, and prisoners. Sheridan, with his own cavalry, Fifth Corps, and part of the Second, is coming in from the west on the enemy's flank, and Wright is already tearing up the South Side Railroad.[12]

In his note covering the release of this message (time stamped 12:30 p.m.), Secretary of War Stanton wrote that the "President in the subjoined telegram gives the latest news from the front."[13] Readers across the nation hung on every sentence.

The massive scope of the Union attack on his lines this morning had shaken General Lee's balanced demeanor. He met just before dawn with two of his three corps commanders: Lieutenant General Ambrose Powell Hill, whose Third Corps troops held a long section of the lines under attack; and Lieutenant General James Longstreet, who was moving his First Corps to Petersburg from Richmond. Lee's first thought was to reinforce the broken flank near Five Forks, but with daylight the long-foretold crisis was upon him.

The generals heard a commotion south along the trench lines and went outside, where they could see that matters were not as they were supposed to be. A frantic General Hill mounted up and rode off to the trouble spot, accompanied by a staff officer and two enlisted men. After only a short time, one of the enlisted men returned to report that they had been ambushed by Yankee soldiers and that the Third Corps commander was dead. (Hill had dispatched the staff officer and other enlisted man elsewhere before the incident.) "He is now at rest," was Lee's response, "and we who are left are the ones to suffer." When he sent another aide to inform Hill's wife (who had wintered at Petersburg with her husband), he cautioned him to "break the news to her as gently as possible."[14]

Before turning his attention to the urgent task of reorganizing Petersburg's defenses, Lee dashed off a message to the Confederate

Secretary of War. "I see no prospect of doing more than holding our position here till night," he wrote. "I am not certain that I can do that. . . . I advise that all preparations be made for leaving Richmond to-night."[15]

Admiral David Porter called on Lincoln between 10:00 and 11:00 a.m. The President had just dispatched his summary to the press and the telegraph had been quiet for a while so the two took a break. Porter had an open two-seated carriage at the ready; Lincoln gathered up Tad and they were off on an impromptu tour of City Point's main defensive lines some two miles distant. As they drew up to Fort McKeon, Porter recognized an acquaintance from his youth and stopped. He introduced the President to Darwin C. Pavey, a private in the 15th New York Engineers. Lincoln eyed the lanky soldier as he shook his hand. "One of my tall boys, I perceive," he observed.

Porter escorted Lincoln and his son to the fort's parapet where they were seen by a member of the garrison band. The admiral, he recalled, "pointed out to the President the positions of the two lines and dilated upon the hardships and dangers encountered while erecting them in the face of the enemy's guns and during the rigors of the severe winter; he also recounted the suffering and deprivations incident to that long siege. Lincoln was greatly moved, his feelings apparent in his rough-hewn features. As they joined arms and retired, this remark the President made: 'The country can never repay these men for what they have suffered and endured.'"

A crowd of bluecoats was waiting as the three visitors returned to their carriage. "Well, my boys," Lincoln said, "I know you are glad the war is practically over and that you will gladly exchange raw pork and hard tack for some more of 'Ma's' cooking—and I don't blame you."

"As the carriage moved away I led in three cheers for the President," Pavey remembered, "to which he responded by taking off his hat with his left hand and holding his right hand at the side of his head until the carriage passed from sight."[16]

Lieutenant Colonel Bowers received a message around noon from Major General Ord, who was anxious to divest himself of several hundred prisoners. Bowers checked with Admiral Porter when the tour party returned, who promptly agreed to supply the necessary guards and hurried back to the *Malvern* to get matters organized. According to the flagship's log: "At 2.30 [p.m.] expedition left the fleet composed of all men able to bear arms to go on shore." Bowers further noted that Porter "kindly furnished [an

Rebel prisoners began passing through City Point in large numbers (seen by Lincoln) on April 2, 1865. This image shows actual Confederate soldiers taken in the fighting. LOC

escort force of] five hundred, which I sent to the front." They were back five hours later with over 3,000 prisoners in tow. (An amused engineer wrote that it "looked very queer to see a sailor in a rifle-pit, and the rebs could not see the meaning of 'get over on the starboard side, and heave ahead.'"[17])

It was reported in Washington that "Secretary Seward and his party returned from their excursion to City Point [Sunday] . . . afternoon, much refreshed by their trip." According to a diary kept by the Secretary's daughter, their itinerary included stops at City Point, Dutch Gap, Norfolk, and Jamestown, along with a touristy walk around Mount Vernon. In a piece he would file this day from City Point, the *New York Herald's* Thomas M. Cook stated "the fact upon the best authority that neither Mr. Lincoln's tarrying here nor Mr. Seward's hasty visit has any reference to the mooted question of peace. . . . The day for conferences is past. Peace, now, can only come with victory."[18]

At Petersburg, the battle plan Lieutenant General Grant had initiated was running its course. Once Wright's Sixth Corps had cracked the Confederate defenses southwest of Petersburg, improvisation took over. As

Major General Meade's aide Lieutenant Colonel Theodore Lyman summed things up, Lee's center "was thus destroyed, his left wing driven into the interior line of Petersburg, and his right taken in flank and left quite isolated." Now through the enemy's main line of resistance, Wright turned the bulk of his command southward to begin rolling up the Rebel line down toward Burgess Mill. A reporter present wrote of it as "a series of actions rather than a continuous battle."[19]

As Rebel units shifted to meet this new threat or withdraw westward, the lines in front of Humphreys (Second Corps) and Ord (Twenty-fourth Corps) were denuded of Confederates and the Federals advanced. "We broke their lines," crowed a New Yorker under Ord, "though they fought in places like tigers." Humphreys generally took up the westward pursuit, while Ord turned northward to meet Wright. A reporter for the *Philadelphia Inquirer* observing the Union soldiers marveled that each "man seemed to be endowed with intuitive power to understand the full significance of the mighty events they had been enacting."[20]

The only sector where no comparable progress was being made was that of the Ninth Corps, whose attack along the Jerusalem Plank Road had stalled in the face of fierce counterattacks and a maze of trenches that made it difficult for the attackers to sustain any momentum. Parke called for help. All that was available was the Independent Brigade based at City Point led by Brevet Brigadier General Charles H. T. Collis. These troops, including the distinctively red-panted Zouaves of the 114th Pennsylvania, responded and attacked as ordered, taking heavy losses. By day's end, Parke had to settle for the slight foothold his men had initially gained at high cost.

Right after sending his 8:25 a.m. message to Lieutenant Colonel Bowers, Grant and his staff rode into the breach opened by the Sixth Corps assault. He passed a long coffle of prisoners at one point (Horace Porter estimated the number at 3,000) and, observed the staff officer, "was enjoying his usual satisfaction of seeing so large a capture." Grant was not known for his charisma, but on this day many of the soldiers he passed "cheered him long and lustily." The general, observed the *New York Herald's* man on the scene, "rode with his head uncovered, and bowed his thanks for the soldiers' hearty greeting. His strongly marked and sun-browned face lighted up with stern pleasure as he rode along through the rebel works."[21] The command party encountered Major General Meade and his staff on a similar mission; notes were compared, and new plans fashioned on the spot. One of the key decisions made was to reorient the effort toward Petersburg utilizing the only army unit still relatively intact: the Twenty-fourth Corps, under the direct command of Major General John Gibbon.

General Lee had anticipated a catastrophe and had previously ordered two small forts built close to Petersburg at a right angle to what was then the main line of resistance. Behind them loomed a final defensive line, lacking sufficient troops as the Federal tidal wave surged northward. Lee was now fighting for time. Longstreet's men were on the way but not yet present. Hill's Corps was scattered with its commander dead. Gordon's Corps had its hands full fighting along the Jerusalem Plank Road. The Virginia general needed men to hold the final line and he found them in a brigade of Mississippi soldiers who were part of Hill's command but who had been spared much of the day's combat. He ordered them to occupy the two small strongpoints—Fort Whitworth (north) and Fort Gregg (south)—all that stood between the advancing Federals and the capture of Petersburg, and with it most of Lee's army.

The First Division of the Twenty-fourth Corps launched a series of attacks against the positions beginning around 1:00 p.m. Resistance was furious, and the constricted nature of the ground made it difficult for the Yankee soldiers to take advantage of their superior numbers. For nearly three hours, successive waves of Federals attempted to storm the positions, only to be forced to take cover or fall back. Troops advancing in the later phases faced the gruesome chore of charging over a field littered with the bodies of those who had preceded them.

General Lee refrained from committing any of Longstreet's arriving troops to assist the beleaguered Mississippi men, instead having them occupy the final defensive line covering Petersburg. The Federals kept coming and kept getting stopped. Only when Lee decided that his last line was ready did he authorize that the two positions be abandoned. The troops in Fort Whitworth were able to pull back, but those in Fort Gregg were too closely engaged to withdraw. The moment Whitworth ceased firing the Yankees surrounded Gregg and poured over the walls. It was all over by a little after 4:00 p.m.

Lincoln's 11:00 a.m. dispatch to Secretary of War Stanton had barely cleared the wires when a summary sent by Grant at 10:45 a.m. to Bowers was processed at City Point. The President decided to wait to see what else the wires might bring. What they brought were messages of a personal nature. A telegram arrived around midday from Secretary of War Stanton with the welcome news that "Mrs. Lincoln arrived safely this morning." After mentioning a fire (origin unknown) in the quarters of the regional military commander, Stanton passed along his congratulations to the President and General Grant "upon the prospect of great success. Every one is eager for news."[22]

One message from Mary herself came through about the same time. She reported her safe arrival in Washington, asked after Tad, and instructed her husband to give her "all the news." She also signaled her intention to return to City Point "with a little party."[23]

For the moment the President had no news to give. When nothing more from Grant had arrived by early afternoon, he decided to share what he had with the nation:

At 10:45 a.m. General Grant telegraphed as follows:

> Everything has been carried from the left of the Ninth Corps. The Sixth Corps alone captured more than 3,000 prisoners. The Second and Twenty-fourth Corps both captured forts, guns, and prisoners from the enemy, but I cannot tell the number. We are now closing around the works of the line immediately enveloping Petersburg. All looks remarkably well. I have not yet heard from Sheridan.

His headquarters have been moved up to T. Banks' house, near the Boydton road, about three miles southwest of Petersburg.[24]

Stanton apparently decided that this note covered much the same ground as the first one the President had sent earlier, and he decided to hold its release to see what else would come from the commander-in-chief at City Point.

This day's battles had stretched along the entire length of the Confederate entrenched lines shielding Petersburg. Once the Sixth Corps had broken through the enemy's positions it became combat on the fly, with Grant monitoring events as best he could, intervening only when necessary to maintain the momentum. The first fighting had been at dawn south and southwest of the city; the last ended around 4:00 p.m. at Sutherland's Station, some eight miles to the west, where retreating Rebels attempting to regroup were assailed by a division of the Second Corps and scattered after a sharp engagement. Now Grant had to clear his mind to assess the overall picture, try to project what his opposite number would do next, and take the appropriate steps to exploit this day's victory.

He allowed for two possible situations in the morning. If dawn found the enemy hunkered down behind the earthworks that were now wound tight around Petersburg, he would renew the attack and issue orders for a "bombardment to be commenced the next morning at five A.M., to be followed by an assault at six o'clock." But he felt it more likely that Lee would evacuate Petersburg, which would also mean abandoning Richmond. So an alternate set of orders was prepared which, noted his aide Horace Porter, disposed the "troops for a parallel march westward, . . . [to] try to head off the escaping army."

"We may have some more hard work," Grant wrote his wife this night, "but I hope not."[25]

The general made one additional decision that suggested he strongly believed that Lee would be gone in the morning. At 4:40 p.m. he sent Lieutenant Colonel Bowers an extensive summary of the situation ending with an invitation. "All seems well with us, and everything quiet just now. I think the President might come out and pay us a visit to-morrow."[26]

Robert E. Lee's warning of his army's imminent departure from Petersburg reached Confederate President Jefferson Davis late in the morning while he was attending services at St. Paul's Episcopal Church. An emergency cabinet meeting was called and officials were tasked with activating contingency plans for an evacuation. The entire government would leave on trains that would carry them 160 miles to the southwest to Danville, a symbolic final Virginia stop on the North Carolina border. Davis held off implementing the action until the last possible moment, still believing that somehow General Lee would prevail at Petersburg. When it became clear that this was not the case the exodus began.

The Confederate capital's military commander, Lieutenant General Richard S. Ewell, hopped a train for Petersburg where he had a late-day meeting with General Lee. At numerous government offices in Richmond, employees began destroying sensitive documents in large bonfires (an ominous sight that filled observers with dread) as they wrestled with the question of whether to stay or go. As a general rule, workers with families were urged to remain and many did.

In wars of old, enemy prisoners might well be put to death, but in this war of brothers the Yankees (some captured as recently as Saturday) were hustled onto river transports and taken to the exchange station at Varina Landing. On their way, they passed the impressive looking ironed warships of the Rebel's James River Fleet, now slated for destruction at the direction of Admiral Raphael Semmes. Also scheduled to be destroyed were Richmond's liquor stocks. Frantic city fathers decided that there was more to fear from their own people than the Federals and issued the orders, though carrying them out was something else again. Part of the problem was that as fast as a militia unit could be called together, most of the men slipped away once they figured out what was happening. Also atop the list of doomed items was the tobacco stored in warehouses throughout the town.

Because it was Sunday many railroad workers were off duty, and it wasn't until evening that the trains began leaving Richmond for Danville, each crammed beyond safety limits. For Jefferson Davis it had been a painful parting from the three-story Italianate mansion that had been his home for the past four years. He had sent his wife and four children out of town for their safety on March 31—a critical day in Grant's Petersburg operation. Now, his official duties completed, Davis sat for a last time on a divan in his study in the Executive Mansion, and then left in a carriage for the Richmond & Danville Railroad depot. There was a short wait in the office of the railroad's president as a special train was prepared. Finally, accompanied by all of his cabinet save his Secretary of War (who would come later), President Davis boarded the train, which left the station around 11:00 p.m.

Lincoln's earlier observation that dispatches were frequently coming in would have applied to the afternoon as well as the morning. There were several exchanges passing through City Point between Grant and Major General Godfrey Weitzel, commanding the Army of the James units left outside Richmond. Grant advised Weitzel of the progress being made at Petersburg, pumped him for any intelligence regarding enemy troop movements, and reminded him to be ready to advance if he felt "the right time has come."[27] (The cautious Weitzel didn't move.)

Lincoln had heard enough and seen enough by 8:15 p.m. to convince him that Union arms had won an important victory this day and he told Grant so in a message:

> Allow me to tender to you, and all with you, the nation's grateful thanks for this additional, and magnificent success. At your kind suggestion, I think I will visit you to-morrow.[28]

The President also decided to release the long battle summary received four hours earlier. All he had heard by word of mouth from the front confirmed everything Grant said in that note still was true. He provided the briefest of introductions ("At 4:30 p.m. to-day General Grant telegraphed as follows"[29]), and remembered to delete Grant's invitation for him to visit.

Stanton promptly bundled this note with Lincoln's previous message and released the pair to the press, commenting only that "The following telegrams from the President report the condition of affairs at half-past four o'clock this afternoon."[30]

Lincoln wasn't done; the note from his wife still required an answer. He briefed her on Grant's accomplishments and indicated his decision to take the general up on his offer to visit. He closed his note saying that "Tad and I are both well, and will be glad to see you and your party here at the time you name." Observed Captain Penrose, "If there was ever a happy man I think it was the president that night."[31]

For his part, Admiral Porter was busy throughout the late afternoon and evening. He saw off his prisoner escort force (sometimes described as just marines, but noted by a reporter on scene as "marines and sailors from Porter's fleet"[32]) and was present when they returned. Since he fully expected there to be more prisoners in need of oversight, some of the armed escorts may have remained at City Point, while the admiral and his officers returned to the *Malvern* at 6:15 p.m.

Porter immediately gave instructions to begin making plans to clear the river of enemy torpedoes. Then he was off again to rejoin the President for a late dinner aboard the *River Queen*. They sat afterwards on the vessel's upper deck, "enjoying the evening air." At some point before 10:00 p.m. Provost Marshal Patrick paid his respects. Top of mind would have been the steady influx of prisoners from the front and how they were being managed. Like the flag brought yesterday by the reporter Cadwallader, the long queues of captured Rebels were a physical manifestation of victory that would have deeply impressed the President. Patrick left with Lincoln's best wishes for the ladies on his next stop, Mrs. Grant and Mrs. Rawlins.

The steady rumbling of distant fighting that had been constant throughout much of the day noticeably diminished not long after the provost marshal departed, though there were still occasional outbursts. The messages sent by Grant had given numbers for enemy soldiers captured and enemy cannon taken. Missing was the most important number: the Union killed, wounded, and missing. It was a grim accounting that the President knew would fill newspaper columns around the country. Mr. Lincoln, Porter remembered, was for "some time quiet."[33]

Chapter Eleven

Monday, April 3, 1865

"I have had a sort of a sneaking idea for some days that
you intended to do something like this."

THE Confederate troop evacuation from Petersburg and Richmond was well underway by midnight on April 2 and filled the early hours of April 3. Lee's orders stressed that it was to be done "quietly and rapidly." The operation that the Rebel chieftain deemed "difficult" but "not impracticable" was aided by the general weariness of the Yankee troops at Petersburg and the deeply defensive mindset of Major General Godfrey Weitzel, commanding north of the James, none of whom seemed to notice that the Confederates were hurriedly decamping.[1] Lee's columns were navigating for the most part under a directive that he had circulated in February to his senior commanders specifying the routes to be taken and the concentration points in just such a circumstance.

The basic operation was fairly straightforward. Picket lines were maintained to the last, providing cover to the main body to depart following their assigned routes. Only after the principle force had left would the pickets be allowed to hustle off and hope to catch up. The route for many of the Southern troops holding lines east of Richmond was west via pontoon bridges across the James River, causing a number to pass through their capital; while for those in Petersburg the course was north across the Appomattox River and then westerly. A village 40 miles distant on the Richmond & Danville Railroad line named Amelia Court House was the designated rally point.

Confederate Brigadier General Edward Porter Alexander observed on entering Richmond that every "private house in the city, & public ones as well, were open & lit up, & the streets swarmed like bee hives." The limited number of bridges across the Appomattox River meant that large numbers of infantry transited Petersburg on the retreat. One soldier recollected that "the sidewalks of the city were filled with weeping women and children, lamenting the fate which they knew daylight would bring upon them."[2]

Soldiers in both cities were ordered to burn tobacco warehouses (a task generally executed just before dawn) and to destroy the bridges after the last of them had crossed. A young girl in Petersburg never forgot the "great clouds of smoke; acrid, stinging smoke." Fortunately, there was no widespread destruction or looting in the Cockade City, though some of both occurred. It was a different story in Richmond, where the decision by city leaders to dump liquor in the streets, followed by the torching of the tobacco warehouses, proved a recipe for catastrophe. With no effective civil authority, crowds turned into mobs, looting spread, and the specifically targeted burnings roared out of control. The glow of individual fires in the lower part of the city meshed and merged as the sun began to rise until most of the Shockoe warehouse district running along the James was ablaze. "The whole river front seemed to be in flames," recalled Alexander, "amid which occasion heavy explosions were heard, & the black smoke spreading & hanging over the city seemed to be full of dreadful portents."[3]

The grand punctuation to all this destruction was the end of the Rebel ironclads. The powerful craft had been shifted northward from their blocking positions and anchored below Drewry's Bluff. While the sailors gathered their belongings and departed (to serve as infantry in the upcoming campaign) demolition teams laid charges, and then lit the fuses. The first to go, around 4:30 a.m., was the *Virginia II* (named after the iron warship that fought the USS *Monitor* in 1862). "Her shell-rooms had been full of loaded shells," Admiral Raphael Semmes wrote. "The explosion shook the houses in Richmond, and must have waked the echoes of the night for forty miles around."[4]

The other two Southern ironclads—CSS *Richmond* and CSS *Fredericksburg*—suffered the same fate roughly 30 minutes later along with two wooden gunboats anchored nearby. The "fleet in being," whose presence had kept the U.S. Navy at bay for three years, was no more. A Virginia artilleryman passing between the two apocalypses while retreating from Chaffin's Bluff, remembered that it was a "scene more awful, and at the same time sublime, I never witnessed certainly, or even conceived, than that presented by the burning of the Confederate capital in the distance, rendered . . . the more impressive by the explosions on the river not far distant, which almost deafened us. It is a scene I shall never forget."[5]

It took the sound of the *Virginia II's* explosive death less than a minute to travel the 12 miles to City Point, where it was heard by President Lincoln and Admiral Porter, still together aboard the *River Queen*. Sleep had a way of eluding the chief executive during periods of great stress, and the night of April 2-3 certainly qualified. Lincoln had learned a bitter lesson in the course of the war; that it was one thing to *win* a victory and quite another to *complete* it. He had been greatly disappointed by the follow-through failures of McClellan after Antietam and Meade after Gettysburg. This morning would show him whether Grant was cut from another cloth. Lincoln believed it was so, but he wouldn't know until he met with the man and looked him in the eyes.

There had been a steady, if occasional, rumbling of gunfire and distant explosions during the night but the blast that careened down the James at about 4:30 a.m. was startling in its power. Lincoln jumped up from his chair at the sound, momentarily convinced that it came from one of the Union warships he had reviewed near Trent's Reach.

"I hope to Heaven one of them has not blown up!" he exclaimed.

"No, sir," Admiral Porter replied. "My ear detects that the sound was at least two miles farther up the river [from Trent's Reach]; it is one of the rebel ironclads. You will hear another in a minute."

It was actually 30 minutes later that there was a second explosion, and then two more. "That is all of them," Porter said. The President commented to Captain Penrose that the "end of the war was now in sight."[6]

All along the Union lines confronting the two abandoned cities the soldiers began to realize that this day would be different from the 291 preceding it. The fires and explosions occurring after midnight signaled something out of the ordinary, and the uncharacteristic quiet that followed in the morning's early hours seemed to confirm it. Picket James Ford of the 60th Ohio (Ninth Corps) was one of dozens of plucky individuals outside Petersburg who decided to investigate. He crawled up to the Confederate lines in front of Fort McGilvery and found them empty. "Come on, boys, the Johnnies are gone," Ford shouted back to his companions on the outpost line.[7] First in irregular groups, then in more organized formations, the Yankees began to filter through the enemy earthworks and enter Petersburg.

For the Federals watching Richmond, the deafening immolation of the Rebel ironclads also blew away the healthy caution that had kept them alive for months of deadly trench warfare. How deadly was made chillingly clear to Colonel George A. Bruce who led an advance party forward toward the silent enemy works. Fortunately the men who probed first had scooped up a Rebel prisoner who knew his way through the entanglements and, more important, the mine field. This process was repeated up and down the line, so by dawn the Federals held the enemy forts and trenches. The next order was to march the several miles into Richmond. The Yankee boys were now freed from the dungeons of the trenches, and, recalled Colonel Bruce, "pressed on joyously, with a quick step and light hearts." Added a nearby New York officer: "There was no occasion to caution the boys to 'go slow' and 'preserve their intervals.'" "One of the grandest sights of the war was that when our troops entered the city," contributed a Vermonter. "Such a shouting, long, loud and deafening, may possibly be imagined, but not described."[8]

Claims for who first entered Petersburg and Richmond would be argued for years and continue well past the death of the last veteran with no clear winner. In both cases U.S. flags were mounted on prominent buildings and greeted the rising sun. The fires in Petersburg were relatively minor and quickly brought under control. The conflagration in Richmond was of another magnitude. "The heated air, dim with smoke and filled with the innumerable particles that float from the surface of so great a fire, rendered it almost impossible to breathe," related Colonel Bruce.[9] In both cities civil policing began even as the soldiers fought and eventually defeated the fires. Petersburg and Richmond were now captured citadels.

Petersburg's general calm this morning allowed the various regimental bands to find open spaces and cut loose with what one reporter termed "the grand old round of national airs." The feelings of the Yankee soldiers were encapsulated in the experience of the sergeant of a Michigan regiment whose squad had first displayed the American flag from Petersburg's clock tower. "Our hearts were too full for utterance, so we clasped hands and shed tears of joy," he recollected, "for we knew that the beginning of the end had come."[10]

At some point during the early morning hours, a courier from Lieutenant Colonel Bowers came aboard the *River Queen* and handed Lincoln a copy of an untimed message just received from General Grant announcing Petersburg's occupation and that pursuit of Lee's retreating forces "will be immediately made."[11]

There was time for breakfast before Lincoln and Admiral Porter headed up the hill. As they were sitting down to dine, Lincoln welcomed back Captain John Sanford Barnes whose fast steamer had returned after transporting General Sherman to North Carolina. The President, as Barnes remembered, "expressed great satisfaction in knowing that the General was again with his army, read the dispatches sent by him, and told me that Petersburg was evacuated and our troops in possession, and that if possible he would visit that city that day."[12] An invitation to join the party was extended and gratefully accepted, especially when Barnes learned that Mary Lincoln had returned to Washington.

The fluid situation at the front presented Ulysses S. Grant with something of a protocol problem. A battle may have been won, but the campaign was far from over. Lee's forces had a 12-hour head start and Grant was determined not to give them any chance to catch their breath. His objective, as he would explain to Sherman in a message sent later this day, was to "capture or disperse a large number" of them.[13] He knew he had to keep tight hold of the reins to ensure that there was no letting up in the pursuit made by Sheridan's troopers, the Army of the Potomac, and the Army of the James, but he also had a responsibility to brief his commander-in-chief in person.

Grant initially opted to set off with his columns. He sent a message to Lieutenant Colonel Bowers extending his regrets for not being able to meet the President in Petersburg, certain that Lincoln would accept and approve the reason he gave. "I want to cut off as much of Lee's army as possible," Grant said.[14] However, shortly after sending that note he reassessed conditions and changed his mind. There would be time to meet the President after all.

According to Lieutenant Colonel Porter, Grant selected a "comfortable-looking brick house with a yard in front, No. 21 Market street, the residence of Mr. Thomas Wallace, and here he and the staff dismounted and took seats on the piazza." General Meade arrived at Grant's headquarters after enjoying a little sightseeing tour with his staff, who wanted to view some of the positions that had defied them since last June. While the two reviewed plans, Meade's aide, Lieutenant Colonel Theodore Lyman, ambled around.

"There was a large tobacco warehouse near, where one could see the various forms of chewing & smoking weed," he noted. "There were little leaves on the tulip trees as big as a dollar, also the strawberries were in bloom." He was approached by several blacks offering to sell him Confederate paper money and accepting any amount offered in return. "They were all as plainly pleased," Lyman quipped, "as were the whites not so."[15]

Grant and Meade had their meeting of the minds; or rather, Grant impressed his thinking on his subordinate. Meade was initially concerned that Lee was going to consolidate his forces and make a stand, but Grant was convinced that there was no suitable ground in the vicinity. He believed that the Rebel general would make a bee-line for the Richmond & Danville Railroad to access his best pathway south. Grant wanted Meade to understand that the objective was to prevent that from happening; not to follow after the retreating Confederates, but to get ahead of them and block them from turning south. Meade got it, and in a letter to his wife written this day said that the Army of the Potomac was "now moving after Lee, and if we are successful in striking him another blow before he can rally his troops, I think the Confederacy will be at an end."[16]

Meade departed with his staff to carry out his part of Grant's program. Grant settled in, now satisfied that the pursuit would proceed as he intended and determined to wait at the Wallace House for the President.

Grant had instructed Captain Robert Lincoln to organize a small escort to bring the President into town. Company C, 5th United States Cavalry got the call when Sergeant Jacob Buch was instructed to pick eight men for an escort detail and present himself to the major in charge. "When I reported," Buch recalled, "I found Maj. Duncan and Capt. Lincoln ready to mount, and an Orderly had one le[a]d horse ready saddled and bridled for us to take along." The noncom didn't identify the extra animal, but other accounts say it was "Cincinnati," the larger of the two horses General Grant used on a regular basis. Now that the Union army occupied Petersburg, the railroad stop with the easiest access was Hancock Station.

The party immediately departed and wriggled eastward along city streets until eventually heading southbound on the Jerusalem Plank Road. Their route took them through the Rebel defenses attacked on April 2 by the Ninth Corps. The sergeant never forgot passing "one rebel fort which had kept shooting our infantry down long after the other forts had surrendered, which fact was shown by our dead lying where they had fallen, piled one across the other for quite a distance all around the fort. . . . In the ditch in front of the rebel fort we saw one of our infantrymen, who had been one of those to charge this fort, standing upright, with left foot forward, the right foot a little behind, his musket tightly grasped in his right hand, his forage cap on his head, with a large hole through his cap and skull. He was stone dead, but being over knee deep in the mud and mire of the ditch, could not fall over. We passed those horrible sights (which I had often seen, but not in such a fearful way as this last mentioned) and went on to the railroad which ran from City Point in rear of our army to a station."

Robert Lincoln sent his message from there. It was even more succinct than Grant's first had been. "I am awaiting you at Hancock Station," it read.[17]

By this time most, if not all, the soldiers wounded in the fighting here had been picked up by ambulances, stabilized at nearby aid stations, and then put aboard military railroad cars for delivery to the Depot Field Hospital, a nearly 200-acre log-and-canvas establishment about a mile from where the President received Robert's message. It was at the Depot Field Hospital that the cost of victory was being counted. Private Cyrus T. Goodwin, a member of the 59th Massachusetts (Ninth Corps), wrote home from the hospital this day that this "victory is causeing a good many woman and children pain and anguish, for there many killed and a grate number of men wounded. There was two trains come in last night twenty car loads mostly wounded men. . . . Some of these are wounded very bad, some in the face[,] head[,] neck[,] back[, &] shoulder[,] . . . in fact in all parts of there bodies. . . . Two or three men died on there way down here this the sadest sight I ever saw, so many young men that will be crippled for life, and there will be so many widows and orphan children it makes me feel sad when I think of it, although we have gained a grate victory."[18]

A train had been arranged for 9:00 a.m. and Robert's message specified the destination. Lincoln used the time before departure to put together another message to the nation, which zipped off to Washington at 8:00 a.m. Secretary of War Stanton immediately released it to the press with this introductory statement: "The following telegram from the President, announcing the evacuation of Petersburg, and probably of Richmond, has just been received by the War Department."[19]

This morning Gen. Grant reports Petersburg evacuated; and he is confident Richmond also is. He is pushing forward to cut off if possible, the retreating army. I start to him in a few minutes.[20]

President Lincoln and his son, Captain Penrose (watching over Tad), Admiral Porter, and Captain Barnes were still at the telegraph office waiting to hear that the special train was ready when they saw the *New York Herald* reporter Thomas M. Cook hurrying toward them. "When asked where I came from, and replying Petersburg, the President very dryly asked if I saw anybody there I knew," Cook noted. "The joke was scarcely perceptible, but still, under the circumstances it will do." Never at a loss for words, Admiral Porter chimed in that the capture of Petersburg might be reckoned a naval victory, provoking a questioning look from the President. "Why," explained Porter, "my Monitors up the river the other night scared the rebels away." Looking conspiratorially at Cook, Porter asked him, 'Didn't they tell you so in Petersburg?"

Ever the diplomat, the *Herald* man answered that he hadn't heard exactly that remark. "Well," continued the Admiral, "Mrs. Grant says I can have Petersburg for my victory if I won't claim Richmond, and I think I had better accept the terms, or Grant will have all the honors." Here, recalled Cook, President Lincoln "suggested that there was glory enough for all." The naval officer also advised Cook that he had "ordered such of his vessels as can go to feel their way up to Richmond and open the river."[21]

Word arrived that the train was ready and everyone trooped down the bluff to the framework station platform and clambered aboard. The weather was cooperating; it was clear, pleasant, and warm. With word spreading that Petersburg was wide open, every departing train attracted people eager to visit. Admiral Porter prevented a pair of uninvited riders from boarding the President's car, something he considerably embellished when he wrote about it in later years.

Even as Lincoln was settling in for the ride, Washington officials were receiving the electrifying news that would halt the government for the rest of this day. The confirmation that Richmond had fallen was being flashed throughout the country even as Lincoln was enroute to Petersburg, where telegraph circuits had yet to be reconnected.

In this age before child labor laws it wasn't unusual that 15-year-old William E. ("Willie") Kettles was working. What was out of the ordinary was the specialized task he performed. Kettles was a trained and experienced telegraph operator assigned to the War Department in Washington. He was on duty a little before 9:00 a.m. and idly listening to a colleague's exchange with a field operator when his own instrument came alive. It was Fortress Monroe calling with an urgent instruction for him to "Turn down for Richmond, quick." Although momentarily taken aback, Kettles did as instructed and made the necessary adjustment for a weak incoming signal.

In another moment he was exchanging identifications with an operator who reported his location as the Rebel capital. (In actual fact, he was set up just outside city limits at the nearest station hooked into the army network.)

"Do you hear me well?" queried the distant telegrapher.

"I do; go ahead."

"All right. Here's the first message for four years."

RICHMOND, VA., April 3, 1865.
Hon. E. M. Stanton, Secretary of War:

We entered Richmond at 8 o'clock this morning.
G. WEITZEL,
Brigadier General Commanding.[22]

The next few moments were something of a blur for the young operator. He brought the message to his boss, Thomas Eckert, who promptly rushed it to its addressee. Kettles's colleagues in the main receiving room had gotten wind of the historic communication and crowded around his work station, but the distant operator had done the telegraphic equivalent of hanging up. Young Kettles knew no more than what the brief note had said, but everyone questioned him as if he were sitting on more information. Meanwhile, the cat leapt out of the bag when a colleague spotted a friendly newspaper reporter lounging outside the building and opened a window near him.

"Any news?" the correspondent called out.

"Richmond's fallen!"

"It was not many minutes before the news spread like wild-fire through the city, the doubted intelligence being speedily made positive by the circulation of thousands of newspaper extras containing the news in the official telegrams," wrote the reporter filing for the *Sacramento Daily Union*. "Almost by magic the streets were crowded with hosts of people, talking, laughing, hurrahing and shouting in the fullness of their joy. Men embraced each other, treated each other, made up old quarrels, marched along the streets arm-in-arm, singing or chatting in that happy sort of abandon which characterizes people when they don't care whether school keeps or not."[23]

Lincoln's relatively short train ride from City Point to Hancock Station was not without incident. The *Boston Evening Journal* reporter "Carlton" (Charles Coffin) spoke afterward to someone aboard who related that just "before reaching the station it was stopped by a procession of several thousand Confederate prisoners crossing the track. They were . . . in rags, and had no blankets. Many had neither shoes nor hats. Mr. Lincoln watched them in silence a while, then said, as if in soliloquy: 'Poor boys! poor boys! If they only knew what we are trying to do for them they would not have fought us, and they would not look as they do.'"[24]

Captain Lincoln and the escort were waiting as the special train halted at Hancock Station. Sergeant Buch counted heads and realized that instead of one person to convey there were actually four men and a boy. He ordered four of his troopers to turn their mounts over to the additional people traveling with the President, and the group set off. "When we came to the rebel fort before mentioned," Buch later wrote, "the Ambulance and Burial Corps had very nearly all the dead taken off the field; still there were enough lying around to show what had been going on here, also the dead man was still standing in the ditch." One account (probably Penrose, uncredited) mentions the sight of "one man with a bullet-hole through his forehead, and another with both arms shot away." Hard-bitten Sergeant Buch "saw big tears run down the President's cheeks."[25]

The noncom also recollected that Tad Lincoln started "complaining that the horse which he rode was such a rough trotter . . . [so much that] we halted and I exchanged horses with him."[26] The riders pushed northward along the Jerusalem Plank Road and covered slightly more than a mile when they crossed what in July 1864 had been the staging area for Confederate counterattacks at the Battle of the Crater. They overtook and began passing the First Brigade of the Second Division (Ninth Corps) which had halted to draw rations in a field near Cemetery Hill. For many of these men their encounter with Lincoln was something to be long remembered and fondly recalled:

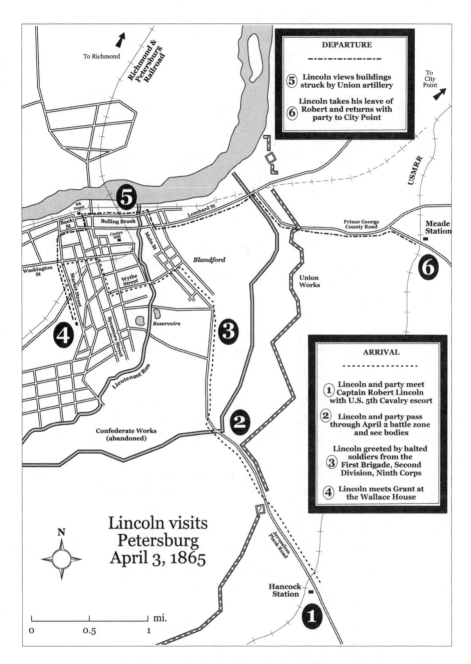

DEPARTURE

⑤ Lincoln views buildings struck by Union artillery

⑥ Lincoln takes his leave of Robert and returns with party to City Point

ARRIVAL

① Lincoln and party meet Captain Robert Lincoln with U.S. 5th Cavalry escort

② Lincoln and party pass through April 2 battle zone and see bodies

③ Lincoln greeted by halted soldiers from the First Brigade, Second Division, Ninth Corps

④ Lincoln meets Grant at the Wallace House

Lincoln visits
Petersburg
April 3, 1865

Corporal George H. Allen, 4th Rhode Island: "Immediately the whole force was in commotion, and without stopping to form a line, we gathered in a crowd alongside the road, and prepared to give him a joyful welcome. As he reached us he took off his hat and held it down at his side."[27]

Unknown Soldier, 35th Massachusetts: "They rode swiftly through the column amid the enthusiastic cheering of the troops. It was a day of compensations for the long-tried, much-enduring Lincoln."[28]

Captain Albert A. Pope, 35th Massachusetts: "They were received by the soldiers with rounds of applause."[29]

Sergeant Eugene Beauge, 45th Pennsylvania: "Riding at a slow gallop through our division, guiding his horse with one hand, his stove-pipe hat in the other, Mr. Lincoln seemed very contented that morning as he bowed and smiled in response to our cheers."[30]

Private Frederick E. Cushman, 58th Massachusetts: "Here President Lincoln passed us on horseback, and as he went by our boys cheered him, as the rebs used to say, 'right smart.' The good man acknowledged the compliment by doffing his hat."[31]

Lieutenant James F. Merrill, 7th Rhode Island: "We rushed along the way to greet him and I never will forget the mournful smile that he gave us as he passed thro on his way to the city."[32]

Unknown Soldier, 36th Massachusetts: "As the men recognized Mr. Lincoln their enthusiasm could not be restrained, and amid the thundering cheers which he graciously acknowledged, the President rode on toward the city."[33]

The route the Lincoln party followed into town was charted years later by Charles A. Clark, a young Petersburg resident at the time. After clearing the halted brigade, the party continued along the Jerusalem Plank Road before coming down a long hill where the riders turned left (west) onto Wythe Street, which they followed a short distance before jogging north (Sycamore Street), then west (Washington Street) to Market Street, where a turn to the north brought them to No. 21, Grant's temporary headquarters at the Wallace House.

Lincoln "dismounted in the street," wrote Horace Porter, "and came in through the front gate with long and rapid strides, his face beaming with delight. He seized General Grant's hand as the general stepped forward to greet him, and stood shaking it for some time, and pouring out his thanks and congratulations with all the fervor of a heart which seemed overflowing with its fullness of joy." Added Grant, "About the first thing that Mr. Lincoln said to me, after warm congratulations for the victory, and thanks both to myself

This postwar illustration depicts President Lincoln meeting General Grant at the Wallace House in Petersburg, with Admiral Porter and Tad Lincoln as interested observers. *Petersburg National Battlefield Park*

and to the army which had accomplished it, was: 'Do you know, general, that I have had a sort of a sneaking idea for some days that you intended to do something like this.'"[34]

Certainly item number one on Lincoln's mind at this point was to learn the latest news on the fate of Richmond. Here Grant could shine no light in the darkness. He'd been on the move since dawn and, while he strongly suspected that it had been evacuated like Petersburg, he had not received any official word. The inhabitants of No. 21 had been quietly observing up to this point, so much so that several accounts describe their place as deserted. Owner Thomas Wallace now appeared. He happened to have known Lincoln back when the President was a Whig Party Congressman from Illinois, and invited his guests to come inside, but Grant displayed his burning cigar as his reason to decline the offer. Lincoln formally asked permission for them to use Wallace's porch, which was granted, the owner even bringing out a high-backed chair for the President. Lincoln moved the chair to the porch edge so that when he sat down his long legs could dangle over the side.

Wallace retreated inside as the two men continued their conversation. "Our movements having been successful up to this point," Grant later explained, "I no longer had any object in concealing from the President all my movements, and the objects I had in view." The lieutenant general likely used language he had employed in a message sent to Phil Sheridan less than an hour earlier, when he said that he believed "that the enemy will make a stand at Amelia C[ourt] H[ouse] with the expectation of holding the road between Danville and Lynchburg. The first object of the present movement will be to intercept Lee's Army and the second to secure Burkesville."[35]

A crowd gathered to gawk at the two famous men. Among them were the *Boston Journal* reporter Coffin and a minister with the U.S. Christian Commission named Charles C. Carpenter. The savvy Coffin quickly realized that the big story of this day wasn't in Petersburg at all. He watched the general and the President for "a few moments, and then, comprehending that Richmond was the objective point for a correspondent, hastened to Meade station, on the military railroad."[36] Carpenter remained behind and struck up a conversation with an "old family slave" who was standing "just inside the yard."

"Aunty," he asked her, "do you know who that old man is?" When she shook her head he continued, "That is the man who made you free Abraham Lincoln."

She looked again at the lanky man on the porch, her eyes showing her understanding. "Lor' bress him!" she said, "is dat Massa Linkum?" For the blacks of Petersburg this day was a day of liberation, a time when their lives changed in ways beyond their comprehension. A Union soldier walking through the town asked one of the African-Americans: "What did you do when you knew you was free?" According to the infantryman, the now ex-slave struggled to find the words to express his feelings before explaining, "Oh! I jes' laid down and rolled."[37]

The pair on the porch talked about William Tecumseh Sherman. Lincoln knew from the conversations aboard the *River Queen* that Sherman had hoped to move his army up from North Carolina in time to help Grant finish off Lee, and he wondered if that was still part of the plan. Grant indicated that such a junction was unlikely, and further, he preferred it that way. In response to Lincoln's questioning look, Grant explained that he wanted to avoid any tensions between the eastern and western armies. "I said to him that if the Western armies should be even upon the field, operating against Richmond and Lee, the credit would be given to them for the capture, by politicians and non-combatants from the section of country which those troops hailed from. It might lead to disagreeable bickerings between members of Congress of the East and those of the West in some of their debates."[38]

"I see, I see," said Lincoln; "but I never thought of it in that light. In fact, my anxiety has been so great that I didn't care where the help came from, so that the work was perfectly done."[39]

The others who came with the President found ways to amuse themselves. The two navy men set their sights on securing some tobacco. Admiral Porter noted that several undamaged tobacco warehouses had been thrown open and "every one seemed to be helping himself to the delicious weed. It was mostly put up in small bales of three pounds each. Some one presented me with four packages, and I tied them upon the saddle of my horses." Nor could Captain Barnes resist sampling some of the "great quantities of which were lying about, eagerly seized by the soldiers."[40] He claimed a bag of tobacco as his trophy. A grateful Tad Lincoln seized some sandwiches as his prize, provided by no less than Grant's head of intelligence, Brevet Brigadier General George H. Sharpe.

"Here, young man, I guess you must be hungry," the staff officer said as he handed them over. Lieutenant Colonel Horace Porter thought that the way the boy grabbed the food reminded him of the manner "a drowning man would seize a life-preserver."

"Yes, I am; that's what's the matter with me," Tad said as he began to wolf the food down, much to the amusement of his father and General Grant.[41]

Lieutenant Colonel Adam Badeau observed that Lincoln evidenced "a dash of anxiety" with his satisfaction. The chief executive, continued Badeau, "foresaw the imminent civil complications that success involved. His great heart was full of charity, however, and he was planning already what merciful magnanimity he could show to those who had resisted and reviled himself and his government so long. Some of these plans he unfolded now to Grant."[42]

Their impromptu conference was interrupted after about an hour by the passage of a Sixth Corps brigade on its way to join the chase after Lee's army. Lincoln looked on approvingly while Grant puffed on a cigar. "Passing along through the city," recollected a member of the 121st New York, "we saw President Lincoln and General Grant, and gave them a marching salute." To one soldier, the commander-in-chief "looked pale and thin," while to another his "careworn countenance was illumed with a benignant smile." The President, recollected a third, "looked good to us all." A Vermont man noticed that word had spread so that now there was a "big crowd of colored people, who were shouting 'God bless Massa Lincoln!' They appeared to be fairly crazy with delight."[43]

It was about 12:15 p.m. when Grant briefly excused himself, went inside, and began to write out two dispatches on a marble-topped table near the entrance. The crowd of African-Americans had grown quiet. Brevet Brigadier General Michael R. Morgan of Grant's staff arrived at this time and was deeply moved by what he observed. "I saw the President seated looking down on a yard full of negroes and they all looking up at him, not a word being spoken on either side," he commented.[44]

Grant emerged and shared the dispatches with the President. In the first, to Major General Weitzel, he asked, "How are you progressing? Will the enemy try to hold Richmond? I have detained the division belonging to your corps, and will send it back if you think it will be needed. I am waiting here to hear from you. The troops moved up the Appomattox [River] this morning." The other went to the officer commanding the U.S. forces on Bermuda Hundred. "What do you learn of the position of the enemy in your front?" it read. "If the enemy have moved out, try to connect pickets with the forces from Petersburg."[45] Grant passed the messages to a courier to be delivered to the nearest operating telegraph terminal along the old Union siege lines.

Lincoln and Grant were together for perhaps 90 minutes. Grant needed to catch up with the troops chasing Lee's army, and the President was loath to detain him, so they parted, though not without a moment of unexpected humor that was observed by the minister, Charles Carpenter. "Directly in front of the house, at the edge of the street, in the midst of the soldiers, sat President Lincoln upon his horse, about to depart," he recalled. "It was a beautiful picture as his tall form bent down to listen to a plain old man who had ventured in among the troops." Suddenly an officer in the crowd called out "Lincoln!" prompting the President to look right at him. "*Captain* Lincoln!" the embarrassed officer quickly corrected himself. A biographer not present recorded Lincoln's parting words to Grant as "God bless you!" (According to another witness, just five minutes after the Lincoln party departed, "the Lieut. General and all his attendants had rapidly ridden away.")[46]

Sergeant Buch had remounted his stranded men so his squad was back up to eight riders. As Grant and his staff headed west, Captain Lincoln led the Presidential party eastward instead of southward back to Hancock Station. No explanation was given for the change in route. Perhaps the President wanted to see more of Petersburg, or Captain Lincoln had learned of a clear path through the opposing lines to Meade Station. It was about the same traveling distance, but Meade Station was several miles closer to City Point. Possibly on this return leg Lincoln observed a bit of Yankee opportunism: enterprising newsboys from City Point posted on Petersburg street corners hawking the March 31 edition of the *New York Herald*.

The route reconstructed by Charles Clark was north several blocks along Market Street, an eastward jog on Bank Street, a block south on Sycamore Street, then east along Bollingbrook Street for a while. This leg of the journey would have vividly brought home to the President the impact of the war on infrastructure. Located directly in line with massed Union batteries, just two miles east, the residential area had been heavily damaged during nine months of constant shelling. Northern photographers would soon document the worst of the destruction, with several damaged houses that Lincoln rode past this day being especially prominent in the gallery of images that emerged. According to Charles Clark, the "house that attracted his attention more than any other was the old Dunlop Mansion. . . . which had been struck more than one hundred times by shells, and fragments of shells.

One of the houses on Bollingbrook Street, Petersburg, that President Lincoln viewed on his return to City Point after meeting with General Grant. According to a young observer, the President "looked and shook his head." LOC

He stopped at this place for a moment, looked and shook his head and rode off."[47]

The Presidential group eventually made a turn southward onto Main Street, then a quick jog back east onto Lombard Street. This took them to the Prince George County Road, which passed through the opposing lines to Meade Station. Throughout the return journey the horse that had been provided to Admiral Porter (not the one he had ridden earlier, which had been returned to its cavalryman) was proving difficult to control. Watching the naval officer struggling to steer his beast, Lincoln joked, "Admiral, you mistook your profession; you ought to have been a circus-rider. I don't think there's another man in the United States, besides his owner, who could ride that horse half a mile."[48]

Captain Robert Lincoln presumably had the presence of mind to send a rider ahead to telegraph for the President's train so that it would be waiting when they arrived. There was an emotional parting for the President before the travelers boarded for the run back to City Point. (Admiral Porter got even for Lincoln's joke at his expense. He made a big deal of wanting to purchase the rambunctious animal, finally prompting the President to ask him why. "I want to buy it and shoot it," answered Porter, "so that no one else will ever ride it again.") On the way back, Lincoln's train passed another filled with the curious flocking to see fallen Petersburg. "Of course he attracted no little attention," said one of the tourists. "There was no mistaking his face as we saw him seated in the car."[49]

As soon as the train halted at City Point, Admiral Porter hurried to his flagship to see how the work clearing the James River was progressing. Tad and Captain Penrose probably went back to the *River Queen*, while Captain Barnes remained with the President. Overall, the trip to Petersburg had been a tonic for the anxious commander-in-chief. "He was in high spirits, seemed not at all fatigued, and said that the end could not be far off," Barnes recalled.[50]

It would have been hard for Lincoln to miss the encouraging sight of long queues of Confederate prisoners at City Point. A Massachusetts soldier named Cyrus T. Goodwin observed a group of captured Southerners marching through and recalled that "they were a rough looking set, and did not look much like Soldiers, they had on all sorts hats and caps coats and pants[.] Some of them had on our uniforms but the most of them had on dirty grey cloth[e]s. Some of them were quite saucy[.] I heard one them say you dam yankey Sons of bitches we will blow you sky high before you get Richmond."[51] Goodwin thought about telling them that Richmond had fallen but decided against it.

Lieutenant Colonel Bowers greeted Lincoln at the telegraph office with the much anticipated news that had arrived not long after the President departed for Petersburg. A message from Major General Weitzel confirmed that his forces had occupied Richmond this morning, that they had found portions of the city on fire, were doing their best to extinguish the flames, and that their reception by the residents had been enthusiastic. (This information would not reach General Grant for another hour or so.) Bowers also handed Lincoln a note of congratulations sent at 10:30 a.m. by the

Secretary of War, which also expressed concern for the President's safety. "Allow me respectfully to ask you to consider whether you ought to expose the nation to the consequences of any disaster to yourself in the pursuit of a treacherous and dangerous enemy like the rebel army," Stanton wrote. "If it was a question concerning yourself only I should not presume to say a word. Commanding generals are in the line of their duty in running such risks; but is the political head of a nation in the same condition?"[52]

Lincoln answered Stanton's note, but not until 5:00 p.m. The most likely explanation is that having been up for most of the night and on the go since dawn, the President was finally overtaken by fatigue. He returned to the *River Queen* for a long-deferred nap. The reply he eventually sent was a brief summary of what he'd done this day, closing with a firm statement of intentions. "It is certain now that Richmond is in our hands, and I think I will go there to-morrow, I will take care of myself."[53]

There was also a note to Mary to tell her that "Petersburg & Richmond are both in our hands; and Tad & I have been to the former & been with Bob four or five hours. He is well & in good spirits."[54]

These he handed to Captain Barnes, who carried them up the bluff to the telegraph office before returning to the *Bat*. Then there was time for a visit with Mrs. Grant aboard the headquarters boat. "The President returned that evening, calling to tell me he had left General Grant looking well and full of hope," she recollected. "The President was radiant when he told us of the fall of Petersburg."[55] After a quiet dinner aboard the *River Queen*, Lincoln strolled on the upper deck in the company of Captain Penrose. He caught sight of a nearby transport, which was being loaded with Confederate prisoners captured in the recent fighting.

"Poor fellows!" Lincoln said. "It's a hard lot. Poor fellows."[56]

Chapter Twelve

Tuesday, April 4, 1865

"It is well to be humble."

WHILE the President slept, scores of sailors and naval officers were engaged in a deadly game of hide-and-seek along the James River from Trent's Reach northward. Just before departing City Point to visit Petersburg, Admiral Porter had issued orders for the "river to be at once cleared of torpedoes as far up as Richmond."[1] It took until the evening for the operation to begin in earnest, and it was still going on well into the morning of April 4, which fortunately looked to be another fine one weather-wise.

The Rebel torpedoes (mines) consisted of gunpowder charges in watertight containers that were often anchored to the riverbed, but sometimes allowed to drift free. Detonation occurred in one of two ways: either through physical contact with a passing vessel, or via an electrical signal sent from shore through an insulated cable. The process of removing these deadly obstacles was often referred to as dragging for torpedoes. Teams of shallow draft boats (usually cutters) moved methodically through a seeded area with cables strung between them at river bottom depth or hauling an array of grapples well behind them. The cables would snag the torpedo anchor chain, allowing the sailors to work the infernal device to the surface, where they would either explode it with gunfire or cut it open to dump the powder into the river. The grapples would sometimes trigger the explosion so the trick was to be far enough away when that happened. The electrically triggered torpedoes would occasionally be pulled to shore, beached, and kept for later inspection by ordnance specialists.

A corresponding action took place along the shoreline, as armed parties kept pace with the boats on the lookout for cables snaking out of the river leading to camouflaged firing positions. These squads also drove off any sharpshooters sent to harass the sailors. Porter's orders had the sailors working through the night, which was only possible because the defenders had fled, allowing torches and lanterns to be employed. Still, it was a tense and nerve-wracking procedure in which a mistake or bad luck could have fatal consequences. "Let the work be pushed ahead," read the operational orders, "but be careful that no accidents happen."[2]

A grand final sweep was initiated this day at 6:00 a.m. Twenty boats were employed in pairs (two from each of ten ships) and deployed in a diagonal formation from one side of the channel to the other, while shore parties moved just ahead of the group to double check for wires. Admiral Porter wanted an open route to Richmond for Lincoln, and the men of the James River squadron risked their lives to give it to him.

This would prove to be the first of three consecutive days that Virginia war dispatches did not appear in newspapers over Lincoln's signature. Making the matter somewhat curious is the fact that the President did send off a signed note to Stanton this morning clearly intended for national release. It was a "just the facts" note, mentioning railroad stock Weitzel found intact in Richmond and passing along an update from Grant about Sheridan's movements. Yet when it was released to the press Lincoln's name was removed with Stanton's introduction reading: "The following particulars, dated at City Point, April 4, 8 A.M., give the latest information received from Richmond."[3] It would be followed by a second bulletin this day, released near midnight, containing a longer summary from Grant addressed to Secretary of War Stanton via Lieutenant Colonel Bowers, and received at 6:30 p.m.

Lincoln likely sent his note from the telegraph office where he had gravitated first thing to catch up on the latest news. He then returned to the *River Queen* to wait for Admiral Porter's all clear. According to Captain Barnes, the word came at 8:00 a.m., though none of the ships moved for an hour. As Barnes wrote, "The Admiral sent me word that he was going up to Richmond and would take the President along, and that the *Bat* could follow." In this case, "take the President along" meant in the *River Queen*. Barnes observed the President standing on her upper deck as the passenger ship moved past the *Bat*. Lincoln, the captain recollected, "waved his hat in answer to my salute as he passed."[4] Not mentioned by either Porter or Barnes was a fourth vessel, the transport *Columbus*, said to be carrying riding horses and a carriage.

From the logbooks kept by the *Bat* and *Malvern*, it appears that the *River Queen* departed first, followed by the flagship and then Captain Barnes' vessel. The *River Queen's* skipper was taking no chances and proceeded cautiously enough that she was quickly overtaken by the two warships. The swift *Bat* forged ahead so rapidly that she had to halt and hold for the others to join her. Something of her crew's impatience was reflected in the log entry which reads: "stopped & drifted waiting waiting [sic] for the *Malvern* & Queen to come up."[5] The *Malvern* arrived first, followed 30 minutes later by the *River Queen*. The little convoy passed Aiken's Landing at noon, with the *Bat* now last in line. Twenty minutes later the ships steamed through what had been the navy's front line at Trent's Reach.

They were now cruising into what was once enemy territory. As the vessels eased into the first of two hairpin turns, several powerful Confederate batteries were visible off to the port side, the unmanned positions now silent. A bit farther on and there was clear evidence of the hard work performed by Porter's sailors. The Admiral appears to have kept a weather eye on the President. As the three ships entered the mined area (now presumably cleared), Lincoln recalled, Porter "glanced rather askance at the ugly torpedoes that now and then showed their heads along the banks where our boats had hauled them out of the way." Fort Brady was located at the peak of the second hairpin representing the southern end of the Federal lines outside Richmond. Admiral Porter was setting a brisk pace, which the President's boat matched, a matter of no small concern to Captain Barnes. "I could not avoid a feeling of anxiety for the *Malvern* and the *Queen*, as they pushed ahead rapidly," he reflected, "lest some undiscovered mines should be touched and the vessels blown to pieces."[6]

As the river began to straighten out, the little procession passed through Graveyard Reach; empty now, where Rebel ironclads had been regularly stationed throughout the Petersburg operation. The James made a sharp twist to the west some two miles past Graveyard Reach before another abrupt bend north for the final leg to Richmond. Approaching that turn about 1:40 p.m. the passengers and crew sighted the major Confederate defensive position blocking the river—Fort Darling, perched to the west atop the 90-foot high Drewry's Bluff. Its guns were also silent, but the passive obstacles in the water still functioned.

There were three major elements to the obstructions here, where the river was 175 yards wide. First were three distinct rows of stone-filled wooden cribs roughly at a right angle to and tight against the western shore line. Parallel and between the cribs were rows of wooden pilings driven deep into the river bottom. Finally there were several scuttled vessels positioned to block channel openings, portions of their wheelhouses and superstructures clearly visible. The only passageway was a narrow route hugging the eastern bank, within point-blank range of the fort's powerful (but now abandoned) cannon. Several vessels from Porter's flotilla had grounded here or been forced to halt in the efforts by their eager captains to maneuver past the obstacles and be the first into Richmond. The logbooks for the *Bat* and *Malvern* indicate that both ships were temporarily unable to squeeze past the grounded craft and so anchored at this point. (Admiral Porter and Captain Barnes claim in their postwar recollections that the Malvern grounded, though her log doesn't admit as much.) The three ships were about seven miles below the former Confederate capital.

Admiral Porter had become fixated on reaching Richmond with the President. Common sense and prudence dictated waiting here until the river route was open, or going overland, but Porter never considered these options. The navy had promised the President he would visit the Rebel capital this day and the navy delivered. "Not to be delayed," Porter later

These models of Admiral Porter's barge (above, and next page) are based on the small boats known to be carried by the *Malvern* and *Boston Journal* reporter Charles Coffin's information. Note the wraparound bench in the stern where Lincoln would have sat.

Naval Surface Warfare Center, Carderock Division

recorded, "I took the President in my barge, and, with a tug ahead with a file of marines on board, we continued on up to the city."[7]

The admiral's barge in this case was likely a 30-foot cutter with 12 sailors powering six oars (two men apiece) and helmed by a coxswain. Sitting on the stern bench would have been Admiral Porter plus two aides, President Lincoln, and Captain Penrose. Also present was Tad who likely shared a thwart with two oarsmen. This was turning out to be quite an adventure for Lincoln's youngest, especially as it was his twelfth birthday. Once Captain Barnes observed what was happening, he manned his own gig "and pulled after him with all the speed possible."[8]

The small boats first had to maneuver past some grounded Union warships jamming the narrow channel, one of which was the single-turreted monitor USS *Mahopac*. "As he passed our vessel the crew lined up on the side and saluted," remembered a sailor. "He arose in the stern of the launch and returned the salute." Another craft in the way was the 143 foot-long, 520-ton USS *Perry*, an armed side-wheel ferry carrying five guns. Before the admiral's barge could hook up to its towing tug, she had to get clear of the congestion, which meant getting by the *Perry*. According to the *Perry's* signal officer, Elisha N. Pierce, his captain was working the engines to try to break free when Admiral Porter's barge passed and was drawn in by the current toward one of the great paddle wheels, which was about to start rotating. The *Perry's* captain managed to stop the engines, but Pierce claimed it was a near thing. In a letter describing the incident he insisted that "had the wheel gone over once more, it would have caused the death of most of those in the barge."[9]

(Most likely the wheel wasn't turning as the President passed. The incident is not noted in the Perry's deck log, nor does Admiral Porter nor Captain Barnes mention it, suggesting that Pierce was recollecting 20 years later something that *could* have happened rather than something that *almost* happened.)

Once clear of the gridlock a tow line was attached from the tug to the bow of the admiral's barge and the party began made better time against the current. The *Bat's* gig with Captain Barnes, struggling to keep pace, slowly dropped behind. The tug and the admiral's barge had covered about six miles when they approached the remains of the Tree Hill Bridge and spotted the Rebel flag-of-truce boat, the *William Allison*, anchored on the Richmond side. There were people aboard, so the tug eased over to investigate. David Dixon Porter now got the surprise of his life, for among the passengers was none other than Vice Admiral David G. Farragut, the hero of Mobile Bay.

"Is that you, Farragut?"

"Yes, sir, it is. We have come down from Richmond to meet you."

Farragut had been in Norfolk on a loose Navy Department assignment when the news of Richmond's fall crackled along the telegraph wires. The Vice Admiral gathered some staff and associates and promptly steamed up the James, passing City Point early this morning. They had gotten as far as Varina Landing before they were held up by the torpedo-clearing operations. Farragut and a few others went ashore, where they acquired some horses and headed for Richmond. They entered the city around 10:00 a.m., enjoyed a tour, and met with the army commander, Major General Weitzel. The vice admiral was determined to take the water route for the trip back and used his rank to commandeer the abandoned Rebel flag-of-truce boat. They had steamed slightly more a mile out of town when they encountered the bridge whose hinged section, designed to permit riverboat traffic, was jammed. They were working to raise it when Admiral Porter's party appeared.

Observing their exchange of greetings, an army officer traveling with Farragut noted that "Porter's expression was one of blank amazement." As the army man phrased it, Farragut had "cut in and investigated" Richmond "while the naval commander to whom the work belonged [Porter] was sounding and feeling his way cautiously up the James." President Lincoln broke the awkward silence between these two highly competitive men by asking, "How is Libby?" When Farragut answered that the infamous lockup was "Very full of Rebel prisoners," the President displayed "an audible and very open smile."[10]

Farragut's unexpected (and unwelcome) appearance not only had taken the wind out of Porter's sails, but it had taken him aback. He now made an unwise decision, instructing the tug to drop the tow line to assist Farragut in getting the passageway cleared for full-sized boats. Porter then directed the barge crew to set to their oars, and the boat (small enough to slip through the jumbled structure) proceeded steadily toward Richmond. In detaching the tug, Porter had also detached the Marine guard, so he was bringing the President of the United States into a city evacuated by the enemy some 36 hours earlier with the commander-in-chief's only immediate protection being those in the barge, one of whom was a child.

Something in Porter's worried look prompted Lincoln to tell a story. "Admiral," he said, "this brings to my mind a fellow who once came to me to ask for an appointment as minister abroad. Finding he could not get that, he came down to some more modest position. Finally he asked to be made a tide-waiter. When he saw he could not get that, he asked me for an old pair of trousers. But it is well to be humble."[11]

After about a mile of effort they passed by the Richmond docking area called "Rockett's" off the starboard side. This is where Porter had intended to bring the President and the *River Queen* but it was configured for full-sized ships, not a cutter with barely a foot of freeboard. Besides, the smoke from the recent fires still filled the air, masking everything behind a faint scrim. They kept rowing. "We saw few or no signs of our army in the lower part of the city, and not knowing where to land we pulled on up until we got ashore among the rocks in the rapids, which brought us to a standstill," recalled the Admiral.[12]

Porter was no stranger to river vexations. He had commanded the Navy's part in a combined arms operation along the Red River in Louisiana just a year earlier. The river level had begun to fall precipitously, trapping Porter's flotilla on the wrong side of shallow rapids outside Alexandria, Louisiana. The officer faced a career-ending decision of scuttling his force, but U.S. Army engineer Lieutenant Colonel Joseph Bailey conceived and constructed a series of small localized dams that raised the water enough for the warships to escape.

Lincoln laughed as he observed Porter's discomfort and remarked: "Admiral, you will have to send for Colonel Bailey." The navy man was not in a mood for humor. "No, sir," he muttered, "we don't want Colonel Bailey this time. I can manage it." Some of the sailors slipped overboard and soon pushed the boat back into deeper water. According to Porter, "We then put

In this magnification of a larger photographic image, the area where the Lincoln party landed is just to the right of the pontoon bridge (opposite page), which was built after the President's visit. Only a few workmen were visible at the time.

LOC, magnified view courtesy of Mike Gorman

our head down stream again and hauled in to the only practicable looking landing that we saw, where twenty or thirty negroes were at work throwing up some dirt."[13]

In this manner did Abraham Lincoln enter the city of Richmond, Virginia.

A short distance from the landing beach the *Boston Journal* reporter Charles Coffin was adding some jottings to the notebook he was keeping of his recent adventures. Just 24 hours earlier he had been in Petersburg, where he observed Lincoln's arrival and calculated that if the President was visiting Petersburg and all the army troops he had seen were marching west, it was very probable that Richmond had been abandoned. The major story that the North had been hungering for since 1861 was just 30 miles away and that was where he needed to be.

Coffin hustled out to Meade Station where he hopped a military train that brought him to City Point around noon. "I was soon in the saddle," he reported to his readers, "galloping 'On to Richmond.' Crossing the Appomattox [River] at Broadway [Landing, site of a Union pontoon bridge], riding to Varina [Landing] on the James, crossing on the pontoons and approaching the city by the New Market road, overtaking the twenty-fifth corps on the outskirts of the city," and arriving in the Rebel capital at 5:00 p.m., April 3.[14]

Locating the U.S. command headquarters at the former Confederate executive mansion on Clay Street, Coffin chatted up some friendly officers and began to fill in the story of Richmond's last 24 hours. Talks with a few citizens and a quick visual tour of damaged areas (plus the notes he had been taking at Petersburg) gave him what he needed to file his first report from Richmond. He secured a room at the Spotswood House (itself under threat from the city fires) and before midnight had produced 2,700 words that he handed to a messenger. It would appear in the April 8 edition alongside the next piece he would file.

Coffin rose early in the morning of April 4 and was stunned by what he saw. "The ruins were still smoking," he scrawled. "The fire was still flaming furiously in several places. The pavements were hot to my feet, so intense had been the flames." The reporter made his way over to the Capitol grounds which in pre-war times had been a well-tended oasis of tranquility but now seethed like a refugee camp, filled with random bunches of people and piles of belongings hastily snatched from yesterday's fires, which had destroyed much of the city directly south from the Capitol to the river. He wandered into the statehouse, curious about the place where the Rebel legislature had tried and failed to govern the upstart nation. "The windows are broken, the carpets faded, the paint dingy, the desks rickety," he noted with smug satisfaction.[15] Coffin encountered Major General Weitzel reviewing occupation protocols with several officers, including Brigadier General George F. Shepley, just appointed the city's military governor. Coffin had watched for just a few minutes when the door opened and in strode Vice Admiral Farragut on his personal tour of the fallen citadel.

Coffin enjoyed a brief exchange with the celebrated sailor before moving along. He was eager to visit one of the most infamous Confederate prisons of the war and so ambled south and east to view Libby Prison. He was working on his notes when he caught sight of Admiral Porter's barge and hurried over to where it was making landfall. While he would recall the time in his postwar writings as being around noon (his April 4 dispatch has no time notation), the logs of the *Malvern* and *Bat* indicate that the Admiral's barge pulled clear of the Drewry's Bluff obstructions a little before 2:00 p.m., so the time was more likely around 3:00 p.m.

The spot Admiral Porter chose to ground his barge was a sandbar separated from the shoreline by a 150-foot-wide channel which was crossed by a somewhat ramshackle but usable footbridge. "The street along the river-front was deserted," he recollected, "and, although the Federal troops had been in possession of the city some hours, not a soldier was to be seen. At the landing was a small house, and behind it a dozen negroes were digging with spades." From the beginning of this day's adventure, the naval officer had blithely assumed that the army would be present in force when they landed, but the reality was quite the opposite. "For the first time I realized the danger in which the President was placed," Porter admitted.[16]

He ordered the 12 rowing sailors to take up their carbines and join them. The coxswain remained behind to protect the admiral's barge. The group made its way across the footbridge and, once ashore, Porter set the

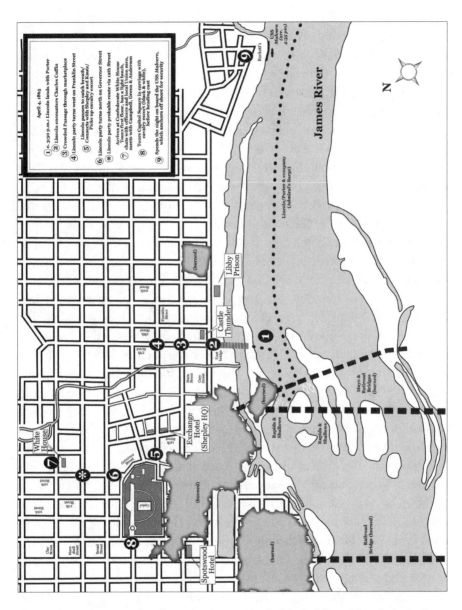

formation: six armed sailors in front, six behind, himself and the others covering the flanks. An army officer in the city later took the admiral to task because "instead of delaying landing to notify him [i.e., Weitzel] of their presence, and awaiting his arrival with a carriage and strong military escort to protect the President from any possible danger, as it was his duty to do, [Porter] formed his little party and set out on his hunt for the Headquarters of Gen. Weitzel."[17]

President Lincoln at once attracted attention. The workers Porter had observed dropped their tools and began to cluster near the group. Reporter Coffin pointed him out to a black woman. "There is the man who made you free," he said. When she asked who he meant, he said Lincoln's name and pointed: "There he is, that tall man." According to Coffin, the black woman "gazed at him a moment, clapped her hands, then jumped straight up and down, shouting 'Glory, glory, glory!'"[18]

The correspondent dutifully took down the names of those in the entourage. Present this day were "President Lincoln and his son [Tad], Admiral Porter, Capt. [Charles] Penrose of the army, Capt. A. H. Adams of the navy, Lieut. W. W. Clemens of the signal corps," plus the dozen sailors (outfitted with "round blue caps and short jackets and bagging pants"). The President, Coffin noted, "wore his overcoat which was quite long, & reached below the knees, & a stove pipe hat."[19] Their intention was to reach General Weitzel's headquarters at the former Confederate executive mansion. Although Coffin would later claim to have supplied directions, his first account says that a black man initially assumed the role of guide.

What had begun as a small group of African-American laborers working along the waterfront began to grow with the addition of others drawn by the happy shouting. "They pressed round the President, ran ahead, and hovered upon the flanks and rear of the little company. Men, women, and children joined the constantly increasing throng," Coffin noted. While their numbers would not become huge, the narrow streets choked with debris from the fire and looting served to compress the assemblage so that it fast became a challenge to press ahead. "We at once found that we had a hard road to travel as the crowd was getting more dense at every moment, almost impossible to get through as it was not an ordinary task to keep the people back or prevent them from enveloping us entirely—whilst there was one incessant roar of cheering from the almost frantic population, and at every corner it was augmented and the streets on all sides were filled with people running to get a glimpse of Old Abe," recollected Lieutenant Clemens.[20]

Admiral Porter saw enemies at every turn and filled his postwar narratives with incidents he alone witnessed. Still, there was danger in the crush of so many people jammed into such a constricted roadway. Captain Penrose felt that it was "foolhardy" to push on, but nobody suggested turning back. In the end the army officer had to admit that the President throughout showed "great courage." They continued to walk north along 17th Street. When they crossed Main Street, the view to the west was one of

A seldom seen depiction of Lincoln's walk through Richmond by illustrator James
Carroll Mansfield from the early 20th century. It captures something of the
grim determination of everyone involved. *Archive.org*

smoldering timbers and collapsed buildings representing the upper portion
of an area that would hereafter be known as the "burned district." An
unidentified witness (likely Penrose) observed that the President's gaze at
this time "had the calm in it that comes over the face of a brave man when he
is ready for whatever may come."[21]

Their passage through the area that housed the city's farmers' market
likely encountered the largest crowd of the journey since this was also a
ration distribution point. Thanks to the general tumult accompanying the
President's visit, everyone within earshot would have converged by this
time. This was likely the section Coffin was writing about when he described
"a surging mass of men, women and children, black, white and yellow,
running, shouting, dancing, swinging their caps, bonnets and handkerchiefs.
. . . All could see him, he was so tall—so conspicuous." Passing one doorway
the reporter heard a black woman chanting: "Thank you, dear Jesus, for this!
thank you, Jesus!" and another "Bless de Lord!"[22]

Captain Barnes had landed in his gig back at the river's edge after
gamely trailing the admiral's barge for seven miles. "I saw them some
distance off, surrounded by a dense mass of people, mostly negroes, the tall
hat of the President looming up above the crowd," recalled the captain. "A
few sailors with carbines were their only escort. Not a soldier was in sight,
while the mob seemed frantic, edging up and rushing against the little party,
shouting and praying aloud in negro fashion."[23]

A short block north brought the President's party to Franklin Street
where they turned left and walked to Governor Street at the foot of a

precipitous hill. Here the men and boy paused to catch their breath before chugging up the steeper slope. (The President, Coffin noted, "halted a moment to rest and wipe the perspiration from his brow.") An elderly black man stepped forward and prayed aloud for Lincoln's safety. Much to Coffin's surprise, the President "lifted his own hat from his head and bowed to the old man."[24]

Up until now the procession had consisted of the group that came off the admiral's barge, the reporter Coffin, and the crowd of noisy, happy, pressing civilians. That was about to change. They were being observed by two Union army officers, Brigadier General George Shepley (the military governor) and Brevet Major General August V. Kautz (commanding a Twenty-Fifth Corps division). Kautz was in his office in the Richmond House, facing Capitol Square, while Shepley was outside on horseback, accompanied by an aide whom he sent to investigate. The subordinate was back in a few minutes with the information. "General, they say it is the president," he reported. Sending the aide off for reinforcements, Shepley spurred forward, halted at the head of the procession, and dismounted.

"Hullo, general! Is this you?" Lincoln asked. "I was walking round to find headquarters." A few moments more and Brevet Major General Kautz arrived, followed by a detachment of the 4th Massachusetts Cavalry. The mounted men, observed Captain Barnes (who had nearly caught up by now), "cleared the street without ceremony, pushing and striking out right and left at the crowd." (A vastly relieved Admiral Porter noted that for "the first time since starting from the landing we were able to walk along uninterruptedly.") Kautz assumed command as ranking officer, later taking full credit for guiding the President to Weitzel's headquarters (as did Shepley). No accounts mention this, but let us imagine that a sympathetic cavalryman allowed young Tad to ride double for the final three-quarters of a mile to the headquarters. The time, according to Kautz, was "between three and four p.m."[25]

Another ten minutes or so and they were in front of the three-and-a-half story mansion at 12th and Clay streets (in the well-to-do section of town known as Court End) that had been the home and a sub-office of Jefferson Davis since August 1861. Captain Barnes remembered it as "a modest and unpretentious building, brown in color, with small windows and doors." There was a mostly black crowd waiting as they arrived, one that grew steadily in size as the time passed, eventually reaching 500 or so. According to Shepley he "presented the president to the people, and he acknowledged

The Richmond residence of Jefferson Davis, aka "The White House of the Confederacy." On April 4, 1865, the area would have been packed with hundreds of onlookers for Lincoln's visit. LOC

their hearty cheers by a few simple, sensible, and kindly words." The diary of a Richmond lady present in the town this day (but not near the executive mansion) reports Lincoln's "telling them they were free and had no master now but God," while a six-year old who was present never forgot him "speaking in friendly tones to all whom he met." A Christian Commission minister who was there long remembered the image of "that homely, awkward, great good man."[26]

A fragment from several longer speeches recollected by Admiral Porter as having been made this day may well reflect some of what Lincoln said in front of the Confederate White House: "My poor friends, . . . you are free— free as air. You can cast off the name of slave and trample upon it; it will come to you no more. Liberty is your birthright. God gave it to you as he gave it to others, and it is a sin that you have been deprived of it for so many years."[27]

A carriage with mounted escort came up to the house toward the end of this briefest of speeches, prompting another round of cheers from the crowd. Out of it popped Samuel Beckwith, the President's telegrapher, who made his way to his chief. "Young man," chided Lincoln, "'I am afraid you have been stealing somebody's thunder." "The enthusiasm of the colored people was something indescribable," Beckwith observed.[28]

Shepley introduced the crowd to some of the other notables present (Admiral Porter and Brevet Major General Kautz among them) and then ushered the President inside. According to a letter Lieutenant Clemens wrote this day, those gathered here were "swaying to and fro constantly increasing until there . . . was one incessant cheer from old and young white and black— the latter being almost unable to restrain themselves and it was amusing to see their gyrations and performances gone through by them."[29] The Massachusetts troopers cleared the immediate area and established a security perimeter.

Charles Coffin reported in a later recollection that the sailors formed in two lines and presented arms as Lincoln entered the building. (After a short rest and some refreshment the dozen tars who had guarded Lincoln for much of his walk formed up and headed down the hill back to the admiral's barge. No one thought to take their names, and none left any recollection that has come to light.)

The first sight to greet Lincoln upon entering the Rebel executive mansion was a pair of gas powered lamps in the form of life-sized statutes representing "Comedy" and "Tragedy." Colored and polished to look like stone, they were in fact painted plaster. The President was likely steered into a room immediately on the right that had often been used by Jefferson Davis as a place to receive visitors. Someone would have brought him a glass of water while a few officers made small talk, stalling until the general in charge arrived. Possibly while everyone was waiting, Lincoln was shown around the first floor of the mansion. While some accounts have him visiting upstairs it is unlikely he would have spent any time in what was formerly the Davis family's private living space and presently General Weitzel's offices and sleeping area. The often repeated story of him sitting in Jefferson Davis's chair did not happen.

The formal reception began once Richmond's military commander arrived. Major General Godfrey Weitzel later explained that the information he had received from City Point concerning the President's arrival sent him to the wrong place at the wrong time. As Lieutenant Clemens wrote in a letter home, "All the Army officers in the vicinity came to pay their respects and the house was soon filled with the shoulder strap gentry of all grades." Among them was Colonel Samuel H. Roberts, who reminded the President that during the March 26 review of the Army of the James, General Grant had prophesied that his brigade would be among the first to enter Richmond. Lincoln, Roberts remembered with pride, "had a hearty laugh over it." To officers he didn't know, Lincoln's comment was a standard "I am very happy to meet you." A small piece appearing in a Washington newspaper six days hence may well have caught something of the light mood of the moment. "When Mr. Lincoln heard that Weitzel's negroes had taken Richmond, he said, 'Well, the people in Richmond have been wanting black soldiers for some time past, and now they've got them.'"[30]

Coffin says that several white citizens who had maintained their allegiance to the Union throughout the war were also present. A Federal officer noted that one of them, a former U.S. Congressman named John Minor Botts, who had suffered imprisonment for his sentiments, "quickly stepped forward [and] he flung his arm about Mr. Lincoln's neck in the most tragic manner." All he could do was say: "Thank God, I have lived to see this day." The President renewed his acquaintance with Dr. Moses Parker, who had shown him about the hospital at Point of Rocks. "I was proud to be remembered," Parker recalled, "and shall never forget his kind and pleasant face and manner as he said when taking my hand, 'the war is nearly over.'"[31]

Food had been prepared and a meal was served (Captain Barnes described it as "a soldier's luncheon, simple and frugal"[32]). Lincoln hadn't eaten since breakfast so most accounts label it as "lunch," although it was now past 4:00 p.m. Likely while they were eating came the distant rhythmic booms of cannon firing a salute as Admiral Porter's flagship at last reached Rockett's and anchored just offshore. (The *Malvern's* log notes the time as 4:35 p.m.) General Weitzel was called out of the room not long after, and when he returned he took the President aside to say that a small delegation of prominent citizens headed by former Supreme Court Justice (and Confederate assistant secretary of war) John A. Campbell wanted a few words with him. Campbell had been one of the three commissioners Lincoln met at Hampton Roads in February, and he took the meeting behind closed doors in the reception room.

Coffin described the judge as tall and looking "pale, care-worn, [and] agitated." He "bowed very low to the President, who received him with dignity, and yet cordially." Much to Lincoln's surprise, there was another man present very familiar to him named Duff Green, dressed in Confederate gray and carrying a smoothly polished white pine walking stick. The two had known each other since 1847 when Lincoln was a Congressman and Green was already esteemed and feared as a power broker. Green was first and foremost a Southerner. It was during the political maneuverings between Lincoln's election and inauguration that he had tried to convince his friend that all the South needed to remain in the Union were constitutional guarantees regarding slavery. The plan, such as it was, failed to gain traction and, as Lincoln remarked in his second inaugural, "The war came."[33] Green threw his lot in with the Confederacy to run a factory in Tennessee that produced military supplies.

Lincoln had hoped that Campbell bore a private note from Jefferson Davis, but that was not the case. Campbell and the others, including Joseph Reid Anderson, a Confederate general at the start of the war who resigned to manage the Tredegar Iron Works, had come as private citizens, anxious to find an honorable, though unofficial, end to the fighting. The judge stated that he had told Jefferson Davis that no victory was possible on the battlefield and that they should seek terms. Green reminded Lincoln that they had tried together to avert war in 1861 and "I come now to ascertain upon what terms we can make peace."

Lincoln answered with words that Judge Campbell had heard at Hampton Roads. "If you desire peace, all that will be required of you is to acknowledge the authority of the United States," the President said, adding that "he did not commence the war, and was anxious for peace."[34] Always ready to deal when lives might be saved, Lincoln was willing to talk further, but this was not the time or place. A hasty appointment was made to meet again tomorrow morning aboard the *Malvern*.

Captain Barnes recollected that at this point carriages were "sent for, and under military escort Mr. Lincoln was driven to places of interest about the city."[35] The complexion of the cavalry escort had changed with the addition of troopers from the 5th Massachusetts, an African-American regiment. Brevet Major General Kautz left a brief description of this portion of Lincoln's visit. He did so in two accounts, one an unpublished memoir, the other as part of a series of articles he contributed to a weekly newspaper aimed at veterans called *The National Tribune* (in this descriptive passage, the *Tribune* contributions are italicized):

> Mr. Lincoln, Admiral Porter, Genl. Weitzel, Genl. Shipley and I occupied one [carriage] and a number of the staff took the other and we drove about the city and into the capitol grounds. *I remember Mr. Lincoln's nervousness, as the wagons turned the southeast corner of the Capitol building where the road ran very close to the step declivity on his side and made him shrink and seize the back of the seat in*

front of him as we whirled swiftly around the corner, in evident fear that we might
go over the bank. We completed our drive at the landing where lay the gunboat
Malvern.[36]

The correspondent for the *New York Times* reported that the President's
conveyance paused briefly in front of the large statue of George
Washington, but there was no stopping at the statehouse itself. Crowds of the
curious gravitated toward the vehicles as they passed along the city streets.
"The President," Coffin noted in a later recollection, "was much affected as
they crowded around the carriage to touch his hands." Lincoln appeared to a
devoted Southern matron "tired and old" and she thought him "the ugliest
man I had ever seen." Another white resident, watching from her window,
overheard several ex-slaves talking. "Jeff Davis did not wait to see his
master but he had come at last," she recalled them saying.[37]

It was during this ride, as Major General Weitzel recollected, that he
"had considerable conversation with him in regard to the treatment of the
conquered people. The pith of his answers was that he did not wish to give
me any orders on that subject, but as he expressed it: 'If I were in your place,
I'd let'em up easy—let'em up easy.'"[38] Captain Penrose made no
observations about this moment, even though he had spent time in Libby as a
prisoner in 1862.

Once at Rockett's a small cutter took the President, his son, Admiral
Porter and the officers with him out to the *Malvern*, which was anchored a
short distance away from the wharf for security reasons. A black woman in
the crowd, watching him go, shouted, "Don't drown, Massa Abe, for God's
sake!" Lincoln, Admiral Porter observed, "was tired out, and wanted the
quiet of the flag-ship." The naval officer also made a vow that "the President
should go nowhere again, while under my charge, unless I was with him and
had a guard of marines."[39] Also parked nearby was the USS *Bat*, Captain
Barnes's ship. (Barnes had returned to his gig when Lincoln left in the
carriage.)

Porter reports that Lincoln spent part of the evening relaxing on the
ship's upper deck. In his various accounts, he records several suspicious
happenings; a foiled attempt by a stranger on shore to come aboard the
Malvern with dispatches for the President, and another effort to board the
boat by a person claiming to be a wayward sailor from the USS *Saugus* who
disappeared before his identity could be verified. While it is apparent that
security in Richmond was rather loose at this time, Porter seriously

undermines the credibility of his statements by insisting that one of the two strangers was none other than John Wilkes Booth.

What's clear from Porter's account is that the navy was not yet in contact with the world beyond Richmond. There are no communications from the admiral noted for this day, nor any evidence that Lincoln received dispatches from City Point. General Weitzel was still depending on couriers operating from his headquarters to the nearest telegraphic station on the old siege lines. He exchanged several messages with General Grant and Army of the James officers posted to Bermuda Hundred today, not once mentioning Lincoln. A dispatch sent by Grant and acknowledged by Weitzel was an order to arrest "all editors and proprietors of Richmond papers still remaining in the city and send them to Fort Monroe for confinement," adding he should "be quiet about it."[40] There is no evidence that Lincoln knew about these orders.

The President's visit inspired reflections by others present who tried to sort out what it all meant. Sergeant John C. Brock of the 43rd USCT imagined Lincoln savoring his victory and celebrating the war's one clear accomplishment:

> After four long years of patient watching, filled with many doubts, fears and anxieties, he was rewarded by seeing treason and rebellion pale before the victorious armies of the Union. He saw with his eagle eye rebellion crushed, the supremacy of the government reestablished, Slavery forever blotted from off the statute books of America.[41]

Although the reporter Charles Coffin wrote in later years about the greater meaning of what he witnessed this day, his newspaper account dated April 4 reveals the impressions that were strongest and most vivid in his mind while the events themselves were still fresh:

> No wonder that President Lincoln who has a child's heart, felt his soul stirred; that the tears almost come to his eyes as he heard the thanksgivings to God and Jesus, and the blessings uttered for him from thankful hearts. They were true, earnest and heartfelt expressions of gratitude to God. There are thousands of men in Richmond to-night who would lay down their lives for President Lincoln—their great deliverer—their best friend on earth. He came among them unheralded, without pomp or parade. He walked through the streets as if he were only a private citizen and not the head of a mighty nation. He came not as a conqueror—not with bitterness in his heart, but with kindness. He came as a friend, to alleviate sorrow and suffering, to rebuild what has been destroyed.[42]

Chapter Thirteen

Wednesday, April 5, 1865

"I cannot bring myself to believe that any
human being lives who would do me any harm."

THEY had been gathering throughout the night from all around Richmond as word spread that the man who had broken the chains of bondage was present among them. Some in the enslaved African-American communities insisted this would be the second time that Lincoln had been present. Charity Austin recalled that when she was a young girl she had met a ragged man walking along the railroad tracks near her home. "He said he wus huntin' his people; and dat he had lost all he had," she remembered in later years. "Dey give him somethin' to eat and tobacco to chew, and he went on. Soon we heard he wus in de White House then we knew who it wus come through. We knowed den it wus Abraham Lincoln." Others recognized him as an itinerant man of God who "went all through de country just a-rantin' an' a-preachin' about us being his black brothers. De marster didn't know nothin' about it, cause it was sorta secret-like."[1]

Sunrise this morning was 5:49. The weather was warm and pleasant with clouds that would thicken throughout the day. President Lincoln rose early, had breakfast, and informed Admiral Porter he wanted to see a little more of Richmond before Judge Campbell arrived. This time Porter was taking no chances. There were 30 U.S. marines aboard the *Malvern*, and he detailed 24 of them to accompany the President. The senior Marine officer present was Orderly Sergeant William J. Givin, who made the selections. The men were kitted out as light infantry with rifles and bayonets. On shore was the carriage carried by the *Columbus*, hitched and ready to go, plus there was some cavalry on hand as additional escort. Samuel Beckwith, the telegraph operator on loan to the President from General Grant, put the time around 9:00 a.m. when things got underway, though an hour earlier seems more likely.

The marines landed first followed by the President, Tad, Admiral Porter, and two officer-aides. For this day's escort duty Porter had chosen Ensign Aaron Vanderbilt and Lieutenant Silas Terry. (Captain Penrose appears to have remained behind, perhaps not wishing to see Libby Prison again.) As they clambered into the carriage, Lincoln indicated he wanted to tour more of the burned district, so the group turned west and followed Cary Street.

"The streets seemed to be suddenly alive with the colored race," recalled Admiral Porter. "They seemed to spring from the earth. They came, tumbling and shouting, from over the hills and from the water-side, where no one was seen as we had passed. The crowd immediately became very oppressive. We needed our marines to keep them off." The naval officer ordered the leathernecks "to fix bayonets to their rifles and to surround the President, all of which was quickly done; but the crowd poured in so fearfully that I thought we all stood a chance of being crushed to death."[2]

This gathering of Richmond's former slaves was an epiphany. Some of their words were recalled by the white men present, many of whom recalled the dialect through the filters of their racism. An officer of an African-American regiment remembered the repeated cry of "Fodder Abraham hab don come! Fodder Abraham hab don come!" A brigade commander in the Twenty-fourth Corps heard lots of "God bress Aburn Linkum." Included in the patois related by Admiral Porter was: "Bress de Lord, 'dere is de great Messiah! I knowed him as soon as I seed him." The black reporter Thomas Morris Chester spoke afterwards with an "old negro woman" who told him: "I know that I am free, for I have seen Father Abraham and felt him." When Booker T. Washington spoke of this event in later years he reflected that Richmond's blacks "greeted the strange, kindly figure of the President as if he had been their Saviour instead of merely their liberator."[3]

Despite the armed marines and a cavalry squadron, the crowds were making it difficult for the Presidential party to get very far. "Our progress was very slow," said Porter, "we did not move a mile an hour, and the crowd was still increasing." It took more than 30 minutes to reach the site of Libby Prison, where it became clear that they could not proceed much farther. A soldier on guard duty inside the lockup recollected that he heard noises and "went to the window to see a dense cloud of dust followed by a dark crowd of the colored population (as the boys used to call them) they consisted of men, women and children and . . . were screaming at the top of their voices, 'Massa Linkum, Massa Linkum has come,' they were followed by a squadron of cavalry, then came the carriage with the President."[4]

It was stop and go, mostly the former, and during some of the pauses several black youngsters "taking advantage of the delay, climbed upon the top of the carriage and took a peep at him over the rim, greatly to the amusement of the President."[5] That according to one soldier in the city.

They could have spent another hour just reaching the burned district so it was decided, as Porter related, "to look on the horrid bastille where so many Union soldiers had dragged out a dreadful existence, and were subjected to all the cruelty the minds of brutal jailers could devise." "I was on horseback and saw President Lincoln in the carriage in front of Libby prison, looking at that place of horror, now filled with rebel prisoners, which the day before held our Union soldiers," recounted Dr. Moses Parker. "We all enjoyed this sight—the tables were turned and we had the fun of asking these 'rebs' how they liked it."[6]

The officer in charge of security for Libby Prison and nearby Castle Thunder was Colonel Lucius Mattison of the 81st New York, who turned out the guard to honor the commander-in-chief. "The President spoke a brief word of congratulation to our men both at Libby and the Castle," he recalled. "The halyards to the flagstaff on the Castle had been unwove. Captain William P. Babcock and another officer of the 81st ascended to the roof in great haste to raise a flag before the President should arrive. The staff had to be taken down. They rove the halyards, but seeing the staff could not be replaced in time, they ran the butt down through the roof hatch, and made the staff fast to a beam that left the staff leaning to one side. But the flag was hoisted. One of the proudest things I have to say of my life was that I have shaken hands and spoken to Abraham Lincoln twice. This was the last occasion. His eyes happened to catch sight of the flag on the prison and he said 'Boys, I'm glad to see you have the flag up, but straighten that staff.'"[7]

Then it was back to the *Malvern* where Lincoln found his first appointment waiting. It was Richmond provost marshal Brevet Brigadier General Edward H. Ripley bearing disturbing news. The President met him in the admiral's cabin and brought his son along. Lincoln, recalled Ripley, "sat down on the long cushioned seat running along the side of the ship behind the dining table, I taking my seat opposite him. Little Tad, who was

Admiral David Porter and his officers aboard his flagship USS *Malvern.* Her noisy
arrival in Richmond (announced by a 35-gun salute) convinced many she
carried President Lincoln aboard at the time. LOC

then a small and very restless boy, amused himself by running up and down
the length of the sofa behind his father and jumping over his back in passing.
As I progressed in the explanation of my errand, Mr. Lincoln let his head
droop upon his hands as his elbows rested on the table, his hands supporting
his chin and clasping either cheek in an expression of the most
heart-breaking weariness, his great, melancholy eyes filling the cabin with
the mournful light they emitted."

Ripley had spoken yesterday with a former Confederate agent who
reported a plot afoot to assassinate the President. While the informant's
credentials seemed solid enough, he had precious few facts to back up what
he was saying. Ripley had his doubts but felt he could not ignore the man and
had come to urge Lincoln to take more precautions regarding his safety. He
had even brought the informant with him in case the President wanted to ask
his own questions.

"No, General Ripley, it is impossible for me to adopt and follow your
suggestions," Lincoln said after some thought. "I deeply appreciate the
feeling which has led you to urge them on me, but I must go on as I have
begun in the course marked out for me, for I cannot bring myself to believe

that any human being lives who would do me any harm."[8] With that he indicated the meeting was over. Ripley left, not satisfied with Lincoln's answer, but powerless to do anything more to influence events.

(Lincoln afterward said little about his time in Richmond. One comment was made to a minister who asked about the reception he received from the people. "Why, Doctor," the President answered, "I walked along on the street, and any one could have shot me from a second story window."[9])

It was a little after 10:00 a.m. when General Weitzel arrived in the company of Judge John A. Campbell, who had brought along a well-known attorney and state legislator, Gustavus A. Myers. (Apparently, no one else Campbell approached was willing to risk the possible backlash of meeting with the long-demonized U.S. Chief Executive.) What happened in the next hour would prove to be an irksome footnote to Lincoln's Richmond visit.

From the moment on April 4 that he learned that Judge Campbell carried no letter from Jefferson Davis or authority to negotiate, Lincoln wisely scaled back his expectations. He still held out some hope that Campbell had enough personal authority to convene a meeting of distinguished Virginians who might publically repudiate the state's act of secession. That could incite wholesale desertions of Virginia troops from the armies of the Confederacy and hasten the inevitable collapse of rebel power. Campbell, for his part, was trying to slow down the Confederacy's cascade failure long enough for its civilian leaders to mount a common effort to limit the degree of social upheaval and political turmoil that would follow a Union victory. These were diverging agendas, but Lincoln was so anxious to limit further casualties that he was willing to expend the personal capital involved in having such a meeting.

Lincoln never set down his own version of events, while Myers would write about it once, Weitzel a couple of times, and Campbell often. Admiral Porter would have something to say as well, but he was not present. Myers, who set down his notes later this day, said that the President "commenced by stating that he understood we came in no official capacity and that we were unauthorized to act on any matter that might be the subject of our conversation, which we of course confirmed. He then told us that he had written a paper which he would read to us, accompanied by a verbal running commentary of his own when he considered explanation necessary."[10]

"Mr. Lincoln had reduced to writing his terms of peace," continued Campbell. "There were three indispensable conditions: 1. Recognition of the national authority. 2. No cessation of hostilities till this was entirely done. 3.

No receding by the Executive in reference to slavery, as manifested in his [emancipation] proclamation and other official papers. All other questions to be settled on terms of sincere liberality." Lincoln, added Myers, "professed himself really desirous to see . . . an end of the struggle, and said he hoped in the Providence of God that there never would be another." Campbell was convinced that the President "felt a genuine sympathy for the bereavement, destitution, impoverishment, waste, and overturn that the war had occasioned at the South."[11]

It was the recollection of the former U.S. Supreme Court justice that he suggested a gathering of notable Virginians to "have their counsel and cooperation in reconstructing its political and social systems to meet the new and extraordinary conditions of society." He insisted that it was Lincoln who desired that such conference take place with just one item on the agenda. "He wanted the very Legislature that had been sitting in Richmond to vote the restoration of Virginia to the Union," Campbell recorded years later.[12]

With the big points having been made, the conversation turned to some smaller ones. Both Southerners were unhappy with rumors about that every citizen would have to take an oath of allegiance to the Federal government. Lincoln, Myers wrote, "remarked that he had never attached much importance to the oath of allegiance being required," then turned to General

Weitzel with the observation that whatever happened in Richmond would be a decision made on the local not national level. The military officer contributed that he had required the oath to a limited degree when he was second in command of the Union forces occupying New Orleans and saw no reason why Richmond should be any different.

A pre-war Supreme Court justice and wartime Confederate government official, Campbell came to Lincoln hoping to limit the social and political upheavals facing a defeated South. LOC

Major General Godfrey Weitzel, the officer initially in charge of the Union occupation of Richmond. Lincoln's desire to get Virginia out of the Confederacy would put the soldier in a difficult diplomatic position. LOC

"Other conversation occurred," Myers continued, "in which the President declared his disposition to be lenient towards all persons, however prominent, who had taken part in the struggle, and certainly no exhibition was made by him of any feeling of vindictiveness or of exultation." There were two exceptions to his leniency. The first, as Judge Campbell noted, was that "he said it would not be proper to offer a pardon to Mr. [Jefferson] Davis—whom we familiarly call Jeff. Davis,—who says he will not take one." The second, as Lincoln later explained to U. S. Grant, was "that if the war be now further persisted in by the rebels confiscated property shall, at the least, bear the additional cost; and that confiscations shall be remitted to the people of any State which will now, promptly and in good faith, withdraw its troops and other support from resistance to the Government."[13]

Campbell insisted on presenting a draft proposal for a military armistice (already rejected in Lincoln's second condition) which the President politely pocketed. At that point, wrote Myers, "our interview ended. Throughout, it was conducted with entire civility and good humor." General Weitzel remembered that the President took him aside and "told me that he would think over the whole matter carefully and would probably send me some instructions from City Point on the next day."[14]

Now it was time for Lincoln to return to City Point to better monitor Grant's progress as well as events in Washington. (Richmond's telegraphic blackout would not be resolved until later this day.) The question was, how would the President travel? Admiral Porter needed the *Malvern* on station for another day. He had already given Captain Barnes permission to weigh anchor and the *Bat* had dropped down the river. The *River Queen* was

Lincoln's first choice, but Captain Bradford had not attempted to squeeze through the tricky opening at the Tree Hill Bridge but anchored just below it. The decision was made to trust the President's person to the Admiral's barge to ferry the party as far as the *River Queen*. The barge departed shortly after noon with Lincoln, Tad, Captain Penrose and Samuel Beckwith aboard (and possibly a couple of marines as well.) Once the passengers clambered aboard the *River Queen* the steamer started downriver escorted by the USS *Bat*, helmed by Captain Barnes.

Lincoln's boat passed through Trent's Reach about 1:30 p.m. where the President was seen by the sailors about the USS *Monodnock* and *Casco*. The logbooks note that the men of the former gave him "three cheers," while those on the latter did the same as he passed. The little convoy anchored off City Point at 3:30 p.m. According to Beckwith, Lincoln went directly to Lieutenant Colonel Bowers's cabin while he attended "to my post of duty in the telegraph tent adjoining, where a number of ciphers for the President were awaiting translation."[15]

A quick review of the messages from Grant to the War Department showed that the pursuit of Lee's army had not relented in the slightest since Lincoln had dropped off the telegraphic grid. The lieutenant general was last heard from at Nottoway Court House, maybe ten miles from Burkeville Junction—a point Lee would have to hold if he were intent on retreating south toward Danville, where most of what remained of the Confederate government had gathered. The Union force was advancing in two columns. The left (or southern wing), consisting of Sheridan's cavalry, the Army of the James divisions under Major General Ord, and the Fifth Corps, was following the Southside Railroad. The right (or northern wing), representing the Second and Sixth Corps of the Army of the Potomac under Major General Meade, was marching more directly west. The Ninth Corps trailed behind repairing the railroad and restoring the telegraph lines. Communication with his far-flung units was spotty at best, but Grant's hope this morning was that one or both columns "have come up with and captured or broken up the balance of the Army of N. Va."[16]

The men and officers manning the City Point station knew very little beyond that, and Lincoln likely advised them on the Richmond situation. A message had been waiting for him from Secretary of State William H. Seward. There were papers that needed signing, though the Secretary readily allowed they were "not at all critical or serious." If the President wasn't planning to return soon, Seward was ready to come down to City Point. "The public interest will not suffer by you remaining where you are," he said in closing.

Lincoln promptly replied:

> Yours of to-day received. I think there is no probability of my remaining here more than two days longer. If that is too long come down. I passed last night at Richmond and have just returned.[17]

A message arrived toward evening for the President from Major General Nathaniel P. Banks, an officer he had entrusted with managing one of his reconstruction experiments in Louisiana. Banks was returning there after having taken leave for a family matter and now requested instructions. Lincoln answered without much pause, confessing that he had "been so much occupied with other thoughts that I really have no directions to give you."[18]

Lincoln had yet to advise Seward or Stanton of his talks with Judge Campbell and others in Richmond. This time the President lost control of the message thanks to an active assistant to the Secretary of War named Charles A. Dana. Serving as Stanton's agent, Dana spent the morning at City Point before heading overland to Richmond, which he reached early in the afternoon even as the President was steaming south. Dana promptly cornered General Weitzel who briefed him on the particulars of the President's morning's meeting. Dana communicated it all in a message sent at 4:00 p.m. Just about every newspaperman in the former Rebel capital knew about it as well, and their reports plus speculations were speeding north by various means.

A few officers made courtesy calls when word leaked out that the President was back at City Point, among them Brevet Brigadier General Charles H. T. Collis. As commander of the independent brigade based at City Point, Collis was alerted when any high ranking Confederates were brought in. One who came to his attention was Brigadier General Rufus Barringer, who had been captured April 3 in a fight near Namozine Church, west of Petersburg. Collis, who believed in military decorum, played host to Barringer at his headquarters.

The Union officer found his Confederate counterpart to be a "polished, scholarly, and urbane gentleman," as well as a proper house guest. When Collis mentioned Lincoln's extended stay at City Point, the captured officer expressed an interest in seeing the President, if only from a distance. Collis mentioned this as he chatted with Lincoln, who immediately suggested that he bring Barringer over to meet him. As the Federal rose to get his guest, the President mused with a smile, "Do you know I have never seen a live rebel general in full uniform."

Collis returned with the gentleman in tow and made the introductions. Lincoln shook hands and offered the Rebel a seat, but when Barringer saw that there was only one chair for all of them he politely declined. The President chewed on the name for a few moments.

"Barringer? Barringer? from North Carolina? Barringer of North Carolina? General, were you ever in Congress?"

"No, Mr. Lincoln, I never was," the Rebel officer answered.

"Well, I thought not," the President continued. "I thought my memory couldn't be so much at fault. But there was a Barringer in Congress with me, and from your State too!"

"That was my brother, sir."

Watching the two closely, Collis saw Lincoln's expression change from one of puzzlement to realization. He likened it to "a great sudden burst of sunshine in a rain storm."

"Well! well!" the President exclaimed. "Do you know that that brother of yours . . . sat at the same desk and ate at the same table. He was a Whig and so was I . . . and I was very fond of him. And you are his brother, eh? Well! Well! shake again."

By now a couple of additional chairs had been slipped into the space and everyone sat down. There was an easy conversation, touching some memories, and setting out some light reflections on the present times. Barringer tried more than once to depart, worried that he had overstayed his welcome, but Lincoln would not hear of it. As Collis recalled, the President remarked "that they were both prisoners, and he hoped the General would take some pity upon him and help him to talk about the times when they were both their own masters, and hadn't everybody criticizing and abusing them."

After a while, Barringer rose again to leave and this time Lincoln let him go, but not without a final word.

"Do you think I can be of any service to you?" he asked.

It wasn't what Barringer or Collis were expecting. Finally, the Confederate officer said, "If anybody can be of service to a poor devil in my situation, I presume you are the man."

Lincoln drew a blank card out of his coat pocket without any prompting, sat down and began to write, chattering about Washington as he did so. He then passed over the handwritten note, addressed to the Secretary of War:

> This is General Barringer, of the Southern army. He is the brother of a very dear friend of mine. Can you do any thing to make his detention in Washington as comfortable as possible under the circumstances?

Barringer was overwhelmed by the kindness shown him by the man who had been his enemy. When words of thanks didn't come, Collis diplomatically steered him out of the tent and back toward his quarters. He couldn't be sure, but as they walked together he guessed that the Rebel warrior was softly sobbing. Once Barringer returned to his quarters he made a diary entry about the events of this dramatic day. "Pleased with him," he wrote of Lincoln. "His leadership & manners have been misrepresented [by the] South."[19]

Someone brought Lincoln something to eat because he was still in Colonel Bowers's cabin when Provost Marshal Patrick called a little before 9:00 p.m. The general noted in his diary that he "spent about an hour . . . with the President. Talked fully and freely of Richmond Matters which appear to be in a bad State." He added some observations that may reflect Lincoln's, "Richmond is one great mob—There does not appear to be any Military control—The works along the River are of astonishing Strength and there are quantities of Torpedoes on the banks fished out by our Navy."[20]

After Patrick left, Beckwith rushed in with an urgent message from Edwin Stanton that he had just deciphered. There had been a carriage accident in Washington about 4:00 p.m. involving William Seward. Stanton reported Seward's "shoulder bone at the head of the joint broken off, his head and face much bruised." All in all, the Secretary of State was "dangerously injured," in Stanton's opinion and he felt that Mr. Lincoln should return at once. A brief follow-up message two hours later indicated that the "fracture of Mr. Seward's shoulder has been set and he has revived and appears better."[21] For the moment Lincoln did nothing, probably waiting to see what news the morning would bring.

It was close to midnight when he returned to the *River Queen* at the end of two very long but important days.

Chapter Fourteen

Thursday, April 6, 1865

"Nothing I have done is to interfere with you in your work."

UPDATES from the Secretary of War regarding the condition of injured Secretary of State Seward trickled in to City Point overnight. The situation was dire enough that the President likely asked to be awakened for each message, one probably arriving every few hours. The story they told was generally positive:

> Mr. Seward is now quite easy & that there appears no dangerous symptom in his case. I have also seen and conversed with him and although suffering much pain he is composed and entirely in possession of his faculties.

> Mr. Seward is still doing well . . . but his lower jaw is broken. I have seen him and read him all the news. His head received no injury. His mind is clear and spirits good.

> Mr. Seward is doing very well. There is no need for your leaving City Point before Mrs. Lincoln reaches there.[1]

When Lincoln returned to the military telegraph office on the morning of April 6 he knew that the crisis in Washington was manageable and that he need not rush back. He wanted very much to be on the scene when news arrived that Grant had captured or destroyed Lee's army. He was disappointed to find nothing fresh had come in during the night; the last missive was one from Grant to Sherman providing an estimate of Lee's force of 20,000 and hoping soon to "reduce this number one half." The grand plan now was for each general to deal with the force in his front and, as Grant said, "let us see if we can not finish the job. . . . Rebel Armies now are the only strategic points to strike at."[2] Lincoln would have had no disagreement with anything Grant said.

Also in the message queue was a note sent at 4 o'clock this morning from Mary Lincoln, who was at Fortress Monroe en route to rejoin him. As soon as she had learned of Richmond's fall she organized a return expedition to City Point. This time, however, she would be surrounded by her friends. Mary and company departed Washington on April 5. She had received a broad summary of the news that War Secretary Stanton was reporting to the President. Her focus at the moment was her pleasure and that of her guests, all of whom would be better off on the *River Queen* than the army transport they were using. She urged her husband to delay any departure as she and her friends "would prefer seeing you & returning on your boat, we are not comfortable here."[3]

There was dampness in the morning air that made it less attractive outside and easier for Lincoln to focus on two letters he had to write. One contained the instructions he had promised to provide Major General Weitzel regarding Judge Campbell's efforts to convene a facsimile of the Virginia legislature. Lincoln had no illusions about Campbell's motives. The Southern jurist had made it clear that achieving a ceasefire was first on his agenda and empowering a Confederate state legislature to negotiate directly with the Federal government was a close second, neither of which Lincoln would condone. The President did not want to pause the war, he wanted to finish it. Besides, as part of his various experimentations with reconstruction schemes, he recognized and fully supported a pro-Union government of the "restored" state of Virginia headed by Francis Harrison Pierpont, which he would not repudiate.

The only reason Lincoln continued to treat with Campbell was the prospect, however faint, that he could gather enough distinguished Virginians to publicly void the state's Ordinance of Secession so that its soldiers would become conflicted in their loyalties. Take the Virginia regiments out of the Army of Northern Virginia and there would be very few left to fight. It was the longest of long shots, but the President wanted to do everything possible to help Grant end the war with minimal additional casualties.

Lincoln used all his legal skills to craft language that granted no recognition to this body or acknowledged that it had any authority, but which provided permission for a group of gentlemen to meet for the sole purpose of professing their disapproval of the legal document that had propelled Virginia out of the Union. "The drafting of that order, though so short, gave me more perplexity than any other paper I ever drew up," he remarked a few days later. The President was walking a very fine line, and he could only hope that Weitzel understood the extremely narrow range of action he was allowing. At some point during the morning it was finished.

> It has been intimated to me that the gentlemen who have acted as the Legislature of Virginia, in support of the rebellion, may now . . . desire to assemble at Richmond, and take measures to withdraw the Virginia troops, and other support from resistance to the General government. If they attempt it, give them permission and protection, until, if at all, they attempt some action hostile to the United States, in which case you will notify them and give them reasonable time to leave; & at the end of which time, arrest any who may remain. Allow Judge Campbell to see this, but do not make it public.[4]

Lincoln did not want the message to be "official," so he would not consign it to the military telegraph; he needed it to be delivered by hand. The means to do this appeared at his cabin door in the person of Morton S. Wilkinson, a former U.S. Senator from the state of Minnesota. The Republican, on his way to visit Richmond, had stopped at City Point to pay his respects. "He gave me a letter," Wilkinson recalled, "and requested me to take it to General Weitzel at Richmond, who was in command of the Union forces in that city."[5] Wilkinson did so not knowing its contents. He passed it along as promised, walked the city streets for a while, and returned to Weitzel's headquarters, where its contents were being openly discussed by the general and his staff.

Wilkinson had just seen the war's effect on Richmond and believed he understood the President's intentions. "I think that Mr. Lincoln appreciated this state of things fully," he said, "and while he was not willing that anything should be done that would cause the loss of a single drop of blood to the Union army, still I think it was very gratifying to him to have an opportunity to do acts of kindness to that people, and to get them back into the Union again, with the same kindly relations that existed between them personally before the war broke out."[6] If Lincoln believed that his small initiative would soon be forgotten, he would soon (and ruefully) learn otherwise.

Lincoln's work on the Weitzel note was probably interrupted by the delivery of a second telegram from Mary, dispatched from Fortress Monroe at 9:00 a.m. She remained anxious about securing the *River Queen* for her and her entourage. "I know you would agree with me," Mary said.[7] The President (who had not replied to the first message) sent no answer to this one, likely assuming that his wife and her party were in transit. (The timing of their arrival suggests that they had departed Fortress Monroe some time before the second telegraph was actually transmitted.)

The other communication Lincoln had to write this day was for General Grant, filling him in on the news from Washington regarding the Secretary of State, and briefing him on the instructions he had provided Weitzel. The note that he produced shows his trust in Grant's judgment and the respect he had for his general by sharing his confidential thoughts on the matter.

Secretary Seward was thrown from his carriage yesterday and seriously injured. This, with other matters, will take me to Washington soon. I was at Richmond yesterday and the day before, when and where Judge Campbell, who was with Messrs. Hunter and Stephens in February, called on me and made such representations as induced me to put in his hands an informal paper, repeating the propositions in my letter of instructions to Mr. Seward, which you remember, and adding that if the war be now further persisted in by the rebels confiscated property shall, at the least, bear the additional cost; and that confiscations shall be remitted to the people of any State which will now, promptly and in good faith, withdraw its troops and other support from resistance to the Government. Judge Campbell thought it not impossible that the rebel legislature of Virginia would do the latter if permitted, and accordingly I addressed a private letter to General Weitzel, with permission for Judge Campbell to see it, telling him (General W.) that if they attempt this to permit and protect them, unless they attempt something hostile to the United States, in which case to give them notice and time to leave and to arrest any remaining after such time.

I do not think it very probable that anything will come of this, but I have thought best to notify you so that if you should see signs you may understand them. From your recent dispatches it seems that you are pretty effectually withdrawing the Virginia troops from opposition to the Government. Nothing I have done, or probably shall do, is to delay, hinder, or interfere with you in your work.[8]

Not long after this went on its way (by telegraph to the end of the line at Nottoway Court House, then by courier to Grant's mobile headquarters)

Lieutenant Colonel Bowers sent the general a query requesting his instructions for two regiments of Army regulars and several hundred of Sheridan's dismounted troopers waiting at City Point for orders. He also indicated his plans to personally visit Grant in the field (departing early the next morning) and reminded his boss that the "President is in the office, anxious for any news you may have leisure to send him."[9]

Some 65 miles west of City Point, there was a great deal more bloodletting on the road to peace.

Grant's decision to rely heavily on Philip Sheridan in the current campaign continued to pay enormous dividends, as did his subordinate's willingness to argue an order he believed unwise. Sheridan had convinced Grant not to let up the pressure on March 31, and the result was a resounding victory at Five Forks. On the morning of April 3, when Grant still believed Lee was holding Petersburg, he wanted Sheridan to cross to the north side of the Appomattox River to block any retreat. Sheridan correctly divined that Lee was already in motion and that such a movement would put him in the wake of the enemy's passage—not on the flanks where cavalry ought to be. He made his protest to Grant who reassessed, agreed, and unleashed his cavalrymen to harry Lee's retreating army.

Part of what made Sheridan so effective in this campaign was his unwavering focus on a simple, basic mission. According to his chief of staff, it "was to pursue and attack the left flank of the retreating army at any possible point with the cavalry division that first reached it, and, if possible, compel it to turn and defend its wagon trains and artillery, then to send another division beyond and attack the Confederate army again at any possible point, and to follow up this method of attack until at some point the whole army would be obliged to turn and deliver battle." Another officer riding with the general pared the equation down to "turn his flank; head him off; attack him—never mind the rear of his column; never mind the stragglers, but get to the head and front; stand across his path and cry 'no thoroughfare,' and let the enemy fight for the right of way."[10]

Sheridan's tactics could set the table for a Union victory, but it would take the infantry to seal the deal. The corps commanders that Grant now had in place understood the part they were to play and relentlessly pushed their columns forward. Aide Horace Porter wrote that "the troops were made to realize that this campaign was to be won by legs; that the great walking-march had begun, and success depended upon which army could make the best distance record."[11] During the two days Lincoln had visited Richmond, the Union infantry outran its supply trains in its efforts to close with Lee's army, while Sheridan's troopers struck again and again into any opening they found. All the pieces came together on this day: Sheridan's cavalry cutting into the line; Federal infantry closing up from behind; and caught between them nearly half of what remained of the Army of Northern Virginia.

The place involved was not near any large settlement but was on ground drained by a stream that gave the battle its name, Sailor's Creek. It was midday when the rear of Lee's retreating column began to pass through this area—troops, artillery, and supply wagons. March discipline was getting ragged, and gaps opened between major units. Into one of those spaces charged Federal horsemen commanded by Major General George Armstrong Custer. Even as the weary Confederates reacted to this roadblock, other troops closed on their rearmost elements: portions of the Sixth Corps under Major General Horatio G. Wright. A segment of the Rebel column with most of the supply wagons veered off to the northwest, while those remaining turned west to take defensive positions behind Little Sailor's Creek (a tributary of the main branch).

The Federals began their attack around 5:00 p.m. with General Sheridan in overall command. On paper, at least, it should have been no contest. There were perhaps 8,000 Yankee infantry on hand, weary from the hard marches but grimly committed to ending things. Facing them were perhaps 4,000 men under Lieutenant General Richard S. Ewell, half of whom had never engaged in a pitched battle, including one small unit made up of sailors and marines from the James River Squadron. Not three-quarters of a mile behind them, 6,000 more Confederate soldiers were confronted by 8,000 mounted Federals. Yet it would be several hours before the battle would be determined, a period that witnessed some of the most desperate and intense combat of the entire campaign.

Following a 30-minute bombardment of the Rebel positions, spiky lines of Wright's infantrymen moved down a long slope and struggled across the marshy banks of Little Sailor's Creek. They were met by a blast of musketry and a countercharge that slashed into the center of the advancing formation. A couple of Federal regiments scattered under the violent assault, but reserves came up and the flanks continued their advance. As the blue-coated wings enfolded the battered Confederates the violence went off the charts. A Kentucky-born officer fighting for Virginia recalled that "quicker than I can

Alfred Waud's sketch of the surrender of Ewell's command after the bloody fight at
Sailor's Creek. It was bloodshed Lincoln had hoped to avoid. LOC

tell it the battle degenerated into a butchery and a confused melee of brutal
personal conflicts. I saw numbers of men kill each other with bayonets and
the butts of muskets, and even bite each others' throats and ears and noses,
rolling on the ground like wild beasts." "The bayonet was freely used on
both sides," added a Federal officer present, "and men with clubbed muskets
fought as if individual deeds of valor could carry the day."[12]

Just to the west of this cauldron, undulating waves of Federal
cavalrymen charged thin but defiant Confederate battle lines. An Ohio
trooper in the middle of it wrote that "the fire as they neared the rebel line
was terrific, opening gaps in their lines, but if a horse was shot & the rider
unhurt he would jump up [and] take his place, firing as he went." "The earth
trembled beneath the tread of thousands of hoofs; the air rang with bugle
blasts and soul-thrilling cheers," a correspondent recorded. "Many saddles
were emptied," added a Union staff officer, "but on they came, jumping over
the [enemy's] works and killing many with the hoofs of the horses."[13]

Both Confederate positions collapsed, with roughly 4,000 Rebels
scampering wildly to the west, while about 6,000 soldiers (including eight
generals, Richard Richard Ewell among them) were captured along with
artillery, animals, and wagons. Compounding this day's catastrophe, the
force farther north protecting the wagons was assailed by the Federal Second
Corps, and while the Rebels extricated themselves in a more orderly manner,
they left behind another 1,700 irreplaceable men, mostly prisoners. When

General Robert E. Lee was informed of the disaster his guard momentarily dropped. "A few more Sailor's Creeks and it will all be over," he said.[14]

There were some 1,100 men killed, wounded, or missing on the Union side in the fighting against General Ewell at Sailor's Creek. But the Federals did not have it all their way. A small mixed cavalry-infantry force sent ahead to destroy a large railroad span called High Bridge was instead overwhelmed by defending Confederate units and wiped out, some 780 Yankees marching into captivity and several promising young officers killed or mortally wounded. It was in the hope of avoiding more such bloody encounters that President Lincoln persisted in playing out his poor hand with Judge Campbell.

Mary Lincoln and company reached City Point aboard the *Monohassett* about 11:45 a.m. Everyone trooped over to the *River Queen* where the President was awaiting them. Accompanying Mrs. Lincoln were Massachusetts Senator Charles Sumner, Attorney General James Speed, Secretary of the Interior William T. Otto, plus Iowa Senator James Harlan, his wife Ann and their daughter Mary. From all accounts the bright and cultured Miss Harlan enjoyed the affections of a number of beaus including a certain Robert Lincoln. In time the two would marry. Also along was an engaging 35-year-old Frenchman—a quasi-diplomat, thoughtful observer, closet philosopher, and friend to all named Charles Adolphe Pineton, known as the Marquis de Chambrun.

Present as well was Mary's African-American dressmaker and occasional companion, Elizabeth Keckly. Mrs. Keckly had a reason greater than curiosity for being here: She had been born in nearby Dinwiddie County and had spent time in Petersburg as a slave, so this was something of a pilgrimage for her. Also now on hand, according to Charles Forbes, was William H. Crook, who wasted no time learning everything he could about the President's activities since he had been at City Point.

Lincoln welcomed everyone in the upper saloon, the same space where he had discussed the war with Grant, Sherman, and Porter; and where, before that, he had met the Rebel commissioners. He spoke in broad terms about what had happened on that latter occasion. According to the Marquis, he then pulled a bundle of papers from his pocket and proceeded to read from them. They were copies of recent dispatches he had received from General Grant. The lieutenant general had written them knowing Lincoln had access to area maps so the President paused his presentation long enough to fetch some. "He soon returned holding them in his hands," recalled Chambrun, "and spreading them on a table, he showed us the place of each army corps."[15]

Mrs. Keckly noticed that the moment the President mentioned his visit to Richmond "Mrs. Lincoln was much disappointed . . . as she had greatly desired to be with him when he entered the conquered stronghold." Lincoln, according to the Marquis, admitted that he was preoccupied with "the necessity of wiping out the consequences of the civil war, and to drive the war itself from the memory of all, nay, even of its criminal instigators."[16] Mrs. Lincoln wanted very much to see Richmond, so to accommodate her wishes the President let her use the *River Queen*. He would stay behind and continue to monitor events at the front while Tad would travel with his mother. It was a little after 1:00 p.m. when the *River Queen* departed City Point on her second journey to the wrecked rebel citadel in three days.

(Mary Lincoln's Richmond visit was very different from her husband's, for she came as a victor and not a healer. "We had a gay time I assure you," she wrote afterward to a friend, "Richmond . . . & 'the banquet halls' of Jeff Davis looked sad and deserted. Each & every place will be repeopled with our own glorious & loyal people & the traitors meet the doom which a just Heaven ever awards the transgressor." The Marquis de Chambrun was far more affected by the "painful sights" of the battered city. "Devastation is complete," he exclaimed.[17] Evening twilight had come by the time they returned to the *River Queen*, too dark to attempt a run down the unmarked James until next morning.)

Lincoln returned to City Point after seeing off Mary and company, where he was joined just after 3:00 p.m. by Admiral Porter, who had arrived with the *Malvern* around 10:30 a.m. Porter offered temporary accommodations on the flagship, an offer that the President gratefully accepted. News that the Confederates had abandoned Richmond had unleashed a flood of visitors from government officials to the plain curious on City Point. Lincoln had no interest in meeting any of them, not even Vice President Andrew Johnson, who arrived unannounced today on his way to Richmond. Johnson would continue to the fallen capital the next day, never having spoken with the President.

Also traveling to Richmond was Mrs. Grant and her friends, using the general's personal boat. Her feelings toward Mary Lincoln had not improved with the First Lady's return; if anything, she was even less willing to extend courtesies toward someone who consistently treated her as an inferior. It was seeing the *River Queen* depart while she, "not a hundred yards from them, was not invited to join them," that prompted her to make a separate visit with people of her circle.[18]

This was all unknown to the President, who was marking time hoping to hear something from General Grant. At 5:00 p.m. Lincoln and Porter dined aboard the Malvern, returning to City Point a little before 8:00 p.m. He was there when Provost Marshal Patrick came to visit Bowers for any news and chatted briefly with the officer, who could add nothing to the little that was known. Patrick and Bowers were determined to visit Grant to resolve some administrative matters and planned to leave early the next morning.

It was after 10:00 p.m. when Lincoln and Porter retired to the *Malvern*. The ship's log indicates that at 11:00 p.m. Lieutenant Colonel Bowers came aboard with dispatches. The important one was from General Grant at Burkeville, now an active station for the U.S. Military Telegraph. It summarized all that he knew when it was sent, perhaps 6 or 7:00 p.m. Instead of fighting for the railroad line as Grant had expected, Lee's army had moved off this morning "by the roads west of this place." The lieutenant general had immediately spread his forces in a broad-front pursuit that snared "many of the enemy's stragglers and forced him to burn many of his wagons." The Union soldiers were in the "finest spirits" despite most having had "no rest for more than one week." Grant remained hopeful that his combinations would soon "totally break up the Army of Northern Virginia."[19]

Lincoln anticipated that there would be news of even greater importance coming very soon.

CHAPTER FIFTEEN

Friday, April 7, 1865

"Every day brings new reason for confidence in the future."

A messenger from the City Point military telegraph office came aboard the *Malvern* just before dawn, April 7, with an important update from General Grant: a preliminary report on the great victory at Sailor's Creek. Not since Five Forks and the fall of Petersburg had there been news of such importance, and the President was anxious to pass it along to the nation. His emendation was brief, noting just that at "11.15 p.m. yesterday, at Burkeville Station, General Grant sends me the following from General Sheridan."[1]

Lincoln came ashore in the company of Admiral Porter and walked up the hill to the headquarters area. The capable and efficient Lieutenant Colonel Bowers was no longer at this post. He and Provost Marshal Patrick had taken a 5:00 a.m. train out to Sutherland's Station, where the line ended, and there changed over to horses for the ride to Grant's Burkeville headquarters. (Bowers's replacement is not otherwise identified.)

Lincoln had just settled in Bowers's cabin when army postmaster David B. Parker came calling with a postal clerk in tow named William H. Proudfit. "A broad and kindly smile wreathed Lincoln's plain, gaunt features," Proudfit remembered, "as he sat there reading those dispatches [from Grant]." The President's mood remained upbeat after they left, when he spotted an officer he knew and called him over. It was Lieutenant Colonel Henry S. Huidekoper, whose regiment had briefly provided security for the summer house used by the Lincolns in northeast Washington, and who had lost an arm in battle at Gettysburg. "Mr. Lincoln," as Huidekoper recalled, "rose from a desk and pleasantly made a few inquiries about myself. He then said, 'Oh! let me give you the latest news,' and picking up a paper which lay on his table, he read to me Sheridan's telegram to General Grant, repeated word for word by the latter to the President. . . . Mr. Lincoln was, of course, intensely delighted with the success of the Army of the Potomac in hemming in Lee's army, and, rubbing his hands together in his satisfaction, said, 'The end has almost come.'"[2] Huidekoper had come to visit his brother, an officer in an African-American regiment, and after chatting a few more moments he continued his errand.

He may well have passed telegrapher Beckwith who delivered several long reports just in from the front that provided important details regarding the Sailor's Creek fighting. Lincoln did not want to sit on these, so he rushed them along to the War Department, saying only that the "following further just received."[3]

Problems with the telegraph network in Washington delayed the national release of these battle reports until the afternoon. Grant's 11:50 p.m. April 6 message was joined with the other three, filling nearly two full columns of newspaper print. This would prove to be Lincoln's last message from the front to the people but the information it conveyed electrified readers. "The Army of Northern Virginia has ceased to exist," proclaimed one editorial.[4] Lincoln could clearly see how Grant was closing on the rebel army. Perhaps he had some doubts about the limited leeway he had allowed Judge Campbell, but Robert E. Lee had done the impossible before so nothing was definite.

Assistant Secretary of War Charles Dana stopped by on his inspection tour for Edwin Stanton. He had already been to Richmond, learned of Lincoln's meeting with Judge Campbell, and received Major General Weitzel's version of events. Dana was hoping to get the President's piece of the story and Lincoln obliged by producing two notes. The first was a copy of the non-negotiable conditions he had handed to Judge Campbell, the second his instructions to Weitzel. When the subject moved along to the latest news from the front, Lincoln modified his Grant joke for the occasion, telling the assistant secretary that "Sheridan seemed to be getting Virginia soldiers out of the war faster than this legislature could think."[5] Dana absorbed it all, returned to Richmond, and from there transmitted a full report to the Secretary of War.

Likely not long after the young man departed word came that the *River Queen* had returned, so the President asked for a special train to be put on for Mary and her guests to visit Petersburg. Admiral Porter excused himself at this point and returned to the *Malvern*. Lincoln used the pause to ponder Sheridan's note of late yesterday to Grant, which had closed with the statement: "If the thing is pressed I think Lee will surrender." He had great faith in his lieutenant general's determination to complete the mission, but it never hurt to remind Grant that his personal resolve to bring a swift end to the fighting had not waivered in the slightest. About an hour before midday he put those thoughts into a terse message:

> Lieut Gen. Grant.
>
> Gen. Sheridan says "If the thing is pressed I think that Lee will surrender." Let the *thing* be pressed.[6]

It was the recollection of Lincoln's telegrapher-on-loan Beckwith that one of "Col. Bowers's clerks took the laconic message to the telegraph office. He was very much impressed with its forceful brevity and asked the President if he might retain the original as a souvenir. The face of the nation's chief lightened up with a smile as he said: 'I guess, young man, that the document's yours. Possession is nine points of the law, you know.'"[7]

There would have been some coordination between Lincoln and his wife about the Petersburg visit. Everything was ready midday when Mary's party met the President at the same simple station that had been used when the First Family visited the front on March 25. "Our car was an ordinary American car," wrote the Marquis de Chambrun, "and we took seats in its centre, grouping ourselves around Mr. Lincoln." The Frenchman assumed that they were in a special car reserved for high dignitaries and was taken aback when several officers not part of the group found empty seats. Lincoln showed no surprise, so the Marquis let it pass. He also noted the presence of some of the African-American servants from the *River Queen* and observed approvingly that no one in the Presidential party objected.

The route this time was decidedly more direct than the one they had followed in March or that the President himself had taken on April 3. A military railroad construction crew had reconnected the Union section of the old City Point tracks to the original portions behind the Rebel earthworks, so the locomotive and cars could run directly downtown. The repairs had been

After Lincoln's visit one USMRR passenger car was designated "The President's Car," even though the information is spotty whether he used it once, twice, three times or never while he was at City Point. LOC

necessarily hasty, so speed was little better than a brisk walk. It took half an hour to reach and pass through the Union lines near Fort Stedman, and then they slowed even more as sections of the track bed remained edged with debris.

"Soon Petersburg loomed up in the distance," wrote Chambrun. "Lincoln gazed a while on its first houses," which showed the effects of shrapnel damage. Widespread ruin was evident. "It was Lee's army, said the President, which, on retiring toward Burkesville, had destroyed all lines of communications."[8] Upon reaching the downtown depot they were met by a crowd of curious citizens, black and white. An offer from an African-American boy to help Lincoln "tote" his briefcase prompted an exchange between Lincoln and Senator Sumner set down by Mrs. Lincoln's black assistant, Elizabeth Keckly:

> "Tote," remarked Mr. Lincoln; "what do you mean by tote?"
>
> "Why, massa, to tote um on your back."
>
> "Very definite, my son; I presume when you tote a thing, you carry it. By the way, Sumner," turning to the Senator, "what is the origin of tote?"
>
> "Its origin is said to be African. The Latin word totum, from totus, means all—an entire body—the whole."
>
> "But my young friend here did not mean an entire body, or anything of the kind, when he said he would tote my things for me," interrupted the President.

"Very true," continued the Senator. "He used the word tote in the African sense, to carry, to bear. Tote in this sense is defined in our standard dictionaries as a colloquial word of the Southern States, used especially by the negroes."

"Then you regard the word as a good one?"

"Not elegant, certainly. For myself, I should prefer a better word; but since it has been established by usage, I cannot refuse to recognize it."[9]

Everything Chambrun saw in Petersburg "bespoke desolation." There were passing rain showers in the area and the travelers were not inclined to wander far afoot. Carriages were obtained and the party (minus Mrs. Keckly, who had old friends to visit) went to Centre Hill Mansion, military headquarters for Major General George L. Hartsuff, now overseeing the city's occupation. Lincoln spoke with the general while the others wandered about the house and yard. According to an item that would appear in the soldier-run newspaper Grant's Petersburg Progress, when Hartsuff asked about the government leasing the mansion Lincoln quipped that Union artillery fire had "made rent enough here already." The President also sent word to a captured Confederate general (and former U.S. Congressman) named Roger Pryor, who was in town under house arrest, inviting him to come for a chat. The soldier delivering the message returned one from the general's wife Sara saying that since Mr. Pryor was still a Confederate officer "he could hold no conference with the head of the opposing army."[10]

Everyone clambered back into the carriages as soon as the commander-in-chief emerged from his meeting. Continued Chambrun,

While we were on the road which was to lead us back to the train, Mr. Lincoln noticed on the roadside a very tall and beautiful tree. He gave orders to stop the carriage, looked a while at the tree with particular attention, and then applied himself to defining its peculiar beauty. He admired the strength of its trunk, the vigorous development of branches, reminding one of the tall trees of Western forests, compared it to the great oaks in the shadow of which he had spent his youth, and strove to make us understand the distinctive character of these different types. The observations thus set forth were evidently not those of an artist who seeks to idealize nature, but of a man who seeks to see it as it really is; in short, that dissertation about a tree did not reveal an effort of imagination, but a remarkable precision of mind.

When the carriage again moved on, the topic of conversation changed, and Mr. Lincoln imparted to us the good news which the Federal commanders had given him. Animosity in the town is abating, said he; the inhabitants now accept accomplished facts, the final downfall of the Confederacy, and the abolition of slavery. There still remains much for us to do, but every day brings new reason for confidence in the future.[11]

They returned to the train where Mrs. Keckly awaited them. Her impulse to visit a city where she had lived in bondage had been a mistake. "The scenes suggested painful memories," she reflected, "and I was not sorry to turn my back again upon the city." During the train ride back Lincoln noticed a turtle sunning itself and asked that they halt long enough for it to be brought to him. "The movements of the ungainly little animal seemed to delight him," Mrs. Keckly recollected, "and he amused himself with it until we reached James River, where our steamer lay. Tad stood near, and joined in the happy laugh with his father."[12]

About the time the Presidential party was returning to City Point, Lieutenant General Ulysses S. Grant decided the time had come to offer Robert E. Lee a chance to end the fighting and he wrote him:

> General: The result of the last week must convince you of the hopelessness of further resistance on the part of the Army of Northern Virginia in this struggle. I feel that it is so, and regard it as my duty to shift from myself the responsibility of any further effusion of blood by asking of you the surrender of that portion of the C. S. Army known as the Army of Northern Virginia.[13]

While Mary's party returned to the *River Queen* after visiting Petersburg, Lincoln doubtless climbed the steps to the top of the bluff to see if there was any fresh news. There was none. He retired to the *River Queen*, where nothing formal had been planned for the evening. The President, his wife, and her entourage passed the time discussing recent events. A pair of unexpected but welcome guests appeared in the persons of congressmen Elihu B. Washburne (Illinois) and James G. Blaine (Maine). The two were traveling to the front to connect with Washburne's good friend Grant.

"Mr. Lincoln was in perfect health and exuberant spirits," Washburne recalled. "His relation of his experiences and of all he saw at Richmond had all of that quaintness and originality for which he was distinguished. Full of anecdote and reminiscence, he never flagged during the evening. His son, Robert, was in the military service and with the advancing army, and knowing that I was bound for the 'front' the next morning, he said to me: 'I believe I will drop Robert a line if you will take it. I will hand it to you in the morning before you start.'"[14] Arrangements were made to meet.

It was around midnight when most of the lights dimmed on the *River Queen*. Seventy miles to the west General Grant was at his field headquarters, established in the Farmville village hotel (some called it a tavern), waiting for Lee's reply to his note. He sat on the little piazza for a long time watching some troops tramping past. A staff officer recalled that the "moon shone brightly as Wright's Corps marched through, singing, 'John Brown's Body, etc.' The whole corps joined in the song." Grant was alone by choice and gave no outward recognition of the men passing him below. "Oh, what a night that was!" recollected another officer. "The 'old man' was wonderful."[15] Grant dozed off only to be awakened not long after midnight when the staff officer he had sent with his message returned with Lee's answer:

> General: I have received your note of this date. Though not entertaining the opinion you express of the hopelessness of further resistance on the part of the Army of Northern Virginia, I reciprocate your desire to avoid useless effusion of blood, and therefore, before considering your proposition, ask the terms you will offer on condition of its surrender.

Grant deemed Lee's response "not satisfactory."[16] The fighting Mr. Lincoln so hated would continue.

CHAPTER SIXTEEN

Saturday, April 8, 1865

"I came here to take by the hand the men who
have achieved our glorious victories."

LIEUTENANT General Grant awoke this morning
determined to maintain the lines of
communication with General Lee. He also understood that he was not just
writing to the enemy commander, but that the nation was looking over his
shoulder, since whatever he set down would soon be splashed across
hundreds of newspapers throughout the country. He remembered too his
time with Lincoln, especially the conference with Sherman and Porter
present as he wrote:

> General: Your note of last evening in reply to mine of same date, asking the
> condition on which I will accept the surrender of the Army of Northern Virginia is
> just received. In reply I would say that, peace being my great desire, there is but one
> condition I would insist upon, namely: that the men and officers surrendered shall
> be disqualified for taking up arms again against the Government of the United
> States until properly exchanged. I will meet you, or will designate officers to meet
> any officers you may name for the same purpose, at any point agreeable to you, for
> the purpose of arranging definitely the terms upon which the surrender of the Army
> of Northern Virginia will be received.[1]

"Lee's army was rapidly crumbling," of this Grant was certain. As
proof, he was confronted this morning by what aide Horace Porter described

as "a rather hungry-looking gentleman in gray, wearing the uniform of a colonel, who proclaimed himself the proprietor of the hotel" being used as Grant's headquarters. The man said that his regiment had deserted until only he was left, "and he thought he might as well 'stop off' at home to look after his property." Grant told him to "stay there and he would not be molested." As he and his staff mounted to ride toward the west, Grant reflected that the late colonel's command "was one regiment that had been eliminated from Lee's army by this crumbling process." In another note sent this morning to Sheridan, Grant reported supplying Lee with surrender terms but made clear that the army "will push him until terms are agreed upon."[2]

Senator Elihu Washburne waited patiently on the wharf at City Point until the President "came ashore from the steamer with the letter [for his son Robert] in his hand. He was erect and buoyant, and it seemed to me I had never seen him look so great and grand. After a few words of conversation, he handed me the letter, and I bid him . . . adieu." It may have been at this time that Lincoln shook hands with Private George W. Sutfin, assigned to guard the wharf. It would be something that the young New Yorker would talk about until his death in 1934.[3]

The President likely continued up the hill to the telegraph office to see if there was any breaking news. There was none. On his way back, he encountered Brevet Brigadier General Charles H. T. Collis, who was under orders to transport his troops as far west as the trains were running and there to take charge of all prisoners for escort back to City Point. Given their past pleasant associations, Collis would have held a brief impromptu review for the President, one that was seen by Mrs. Keckly from the *River Queen*. Yesterday's spotty showers had moved on and this day promised to be clear and warm.

Great events may well have been in the making, but the President also had to contend with his celebrity status. Lincoln was not long back aboard the ship when a pair of intrepid Englishmen invaded his privacy. Thomas W. Kennard was a well-to-do engineer and entrepreneur, while Edward Moseley was a successful accountant. Moseley was on a business trip with his son when they met Kennard in New York City and accepted his invitation to join a small party on a jaunt to the war front aboard his newly acquired steam sloop. The *Octavia* (named for Kennard's wife) departed New York on April 1 for a test run to Fortress Monroe.

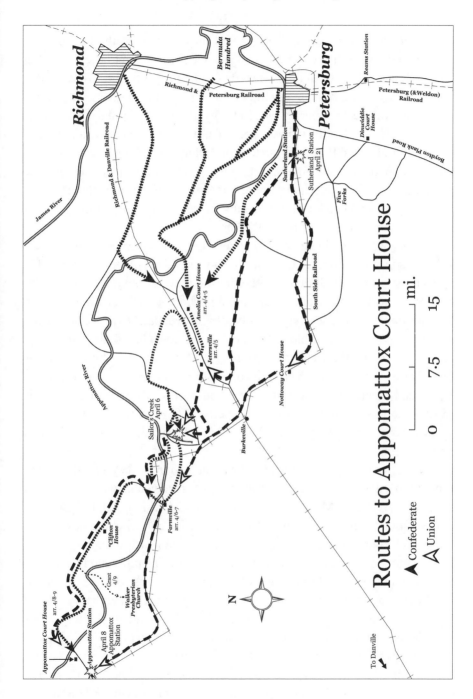

Routes to Appomattox Court House

When the tourists arrived on April 3 they learned of the Confederate capital's fall. No military agent would provide them a pass to Richmond but Kennard decided to flaunt the British flag and hope for the best. They sailed up the James River, passing several boats on a reciprocal course "crammed with Confederate prisoners." Once at City Point they spoke with Brevet Brigadier General Collis, who wished them well, but then they ran afoul of Rear Admiral David Porter (about to visit Richmond with the President) who had little patience for anything English. Met with abject and profuse apologies from the British pair, Porter relented enough to allow them to hang around. The two had a knack for making friends, which soon opened up rail and steamship passage throughout the area.

April 5 was spent in Petersburg, where Kennard observed "huge rents in solid masonry proclaiming too truly the horrors of protracted warfare." On April 6 they traveled along the siege lines to view "ground all strewn with bullets, or torn with shell, where bursting bombs had rent the earth in mounds like rifle-pits; at every footstep dark brown patches attract attention, explaining too truly how blood had poured and souls had fled." On April 7 they rode one of the first trains running north from Petersburg as far as Manchester. From there they walked across a military pontoon bridge to Richmond, visited the devastated city, and observed for themselves "this most barbarous sacrifice of private property."[4] They caught a steamer back to City Point where they spent this morning thanking everyone who had helped them.

While returning to the *Octavia* from their rounds, they had the happy thought to call on Mr. Lincoln. "The President received us with the greatest courtesy," recalled Moseley, "and we enjoyed a long and interesting conversation with him." Kennard recollected Lincoln rocking easily in a chair, and after "graciously receiving our compliments, expressed with a cheerful though somewhat careworn countenance, his unfeigned happiness at the apparent speedy termination of a struggle so disastrous to both North and South; the conversation interspersed throughout with that lively vein of wit and humour so peculiar to President Lincoln." Added Moseley, "The President shook hands with me twice, and was remarkably polite." Then it was on to the *Octavia* and off the stage of history.[5]

Lincoln knew that his time away from Washington was ending sooner than the war would. He had hoped to hear by now from General Grant that Lee's army had been taken, but as much as he wanted to remain at City Point until it happened, he could no longer justify remaining absent from the Oval

A newspaper sketch of Lincoln visiting the wounded at the massive Depot Field Hospital outside City Point that accompanied syndicated articles about his visit.
Wyoming Reporter [New York], May 22, 1907

Office. However, there was one important duty for him to perform, something that now assumed the character of an imperative. He had spoken in his second inaugural address of the importance of caring "for him who shall have borne the battle." In December 1863 he had written of the honor due the citizen who "cares for his brother in the field, and serves, as he best can, the same cause."[6] This day Lincoln was determined to turn his words into deeds—on a grand scale.

Images of wounded soldiers were not unfamiliar to the President, whose lanky form was often seen in various hospital wards around the capital. On occasions when his schedule allowed, he might see and speak with dozens or more. This day he was bound and determined to visit one of the largest hospitals in the United States and personally greet every wounded soldier— at least 5,000, perhaps as many as 6,000. It was something he had to do. A chapter of history was nearing its end, and before he turned to the challenges of a postwar American nation he needed a physical communion with the men whose sacrifices had bought that victory. He had been waiting for the right time to do this, and it had come.

Lincoln made his intentions known during his morning visit to the telegraph office, and word was passed to the medical director of the 200-acre facility. Carriages were waiting when a little after midday, the President, his wife and son, plus Mary's entourage, clambered aboard. The small cavalcade rattled up the bluff onto what is modern Pecan Avenue, and then went left on a long tree-lined lane that led outside the now abandoned U.S. earthworks. The road was only slightly dusty after the recent rains so their passage was comfortable, albeit bumpy at times. Their route eased along the riverbank, crossing a special spur added to the military railroad to facilitate transport of the wounded. Lincoln and his party could see a wooden boundary fence and behind it, row after row after row of temporary buildings and tents marking the Depot Field Hospital.

While not the only sizable medical facility serving the armies before Petersburg (there were three civilian and three other military operations), it was the largest and represented an important advancement in caring for wounded soldiers. At the start of the Civil War each regiment took care of its own casualties, but as the battles grew in size medical directors began grouping hospitals by brigades, then divisions, and finally by corps. At Petersburg they took the next logical step.

Even as Grant's effort to capture Petersburg by force in June 1864 was turning into a siege, army medical officers were staking their claim to a broad wheatfield one-and-a-half miles southwest of City Point atop a 35-foot bluff overlooking the Appomattox River. It was a healthy place, convenient to fresh water and fuel, and accessible to the railroad. A tent city was erected that within days was handling more than 4,000 patients. Here were gathered the general hospitals for all the corps operating against Petersburg. With time came refinements, including more sturdy housing and an exclusive wharf at the foot of the bluff that greatly accelerated the receipt of supplies and evacuation of patients to Northern hospitals. There were easily 735 tents when Mr. Lincoln visited, supplemented by 90 or so log barracks, plus support facilities housing laundries, dispensaries, regular and special diet kitchens, dining halls, staff quarters and offices; also places for the civilian and state welfare agencies, especially the U.S. Sanitary Commission and the U.S. Christian Commission. The Ninth Corps hospital even had its own printing press.

Bureaucratic requirements demanded that each corps keep track of its people, so the Depot Field Hospital remained a collection of distinct corps care centers, serviced through a central command that handled logistics and security, as well as maintaining overall treatment standards. There was nothing haphazard about the layout as the Marquis de Chambrun observed. The Depot Field Hospital, he later wrote, was "organized according to a plan as simple as it was logical. Each army corps had its separate ambulance

An image of the Depot Field Hospital, the largest such along the Richmond-Petersburg front. Lincoln's insistence of visiting all the patients was a deeply personal experience of respect and honor to the nation's wounded. LOC

space. This consisted of a large rectangle of ground divided by open corridors placed at equal distances from one another. Between these corridors stood a row of tents or of frame huts, each of which was capable of containing about twenty wounded. One side of these corridors was given up to officers, the other to privates. At the center of each rectangle of ground was located a pharmacy, a kitchen, and that which Americans consider as always essential—a post office."[7] What the Marquis didn't mention was that the corridors were all graveled; a lesson learned when fall rains had turned the dirt walkways into mud troughs.

The Presidential procession was met by the surgeon in charge, George B. Parker, who initially misread his august guest. He began to steer the President toward one of the kitchens when Lincoln interjected that he had come to see the troops. Then several of Parker's assistants began to explain how the place functioned, which annoyed Lincoln even more. "Gentlemen, you know better than I *how* to Sthese hospitals," he exclaimed, "but I came here to take by the hand the men who have achieved our glorious victories." When someone mentioned the large number of patients involved Lincoln said that he "guessed he was equal to the task; at any rate he would try, and go as far as he could."[8] Parker promptly brought the Lincolns and their group into the nearest ward—the one operated by the Second Corps.

It would appear that the party traveling with the President remained with him to varying degrees. Mrs. Lincoln appears to have dropped out early, prompting a disdainful observation from a regular nurse, "One lady in rich garb sauntered through our worn walks, leaning on the arm of a Congressman, noting what we lacked in our appointments. My bed-tick dress made a sorry contrast to her costly-attired figure, but I looked at my hands, which were not afraid to touch the dirty blouse of a wounded soldier, and wondered if her jeweled fingers would shrink from the contact."[9] The Marquis de Chambrun stayed the course, but not always alongside Lincoln. Senator Sumner seems to have been nearby all of the way. (Of Tad Lincoln there is no mention. Perhaps he remained aboard the *River Queen* with William Crook.)

By the time the President entered the Second Corps compound all the ambulatory patients had been lined up outside their tents to receive their guest. Sometimes it was a straight line, sometimes circular. Lincoln alternated between passing along these lines and ducking into the tents to meet with those who could not stand. Then it was on to the next line and the next tent. He was often preceded by a corps surgeon who announced, "Attention: the President of the United States!"[10]

The Second Corps had taken part in the actions against the White Oak Road, and participated in the April 2 breakthrough of Confederate lines, suffering some 917 casualties, of which 628 were wounded. The corps emblem many of the men wore on their hats was a trefoil.

"Weather clear and pleasant," wrote a Second Corps Pennsylvanian. "Old Abe passed through on a shake hands with all the patients." A New Yorker added that "Uncle Abe gave us each a word of cheer." For many of those standing outside the tents the President's words were a simple "How do you do." Some of those unable to stand heard him say, "I hope you will soon be able to go to your friends."[11] A Vermont man serving as a sharpshooter recalled that they were told we could uncover our wounds, but must not speak to him. I threw the blankets off so he could see that my right leg was gone, above the knee, and when he reached my bed he said:

'What, a leg gone?'

I said: 'Yes.'

He stopped at the head of my bed and looked at the card, saying, 'and a Vermonter.'

I said: 'Yes, sir, I pride myself on being a Green Mountain boy. I was born within seven miles of Mount Mansfield, the highest peak of the Green Mountain range.' He then took my hand in both of his. I asked him: 'Well, Father Abraham, have we done our work well.'

He said: 'Very well, indeed, and I thank you.'

I never shall forget the pressure he gave my hand, nor can I forget that sad, careworn face.

Recollecting this event 50 years later, the soldier wrote: "I often see that sad and worn face in memory, and I can hardly keep back the tears."[12]

Not every Second Corps soldier connected with the President on a first try. Musician John B. Holloway of the 148th Pennsylvania was waiting his turn in an oval formation. "It was my misfortune to stand in one of these circles close to where the President started to go around it," Holloway explained. "He went toward his right which was away from me, and it so happened that before he got around to where I stood some one engaged him in conversation and so he stopped before completing that circle. Then Mr. Lincoln said, 'Well, where will we go now.' So they started across the railroad track to the Fifth Corps Hospital. While on this little walk many were the pulls the President got on his coat tail by persons who wished to meet him, so he would turn about and take them by the hand. As for myself, I pulled the Second Corps badge off my cap, so as not to be known as an interloper, and crossed over and stood in line with the Fifth Corps boys, and then I had the pleasure of shaking hands with President Lincoln."[13]

Also witness to Lincoln's visit were members of the Depot Field Hospital support staff, both army and civilian. An aide known to the readers of a hospital newspaper only as "Frank" said the President "passed around and cordially shook hands with nearly all the boys. It pleased them greatly. He had, as ever, kind words for all, and now and then found utterance in some jokes, for which he is so well known, and thereby would arise the sounds of mirthful laughter."

"He had the manner of a gentleman—I may say of a gentle gentleman;" added an agent for the U.S. Christian Commission, "his voice as we heard it was subdued and kindly; his eyes were mild but all-observing; and his face that he once himself described as 'poor, lean and lank,' was a strong face marked with lines of a mingled gentleness and sadness that redeemed it from being homely. The close grasp of his hand attested the sympathetic great heartedness of the great man."[14]

Many in the Fifth Corps wards had fought at Quaker Road, White Oak Road, and Five Forks, where the killed and wounded exceeded 2,800. A soldier with a shoulder wound recalled the Lincoln mantra, "Be of good cheer, boys; we are at the beginning of the end at last." To another he said, "the war will soon be over and then we'll all go home." In one of the tents the President encountered twelve officers of the Maryland Brigade, Second Division. With them was a Confederate major, who had fallen at the same time as the Union men. According to one of the Marylanders, Lincoln "gave this officer a hearty grasp of the hand and inquired what State he was from and where he resided before entering the Army. . . . He then . . . wished him a speedy and hasty recovery from his wounds and [told him] that in a few days the war would be over and he would be able to see his dear ones at home." After Lincoln left, the dazed Rebel asked who the men was who had spoken him and was stunned by the answer. "My God, is that so?" he exclaimed. "Is that the kind of a man that we have been fighting for four long years?"[15]

There was an even more distinguished Confederate officer in the Fifth Corps wards, Harry L. Benbow, a Rebel colonel captured at Five Forks. Benbow later recalled that the President,

walked down the long aisle between the rows of cots on each hand, bowing and smiling. . . . Arriving at length opposite where I lay, he halted beside my bed and held out his hand. Looking him in the face, as he stood with extended hand: Mr. President, I said, do you know to whom you offer your hand?

'I do not,' he replied.

Well, I said, you offer it to a Confederate colonel, who has fought you as hard as he could for four years.

'Well,' said he, 'I hope a Confederate colonel will not refuse me his hand.'

No, sir, I replied, I will not, and I clasped his hand in both mine.

I tell you, sir, he had the most magnificent face and eye that I have ever gazed into. He had me whipped from the time he first opened his mouth.[16]

Dr. George Mendenhall was not present at the time Lincoln toured the Depot Field Hospital, but arrived just minutes after he departed. "It was like the visit of a father to his children and was appreciated in the same kindly spirit by the soldiers," he wrote. "They loved to talk of his kindness and unaffected manner & to dwell upon the various incidents of this visit as a green spot in the soldier's hard life." From Surgeon Parker, in charge of the facility, he learned that at "one point in his visit he observed an axe which he picked up & examined & made some pleasant remark that he was once considered to be a good chopper. He was invited to try his hand upon a log of wood lying near from which he made the chips fly in primitive style." According to a doctor who was present, Lincoln was "swinging the ax around in a powerful manner, which I would hardly have expected in a man of his sedentary habits."[17] This story would be retold often in later years with unsubstantiated embellishments added.

Those hospitalized from the Ninth Corps had seen hard fighting at Fort Stedman and in the April 2 attacks along the Jerusalem Plank Road, which had resulted in over 2,500 killed and wounded. A Pennsylvanian hit on March 25 remembered this as the day when "Abraham Lincoln came along, took off his hat, grasped him by the hand, asking if there was anything he could do or any word he could send for him to the folks back home." A Massachusetts officer named Cyrus T. Goodwin would write home that the President "looks very thin and as though he has not much rest. [H]e must have had a good deal on his mind the last four years and it would broke many a tougher looking man than what he is. He had a kind word for us all[.] The Dr told me he said the war would be over in six weeks [but] we can tell better about that when the times comes around." Lincoln was a bit more definite speaking with a invalid New York colonel, telling him to "cheer up, and get well . . . for this dreadful war is coming to a close." Another hand taken in compassion was that of Sergeant John H. Strickler, struck down on April 2, who afterwards said that he felt he was "in part . . . recompensed for the wound." A young medical aide trailing the President through these wards was deeply impressed by his "genuine interest in the welfare of the soldiers."[18]

Two of the Ninth Corps boys seen by the President were in the midst of a struggle to survive that would claim the life of one. Pennsylvania Lieutenant Levi R. Robb had been terribly wounded on April 2. A less severely injured soldier lying next to him recalled the moment when the President stopped at his cot. "Suddenly his eyes opened wide and his face lit up with a happy expression of recognition as he spoke in a clear but feeble voice, 'The President.' . . . When he reached Lieutenant Robb's cot he grasped his feebly extended hand as he cheerily said, 'God bless you.' Slowly and deliberately came the reply, 'He has, Mr. President, and may it be your happy portion, too.' The President paused just a moment; as he looked with compassion into the wan face of the wounded officer, and said, 'It is, but cheer up, my boy, we'll meet again,' and then passed on to cheer others."[19] Robb died on April 9.

One of the others was Captain Charles H. Houghton, three times wounded in the Fort Stedman combat and suffering the loss of part of his left leg. A wounded officer next to the captain recorded how Lincoln paused at Houghton's cot, bent over and gently kissed him on the cheek. "In voice so tender and so low that only my near proximity enabled me to hear, he began to talk to him, telling him how he had heard from Dr. McDonald all the story of his bravery in battle, his heroic fight for life and quiet cheerfulness in hospital.

> . . . Poor Houghton could only reply with faint smiles and whispers that were too low to reach my ears, but Mr. Lincoln heard, and a smile came to his grave face. Turning to the surgeon the President asked to be shown the major's wounds, especially the amputated limb. Dr. McDonald tried to dissuade him by saying the sight . . . would be too shocking. But the President insisted, turned down the light coverings, and took a hasty look. Straightening up, with a deep groan of pain, and throwing up both his long arms, he cried out, 'Oh, this awful, awful war!' Then bending again to Houghton with the tears cutting wide furrows down his dust-stained cheeks, and with great sobs shaking him, he exclaimed, 'Poor boy! Poor boy! You must live! You must!' This time . . . [his] whispered answer, 'I intend to, sir,' was just audible."[20]

Captain Houghton did survive his wounds.

Leaving the Ninth Corps wards, the President was momentarily diverted by the Marquis de Chambrun who wanted him to meet one of the interesting people behind the scenes, a hospital matron he called "Miss G," (possibly Helen L. Gilson). At her invitation they viewed what she called "her room"—simply furnished with a well thumbed Bible near her bed. "That is not my only book," she told the President, "here is another I found in the pocket of a German soldier who died a few days ago." It was what in later times might be termed a self-help book. Its title, How to Make One's Way in the World, struck the Frenchman as terribly ironic. "Strange subject for this poor German to meditate;" he reflected, "he who, dreaming of wealth, perhaps of liberty, had come to Virginia to die!" What moved Chambrun most was watching the way that the President opened himself to learning about his hostess's experiences. "It was in the midst of these scenes, so varied in their character, that Mr. Lincoln revealed himself to me," declared the Marquis.[21]

The final ward contained soldiers from the Sixth Corps, whose breakthrough on April 2 had cost them 958 wounded or missing. The President stopped at the bed of amputee patient C. Hull Grant of the 43rd New York. Grant reminded him that he had previously greeted the then president-elect in 1861, during a stop in Albany en route to Washington. As Grant's friends like to tell it, "On the first occasion he shook hands with his own good right hand, but on the second occasion he was obliged to use his left, for the other was on the field."[22]

Another of the injured was a Vermont soldier who recalled years afterward that Lincoln's

> tall form and loving face bent over every one of us. Not one did he pass by. And to every one he had some word of good cheer tenderly spoken, while his homely face became absolutely beautiful as it beamed with love and sympathy. He would say to each, 'God bless you, my boy! Keep up a good heart. You'll come through all right. We'll never forget you!' Ah, I tell you, boys, we felt like reaching up our weak arms to clasp his neck yes, even to press our lips to his rough cheek. We all felt impatient to get well as fast as possible that we might fight as never before for our President, the great heart who came to cheer and love us while we lay disabled from our wounds."[23]

One soldier who had a more comprehensive view of the proceedings was Private Wilbur Fisk, assigned as a guard at the hospital. "Everything passed off in a very quiet manner," he wrote the next day, "there was no crowding or disorder of any kind. . . . Mr. Lincoln presides over millions of people, and each individual share of his attention must necessarily be very small, and yet he wouldn't slight the humblest of them all."[24]

It was late afternoon by the time the President had completed his personal concord with the wounded warriors, each of whom, as he said, "bravely bears his country's cause." It amazed Senator Sumner, who remarked, "Mr. President, you have taken the hand of some thousands of men to-day: you must be very tired." When he afterwards spoke of this day to Secretary of State Seward, the President described it as having "worked as hard at it as sawing wood." Only when he returned to the privacy of his stateroom on the *River Queen* did Elizabeth Keckly hear him tell Mary Lincoln, "Mother, I have shaken so many hands to-day that my arms ache tonight. I almost wish that I could go to bed now."[25]

But protocol (and Mrs. Lincoln) required a reception be held before their departure. Captain Barnes was pointedly not invited, but he was there anyway at Admiral Porter's insistence to keep an eye on the President until they were in safer waters. Mrs. Grant too was noticeably absent. But even remaining at a distance did not free her from Mary Lincoln's pique, as Captain Barnes observed:

> "For convenience in landing and returning, the *River Queen* had been placed alongside the dock and a gangplank connected her with the wharf. The *Martin*, a similar steamboat to the *Queen*, was also fastened to the dock. She was General Grant's headquarters boat, and upon her Mrs. Grant and her family were living. It was sometimes a question as to precedence as to which boat should lie inside —a question not raised by Mr. Lincoln. But Mrs. Lincoln thought that the President's boat should have place, and declined to go ashore if she had to do so over Mrs. Grant's boat, and several times the Martin was pushed out and the *Queen* in, requiring some work and creating confusion, despite Mr. Lincoln's expostulations. The boats came to be called 'Mrs. Lincoln's boat' and 'Mrs. Grant's boat' and the open discussions between their respective skippers were sometimes warm.[26]

Julia did not fade quietly into the night. She was aboard her husband's dispatch boat with a small wind ensemble on hand, setting out on an evening cruise, when they passed near the *River Queen*. "And as bad luck would have it," she remembered, "just as we were nearing the President's boat, the leader of the band came forward and inquired if there was any particular piece of music I wished played, expecting, no doubt, that I would order something patriotic. I coolly answered: 'Yes, play Now You'll Remember Me.' And we passed on up the river."[27]

According to Mrs. Keckly, "As the twilight shadows deepened the lamps were lighted, and the boat was brilliantly illuminated; as it lay in the river, decked with many-colored lights, it looked like an enchanted floating palace. A military band was on board, and as the hours lengthened into night it discoursed sweet music." Early into the soiree the President made a gesture that impressed the Marquis de Chambrun when he asked the musicians to play the "Marseillaise," a tune once considered France's national anthem, but forcibly retired by the country's current ruler, Emperor Napoleon III. Lincoln, wrote Chambrun, greatly enjoyed hearing the piece and had it encored. "He then asked me if I had ever heard *Dixie*, the rebel patriotic song, to the sound of which all their attacks had been conducted. As I answered in the negative, he added: 'That tune is now Federal property; it belongs to us, and, at any rate, it is good to show the rebels that with us they will be free to hear it again.' He then ordered the somewhat surprised musicians to play it for us."[28]

The party began to break up around 10:00 p.m., the guests and band departed, and just after 11:00 p.m. the *River Queen* and *Bat* started down stream. Captain Barnes remained aboard the *River Queen* (and carefully out of sight of Mrs. Lincoln) until it cleared the last vestige of what had been Rebel territory bordering the James River. (In his published memoir he diplomatically wrote, "Mrs. Lincoln was indisposed and I did not meet her.") Looking back at what would be their final time together, Barnes reflected that the "President was more than kind in his manner and bearing toward me, and so endeared himself to me that the affection I felt for him became veneration."[29]

Another keeping a watchful eye on the President was Mrs. Lincoln's guest, the Marquis de Chambrun. "Mr. Lincoln stood a long while looking at the spot we were leaving," he observed. "Above us were these hills, so animated a few days ago, now dark and silent; around us more than a hundred ships at anchor were silent proofs of the country's maritime strength, testifying to the great efforts made. Mr. Lincoln's mind seemed absorbed in the many thoughts suggested by this scene, and we saw him still pursue his meditation long after the quickened speed of the steamer had removed it forever from him."[30]

Abraham Lincoln had seen the face of war up close. He had let the men in the field know how much he valued their service, thanked and comforted the wounded, offered guidance to his military leaders, and seen the devastation suffered by civilian populations in harms way. He had taken all this into himself and found a personal peace for all that he had had to do in the past four years to save the nation. It was behind him now, slipping into the distance as the *River Queen* steamed on for the new challenges to come. He was ready. All that was missing was the final word on Lee's army.

A modest Virginia rural home, some 80 miles west of City Point, was at this moment the headquarters of the Armies of the United States. Ulysses S. Grant and his staff arrived after dark following the Richmond-Lynchburg Stage Road. A few miles east and north of them, elements of the Army of the Potomac were pressing what remained of the Rebel forces commanded by Robert E. Lee. A few more miles eastward and southward Sheridan's cavalry were operating and, if Grant knew his man, they were pushing hard to get ahead of the Confederate columns.

The pressure was taking its toll. "I was suffering very severely from a sick headache," the general later recorded. "I spent the night in bathing my feet in hot water and mustard, and putting mustard plasters on my wrists and the back part of my neck, hoping to be cured by morning."[31] Some of the younger officers were letting off steam by banging away at a piano in the house, but Grant was feeling too ill to complain. It wasn't quite midnight when a courier found his way to the general with Robert E. Lee's answer to the proposal he had sent him this morning:

> General: I received at a late hour your note of to-day. In mine of yesterday I did not intend to propose the surrender of the Army of Northern Virginia, but to ask the terms of your proposition. To be frank, I do not think the emergency has arisen to call for the surrender of this army; but as the restoration of peace should be the sole object of all, I desired to know whether your proposals would lead to that end. I cannot, therefore, meet you with a view to surrender the Army of Northern Virginia; but as far as your proposal may affect the C. S. forces under my command, and tend to the restoration of peace, I should be pleased to meet you at 10 a. m. to-morrow, on the old stage road to Richmond, between the picket-lines of the two armies.[32]

Grant's chief-of-staff, Brigadier General John A. Rawlins, thought that Lee was trying to buy time with something he knew Grant couldn't accept. President Lincoln had carefully drawn the lines of Grant's authority and while he could negotiate the surrender of an enemy armed force he had no power to discuss anything beyond that. "Why it is a positive insult," Rawlins fumed, "and an attempt in an underhanded way, to change the whole terms of the correspondence."[33] Grant saw no trickery here, only a proud military man facing ruination. He knew that the enemy's position had deteriorated since Lee had penned his note because messages received from Sheridan indicated that late this day the Yankee cavalry had captured trainloads of food and munitions at a place called Appomattox Station.

The lieutenant general believed, as he related in later years, "that Lee felt that the war was over; that the South was fought out; that any prolongation of the war would be misery to both the North and the South." Signaling Rawlins to calm down, Grant said: "If I meet Lee, he will surrender before I leave."[34]

It was too late and too dark to send an answer at this moment. Grant would sleep on it—at least try to sleep—and in the morning he would write Lee another note, and perhaps avoid a final bloody battle.

He knew it was what Mr. Lincoln would want.

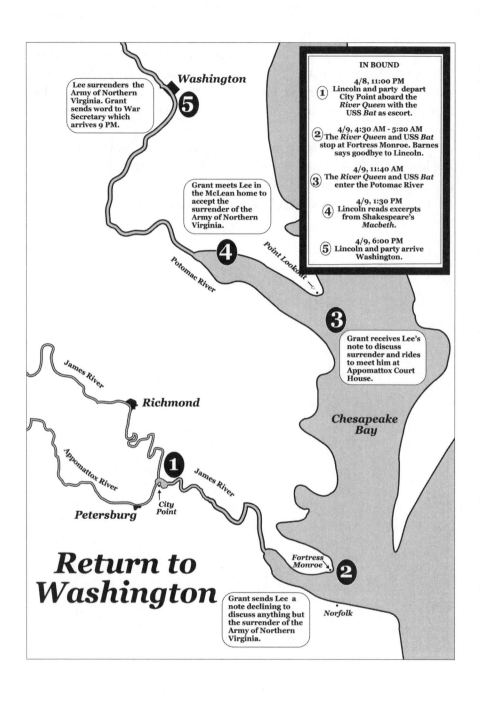

Return to Washington

CHAPTER SEVENTEEN

Sunday, April 9, 1865

"I think we are near the end at last."

THE *River Queen*, in the company of the gunboat USS *Bat*, reached Hampton Roads without incident and—at 4:30 a.m., Sunday, April 9—paused at Fortress Monroe. There were no dispatches waiting so Lincoln knew nothing more about what was happening than when he left City Point. It was time for Captain Barnes to say his goodbyes. Lincoln "was just as kind and pleasant in manner to me as he had always been, was good enough to thank me for what little I had been able to do for his comfort, wished me good luck, and was in the haste of the moment, exceedingly cordial." Reflecting a half century later on his experiences, Barnes wrote: "Probably he never again thought of me; but the memory of his warm hand-clasp and kindly look remained with me and has never left me."[1]

It was about a half hour before sunrise when the pair of vessels shoved off from Fortress Monroe and steamed north into the Chesapeake Bay.

Lieutenant Colonel Horace Porter found his boss this morning outside the Clifton House, "pacing up and down in the yard, holding both hands to his head." Grant's headache—today it would be called a migraine—had not lessened. Porter commented in an attempt at humor that in the past whenever the general had endured a bad headache the next day almost always brought good news. His feeble effort helped a little, as did a cup of coffee and the assembly of more staff officers. Thus fortified, Grant sat down and penned his response to Lee's last message.

General: Your note of yesterday is received. As I have no authority to treat on the subject of peace the meeting proposed for 10 a.m. to-day could lead to no good. I will state, however, general, that I am equally anxious for peace with yourself, and the whole North entertain the same feeling. The terms upon which peace can be had are well understood. By the South laying down their arms they will hasten that most desirable event, save thousands of human lives, and hundreds of millions of property not yet destroyed. Sincerely hoping that all our difficulties may be settled without the loss of another life, I subscribe myself,

Very respectfully, your obedient servant.[2]

Porter took care to emphasize in his account that Grant was rigorously adhering to the limitations on his military authority. What he missed noting were the two lines ending the message, which might well have been dictated by Lincoln. Also at this time Grant sent a note to Secretary of War Stanton bundled with copies of his correspondence with General Lee over the past two days.

Eighteen miles west from where Grant was writing his message, a last-ditch effort was underway by Confederate forces around Appomattox Court House to punch through the ring of U.S. infantry and cavalry inexorably penning them in. For some two hours the fighting would roil as the Rebels tried to burst through the thin line of cavalry Sheridan had pushed up to block their movements south. The Yankee troopers knew that major infantry reinforcements were marching hard to reach them this morning and fought with fierce determination against a force larger than their own. The Union infantry arrived in the proverbial nick of time. Once more the sounds of combat crackled across the Virginia countryside, and once more men were falling killed and wounded.

It took the *River Queen* and *Bat* just under three hours to cross the open expanse of the Chesapeake Bay across from the mouth of the York River and past the Wolf Trap Light Ship. At 11:40 a.m. the paired vessels sighted Point Lookout and turned westward. They were now entering the Potomac River.

General Grant decided on a dramatic personal change of course after he had sent off his reply to Lee's last communication. He had thus far accompanied General Meade's infantry as it continued herding the Rebel army before it. He knew that Sheridan's mixed force of cavalry and infantry (all of the Army of the James divisions plus the Fifth Corps from the Army of the Potomac) was near the head of Lee's columns, if not actually blocking them. That was where he needed to be, so with his staff and escort he began swinging southward then westward to come up toward Appomattox Court House, where he expected to find Sheridan in a fight.

They were overtaken a little before noon by one of George Meade's aides carrying important papers. Lee's breakout effort—about which Grant knew nothing—had failed and he had come out to the nearest Federal picket line (Meade's) pursuant to his April 8 proposal. The Confederate general had been met by a Federal staff officer bearing Grant's message of this morning. Having no more viable options to sustain his retreat Lee was past stringing things along and wrote:

> General: I received your note of this morning on the picket-line, whither I had come to meet you and ascertain definitely what terms were embraced in your proposal of yesterday with reference to the surrender of this army. I now request an interview in accordance with the offer contained in your letter of yesterday for that purpose.[3]

"When the officer reached me I was still suffering with the sick headache," Grant wrote, "but the instant I saw the contents of the note I was cured. I wrote the following note in reply:"[4]

> Your note of this date is but this moment (11.50 a.m.) received. In consequence of my having passed from the Richmond and Lynchburg road to the Farmville and Lynchburg road I am at this writing about four miles west of Walker's Church, and will push forward to the front for the purpose of meeting you. Notice sent to me on this road where you wish the interview to take place will meet me.[5]

Lieutenant Colonel Porter remembered that Grant "handed this to Colonel Babcock of the staff, with directions to take it to General Lee by the most direct route. Mounting his horse again, the general rode on at a trot toward Appomattox Court-house."[6]

According to the Marquis de Chambrun, the conversation among the guests turned to literary subjects as soon as the *River Queen* and her escort left the choppy waters of Chesapeake Bay and entered the calmer Potomac

River about midday. "Mr. Lincoln read to us for several hours passages taken from Shakespeare. Most of these were from *Macbeth*, and, in particular, the verses which follow Duncan's assassination. I cannot recall this reading without being awed at the remembrance, when Macbeth becomes king after the murder of Duncan, he falls a prey to the most horrible torments of mind.

"Either because he was struck by the weird beauty of these verses, or from a vague presentiment coming over him, Mr. Lincoln paused here while reading, and began to explain to us how true a description of the murderer that one was; when, the dark deed achieved, its tortured perpetrator came to envy the sleep of his victim; and he read over again the same scene."

Mrs. Lincoln later recalled that the President also quoted from a poem titled "Resignation." When she offered the observation that Jefferson Davis deserved to be hanged, the President answered, "Judge not, that ye be not judged." And when Senator Sumner wondered if Lincoln ever had any doubts about his "house divided" comment before the war, he was answered, "Not in the least; it was clearly true, and time has justified it."[7]

It was approximately 1:30 p.m. when the little convoy passed Blackistone's Island and drew abreast of the Wicomico River.

As Ulysses S. Grant rode northward toward Appomattox Court House the random rumbling sounds of battle slowly died out. General Meade had reluctantly agreed on his own authority to a request from General Lee for a ceasefire until he could meet with Grant, and an eerie silence spread all down the lines as the word passed along. Once the lieutenant general's party came into the village they were directed to the house of Wilmer McLean, where Lieutenant Colonel Babcock was waiting. The aide ushered Grant into the dwelling while the rest of the general's staff waited outside.

They were a study in contrast: Grant travel-worn and mud-splattered; Lee carefully outfitted in his dress uniform. After they had chatted about nothing of any consequence for a few minutes, Babcock allowed the officers with Grant to enter, including generals Sheridan, Ord, and Rawlins. It was Lee who got them to the point by asking Grant to specify his terms for a Confederate surrender. Grant affirmed that those he had mentioned in his April 8 note were still on the table. Lee asked in a courteous way that they be put into writing and Grant obliged. "When I put my pen to the paper I did not know the first word that I should make use of in writing the terms," he recalled later. "I only knew what was in my mind, and I wished to express it clearly, so that there could be no mistaking it."[8]

The spirit of Lincoln hovered over Grant's shoulder with an approving nod. Lee's soldiers were to return to their homes with a promise not to fight again. Military weapons, save for personal side arms, would be surrendered. The Rebels were officially assured that once they were home they would not "be disturbed by United States authority" as long as they obeyed U.S. laws. Lee had no problem with everything he read, but he wondered if those of his soldiers who actually owned the horses they were riding could keep them. Grant offered to give verbal orders to allow this to happen. He also agreed to send rations over to the Confederate encampments. This was all acceptable.

There was a pause while the necessary copies were made of the surrender document. To help pass the time, Lieutenant Colonel Babcock went to the front door and onto the porch where a number of Grant's staff officers had been waiting. He asked if they would not like to go in to be presented to General Lee, and a queue quickly formed. One can only imagine Lee's thoughts when he was introduced to a young Union captain by the name of Robert Lincoln. The press of the line meant only the briefest moment of contact so, Robert later recalled, because "we crowded the room, [we] almost immediately went out again."[9]

The required copies were made of the surrender document and they were signed. It was all over. Lee and Grant shook hands, and Lee departed first. Grant came out as Lee was turning to leave and in a last gesture he removed his hat in salute, promptly followed by all the officers with him. Lee returned the salutation and went to his army's camps. Turning to his staff, Grant used words that Lincoln might have crafted. "The war is over," he said. "The rebels are our countrymen again."[10]

On their ride to Sheridan's camp, someone mentioned that an announcement should be sent to the War Department. Grant halted, sat on a roadside stone and wrote out the message, which he time stamped 4:30 p.m. The note (plus a copy of the surrender terms) was handed to two military telegraphers assigned to army headquarters along with directions on where to find the closest working connection. In something of an anti-climax, the communications men got lost for a couple of hours before they located the terminal at Appomattox Station. They commandeered a railroad car filled with sandbags, ran the wire inside, hooked up their sending unit, and got in touch with Petersburg. The Petersburg office passed the note plus its large attachment along to the War Department, where it was handed to Secretary Stanton around 9:00 p.m.

The cover message was laconically Grant:

> General Lee surrendered the Army of Northern Virginia this afternoon upon terms proposed by myself. The accompanying additional correspondence will show the conditions fully.[11]

"The *Bat's* boilers under high pressure had a trick of foaming on passing from salt into fresh or brackish water, so that the *Queen* got ahead of me," Captain Barnes noted. Eventually the passenger ship would be running almost an hour ahead, but along this stretch of the Potomac there was little to fear for the President's safety, so, unlike the outward trip, Barnes did not order the *River Queen* to cut her speed to keep the two together. The *Bat* deck officer alerted Captain Bradford, and a little after 3:00 p.m., as the vessels were passing Upper Cedar Point, the warship began falling behind.

The *River Queen* eased past Mount Vernon around 5:00 p.m. The Marquis de Chambrun found the juxtaposition of American presidents too much to let pass without comment. He later recalled observing to Lincoln that "Mount Vernon and Springfield, the memories of Washington and your own, those of the revolutionary and civil wars; these are the spots and names America shall one day equally honor."

"Springfield!" the President answered. "How happy, four years hence, will I be to return there in peace and tranquility!"[12]

It was approaching 6:00 p.m. when the *River Queen* eased into the Sixth Street wharf and docked. William Crook, in one of the few instances of reporting something that he actually witnessed, says that it was here that "Mr. Lincoln parted from Captain Penrose; he took the captain by the hand and thanked him for the manner in which he had performed his duty."[13]

Neither Mr. nor Mrs. Lincoln had sent any messages announcing their pending arrival (at least none has been found), so likely notification to the White House came via the War Department, which would have been informed when the President's party departed Fortress Monroe. Carriages were waiting. The elder Lincolns, Senator Sumner, and the Marquis de Chambrun shared one. Presumably Tad and Crook were together in another. It was during this ride that the Frenchman overheard Mary Lincoln mutter that Washington "is full of our enemies." Mr. Lincoln's answer was quick. "Enemies! We must never speak of that."[14] The President stopped at the

White House long enough to find out that there were no important messages from Grant before continuing alone on to the residence of his injured Secretary of State, William H. Seward.

"It was in the evening," recalled Seward's son Frederick, "the gaslights were turned down low, and the house was still, everyone moving softly and speaking in whispers. The injured Secretary was helpless and swathed in bandages, on his bed in the center of the room. . . . Mr. Lincoln, entering with kindly expressions of sympathy, sat down on the bed by the invalid's side."

Seward's broken jaw made it painful to talk, but he opened the conversation. "You are back from Richmond?" he whispered.

"Yes," answered Lincoln, "and I think we are near the end at last."[15]

Seward's daughter, Fanny, entered and greeted the President, who offered his handshake in what she described as his "cordial way." Writing in her diary this night, she added, "He told us much about his visit to Richmond, & that one of his last acts was going through a hospital of seven thousand men, & shaking hands with each one." Fanny believed that the President "seemed, in his goodness of heart, much satisfied at the labor." Secretary Seward, observed his son, was throughout this "listening with interest, but unable to utter a word without pain. They were left together for half an hour or more."[16] Then Lincoln returned to the White House.

The message he had been desperately waiting to hear finally came through to the War Department a little after 9:00 p.m. Grant's official notification of Lee's surrender prompted a brief moment decidedly out of character for Edwin Stanton, the single-minded, authoritarian, and at times irascible minister whom the President had fondly nicknamed "Mars." A doctor present with the Secretary observed that "his iron mask was torn off, [and he] was trotting about in exhilarated joy." After dashing off a quick congratulatory note to the lieutenant general ("Thanks be to Almighty God for the great victory"), Stanton personally delivered the news to the President. The Secretary of War's confidential clerk afterward "heard that the President hugged him with joy." Stanton later recalled this as "some of the happiest moments of my life; our hearts beat with exultation at the victories, because we believed they would bring the speedy return of an honorable peace, and the re-establishment of the authority of the Constitution and the laws over the whole United States."[17]

As soon as the Secretary of War left to spread the word, Lincoln went upstairs to tell Mary that, as she recalled, "Lee & his Army were in our hands."[18]

Epilogue

PRESIDENT Lincoln's visit to City Point succeeded in restoring him. The news item marking his return to the capital also attested that his "brief relaxation from the wearing duties of his position has had a beneficial effect, and he returns to Washington in excellent health and spirits," while the reporter for the *Sacramento Daily Union* described him as "refreshed in body as well as relieved in mind," to which the *New York Herald* added that the "President is looking much better for his extended absences from the capital." A newsman present at Lincoln's April 11 speech declared that he "appeared much improved in health from his late tour to Richmond."[1]

A new member of his second term cabinet marveled that he "never saw Mr. Lincoln so cheerful and happy," and Navy Secretary Gideon Welles thought that the Chief Executive was "looking well and feeling well." Secretary of the Interior James Harlan, who accompanied the President from City Point, thought that his pre-trip gloom had been replaced with an "indescribable expression of serene joy as if conscious that the great purpose of his life had been achieved." Even Mrs. Keckly, who had seen the President at his worst, now felt that "his face was more cheerful than I had seen it for a long time." The glow was still strong on April 14. Edwin Stanton was leaving the regularly scheduled Cabinet meeting when he turned to a friend and exclaimed, "Didn't our chief look grand today?"[2]

Lincoln's experiences while at City Point, Petersburg, and Richmond, added powerful and deeply personal impressions to his thinking about a number of urgent issues awaiting his attention. He saw first hand the dangerous power vacuum that followed the Rebel collapse in Richmond and returned to Washington increasingly anxious to accelerate the reconstruction process. Virginia was at the top of his mind because of his two meetings with Judge Campbell and other influential Southerners, so it is not surprising that a day after getting back he spoke with the man he supported as governor of the pro-Union "restored" Virginia, Francis Harrison Pierpont.

Pierpont at once offered his congratulations on the capture of Richmond, to which Lincoln responded, "I want it distinctly understood that I claim no part or lot in the honor of the military movements in front of Richmond[.] All the honor belongs to the military. After I went to the front, I made two or three suggestions to Gen. Grant about military movements, and he knocked the sand from under me so quickly that I concluded I knew nothing about it and offered no more advice." The President mentioned his talks with Judge John Campbell and proceeded to pump the loyal governor for his insights regarding issues arising as Rebel Virginians returned to the Union. He urged Pierpont to "keep me advised."[3]

His calculated gamble allowing Judge Campbell to gather select Virginians to vote the state out of the war was drawing lots of fire and producing no results. Instead of men convening for the reason he had approved, there was a lot of palavering, especially by Judge Campbell, aimed at reopening closed topics such as an armistice and formal recognition of the Confederate-elected legislature. Once word spread around Washington regarding the arrangement, Lincoln got sharp pushback from his Secretary of War and Attorney General who both adamantly opposed letting even a facsimile of the wartime Virginia legislature meet for any purpose. Lincoln got the message.

On April 12 he sent Major General Weitzel instructions to withdraw the Campbell offer, or to countermand it, and to allow any individuals who may have come into the city under its protection to return unmolested to their homes. The President admitted at a Cabinet meeting two days later that he "had made a mistake at Richmond in sanctioning the assembling of the Virginia Legislature and had perhaps been too fast in his desires for early reconstruction." To another party Lincoln semi-joked that if he had known

Lee was going to surrender a few days after his meetings "I would not have issued the proclamation."[4]

Still, the doleful images lingered of shattered communities he'd seen, and he needed to act. "Civil government must be re-established . . . as soon as possible," he told Navy Secretary Welles on April 13, "there must be courts, and law, and order, or society would be broken up, the disbanded armies would turn into robber bands and guerrillas, which we must strive to prevent." A way had to be found to allow Southerners "to come together and turn themselves and their neighbors into good Union men." The pensive (and wordy) editor of the *Philadelphia Press* agreed, writing that "President Lincoln is evidently now as thoughtfully intent upon the best means of rearing up a new edifice of order and government in the rebellious States as he has hitherto been vigilant in devising measures to destroy the slave despotism that wickedly sought to exalt itself within our dominions." Reconstruction, Lincoln declared, "was the great question now before us."[5]

He decided to re-energize a political initiative that had gone nowhere—obtaining Congressional recognition for a reconstructed state of Louisiana. Almost from the moment that Federal forces had captured New Orleans in 1862, attempts had been made to get Louisiana back into the Union as a full voting member. Lincoln's method was to encourage and suggest initiatives but never to impose a plan of his own. It might have stood a chance if everyone involved had the country's best interests in mind, but the cultural bias of localized politics resulted in a Union-leaning government that kept African-Americans at arm's length and tried to compensate planters for the slaves they had lost. The racist elements evident in the reconstructed government and Lincoln's indirect support for the process had made few friends on Capitol Hill, so the plan seemed dead. However, after seeing social chaos waiting in the wings at Petersburg and Richmond, the President felt he had to go with what he had.

He used the opportunity of a celebratory public victory speech to press his case. Washington crowds had gathered twice on April 10 to hear the President crow about the Union victory. He put them off the first time; repeating the gambit he had played on the *River Queen* by having the band that was on hand play *Dixie* ("one of the best tunes I have ever heard"). The second time he promised the crowd a speech the next day that would "endeavor to say something, and not make a mistake."[6]

Lincoln's speech on April 11 from the White House could have been tossed off for the occasion, but it wasn't. A reporter friend named Noah

Brooks came to the Executive Mansion to hear it and was surprised to see Lincoln studying a sheaf of papers. "It is true that I don't usually read a speech," he told the surprised newspaperman, "but I am going to say something to-night that may be important, I am going to talk about reconstruction." A large crowd gathered on the White House lawn to hear him. When the President appeared in an upstairs window it was like a dam breaking and releasing a flood of emotion. Brooks was overwhelmed by the way that "cheers upon cheers, wave after wave of applause rolled up, the President modestly standing quiet until it was over."[7]

(As Lincoln began to talk, Brooks could see that he was having a hard time juggling a lit candle and reading in the poor light so he took hold of the dripping wax and held it to illuminate the pages. This prompted a grateful Lincoln to quip afterward, "That was a pretty fair speech, I think, but you threw some light on it." As the President completed reading a page he let it drop to the floor where Tad was lurking to snatch it. Brooks never forgot the sight of the boy "scurrying about, [who] gathered them up as they drifted away, like big butterflies, from the Presidents hand."[8])

Lincoln's opening comments acknowledged that recent events "give hope of a righteous and speedy peace whose joyous expression can not be restrained." He wanted to be sure that due credit went to those who delivered the victories: "To Gen. Grant, his skillful officers, and brave men, all belongs. The gallant Navy stood ready, but was not in reach to take active part." If the audience members were expecting a raucous celebration they were to be disappointed, and many who had come to rejoice instead had to follow an earnestly argued case for letting the President try out his Louisiana plan.

Lincoln made it clear that he was not trying to create a one-size-fits-all template for states rejoining the Union and that there were other approaches worth consideration. The time for talking about it was over, however, and the nation needed to experiment with ways of making it happen. "We all agree that the seceded States, so called, are out of their proper practical relation with the Union; and that the sole object of the government, civil and military, in regard to those States is to again get them into that proper practical relation," Lincoln said. He believed that within every seceded state there was a pro-Union minority that could be harnessed to guide affairs in the short term that would lead to a lasting reconciliation. This brought him directly to the question of the hour. "Can Louisiana be brought into proper practical relation with the Union *sooner* by *sustaining*, or by *discarding* her new State Government?" he asked.[9] His vote was for sustaining it now.

The next day's newspapers would argue the merits of the President's case, some supporting it ("This remarkable speech is wise in sentiment"), others condemning it ("Mr. Lincoln gropes, in his speech, like a traveler . . . without a map").[10] The President was boldly staking out his position and using the bully pulpit provided by the occasion to reintroduce the matter into the national discussion. He would make it a top priority at his April 12 Cabinet meeting, and it was something he fully expected to be spending a lot of time on in the weeks and months to come.

The President's visit to City Point, Petersburg, and Richmond had given him trenchant, first-hand impressions of a wide spectrum of the black experience—from the joyous abandon and guarded apprehension of former slaves, to the determined pride and expectations of long columns of blue-uniformed U.S. soldiers lined up to salute him. Lincoln had followed a reasonably straight course in dismantling the institution of slavery, but he was starting from scratch when it came to what role this large community would play in the nation's future and how best to get there. Until recently he had believed that the two races could never co-exist in a democratic system, but his thinking had changed and was ready to change further.

He utilized the April 11 platform to break new personal ground on the question of black participation in the American political process. The President's evolution on this issue had been almost imperceptible and tentative. In a letter written little more than a year earlier, he had urged the pro-Union governor of Louisiana to consider extending the state voting franchise to some African-Americans in language that was anything but decisive. "I barely suggest for your private consideration, whether some of the colored people not be let in—as for instance, the very intelligent, and especially those who have fought gallantly in our ranks," he wrote. "But this is only a suggestion, not to the public, but to you alone." With the memory of his close encounters with African-Americans at City Point, Petersburg, and Richmond still vivid, Lincoln now publicly proclaimed that it "is also unsatisfactory to some that the elective franchise is not given to the colored man. I would myself prefer that it were now conferred on the very intelligent, and on those who serve our cause as soldiers." Lincoln's time at City Point had resulted in a dramatic transformation of his views on this issue; it was now something he was ready to fight for in his second term. Frederick

Douglass later observed that even though Lincoln's concession seemed small, it "meant a great deal."[11]

Something else he said in this speech suggests that his pride in having been the people's representative at Petersburg and Richmond might well have led him to explore a new public role as communicator-in-chief on the great issues of the age. "I myself, was near the front, and had the high pleasure of transmitting much of the good news to you," he said.[12] However brief they might have been, Lincoln's annotations of the latest news from the front broke new ground for him and pointed the way to his further use of the mass medium as the nation grappled with contentious and even divisive issues in its path back to unity. It foreshadowed a dramatic reinvention of the Office of the President.

The President closed his speech, suggesting that there would be more to come on the subject. "In the present 'situation' as the phrase goes, it may be my duty to make some new announcement to the people of the South," he said. "I am considering, and shall not fail to act, when satisfied that action will be proper."[13]

Themes not brought up in Lincoln's short time back in Washington after his City Point sojourn—but which would have had a prominent place in his policies—included extended care for the war's wounded, restoration of the greatly ravaged areas of the South, reintegration of discharged veterans into American society, and a close partnership with Ulysses S. Grant as the political and military wings of the country joined in common purpose to re-glue the shattered pieces of the Union. During a brief public audience on April 14, Lincoln was asked by a lady if the continuing reports of military successes did not please him. "Yes, madam;" the President answered, "for the first time since this cruel war began, I can see my way clearly."[14]

This would take place under an umbrella of peace. When the Marquis de Chambrun asked Lincoln if the country's civil conflict would be followed by one against France over its imperialist adventures in Mexico he was told, "There has been war enough. I know what the American people want, but, thank God, I count for something, and during my second term there will be no more fighting."[15]

Much of this new thinking and determination had been validated by all that Lincoln saw and experienced while at City Point.

On April 14, 1865, Lincoln's breakfast was interrupted for the best possible reason: the arrival from the front of his son, Robert. The young captain was exhausted and travel-worn but full of stories of Grant's last campaign, including his personal observations at Appomattox Court House, where he had had the brief meeting with the great Rebel chieftain. Robert had managed to procure a souvenir of sorts, a photograph of the Confederate commander. The President looked at the image for a long time before proclaiming it "a good face; it is the face of a noble, noble, brave man. I am glad the war is over at last."[16] The elder Lincoln wanted to know everything that had happened during the campaign, and he had plenty of questions, enough to keep the pair talking for two hours and causing him to postpone a Cabinet meeting scheduled for 9:00 a.m. until 11.

General Grant was also in town and attended the gathering to talk about Lee's surrender and the winding down of the war machine. Lincoln afterwards asked if the General and his wife would join him and Mary for an evening of stage comedy at Ford's Theater. When Grant checked with Julia she "objected strenuously to accompanying Mrs. Lincoln" (her words).[17] As the general's hostess at City Point she was obligated to endure the First Lady's snobbery, but free of such a duty she loathed the prospect of spending another minute with that woman. They decided it was the right time to visit their children in New Jersey and made sure they were on the evening train when it departed Union Station.

Grant was one of two prominent military men profoundly affected by Lincoln's visit to City Point whose own public careers were to be prominently intertwined with the nation's destiny.

William Tecumseh Sherman had begun his offensive operations in North Carolina on April 10 as promised. His advance was carefully matched by the retreat of his opponent, General Joseph E. Johnston, who had unsuccessfully battled Sherman in Georgia in 1864 and whose faith in an ultimate Confederate victory was non-existent. By April 14 Johnston was looking to surrender. "I will accept the same terms as Gen. Grant gave Gen. Lee, and be careful not to complicate any points of civil policy," Sherman assured Grant and Stanton.[18]

The big difference between the conditions surrounding the Grant-Lee capitulation and the Sherman-Johnston one was the fact that Johnston was in regular communication with the Confederate government, which was moving slowly and steadily dissolving along the wrecked railroad line from Greensboro to Charlotte. At his third meeting with Johnston in the Bennett House (outside Durham), Sherman found himself facing Major General

John C. Breckinridge, who doubled as Confederate Secretary of War. What the two enemy soldiers put on the table was nothing less than a comprehensive capitulation of the entire Confederacy—if Sherman would extend his authority into the realm of civil policy.

It was the earnest desire of the two Rebel officers to end the war that finally persuaded Sherman to craft an agreement that went well beyond what Grant allowed Lee at Appomattox Court House. His timing, however, was terrible. It was April 18; Lincoln had been dead three days, but Sherman felt the deceased president was leaning over his shoulder as the surrender document was drafted. Besides disbanding the remaining rebellious armies, Sherman's terms allowed existing state governments to continue as long as loyalty oaths were taken (in cases such as Virginia, where a Confederate government co-existed with the U.S.-backed Pierpont regime, the issue would be decided by the Supreme Court), and there would be a general amnesty with Southerners guaranteed their "rights of person and property." Sherman wanted to reset the national clock to 1861, and he convinced himself that this was what Lincoln would have desired as well. In his way of looking at things, quickly restoring law and order easily trumped any temporary social changes caused by the war.

These and similar terms were sent to Washington for review. Sherman expected there would be some tinkering but he wasn't prepared for what his son, Philemon, later called the "storm of indignation with which they were received in the North." With dark currents of conspiracies real and imagined gripping Washington, Sherman's action was seen by some as a gross overreaching of his proper authority. Even General Grant's unwavering support of his friend was not enough to quell calls for Sherman's head, and the lieutenant general was ordered south to take over his subordinate's command. Grant instead sent Sherman back to the negotiating table to obtain the basic Appomattox deal. With Grant's steadfast refusal to condemn his subordinate, Sherman's career was saved.

Sherman would go on to command the armies of the United States but the rancor over his rejected treaty followed him to the grave. His most enthusiastic advocate was Admiral David Porter, who bent his popular recollections of Lincoln's City Point visit to justify everything Sherman did at the Bennett House. According to one of Sherman's sons, his father "always firmly believed that the substance of those terms expressed the policy of reconstruction outlined by Mr. Lincoln in their interview [aboard the *River Queen*], and which Mr. Lincoln would have followed, had he lived."[19]

Ulysses S. Grant had come away from his last visits with the President deeply impressed by what he heard and saw of the man. Speaking well after the war, he proudly said Lincoln "spent a good deal of time with me at City Point, and I saw him on intimate terms."[20] It would be wrong to say that Lincoln imprinted himself upon Grant's thinking. It would be closer to the truth to say that Lincoln's strong moral core and flexible tactics toward achieving peace validated Grant's own inclinations in that direction. For a man whom history for many years branded a "butcher," Grant in 1865 was equally willing to seek peace as he was to wage war. If it was to be war, however, he would prosecute it without pity. He also understood that the nation's destiny could not be realized if a sizeable section of it was beaten to its knees.

Twenty-four years in the future, after two terms as President of the United States, Ulysses S. Grant reflected on the Lincoln he had come to know at City Point and the values he espoused. "I often recall those days," said Grant. "He came down to City Point in the last month of the war, and was with me all the time. He lived on a dispatch-boat in the river, but was always around head-quarters. He was a fine horseman, and rode my horse Cincinnati. We visited the different camps, and I did all I could to interest him. He was very anxious about the war closing; was afraid we could not stand a new campaign, and wanted to be around when the crash came. . . . He was a great man, a very great man. The more I saw of him, the more this impressed me. He was incontestably the greatest man I ever knew. What marked him especially was his sincerity, his kindness, his clear insight into affairs. Under all this he had a firm will, and a clear policy."[21]

Grant understood—as Lincoln understood—that the true measure of the North's victory would be in the promises kept—especially to those who delivered the victory, white and black. Both men also were pledged to doing whatever had to be done to knit the fabric of the nation together again. Lincoln said, "We must extinguish our resentments if we expect harmony and union." Grant said, "Let us have peace."[22] Seen in this light, Grant's two White House terms were a determined effort (sadly, not always successful) to transform the nation along the lines Lincoln had chalked out during his visits with Grant at City Point.

The sheer vastness of the war had changed America, and there was no going back. Lincoln returned from City Point ready to campaign for his vision of the new and fully united states. Had he completed his second term, modern historians would have regarded his time at City Point as the occasion when a U.S. president dramatically refashioned his agenda. Lincoln left Washington on March 23 a weary war leader; he returned having found his peace with the burdens borne by a commander-in-chief and was energized to lead the country forward. It was an amazing, remarkable transformation whose possibilities would soon be submerged in the turbulent waters of assassination, national vengeance, and a power struggle between branches of government over the nation's future direction.

There is no proving of any speculation regarding Lincoln's second term agenda, but one factor cannot be ignored: his personal power of persuasion. It took an observation by a dedicated Rebel to put that uncanny ability in context.

On April 10, 1865, Lieutenant General Grant—at his request—met with General Lee between the camps of the two armies for an informal conversation. As Grant related the matter, he "suggested to General Lee that there was not a man in the Confederacy whose influence with the soldiery and the whole people was as great as his, and that if he would now advise the surrender of all the armies I had no doubt his advice would be followed with alacrity." According to Lee's principal staff officer, Colonel Charles Marshall, Grant further suggested that the Virginian travel to Washington to meet with President Lincoln. Lee declined, citing the need to check first with Jefferson Davis, something that clearly was not going to happen.

Grant departed greatly disappointed and with a deep sense of regret; feelings that were shared years afterward by Colonel Marshall. "I have always thought that if General Lee and Mr. Lincoln could have met as General Grant proposed," he wrote, "we could have had immediate restoration of peace and brotherhood among the people of these States.[23]

Sources Casebook

CHAPTER ONE: JANUARY-MARCH, 1865
"It was an immense relief to him to be away from Washington."

The memoirs of John Sanford Barnes, published in two 1907 magazine articles, are central to any telling of Lincoln's 1865 visit to the war front. During my research I located a second memoir written in 1910 for private circulation, which he titled *The Egotistigraphy of a Rolling Stone, that Gathered Moss, Herein Scraped off for the Information and Amusement of his Family*. There is no evidence that at the time he set down either of these accounts he had access to the USS *Bat's* log book. When the dates, times, and comments notated in it are compared with Barnes's accounts, a number of discrepancies become evident. I have used the ship's log as the foundation of my narrative, with Barnes's testimony fitted into the new outline. I note also that Barnes penned letters to his wife at the time of Lincoln's visit which he later collated for family eyes only, but even with the generously kind help of several Barnes descendants, I was unable to locate a copy.

Anyone familiar with the events of Lincoln's last weeks will notice that I have not included William H. Crook among the party traveling with the President in March 1865. The evidence I have seen convinces me that he was not at City Point until April 6. I believe that he subsequently drew from his brief time there with the President and conversations with several individuals who had been present throughout to craft a self-promoting story that a ghost-writer turned into a memoir for a *Washington Post* feature piece in 1895. (It went on to become several magazine articles and chapters in a larger autobiography, all ghost-written. Excerpts were often serialized in turn-of-the-century newspapers.)

About the time that Crook's memoirs first appeared questions were raised. A man named Robert Lincoln O'Brien, who clerked at the White House in the early 1890s and personally knew Crook, described him as "an intrinsically stupid man who lived on his pretended intimacy with Abraham Lincoln." There was also Charles Forbes, President Lincoln's personal attendant, who wrote a rebuttal letter to the *Washington Post* in 1895. "Mr. Crook did not accompany the Presidential party on their trip to City Point in the latter part of March, 1865," he declared, "the party consisting only of the President, Mrs. Lincoln, Tad and myself."[1]

Historians before me noted that no other witness to Lincoln's visit mentions Crook as being present, and there are several mistakes he makes that an actual companion would not have made. Where I can determine that witnesses to an event were present who may have spoken afterwards to Crook, I have used their observations.

Another challenge concerns the portrayal of Mrs. Lincoln during this visit. The two key witnesses are Lieutenant Colonels Horace Porter and Adam Badeau of Grant's staff. I believe that pair had strong reasons to amplify the negative aspects of Mrs. Lincoln's personality when they wrote long after the war, since both by then had become valued members of Grant's political family. By making Mrs. Lincoln look bad they made Mrs. Grant look good. Mary Lincoln was an easy target: an emotionally damaged woman with a haughty personality, whose selfish actions, many felt, shamed the memory of the great martyred President. Still, I'm not convinced by the way that Porter and Badeau (especially) pile on, and have utilized their observations with restraint.

Then there's an interesting meteorological piece to the Lincoln story for March 23 that is curiously absent from most accounts. Close on the heels of the departing First Family was a fast moving tempest with a powerful punch. I constructed a storm profile based on contemporary newspaper accounts and meteorological data recorded by the Smithsonian Institution, which I then provided to veteran Washington meteorologist Doug Hill, who kindly reviewed the information and shared it with his colleagues at WJLA Channel 7, an ABC affiliate. According to Mr. Hill, "It was most likely a strong cold front that caused the conditions you described. With that said . . . most likely, it was a squall line . . . of severe thunderstorms. These storms produce strong, straight-line winds."[2]

Finally, what's in a name? For well more than a century historians have understandably taken Ulysses S. Grant at his word when he identified his headquarters boat at City Point as the *Mary Martin*. Lincoln scholar Wayne C. Temple (to whom I am indebted for pointing this out to me) opined that the vessel's name was more likely the *Carrie Martin*. There was a tradition in the owner's family of naming vessels after their women (no Mary), and Temple believes that when an ailing Grant (in a fatal decline from throat cancer) dictated his memoirs, his pronunciation of Carrie was misheard as Mary. It was such a small point that no attention was paid to it in the subsequent completion of the manuscript or in its use by generations of later historians and biographers. I will so identify the craft as the *Carrie Martin*.

CHAPTER TWO: SATURDAY, MARCH 25, 1865
"He typified the very Union itself."

Captain John Sanford Barnes says in his published articles (1907) that Lincoln met Admiral Porter on March 25. I believe that Barnes confuses this day with the next. Porter had his hands very full on March 25, organizing the naval response to the attack on Fort Stedman. Plus there's a message he sends to Grant on March 26 that begins, "I hear the President is at City Point."[3] Finally, the evidence from the log of Porter's flagship places him at Jones' Landing.

This day marks the first of two similar incidents that occur during Lincoln's visit to the Petersburg-Richmond front, and it is not unusual for writers to mix and match them. One involves the wife of Brevet Major General Charles Griffin (Fifth Corps, Army of the Potomac, posted *south* of the James), the other the wife of Major General Edward O. C. Ord (commanding the Army of the James, posted *north* of that river). I believe I have correctly untangled the pair in my narrative.

There are accounts from Ninth Corps soldiers insisting that Lincoln viewed the final stages of the Fort Stedman fight from an old Confederate earthwork known as the Dunn House Battery, located in the center of the rear lines. Lincoln's movements took him nowhere near that point. There also exist several pages describing Lincoln's actions in the war memoir *Down in Dixie* by Stanton P. Allen of the 1st Massachusetts Cavalry. Published in 1893, it is literally too good to be true, and I do not use it.

There was no formal log of Lincoln's railroad journey to the front and no participant identified where they actually detrained. The balloting among historians seems split between Globe Tavern and Patrick Station farther west. Meade's headquarters (Lincoln's first stop) was located northeast of Globe Tavern, making it highly unlikely that the Presidential party would have traveled beyond that point more than two additional miles to then backtrack over rough corduroy roads. I have therefore opted for Globe Tavern.

CHAPTER THREE: SUNDAY, MARCH 26, 1865

"How grateful I feel to be with the boys."

Coming on stage for March 26 is Rear Admiral David D. Porter, a difficult witness to utilize. Two aspects of his character need to be put into the mix when evaluating his memoirs of Lincoln's visit. One was a storyteller's desire to please his audience. Porter recounted his adventures with Lincoln in three full-length writings as well as shorter pieces, and his stories expanded with time. The second trait was his deep friendship for William Tecumseh Sherman, and a predilection to undermine anyone he believed wronged his friend.

Captain Barnes has Porter at Grant's headquarters when Lincoln arrives, yet there's that 10:00 a.m. query from the admiral asking the general if the President is even there. Barnes also mistakenly identifies the review site where Lincoln saw the Army of the James as being near Malvern Hill, when it was actually seven miles *west* of that place, something confirmed by newspaper and soldier accounts.

One often (and still) recounted Lincoln story that also seemed to me to fall into the "too good to be true" category was his encounter with the kittens in the telegraph office. It is mentioned well after the fact by both Porters—Admiral David and Lieutenant Colonel Horace—and each used the occasion to deliver a little homily on Lincoln's character, always a warning sign. I had consigned it to the "probably spurious" bin when I found a third account, this one much more contemporary to the President's visit, appearing in the May 3, 1865, edition of *The Soldiers' Journal*, published in Augur General Hospital, Alexandria, Virginia. While it is hopelessly inaccurate in some of its details, it nevertheless convinced me that the incident did happen. My narrative does not stray far from that 1865 account.

The boat used by Lincoln in his travels this day is identified by Sheridan as being Grant's headquarters steamer, but Captain Barnes and the logbook of the USS *Bat* clearly indicate that the *River Queen* was the vessel in question.

Finally, I note that Captain Robert Lincoln is missing in accounts this day. No one mentions his presence, and I think it's possible that he was back on staff duty. There is a reference to Lincoln coming aboard Admiral Porter's flagship accompanied by his "two sons," with the inference being that both were boys. I suspect that the second was Grant's son, Jesse, roughly the same age as Tad. Had it been Captain Robert Lincoln, in his staff uniform, I doubt that the deck officer making the log notation would have so linked him with Tad.

CHAPTER FOUR: MONDAY, MARCH 27, 1865

"You are joking, General."

One of the higher profile newsmen present at City Point during Lincoln's visit was Charles C. Coffin of the *Boston Journal*, who used his middle name "Carleton" when filing his pieces. It's challenging to separate his recollections based on contemporary notes from the details he added later. In one of his books (*The Boys of '61*, 1886) Coffin writes of seeing Lincoln, Sherman, Grant, Meade, Sheridan, Ord, and Crook (he says "Cook") together on the morning of March 28. This gathering could not have taken place on that day, nor is there any time when all these individuals were in the same place. This has also led some historians to date Coffin's first meeting with Lincoln on March 28; however, a letter written by minister John Heyl Vincent dated March 27 establishes Coffin's initial conversation with Lincoln on that day.

I have added a morning meeting to Lincoln's schedule not to be found in any accounts of his time at City Point. Early news reports of Lincoln's trip included the names of Treasury Department officials Hanson A. Risley and William P. Mellen on the *River Queen* guest list. A March 23 note from Mellen to Lincoln explains that the two decided to travel on their own utilizing a department Revenue Cutter, but promised to meet at City Point. I inserted Risley and Mellen in the day's narrative of events based on a brief notice in the *Chicago Tribune* that has them just returned to Washington on March 28, so they must have departed City Point no later than mid-day March 27. A postwar Risley letter actually describes the meeting.

Admiral Porter claims he had a lot of face time with Lincoln during the City Point visit. Yet he had demanding responsibilities not only for navy vessels on the James River but also for those as far south as Cape Fear, North Carolina. The manuscript log of his flagship, the USS *Malvern*, shows him aboard her on March 27 and anchored near Aiken's Landing all day except for two excursions; from 2:00 to 4:00 p.m., and from 6:30 to 10:30 p.m. The testimony of Captain Barnes placing Porter with Lincoln during the forenoon cannot be substantiated.

His evening absence from the *Malvern* supports Porter's presence at a gathering of officers at City Point that is sometimes confused with the meeting Lincoln has the next day with three of them. This day's assembly was intended as a reception for Sherman, whose stay at City Point was to be brief. Just about every observer makes one or two mistakes concerning who was present. George Meade is placed there but Grant sent him a telegram explaining that he purposely did not invite him since it was more important that he coordinate the placement of Sheridan's cavalry and oversee arrangements for the arrival of Ord's infantry. (Meade paid his respects on the morning of March 28.) Sheridan is also mentioned among the crowd, but he doesn't arrive until near midnight when the "party" is pretty much over. Lincoln does not attend at all, but does meet privately beforehand with Sherman and Grant.

There's one more Barnes statement for this time period that doesn't add up. Referring to Grant's headquarters boat and Lincoln's craft, he places Mrs. Grant and son aboard the *Martin* and says that Mrs. Lincoln demanded that the *Queen* always be tied to the wharf when she disembarked, forcing Mrs. Grant's boat to sheer off. The problem is that Mrs. Grant doesn't transfer her household from shore to the *Martin* until her husband moves his headquarters into the field—which happens on March 29. Plus Mrs. Lincoln, beginning March 28, is secluded in her cabin and doesn't leave the ship. The circumstances described by Captain Barnes more likely reflect the situation at the end of Lincoln's visit, when Mrs. Grant is living afloat and Mary Lincoln is actively going ashore.

March 27 includes a visit to a spot known as Point of Rocks. Some accounts claim the Lincolns travelled on a steamer named the *Greyhound*, which had served as a headquarters boat for the previous Army of the James commander, Major General Benjamin F. Butler. However, she had burned to the water's edge in November 1864, leaving the *River Queen*, (named by Captain Barnes) as the vessel used.

And who came along? The Crook account mentions a stellar cast: General Grant, Admiral Porter, Captain Penrose, Mrs. Lincoln, Tad, and Crook himself. Captain Barnes's list is a bit more modest: Mrs. Grant, Mrs. Lincoln, and Captains Robert Lincoln and Charles Penrose. In point of fact, Admiral Porter was on the *Malvern*, General Grant at his headquarters, and Crook back in Washington. The Barnes account makes sense, though he omits Tad from the calculation, and Mrs. Lincoln's unnamed maid. Likely there but out of sight was Charles Forbes. So the Barnes roster plus those three seems about right.

Chapter Five: Tuesday, March 28, 1865

"You have never found fault with me."

Admiral Porter remained aboard the USS *Malvern* on March 28 except for a midday absence, departing at 11:15 a.m. and returning at 1:30 p.m. This confirms to my satisfaction his presence at the "War Council" with Lincoln, Grant, and Sherman, and sets the time of that meeting from roughly 11:50 a.m. to 1:05 p.m. Of the four men present on that occasion only Sherman and Porter left recollections and the memories of both were very much distorted by subsequent events, so any parsing of the meeting minutes as set down by these two has to allow for that bias.

How did the naval officer get invited in the first place? I believe Sherman got him in. The meeting was set by Sherman and Grant at the end of their March 27 chat with the President. Sherman was shrewd enough to figure that its agenda would be more serious than the first and, always wishing to do a good turn for his great friend Porter, got him on the exclusive guest list. There is no indication that Lincoln asked for him, or that he opposed his being present.

Sherman makes one error of fact when he states in his *Memoirs* that "General Grant explained to the President that at that very instant of time General Sheridan was crossing James River from the north."[4] That's not entirely true. The bulk of Sheridan's cavalry force had passed through some 36 hours earlier and was encamped near Hancock Station on the military railroad line. The horsemen passing during the meeting came from the Army of the James and would soon be attached to Sheridan's command. They numbered 2,000 riders under Brigadier General Ranald S. Mackenzie.

A question remains for which I have no good answer: What about Mary Lincoln? She remains, unseen, aboard the *River Queen*. In fact, she will continue to do so for five days. No contemporary source offers an explanation for why or what she was doing all that time. There is no evidence she left the *River Queen* or that she had any visitors, although I have to believe that Robert would have paid a call before he departed for the front with the rest of Grant's staff on March 29.

The First Lady's modern biographers vary in their rationale for her abrupt vanishing act. Jean H. Baker writes that Mrs. Lincoln was paying "the price for her temper. Mortified and apologetic, she stayed in her cabin. . . . Those who inquired were told that she was indisposed, as indeed she was." Baker brands this "a bad case of self-inflicted shame." Catherine Clinton blames Mary's failure to sway her husband with her "whining and whimsy. Her bad behavior led to a temporary break between herself and the president. She spent the remainder of her time [at City Point] . . . claiming to be 'indisposed.'"[5]

I believe that Mrs. Lincoln may have been truly ill. Whether it was mental (bipolar) or physical I cannot say, but her almost instantaneous turnaround once she returns to Washington is certainly suggestive of someone susceptible to wide mood swings.

Chapter Six: Wednesday, March 29, 1865

"Your success is my success."

The traditional story of Grant's March 29 departure from City Point comes from Horace Porter with a little added by Adam Badeau. Ironically, a Porter letter I found in the New York Public Library led me to a third account. The irony is that Porter wrote the letter to pan the clipping from an unidentified newspaper. Porter was more interested in defending his and Badeau's ownership of that part of the Lincoln legacy franchise than evaluating the piece. I found that there was much plausible in it and have blended it into my narrative.

The *Malvern* log has Admiral Porter together with Lincoln on the *River Queen* from 10:00 to 11:30 a.m. There is no indication when Porter returned to his flagship, and the next day's entries only show him leaving the ship at 3:00 p.m. It seems unlikely he would have remained on the *River Queen* for any substantial period. After all, Grant's operation was in full swing and, while the part assigned to the Navy was small, it was something that Porter would have closely monitored; this is not a day the Admiral would have wanted to be hard to find. So my surmise is that he and the President enjoyed lunch together before he departed for his flagship, and that his comings and goings were common enough that not all were logged.

Chapter Seven: Thursday, March 30, 1865

"I dislike to leave without seeing nearer to the end."

Tracking President Lincoln on March 30 is a real challenge. The weather was lousy; rain all day, sometimes very heavy, not ending until the evening; so it is unlikely that Lincoln would have gone riding. He certainly would not have ventured anywhere near the front. Add to this, all the best witnesses are elsewhere, save Admiral Porter who is only with him for a short while. The *Malvern* log, which locates Admiral Porter on board except from 3:00 to 5:15 P.M., indicates no nautical activity involving the President. Journalists on the scene would have had their hands full processing reports of yesterday's fighting and transmitting them to their home offices. I have to believe that the President spent some time at the telegraph office monitoring events; otherwise, he most likely was on the *River Queen*, perhaps conversing with Mary, certainly playing with Tad. Charles Forbes and Captain Charles Penrose, two potential witnesses who were also on board, have nothing to say. There are two accounts not specific to March 30 that can fit into this day's pattern, and I have utilized both.

One of the great losses to our knowledge of Lincoln at this time would be the untimely death of the man Grant left in charge of the home office while he was at the front, Lieutenant Colonel Theodore S. Bowers. He was one of those bright young men that Grant allowed into his inner circle; sadly and tragically, Bowers would be dead in less than a year. Still faithfully serving his general, he accompanied Grant to a West Point function in early March 1866. To get there from New York City (where the Grants then resided), required a train up the east side of the Hudson River as far as Garrison, then a boat ride to West Point on the opposite bank. At the start of the return leg of this journey, Bowers noticed that the general's valise had been left on the platform. Even though the train was starting to move, he jumped off to retrieve it, but slipped attempting to re-board and was crushed under the train wheels. Grant lost a valued associate and history was deprived of a witness with special knowledge of Lincoln's time at City Point.

CHAPTER EIGHT: FRIDAY, MARCH 31, 1865

"General Grant telegraphed me as follows."

It was rainy on the morning of March 31, but it began clearing at 10:00 a.m. and by afternoon it was pleasant and cool. All of which explains why Admiral Porter remained onboard the *Malvern* until 1:30 p.m., when he left the flagship for four hours.

We first meet this day another individual who would spend some quality time with the President at City Point: military telegrapher Samuel H. Beckwith. I found a serialized extended memoir Beckwith wrote for the *New York Sun* in 1913. Beckwith's regular assignment was to Grant's headquarters and he considered himself the lieutenant general's personal communications specialist. In those newspaper memoirs, Beckwith explains that he "was not present at Lee's surrender at Appomattox April 9. Gen. Grant had assigned me to the President and I accompanied the latter on Admiral Porter's barge from Richmond to City Point. I was to keep him in touch by telegraph with the army in its advance movement and with the War Department at Washington. For the next two weeks out of the three yet remaining to him, Lincoln was my constant employer."[6]

I believe that March 31 was when Beckwith reported for the special duty. The reason is a distinct change I note in the pattern and content of the telegraph messages between the front lines and the President, and from the President to Washington. All this suggests that starting today Lincoln had the undivided attention of a professional telegrapher ready to do his bidding and offer some advice that dramatically changed the President's role at the war front.

One reason that most historians don't credit Seward's quick visit to City Point is the testimony of Admiral Porter. In fact, he goes out of his way to paint the relationship between the two men as badly strained. Porter declares that "Seward telegraphed several times to the President for an invitation to visit him at that place, with other members of the Cabinet; but Mr. Lincoln, on each and every occasion, positively declined to have them come there."[7] This is pure nonsense. There is no evidence of any such telegram(s).

I find the evidence for such a visit to be strong and convincing, beginning with newspaper accounts of Seward's departure from Washington. That the Secretary had reached City Point late on March 30 is indicated in Provost Marshal Patrick's diary. The brevity of his time there is suggested by the *New York Herald* reporter at City Point, Thomas M. Cook, who termed it a "flying visit" and a "hasty visit."[8] Lincoln acknowledges Seward's presence in a message exchange with Grant, and the fragments of a diary kept during the journey by the Secretary's daughter notes City Point as one of the stops. For his part, Admiral Porter (writing after the war) had it in for anyone he believed wronged his great friend Sherman and he considered Seward in that group.

Lincoln's decision to annotate war bulletins from Petersburg added a new dimension to the Office of the President. In a later age and a later conflict, the technology of radio would allow the nation's commander-in-chief to come into the homes of all Americans with information and commentary. This 1865 foreshadowing of Franklin Roosevelt's fireside chats also brought Lincoln into homes across the nation, not as a chief executive but as a neighbor, providing a gateway to the latest official news of the fighting around Petersburg and Richmond. It was an unexpected and exciting new role for the Chief Executive.

Chapter Nine: Saturday, April 1, 1865

"Having no great deal to do here."

April 1 is a day for which there is no indication that Porter spent any time with the President, and for good reason: his wife came aboard the flagship at midday and she was honored with a little party that evening.

It seems appropriate for this April 1 chapter to pull back the curtain on what may well be the greatest April Fool's joke ever played on generations of readers and historians. The culprit: Admiral Porter; the issue, his best Lincoln tale to come out of City Point. The story in brief: When the *River Queen* goes to Norfolk for a couple of days, Lincoln sets up shop aboard the admiral's flagship, the USS *Malvern*. It's a cramped ship; the only room available is 6 by 4 1/2 feet. When the President retires on the first night he leaves his shoes (dirty) and his socks (holes in them) outside the door. Porter had the former cleaned and the latter darned. When Lincoln puts them on in the morning he proclaims it a miracle. While he is ashore Porter realizes that the room was too small so he has it enlarged before the President returns for a second night aboard. The next morning, Lincoln declares it an even greater miracle. The story is spiced with much humorous dialogue.

There is simply no evidence this ever happened. The only time the *River Queen* left City Point without the President aboard was April 6-7, when she carried Mrs. Lincoln and party to Richmond. The log of the *Malvern* does not indicate any Lincoln stay for more than a day. And the crux of Porter's story is that the *Malvern* was a small, limited space vessel, when it fact she was quite large and comfortable, even with a full crew aboard.

We briefly meet Carl Schurz in this chapter. His *Reminiscences* (three volumes) enhances his meeting with Lincoln at City Point when compared to a letter he wrote at the time. In the posthumously published memoirs, Schurz says he "spent the better part of a day with Mr. Lincoln on the steamboat off City Point, on which he lodged." Yet his claim was more modest in a letter he wrote to his wife at the time, "I saw Lincoln for a few moments at City Point."[9] It's another case of the powerful gravitational pull the Lincoln legend had on those writing about him after his death, when every casual encounter with the great martyr was magnified and amplified in memory.

Schurz also proves a mixed witness regarding Mary Lincoln's behavior at this time. On the one hand, as he told his wife, the First Lady was "overwhelmingly charming to me," adding that he "learned more state secrets in a few hours than I could otherwise in a year. I wish I could tell them to you. She is an astounding person." On the other, however, there is the memoir of the noted book editor Ellery Sedgwick, who writes, "I can recall reading in its original manuscript form a chapter excised from the Memories of Carl Schurz as improper to publish. It told of a trip on the Potomac which General Schurz made in company with Mrs. Lincoln and set down verbatim a conversation on her part so vulgar and so venomous that it can fairly be described as outrageous."[10]

The *New York Herald* reporter Sylvanus Cadwallader recounts a Lincoln incident in a postwar memoir that—at first blush—fails the credibility test. He claims to have departed Grant's headquarters late this afternoon and reached City Point (25 miles distant) carrying several Rebel battle flags captured at Five Forks which he presents to the President. There are problems aplenty with this story. The actual combat was just winding down at the time he states he left Grant's headquarters, and we have Horace Porter's testimony that he brought first word of the Five Forks victory to army headquarters at approximately 8:15 p.m., long after Cadwallader says he had reached City Point with the same news.

I nevertheless feel that there is truthfulness here. In Grant's March 31 message traffic, he mentioned capturing four enemy battle flags during Warren's White Oak Road fight and promised to forward one to the President. There's no record of any headquarters aide visiting City Point after that promise had been made, and when Cadwallader (who had been covering Grant since 1862) announced he was riding there to file his latest piece, someone may have had the bright idea to let him deliver the standard. It is also significant that the dispatch Cadwallader files from Grant's headquarters (appearing in April 3 newspapers) is clearly written before the result of the Battle of Five Forks was known.

I believe the newsman did carry a flag to Lincoln—the one Grant promised on March 31—and that he left army headquarters in the early afternoon, before Sheridan's fight brewed up. When Cadwallader came to write his memoir in the 1870s he knew from history that the Battle of Five Forks was a much bigger deal than White Oak Road, so he fashioned his recollections accordingly, cheerfully ignoring any time discrepancies.

Chapter Ten: Sunday, April 2, 1865

"The country can never repay these men."

Another very believable and often quoted Lincoln anecdote from Admiral David Porter goes under the microscope for the events of April 2 and again comes up short. He and Lincoln are sitting on deck of the *Malvern* that evening when the President asks him if the Navy can't "do something at this particular moment to make history?" Porter reluctantly agrees to order his ships to fire in no particular direction except toward the enemy in a message sent to Captain K. Randolph Breese. At about 9:20 p.m. there is "a loud explosion which shook the vessel." Porter interprets the sounds for the President as being that of the Rebel James River fleet blowing itself up. The next morning the way is clear to Richmond.[11]

Let's analyze the story.

"The night before Richmond was evacuated by the Confederate forces" would be that of April 2-3. I checked the logbooks for seven of the largest warships on station in the James River Squadron and none reported firing their guns during the two night watches, 4:00 to 8:00 p.m., and 8:00 p.m. to midnight. In addition, none indicated *hearing* any significant river firing during that time. There is no record of any telegram in the Naval *Official Records* as described by Porter to Captain Breese. Lastly, a review of the story from the Confederate side indicates that the warship self-immolations that occurred near dawn on April 3 did so in response to orders from Richmond and not any Federal artillery intervention.

I also feel that this is another case with elements of truth in it. When Porter penned his recollections some 20 years later, he strung together three actual occurrences, not directly linked to each other. The first was the hour or so of sustained naval gunfire in the waning hours of April 1 supporting the land cannonade ordered by Grant. The second was the large-scale explosions heard on April 3 at 4:30 and 5:00 a.m. This is according to a reporter present with a watch who wrote that the man-made thunder "leaves no doubt in the military mind here that the rebel rams have been blown up."[12]

The third piece lacks any concrete evidence, but I believe that Lincoln and Porter did sit on a ship's upper deck on the night of April 2-3, but that it was the *River Queen*. The deck officers on the *Malvern* may have missed noting some of the admiral's comings and goings, but they would not have ignored the extended presence of President Lincoln. Also, in his generally reliable diary, Provost Marshal Patrick writes on April 3 that at "ten o'clock last night I left the President & Admiral Porter." He continues the sentence: "Staid a few minutes with Mrs. Grant & Mrs. Rawlins."[13] We know the ladies are on Grant's headquarters boat, and from the way he describes the visitations, Patrick seems to be boat-hopping. So I put Lincoln and Porter aboard the *River Queen*.

This day's message traffic clears up a false statement still accepted by some writers, originating with Captain (later Major) Charles Penrose—the officer assigned by the Secretary of War to accompany the President. He wrote a letter to the editors of *The Century Magazine* in early 1890 responding to a series of pieces about Lincoln's Richmond visit that the journal had published a year earlier. The editors printed a brief scratch diary Penrose kept at the time and summarized his letter. According to their paraphrase, "Major Penrose says he has often seen it stated that Mr. Lincoln was accompanied to Richmond by his young son Tad, when in fact he had returned to Washington with his mother on the day the army moved from City Point, and did not come back to the James River until the morning of the 6th of April."[14] You will find in the chapter narrative that Tad is mentioned in one message by Mrs. Lincoln and one by Mr. Lincoln, both of which make clear that the boy is with his father at the time.

A risk analysis of Grant's invitation to Lincoln to visit him on April 3 seems heavily loaded on the negative side. Grant had ridden over the route Lincoln would likely follow and knew that even though Union arms had been successful, there was no way that the captured sections had been fully secured. I am certain that throughout the night armed parties of Rebels prowled the area seeking to escape the Yankee net. Yet Grant felt that the danger was offset by the prospect of having his commander-in-chief on hand for what looked to be the final battle of the Petersburg campaign. Better yet, if Lee had departed by then, so much the better since the President could enter Rebel Petersburg. Still, for me, it remains a puzzling decision on Grant's part.

CHAPTER ELEVEN: MONDAY, APRIL 3, 1865

"I have had a sort of a sneaking idea for some days that you intended to do something like this."

April 3 is another day when the *Malvern* log is not the final word. It registers Admiral Porter leaving the ship at 1:30 p.m. and returning at 5:15 p.m. Porter says he accompanied the President to Petersburg in the morning. Grant does not identify Porter as present when he met with Lincoln. However, Grant aide Horace Porter (no relation) does mention the admiral being there, and a news piece filed from City Point at 9:00 a.m. records that Admiral Porter and Lincoln were about to visit the fallen citadel. So I believe that the weight of the evidence supports Porter entering the town with Lincoln. This leads me to conclude that Porter spent the night aboard *River Queen*, and after he and the President returned to City Point from visiting Petersburg the naval officer popped on (not logged) and off (logged at 1:30 p.m.) his flagship.

A familiar figure returns this day. Captain John Sanford Barnes and the USS *Bat* returned at 4:00 p.m., April 2, after transporting Major General William Tecumseh Sherman to North Carolina. The ship immediately tied up to a coal barge and the crew mustered to replenish her bunkers. That labor-intensive and gritty process lasted until 9:00 p.m., making April 3 Barnes's first full day back at City Point, still charged with keeping an eye on the President. I am sorry to say that his memoir for April 3 is a jumble of information, some on point, other parts hopelessly muddled in memory.

Accounts of Lincoln's visit to Petersburg are filled with other little errors that have a way of popping up in modern histories. The spot where he disembarked from the military railroad car is sometimes noted as Patrick Station or as Meade Station. Patrick was the choice as long as Lee held Petersburg, but it was no longer necessary once Grant entered the town. Meade Station is directly east of Petersburg and certainly a plausible candidate; however, the telegram sent to the President this morning by Robert states very clearly that his father was to come to *Hancock*

Station. I will add that Robert, who was notoriously tight-lipped about his experiences on Grant's staff, did confirm in 1879 to Alexander K. McClure that he "with a guard of cavalry escorted him [i.e., President Lincoln] to Petersburg & back to City Point."[15]

The makeup of the Lincoln party is also open to different interpretations. Admiral Porter would have us believe that he, the President, and Tad were the only ones along. Captain Barnes says he was there, and someone was later feeding information to William Crook – I suspect it was Captain Penrose. I believe that the determining piece of evidence is an 1890 letter to the *National Tribune* from one Jacob Buch, who identifies himself as a sergeant in the 5th United States Cavalry assigned to escort the President this day. A check with the National Park Service Civil War Soldiers and Sailors database confirms he is who he claims to be. His story recounts the kind of annoying circumstance that an overworked army sergeant would recall.

The route Lincoln followed for his Petersburg visit comes entirely from a letter written by Charles A. Clark to the Lincoln biographer Ida Tarbell in 1898. While other witnesses identify certain moments of the President's journey, the Clark letter is the only one that specifies the entire route. Clark was a boy at the time of Lincoln's visit and observed him briefly on the return leg of his trip. He studied the matter in succeeding years, as his letter includes material gleaned from Horace Porter and cites scenes that he could not have personally witnessed. I suspect he asked around and reconstructed the tour route from the information he gathered. When charted on a map it all makes perfect sense to me.

CHAPTER TWELVE: TUESDAY, APRIL 4, 1865
"It is well to be humble."

With Admiral Porter in charge of the President's journey to Richmond I am sure that an overland route was never considered. And what ever happened to the message sent to Major General Godfrey Weitzel alerting him to Lincoln's pending visit? Weitzel says it provided the wrong time and wrong place so he wasn't there to greet the President. One would think that a note of such historic importance would have been prominently preserved, but I have been unable to find a copy.

One mystery that I believe I have solved concerns the admiral's barge that carried Lincoln to Richmond. There is no standard model for such a craft; it is the name given to whatever small boat the admiral uses. I was able to consult with Dana Wegner, who is Curator of Ship Models at the Naval Surface Warfare Center in

Bethesda, Maryland. Fortunately for me, he is the kind of person who loves a challenge. I told him all that I knew. He provided me with the descriptive material I used and even worked up several pictures, some of which I used also. Wegner also said there had to be one additional crewman not previously listed, the coxswain, who steered and directed the rowers. This would have been a hand-picked team with well practiced skills for the smoothest and most efficient ride (ruling out using Marines to row). A crack boat crew was an officer's pride, and with the President as passenger Admiral Porter would have wanted the best.

I'm not surprised that when Porter wrote about this day, his encounter with Admiral Farragut was largely ignored (the boat is mentioned in his various accounts but not its illustrious passenger). To give the devil his due, all accounts (save one) from Farragut's side claim his ship passed Porter's without any need for assistance. Yet we know that when Porter left Drewry's Bluff his barge was being pulled by a tug holding a small Marine guard, and when he reaches Richmond the tug and the Marines are nowhere to be found. Detaching it to aid the steamship that Farragut had commandeered is the only scenario that makes sense. Besides, leaving a superior officer stranded while one undertakes a sight-seeing tour is just not a smart career move.

Exactly *where* Lincoln stepped ashore at Richmond has confused more than one writer. Had Admiral Porter carried out his original plan, the *River Queen* would have docked at the city's principal wharf area, known as "Rockett's" (named after an 18th-century gentleman who operated a ferry there). But, as you will find out, Porter's plan was pretty thoroughly scotched. National Park Service historian Mike Gorman has done an excellent job researching the matter and identifies that point where Lincoln came ashore as 17th and Dock Streets, a good mile *west* of Rockett's.

Further confusion comes from the low-key nature of Lincoln's arrival which went unnoticed by almost everyone. In contrast, when Porter's flagship at last reached Richmond at 4:35 p.m. and halted at Rockett's, she fired a 35-gun salute, which attracted a lot of attention. Observers not present put one and one together—the gunboat salute, Lincoln in town—leading them to conclude that he must have arrived on the *Malvern*, and they wrote it up that way. The only certified witness to Lincoln's arrival was the reporter Charles Coffin. In my narrative I have relied heavily on the news pieces he immediately filed for the *Boston Journal*, and less of his later writings about the incident.

I have generally eschewed quoting black dialogue as set down by white witnesses imitating minstrel show dialect. Gone too are most of the scenes set down by Admiral Porter, which are heavily freighted with dramatic emphasis and loaded with improbable dialogue. The evidence is that Lincoln said little on his walk from the James River to the Confederate White House and certainly not the florid passages whipped up by Porter, who, by the way, also essayed a postwar career as a novelist.

In this vein, I believe that one aspect of Porter's construction of the Lincoln walk was a product of his racist point of view. In his narrative, which portrays nearly empty streets that are almost instantly filled with black masses, there is the suggestion of a "jungle" telegraph to summon them. This is clearly a white man writing for a white audience at a time when blacks were often cast as exotic comic relief. While I agree that there was a crowd around Lincoln as he moved from the riverbank to the Confederate executive mansion, I do not believe it approached the large swarm that Porter describes. Certainly all within earshot would have been drawn by the calls and cries of the first dozen or so to meet the President, but much beyond that seems a stretch to me. My guess is that a crowd of 75-150, pressed into an untidy mass by streets narrowed with debris, did encircle the President's party, and from inside the ring the view would have been quite daunting. Once everyone was at the White House, I am willing to triple that number.

(A pause here to express my gratitude and admiration for Mike Gorman, a Richmond-based historian on the staff of the National Park Service. He has studied Lincoln's visit for years and walked the route many times thanks to the tours he guides. He readily shared his research materials with me and was ready to discuss any aspect of Lincoln's time in the city. There is much we agree upon, and a few things over which we differ. Mike accepts a crowd number swelling to the thousands on this day, while I am more comfortable with 500 or so.)

Symbolic events of Lincoln's visit to Richmond became one of the principal elements in the popular story of his life emerging in the next decades that consistently reshaped what actually happened to craft an idealized scenario of the great martyred president. The national narrative needed the powerful image of the U.S. President sitting in the chair of Jefferson Davis, so even though he never made it to the Rebel Chief Executive's second floor office area, the "fact" of Lincoln doing so became chiseled in stone and continues to seduce modern historians. The transformed story also demanded his presence in the halls of the Confederate Congress. Once aboard the carriage on April 4, a by now very weary Lincoln took a slow ride to the *Malvern*, not getting out until he reached the warship. Yet the Lincoln legend demanded that he enter that building. Among those convinced it had to be so was the fine popular historian Richard Hanser, who proclaimed it the "clearest symbol of all" that the South was defeated.

Another Admiral Porter concoction concerns the political figure named Duff Green. The admiral's account records quite a dust-up between the two on April 5 aboard the *Malvern*. Green's own account is quite different. His version resets the date to April 4, when he says that his meeting with Lincoln took place "in the presence of Judge Campbell."[16] Since we know that Campbell brought just one "friend" with him to his April 5 Lincoln meeting and it wasn't Green, he must have been with the small group at the Confederate White House.

While Porter paints an exchange filled with rancor, Green's is far more tempered and civil. Lincoln and Green had been friends before the war; they had never crossed swords though they had disagreed, but always with mutual respect—a quality that appears to have been generally present in the room on April 4. According to Green's grandson, "Gen. Green knew and admired Mr. Lincoln before his election to the Presidency, and his admiration continued to the day of his death." The Green that Porter describes on April 5 is not the Green who told his daughter right after the assassination that it was "the greatest misfortune which could have happened to the South," adding that "Mr. Lincoln could do more, and I believe, would have done more to make peace, than any other man."[17]

Chapter Thirteen: Wednesday, April 5, 1865

"I cannot bring myself to believe that any human
being lives who would do me any harm."

This chapter presents a carefully reshaped narrative of Lincoln's April 5 activities in Richmond containing scenes and incidents not previously associated with the day's events. Contrary to the traditional story that he remained aboard the *Malvern* this morning before departing for City Point, there is evidence Lincoln made a brief run ashore, though it remains circumstantial. Admiral Porter had vowed the previous evening that "the President should go nowhere again, while under my charge, unless I was with him and had a guard of marines." An examination of the USS *Malvern* logbook reveals this entry for April 5: "A marine guard of 24 men left the ship as guard to the President."[18] My efforts to locate more details about this escort mission from Marine historical records were unsuccessful.

Research turned up two items that added provocative tidbits to the mix. In the *Boston Evening Transcript* for March 27, 1913, I found an obituary notice for Aaron Vanderbilt, who was an ensign aboard the *Malvern* on April 5. Listing his wartime accomplishments the notice says that he "was part of the escort of President Lincoln at the fall of Richmond." Then, in a 1906 biographical collection titled *Men of Mark in America* I found a summary for Silas Wright Terry (also a *Malvern* officer on April 5) that describes him as "one of the suite accompanying President Lincoln when he entered Richmond."[19] I found no other naval officers making this claim.

Both men enjoyed distinguished postwar careers. Terry remained in the navy to retire with the rank of rear admiral, while Vanderbilt became a civilian marine engineer and shipping executive. Neither, as far as I can tell, ever spoke or wrote about their Lincoln association, and it only appears in their obituary/biographical copy. We know from Coffin's account that neither of these men accompanied Lincoln on April 4. It makes sense that Admiral Porter would have assigned different individuals to escort duty on April 5. He knew what an honor it was to participate in this historic event and would have spread the glory among his junior officers.

In untangling Porter's various memoirs, I identified a number of threads that could not apply to April 4. It is possible that they represent the expected liberties a storyteller takes with facts, but it is also possible that Porter was freely combining his memories of events for April 4 and 5, so I have pulled out those threads in this chapter.

I was skeptical that the "jungle telegraph" could have assembled "thousands" of Richmond's African-Americans to mob Lincoln on April 4. I see April 5 as an entirely different scenario. There have been ten or 12 hours for the word to spread throughout the area, so I think it far more likely that the crowds awaiting Lincoln this morning were substantially larger than those who just happened to be on hand April 4.

A final (and oddest) bit of circumstantial evidence is found in a 1915 biography of Tad Lincoln by Frederic Lauriston Bullard. With no source citation, Bullard states that the President on April 5 "again came ashore . . . and spent several hours looking upon the desolation of the captured citadel."[20]

There are conflicting accounts regarding the means by which Lincoln returned to City Point. The *Malvern* can be ruled out, since her logbook places her at Rockett's until April 6. There is no evidence in the accounts of Captain Barnes or the log of the *Bat* that the vessel carried the President anywhere on April 5. From that same source and others we know that the *Bat* was off Rockett's at the end of April 4. Her April 5 log contains this entry: "At 12.30 President Lincoln came down the river. At 1 got underway & proceeded down the River as a convoy to the *River Queen*." This indicates that the *River Queen* was Lincoln's mode of transportation.

Two readily available sources offer an improbable alternative; namely, that Lincoln traveled in the admiral's barge and was towed back to City Point. This makes no sense for a number of reasons. Lincoln was transported in Admiral Porter's barge on April 4 *only* because every full-sized ship was gridlocked near Drewy's Bluff. By midday April 5 there were five or six U.S. Navy warships anchored near Rockett's. That Admiral Porter would have entrusted the President of the United States to a long ride in a towed rowboat fully exposed to the elements is asinine.

I do however think it likely that the President made a short journey by this means. None of the inventories of the ships anchored off Rockett's on April 5 mention the *River Queen*. My suspicion is that only determined warships could scrape past the Tree Hill Bridge at that time, and that Captain Bradford chose to park the *River Queen* below it rather than risk damaging his vessel. Porter must have known this since it would have been the only basis on which he would have let Lincoln leave Richmond in a towed barge—making a short hop to where everyone transferred onto the *River Queen*.

And in the "no good deed goes unpunished" category, Lincoln's gesture giving Confederate General and POW Rufus Barringer a personal card requesting considerations be given him actually backfired. In the wake of Lincoln's assassination, the card made the Rebel prisoner what current law enforcement would call a person of interest. He was questioned several times for a possible role in the conspiracy and held back from release until July 1865.

Chapter Fourteen: Thursday, April 6, 1865

"Nothing I have done is to interfere with you in your work."

Admiral Porter related a story about Lincoln thoughtlessly dashing off the note to General Weitzel sanctioning Judge Campbell's proposal to convene the Virginia legislature, which he sets on April 5 aboard the *Malvern*. Porter further claimed that he instantly recognized the folly of the President's action and persuaded him to withdraw it. The evidence presented in this chapter proves that Lincoln wrote the note on April 6 and entrusted it to former Senator Morton S. Wilkinson for delivery, making this another of the admiral's fictional embellishments to the historical record.

(It is worth noting here that about a decade after the war, Admiral Porter was a prominent party to a lawsuit filed to claim some $3,000,000 in prize money for vessels and material taken by the navy when Richmond fell. The suit made its way through the Federal judicial system until it reached the United States Supreme Court which, in 1883, agreed with a lower court ruling that Porter and the officers and men of the North Atlantic Squadron were ineligible to file such a claim.)

Regarding the unexpected arrival of Vice President Johnson at City Point, early biographers of the soon-to-be seventeenth president wrote of his traveling at Lincoln's invitation and consulting with him. There is no evidence the two met at this time or that Lincoln had summoned him. Presidents and vice presidents then were paired for political reasons, not personal compatibility.

Lincoln's receipt of Grant's telegram very late this day is a guess on my part. The general sent a message to one of his corps commanders at 4:20 p.m. from Jetersville before riding a few miles south to Burkesville, which had a telegraph station in operation this night. The information in Grant's note contains no reference to the Battle at Sailor's Creek, which ended at nightfall. There is no evidence that this note was handed to Lincoln while he was in the City Point telegraph office this evening, but the *Malvern* log shows Lieutenant Colonel Bowers delivering dispatches at 11:00 p.m. I believe that only Grant's note (addressed to Bowers) would have justified the personal delivery.

CHAPTER FIFTEEN: FRIDAY, APRIL 7, 1865

"Every day brings new reason for confidence in the future."

The evidence indicates that Lincoln received his first message from Grant announcing the Sailor's Creek victory during the early morning hours of April 7; further, he penned his little introduction and sent both off to the City Point telegraph office before leaving the *Malvern*, where he had spent the night. His telegram bears a dispatch time of 8:35 a.m. The *Malvern* log registers the President and Admiral Porter leaving the ship at 8:30. Even though the *Malvern* log doesn't show any dispatches arriving during the late night and early morning watches, clearly not every delivered message was noted.

Grant's original message is time-stamped 11:15 p.m. from Burkeville, which had just been patched into the field telegraph network. Allowing time for transmission and deciphering, it was likely 2 or 3:00 a.m. before it was at City Point. I don't believe that a message of this importance would have been withheld from the President until he arrived in person, though the actual delivery may have been delayed to let him sleep to perhaps 5 or 6:00 a.m. Plenty of time for him to read it, write his preface, and then courier it back to the telegraph office, well before he stepped ashore at around 8:40 a.m.

Some accounts place the brief vignette involving Sara Pryor and her husband, Roger, on April 3 during Lincoln's first visit to Petersburg. I don't believe that the President lingered in town after meeting with Grant on that occasion. By April 7, Federal authorities would have been well aware that Pryor was present under house arrest, the kind of casual information that could have been passed to the President after his return from Richmond. Mrs. Pryor's recollection is ambiguous enough to fit into either day, though she does mention Lincoln's visit in the same breath as one from Congressman Washburne, who *only* comes to City Point after hearing the news that Richmond had fallen.

Chapter Sixteen: Saturday, April 8, 1865

"I came here to take by the hand the men who have
achieved our glorious victories."

The little troop review Lincoln conducted this morning at City Point rests on the slender reed of a passing reference in Mrs. Keckly's memoir. She writes, "The day before we started on our journey back to Washington, Mr. Lincoln was engaged in reviewing the troops in camp."[21] I could not find any corroboration in official orders or soldier recollections but decided to accept it. My reason has to do with an awkward transfer of authority that occurred this day as responsibility for City Point passed from the Army of the Potomac to the Army of the James. Brevet Brigadier General Charles H. T. Collis (Army of the Potomac) initially refused to relinquish authority because he lacked orders through his chain of command to do so. It took a flurry of messages among Major General Weitzel (Army of the James), his subordinates, and Grant's staff to clarify matters. Collis was finally ordered to transport his men west for prisoner escort duty, so they would have been boarding the trains in the area Lincoln had to traverse. It does not strain credulity to imagine that Collis (who had spent pleasant times with the President during his visit) organized an impromptu review near the City Point train station and visible from the *River Queen*.

Concerning Lincoln's visit to the Depot Field Hospital this day, I confess I was skeptical of the axe story when I first encountered it in various post-Civil War newspaper columns, usually appearing in February issues, and usually being a story with a moral to it. Then I discovered a May 2, 1865, letter from Dr. George Mendenhall, who arrived at the hospital just after Lincoln had departed and got all his stories fresh from eyewitness sources. He mentions the axe story. Further digging uncovered a 2008 press release from the Abraham Lincoln Presidential Library announcing it had acquired the item in question, an identification verified by an affidavit accompanying the tool from the hospital director Dr. George B. Parker that reads, "I hereby certify that with this axe Abraham Lincoln, late President of the United States, did, on the Saturday before his assassination, chop a twenty inch white oak log in rear of my quarters at the Depot Field Hospital, Army of the Potomac City Point VA."[22] I am a skeptic no more.

My layout of the Depot Field Hospital is speculative, drawn in part from the work of National Park historian Donald C. Pfanz, who produced a well-researched study of the Depot Field Hospital in 1988. Based on his rough layout and the accounts I have found describing Lincoln's tour, I believe he visited the corps hospitals in this order: Second, Fifth, Ninth, and Sixth.

In an age when people were as apt to bow as clasp hands when they met, Lincoln's hand-shakings were an integral part of the man. His gesture on this day was not perfunctory, but an expression of sympathy and honor from his heart to the men who had sacrificed a portion of their lives to reunite a broken nation. In the simple act of a handshake, Lincoln was affirming for each Union soldier the righteousness of their cause, and for the Southerners he encountered, his firm grip said clearly, "Welcome back *to the Union.*"

It took a little investigation to determine the time of Lincoln's departure from City Point. Captain Barnes states that the President's boat left this morning. Given the multiple witnesses to Lincoln's afternoon visit to the Depot Field Hospital this cannot be true. The Marquis de Chambrun sets the time at 10:00 p.m., while the log of the USS *Bat* notes that the little convoy set out at 11:15 p.m. I believe that the Marquis confused the end of the soiree with the actual departure, it then taking an hour more for the ships to get underway. A brief news piece in the April 10 edition of the *Washington Evening Star* announcing the President's arrival says that the group "left City Point at 11 o'clock p.m. Saturday."[23]

Chapter Seventeen: Sunday, April 9, 1865
"I think we are near the end at last."

Details of the President's journey back to Washington come from the logbook of the USS *Bat*, with time calculations made for the period at the end of the journey when the gunboat suffered more engine problems and lagged well behind the *River Queen.*

Lincoln's receipt of the news of Lee's surrender was a powerful moment for him. I am surprised that most histories make so little of it. A few are misdirected by the Crook account which has the news coursing through the city streets when the President's boat docks at 6:00 p.m. A neat trick. Grant's message announcing the surrender (time dated 4:30 p.m.) was answered by the Secretary of War at 9:30 p.m. It strains belief that Stanton would not have responded the instant he was given the news, and despite the postwar recollections of one of Grant's telegraphers that the message went through almost instantaneously, it seems clear that the transmission took time. This timing is confirmed by accounts of Lincoln's visit to his injured Secretary of State; he arrives around 7:00 p.m., spends about half an hour, and leaves. According to Seward's son and daughter, news of Grant's success reaches them at 10:00 p.m.

The significance of Lincoln's presence at the front throughout this dramatic period was ably assessed by the editorial writer for the *New York Sun*, who wrote in its April 4 edition, "This is the first time in the history of war that the President has been personally present to encourage and animate the soldiers, and the fact that in this instance he personally consulted with his military chiefs before the battle, eagerly watched every fluctuation of the tide during its entire course, and personally reported to the country the progress of the great struggle, shows how anxiously he regarded it."[24]

Marine Muster Roll, USS *Malvern*

Below is a muster roll of a detachment of officers, non-commissioned officers, drummers, fifers, and privates, of the United States Marines Stationed on the *Malvern* from the April 1-30, 1865:

Orderly Sgt. William J. Givin

Sergeant George W. Armstrong

Corporal George W. Megillian

Corporal William E. Savage

Musician William Logue

Musician William Mahoney

Private Jacob Coon

Private Thomas Cooney

Private James P. Finley

Private George W. Harris

Private William Horan

Private Andrew J. Joy

Private John Kelley

Private Patrick Kelly

Private Peter Kierman

Private Leonard Martin

Private George W. Neville

Private Joseph Newman

Private Joseph McCollongh

Private William McGinnis

Private Thomas Pritchard

Private William Shannon

Private Henry Smith

Private Charles Sullivan

Private George Thompson

Private Thomas Taylor

Private Thomas Williams

Private Joseph Wilson

Private Aaron Watts

Private George Weeks

Chapter Notes

Preface

1. Basler (ed.), *Collected Works*, 7:282. Foner, "If Lincoln hadn't died," *American Heritage*, volume 58, no. 6, Winter 2009, 47. Basler (ed.), *Collected Works*, 5:537.
2. Basler (ed.), *Collected Works*, 8:333.
3. Basler (ed.), *Collected Works*, 7:18-19, 4:202.

Chapter One: January-March, 1865

"It was an immense relief to him to be away from Washington."

1. Pease and Randall (eds.), *Diary of Orville Hickman Browning*, (entry for February 23, 1865), 2:8. *The Oregonian*, June 2, 1895. Reinhard H. Luthin, *The Real Abraham Lincoln*, 593. *Chicago Tribune*, March 22, 1865. Benjamin P. Thomas, *Abraham Lincoln: A Biography*, 506.
2. Oates, *With Malice Toward None*, 376, 409.
3. Donald, *Lincoln*, 550. Burlingame, *Abraham Lincoln: A Life* (online manuscript version), 3867.
4. Basler (ed.), *Collected Works*, 7:394.
5. Oates, *With Malice Toward None*, 406-406.
6. "Warburton" Letter, March 27, 1864 {sic} in *The Statesman* (Yonkers, New York), April 6, 1865. Simpson, *Ulysses S. Grant: Triumph Over Adversity*, 404.
7. Simon (ed.), *Papers of Ulysses S. Grant*, 14:188.
8. Simon (ed.), *Papers of Ulysses S. Grant*, 14:156.
9. Simon (ed.), *Papers of Ulysses S. Grant*, 14: 173.
10. Glatthaar, *Partners in Command*, 138.

11. Glatthaar, *Partners in Command*, 182.

12. Simon (ed.), *Papers of Ulysses S. Grant*, 14: 80, 115-117.

13. Simon (ed.), *The Personal Memoirs of Julia Dent Grant*, 141-142.

14. Basler (ed.), *Collected Works*, 8:223-224. Simon (ed.), *The Personal Memoirs of Julia Dent Grant*, 142.

15. *OR* 46/3: 50.

16. Basler (ed.), *Collected Works*, 8:367.

17. Emerson, *Giant in the Shadows,* 96. Basler (ed.), *Collected Works*, 8:369.

18. *OR* 46/3: 62.

19. *ORN* 10:548-550. Barnes, *Egotistigraphy*, 252.

20. Barnes, "With Lincoln," 517-518.

21. Barnes, "With Lincoln," 518.

22. Barnes, "With Lincoln," 518.

23. Basler (ed.), *Collected Works*, 8:372.

24. Sandburg and Angle, *Mary Lincoln*, 224.

25. Penrose, "Lincoln's Visit to Richmond," 307.

26. Temple, *Lincoln's Travels on the River Queen*, 15.

27. *Daily National Republican*, March 24, 1865. *Washington Evening Star*, March 24, 1865.

28. Bullard, *Tad and his Father*, 70. *The Holley Standard* (New York), February 12, 1931.

29. *OR* 47/1: 1055.

30. Johnson, *Story of a Great Conflict*, 560.

31. Johnson, *Story of a Great Conflict*, 563, 565.

32. Johnson, *Story of a Great Conflict*, 571. Gordon, *Reminiscences*, 403.

33. Gordon, *Reminiscences*, 405, 406.

34. Turner and Turner, *Mary Todd Lincoln*, 210.

35. *OR* 46/3: 86-87. Barnes, *Egotistigraphy*, 253.

36. Basler (ed.), *Collected Works*, 373.

37. Barnes, "With Lincoln," 521. "Warburton" Letter, March 27, 1864 {sic} in *The Statesman* (Yonkers, New York), April 6, 1865.

38. Porter, *Campaigning with Grant*, 402.

39. Basler (ed.), *Collected Works*, 8:374n.

40. *Daily Morning Chronicle,* 5/30/64.

41. Hopkins, *Seventh Regiment Rhode Island Volunteers*, 248.

42. *New York Herald Tribune,* August 1, 1926.

43. Simon (ed.), *The Personal Memoirs of Julia Dent Grant*, 142.

44. Simon (ed.), *The Personal Memoirs of Julia Dent Grant*, 142.

45. *Troy Daily Times* (New York)*,* December 31, 1877.

46. Simon (ed.), *Papers of Ulysses S. Grant*, 14: 174, 187, 203. Grant, *Personal Memoirs*, 2:426, 427. *OR* 46/1: 427.

47. Grant, *Personal Memoirs*, 2:423. (Some accounts substitute the word "nubbin'" for "ear," but the language in the quote is as Grant recalled it.)

48. Crook, *Through Five Administrations*, 41. Young, *Around the World with General Grant*, 2:358.

49. *Daily Illinois State Journal*, February 17, 1928.

50. Pearce (ed.), *Diary of Captain Henry A. Chambers*, 252.

51. Jones, "Last Days of the Army of Northern Virginia," *Southern Historical Society Papers*, 21:71. Day, *A True History of Co. I*, 95. Pearce (ed.), *Diary of Captain Henry A. Chambers*, 252-254. Trudeau, *Last Citadel*, 330.

52. Gordon, *Reminiscences*, 395.

Chapter Two: Saturday, March 25, 1865
"He typified the very Union itself."

1. Gordon, *Reminiscences*, 407.

2. *Louisiana Capitolian*, September 6, 1881. Walker, "Gordon's Assault," *SHSP 31*, 24.

3. Thomas, *Doles-Cook Brigade*, p. 42.

4. Gordon, *Reminiscences*, 407-410.

5. Walker, "Gordon's Assault," *SHSP 31*, 25. London, Letter of March 25, 1865 (SHSC).

6. Walker, "Gordon's Assault," *SHSP 31*, 25.

7. Barrier, "Breaking Grant's Line," *CV 33*, 417.

8. *Watertown Daily Times* (New York), April 18, 1915.

9. Gordon, *Reminiscences*, 411.

10. Porter, *Campaigning*, 404.

11. Grant, *Papers*, 14:223n.

12. Chambers, *Diary*, 253.

13. Kilmer, "Assault at Stedman," *Century* 34/5, 787. Huyette, Reminiscences.

14. Gordon, *Reminiscences*, 411.

15. Chambers, *Diary*, 253.

16. Thomas, *Doles-Cook Brigade*, 42. *Louisiana Capitolian*, September 6, 1881.

17. Thomas, *Doles-Cook Brigade*, 42.

18. Trudeau, *Last Citadel*, 351. *Wisconsin State Journal*, April 4, 1865.

19. Gordon, *Reminiscences*, 412. Gordon account in Davis, *Rise & Fall*, 654. Johnson, *Story of a Great Conflict*, 576.

20. *OR* 46/3, 114-115.

21. Barnes, "With Lincoln," 521.

22. Porter, *Campaigning*, 404.

23. Reverend G. H. Hartupee letter (dated April 18) in the *Elyria Independent Democrat*, May 3, 1865.

24. "Warburton" Letter, March 27, 1864 {sic} in *The Statesman* (Yonkers, New York), April 6, 1865.

25. Barnes, "With Lincoln," 521. Barnes, *Egotistigraphy*, 254.

26. Barnes, "With Lincoln," 521.

27. *Roman Citizen,* March 17, 1865.

28. Porter, Campaigning, 212. "Warburton" Letter, March 27, 1864 {sic} in *The Statesman* (Yonkers, New York), April 6, 1865.

29. *Roman Citizen,* March 17, 1865.

30. Barnes, "With Lincoln," 521.

31. Kautz, Memoirs, 103.

32. Adelaide W. Smith, "Brooklyn Army Nurse's Recollections of Lincoln," *Brooklyn Daily Eagle,* February 12, 1909. Badeau, *Grant in Peace*, 356-357.

33. Meade, *Letters*, II:268.

34. Lyman, *Meade's headquarters*, 324-325.

35. Lyman, *Meade's headquarters*, 324.

36. Martin W. Brett, *Experiences of a Georgia Boy*, 34. "The Charge on Fort Stedman" [Confederate Veteran Papers/Duke University].

37. Basler, *Collected Works*, 8:374.

38. Barnes, "With Lincoln," 522.

39. McBride, *In the Ranks*, 163.

40. Cheek, *History Sauk Riflemen*, 158.

41. *The Northern Budget* (Troy, New York); April 9, 1911.

42. *The National Tribune,* August 13, 1903.

43. *New York Herald*, March 28, 1865. *Washington Daily Morning Chronicle*, March 30, 1865.

44. Jason T. Butler letter, March 27, 1865, *The Lincolnian*, volume VI, number 1 (September-October 1987)

45. *The Northern Budget* (Troy, New York); April 9, 1911. Jason T. Butler letter, March 27, 1865, *The Lincolnian*, volume VI, number 1 (September-October 1987). *The National Tribune,* August 13, 1903.

46. Anson Buck, letter of March 26, 1865.

47. Porter, *Campaigning with Grant*, 406. *The National Tribune,* February 26, 1920. Lewis, *History of Battery E*, 410.

48. Quoted in Greene, *Breaking the Backbone*, 176. Lyman, *Diary*, 350.

49. Barnes, *With Lincoln,* 521. H.M. Hammond, "From the Sixth Corps," Wisconsin *State Journal*, April 4, 1865.

50. Barnes, *With Lincoln,* 522.

51. Porter, *Campaigning with Grant*, 406.

52. Porter, *Campaigning with Grant,* 407-408. Barnes, *With Lincoln,* 522.

53. Numbers from B&G Stedman, 49; B&G Western Front, 48; Greene, *Breaking the Backbone*, 182-183. Meade, *Life and Letters*, 268.

CHAPTER THREE: SUNDAY, MARCH 26, 1865
"How grateful I feel to be with the boys."

1. Basler (ed.), *Collected Works*, 8:375. *OR*, 46/3:109.
2. Barnes, "With Lincoln," 522.
3. Sheridan, *Personal Memoirs*, 2:126, 127-28.
4. Sheridan, *Personal Memoirs*, 2:128. Grant, *Personal Memoirs*, 2:438.
5. Porter, *Campaigning with Grant*, 410.
6. Barnes, "With Lincoln," 522.
7. *OR* 46/3: 173. Barnes, "With Lincoln," 522.
8. Porter, *Campaigning with Grant*, 413; Sheridan, *Personal Memoirs*, 2:130. *New York World*, February 22, 1870.
9. Bates, *Lincoln in the Telegraph Office*, 67. Beckwith, "Grant's Shadow," *New York Sun*, April 27, 1913. Sheridan actually stood five foot five.
10. Barnes, "With Lincoln," 522. John Heyl Vincent letter, March 27, 1865.
11. Porter, *Campaigning with Grant*, 413-14. Sheridan, *Personal Memoirs*, 2: 130-31.
12. *Malvern* log, March 26, 1865.
13. Barnes, "With Lincoln," 523.
14. Porter, *Incidents and Anecdotes*, 284.
15. Simon (ed.), *The Personal Memoirs of Julia Dent Grant*, 148.
16. Michael J. Callinan, writing as "Garryowen" in the *New York Irish-American,* week ending April 8, 1865. USS *Monadnock* deck log, March 26, 1865. *The Statesman* (Yonkers, New York), February 16, 1911. USS *Casco* deck long, March 26, 1865. Barnes, *Egotistigraphy*, 256.
17. Porter, *Campaigning with Grant*, 413, 413-14.
18. Barnes, "With Lincoln," 523. Wright, "Mary O'Melia," 10.
19. Badeau, *Grant in Peace*, 358. Simon (ed.), *The Personal Memoirs of Julia Dent Grant*, 146.
20. Badeau, *Grant in Peace*, 359.
21. *New York Herald,* March 29, 1865.
22. Redkey, *Grand Army*, 218, 291.
23. Redkey, *Grand Army*, 147. Blackett (ed.), *Thomas Morris Chester*, 276-77. *Philadelphia Inquirer,* March 29, 1865. *Christian Recorder*, May 6, 1865.
24. Basler (ed.), *Collected Works,* 5:423, 6:24, 148. *Springfield Republican*, June 13, 1890.
25. *Sixty-Seventh Ohio Veteran Volunteer Infantry*, 18. Simon (ed.), *The Personal Memoirs of Julia Dent Grant*, 146-47.

26. Porter, *Campaigning with Grant,* 413. Barnes, "With Lincoln," 524.

27. *The Story of One Regiment,* 301. Cunningham, *Three Years with the Adirondack Regiment,* 166. Walraven diary, March 26, 1865.

28. Kreutzer, *Notes and Observations,* 299.

29. Jesse Grant, *Days of my Father,* 23.

30. Wharff, *From Chapin's Farm to Appomattox,* 232. *New York Herald,* March 29, 1865. Browne, *Every-Day Life of Abraham Lincoln,* 562.

31. *The Press* (Philadelphia), March 29, 1865. Beecher, *History of the First Light Battery Connecticut Volunteers,* 653.

32. Simon (ed.), *The Personal Memoirs of Julia Dent Grant,* 147.

33. Porter, *Campaigning with Grant,* 414-16.

34. Porter, "Lincoln and Grant," 944. Simon (ed.), *Papers of Ulysses S. Grant,* 14:211.

35. Young, *Around the World with General Grant,* 301.

36. Barnes, "With Lincoln," 524.

37. Simon (ed.), *Papers of Ulysses S. Grant,* 14:229.

Chapter Four: Monday, March 27, 1865

"You are joking, General."

1. *Malvern* log, March 27, 1865. *ORN,* 12: 84.

2. Barnes, "With Lincoln," 742.

3. Barnes, "With Lincon," 524.

4. Barnes, "With Lincoln," 742.

5. H. A. Risley, "Gen. Grant's Persistency," *Fredonia Censor* (New York), August 12, 1885.

6. John Heyl Vincent letter, March 27, 1865.

7. Coffin, *Freedom Triumphant,* 400; *The Boys of '61,* 512.

8. Barnes, *Egotistigraphy,* 259-60.

9. De Forest, *Random Sketches and Wandering Thoughts,* 153. Coburn, *Moses Greely Parker, M.D.,* 67.

10. Parker, *Recollections of Lincoln,* 18.

11. De Forest, *Random Sketches and Wandering Thoughts,* 152. Parker, *Recollections of Lincoln,* 18.

12. Thompson, "Got Dinner for the President," *National Tribune,* December 22, 1910. Parker, *Recollections of Lincoln,* 19.

13. Basler (ed.), *Collected Works,* 8: 375.

14. Sparks (ed.), *Inside Lincoln's Army,* 483.

15. *Manufacturers and Farmers Journal* (Providence, Rhode Island), March 30, 1865.

16. Barrett, *Sherman's March Through the Carolinas,* 47-48.

17. Korn, *Pursuit to Appomattox,* 52. Barrett, *Sherman's March Through the Carolinas,* 56.

18. Barrett, *Sherman's March Through the Carolinas,* 120.

19. Underwood and Buel, *Battles and Leaders*, 4:257. Sherman, *Memoirs,* 2: 179. 240.

20. Simpson and Berlin (eds.), *Sherman's Civil War*, 828.

21. Gray and Ropes, *War Letters*, 465. *New York Herald*, March 31, 1865.

22. *New York Herald,* March 30, 1865.

23. *Rome Daily Sentinel,* April 4, 1865. *New York Herald,* March 30, 1865.

24. Porter, *Campaigning with Grant,* 417. Tilney, *My Life in the Army*, 196. *Manufacturers and Farmers Journal* (Providence, Rhode Island), March 30, 1865.

25. Grant, *Personal Memoirs,* 2:430. Sherman, *Memoirs*, 2:324.

26. Sherman, *Memoirs,* 2:324-25. Porter, *Campaigning with Grant*, 419.

27. Sherman, *Memoirs,* 2:324-25.

28. Porter, *Campaigning with Grant,* 418.

29. Sparks (ed.), *Inside Lincoln's Army,* 484. Porter, *Incidents and Ancedotes,* 316.

30. Barnes, "With Lincoln," 743.

31. Porter, *Campaigning with Grant*, 420.

32. *Boston Evening Journal*, March 31, 1865.

33. Sheridan, *Personal Memoirs*, 2: 132-33.

34. *Story of One Regiment*, 309. *Naples Record,* July 22, 1925.

CHAPTER FIVE: TUESDAY, MARCH 28, 1865

"You have never found fault with me."

1. Sheridan, *Personal Memoirs*, 2:133.

2. Agassiz (ed.), *Meade's Headquarters,* 327.

3. Beckwith, "Memoirs of Grant's Shadow, *New York Sun*, April 20, 1913.

4. John R. Hamilton letter, March 28, 1865. *New York World,* March 31, 1865.

5. Sherman, *Personal Memoirs,* 2:325. Simon (ed.), *Papers of Ulysses S. Grant,* 14:240.

6. Basler (ed.), *Collected Works,* 8:376.

7. Porter, *Campaigning with Grant,* 423.

8. Sherman letter, January 13, 1868.

9. Grant, *Personal Memoirs,* 2:458-459.

10. Porter, *Naval History of the Civil War,* 794.

11. Porter, *Incidents and Anecdotes*, 314. Porter, *Campaigning with Grant,* 423-24. Arnold, *Life of Abraham Lincoln,* 422. Sherman, "Address of General Sherman," *Eighteenth Annual Re-Union, Society of The Army of the Potomac,* 65.

12. Sherman, *Personal Memoirs,* 2:326.

13. Porter, *Naval History*, 794. *Sacramento Daily Union,* June 28, 1865.

14. Browne, *The Every-Day Life of Abraham Lincoln*, 565-66.

15. Fellman, *Citizen Sherman*, 147.

16. Sherman, *Personal Memoirs,* 2:327.

17. Porter, "Lincoln and Grant," 945.

18. Sherman, *Personal Memoirs,* 2: 327.

19. Sherman, *Address to the Eighteenth Reunion of the Society of the Army of the Potomac,* 64.

20. Dowdey and Manarin, *Wartime Papers of Robert E. Lee*, 919.

21. Simon (ed.), *Papers of Ulysses S. Grant*, 14:243.

22. Berry diary, entry for March 28, 1865.

Chapter Six: Wednesday, March 29, 1865

"Your success is my success."

1. *OR* 46/3, 229.

2. Agassiz (ed.), *Meade's Headquarters*, 329. Rogers: *History of the 189th Regiment*, 99.

3. Newhall, "With Sheridan," 298. Cheney, *History of the Ninth Regiment*, 255. Denison, *Sabres and Spurs*, 451. Humphreys, *Camp Field Hospital*, 232. Lang, *Loyal West Virginia*, 169.

4. Tobie, "Personal Recollections of General Sheridan," 21-22.

5. Simon (ed.), *The Personal Memoirs of Julia Dent Grant*, 149.

6. Porter, *Campaigning with Grant*, 424-25.

7. Porter, *Campaigning with Grant*, 425. Simon (ed.), *The Personal Memoirs of Julia Dent Grant*, 149.

8. Skilton, "Two Great Republicans." Porter, "Lincoln and Grant," p. 946. The source identifying Rawlins is Richardson, *Personal History of U.S. Grant*, 467.

9. Skilton, "Two Great Republicans." Porter, *Campaigning with Grant,* 425-26. Badeau, *Military History of U.S. Grant*, 452.

10. Dowdey and Manarin, *Wartime Papers of Robert E. Lee*, 920.

11. *ORN* 12:175. Porter, *Incidents and Anecdotes*, 291-92.

12. Chamberlin, *The Passing of the Armies*, 47.

13. Porter, *Campaigning with Grant*, 426.

14. *Philadelphia Inquirer,* April 1, 1865.

15. Simon (ed.), *Papers of Ulysses S. Grant,* 14:248n.

16. *OR* 46/1: 847, 848. *New York Herald*, April 1, 1865.

17. *Baldwinsville Gazette & Farmer's Journal*, June 7, 1894.

18. *Baldwinsville Gazette & Farmer's Journal*, June 7, 1894.

19. Simon (ed.), *Papers of Ulysses S. Grant,* 14: 253.

20. Basler (ed.), *Collected Works*, 8:376-77n.

21. Basler (ed.), *Collected Works*, 8:376.

22. Basler (ed.), *Collected Works*, 8:377n.

23. *OR* 46/3:241.

24. Hagar letters, March 30, 1865. *Boston Journal,* April 4, 1865.

25. *Roman Citizen*, April 14, 1865.

26. Basler (ed.), *Collected Works*, 8:377.

27. Newhall, "With Sheridan in Lee's last campaign," 302. Guelzo, "Holland's Informants," 28.

Chapter Seven: Thursday, March 30, 1865

"I dislike to leave without seeing nearer to the end."

1. *New York Sun,* March 31, 1865.

2. Basler (ed.), *Collected Works*, 8:377.

3. Woodward, *History of the One Hundred and Ninety-Eighth*, 38. Linn, *From Richmond to Appomattox,* 10. Haines, *History of the Men of Co. F*, 88. Willson, *Disaster, Struggle, Triumph*, 286.

4. Aubery, *Thirty-Sixth Wisconsin Infantry*, 213. McBride, *In the Ranks,* 171.

5. Mulholland, *Story of the 116th Regiment*, 335. Rogers, *History of the 189th Regiment*, 100-101. Thomas Campbell diary, March 30, 1865.

6. Freeman, *R.E. Lee*, 4:31.

7. *OR* 46/3: 327-28.

8. S.Collis, *A Woman's War Record*, 60.

9. Porter, *Incidents and Anecdotes*, 286. George H. Williams, "Lincoln and Grant," *The Oregonian*, June 2, 1895.

10. Porter, *Campaigning with Grant*, 428.

11. Sheridan, *Personal Memoirs*, 2:145. Porter, *Campaigning with Grant*, 428-29.

12. Sheridan, *Personal Memoirs*, 2:145. Porter, *Campaigning with Grant*, 429. Simon (ed.), *Papers of Ulysses S. Grant*, 14:273.

Chapter Eight: Friday, March 31, 1865

"General Grant telegraphed me as follows."

1. *OR* 46/3:334.

2. Basler (ed.), *Collected Works*, 8:379.

3. *Sacramento Daily Union*, May 8, 1865.

4. Caldwell, *History of a Brigade of South Carolinians*, 270-71.

5. McBride, *In the Ranks*, 179-180.

6. *New York World*, April 4, 1865. *New York Herald*, April 4, 1865. Calkins,"The Battle of Five Forks," 12.

7. Beckwith, "Lincoln's Shadow," *New York World*, April 6, 1913.

8. Beckwith, "Lincoln's Shadow," *New York World*, April 6, 1913.

9. Beckwith, "Lincoln's Shadow," *New York World*, April 20, 1913.

10. Beckwith, "Lincoln's Shadow," *New York World*, April 20, 1913.

11. Simon (ed.), *Papers of Ulysses S. Grant*, 14:273. Porter, *Incidents and Anecdotes*, 283-284.

12. Humphreys, *Field, Camp, Hospital and Prison*, 240-41.

13. Starr, *Union Cavalry in the Civil War*, 2:441. Davies, *General Sheridan*, 229.

14. *Philadelphia Inquirer*, May 16, 1864. *New York Times*, May 12, 1864. *New York Herald*, August 4, 1864.

15. Basler (ed.), *Collected Works*, 8:378.

16. *New York Times*, April 2, 1865. *Philadelphia Daily Evening Bulletin*, April 1, 1865. *Washington Daily National Republican*, April 4, 1865. *Oswego Commercial Advertiser*, April 10, 1865. Address by J.G. Holland, *Springfield Republican*, April 20, 1865. Hanser, "Mr. Lincoln visits Richmond," 10.

17. Porter, *Campaigning with Grant*, 432.

18. Simon (ed.), *Papers of Ulysses S. Grant*, 14:274.

Chapter Nine: Saturday, April 1, 1865

"Having no great deal to do here."

1. Schurz, Reminiscences, 3:110.

2. Basler (ed.), *Collected Works*, 8:379-80.

3. Basler (ed.), *Collected Works*, 8:381.

4. Basler (ed.), *Collected Works* - Supplement Two, 285.

5. Flanagan, *Life of General Gouverneur Kemble Warren*, 340.

6. Calkins, "Battle of Five Forks," 18.

7. *Warren Court of Inquiry*, 2:901.

8. Young, *Around the World with General Grant*, 301.

9. *New York Tribune*, October 24, 1880.

10. Basler (ed.), *Collected Works*, 8:379.

11. Lincoln Financial Foundation Collection, "Reminiscences about Abraham Lincoln," Linus E. Clark. *Lowville Journal and Republican* (New York), February 8, 1940. *Chatham* (New York) *Courier*, April 5, 1934.

12. *Peekskill Highland Democrat* (New York), February 20, 1909.

13. Basler (ed.), *Collected Works*, 7:253-254.

14. Calkins, "Battle of Five Forks," 41. Bearss and Calkins, *Battle of Five Forks*, 110. *New York Herald*, April 4, 1865.

15. Greene, *Breaking the Backbone of the Rebellion*, 241.

16. Rauscher, *Music on the March*, 225-26.

17. Simon (ed.), *Papers of Ulysses S. Grant*, 14: 295.

18. Basler (ed.), *Collected Works*, 8:380.

19. *Philadelphia Inquirer*, April 3, 1865.

20. Basler (ed.), *Collected Works*, 8:379.

21. Thomas (ed.), *Three Years with Grant*, 307.

22. Thomas (ed.), *Three Years with Grant*, 307.

23. Simon (ed.), *Papers of Ulysses S. Grant*, 14: 309-310.

24. Porter, *Campaigning with Grant*, 441-42.

25. Porter, *Campaigning with Grant*, 443.

26. *Peekskill Highland Democrat* (New York), February 20, 1909.

27. *The Republican Advocate* (Batavia, New York), April 18, 1865. *National Tribune*, June 18, 1891. Thomas Campbell diary, April 2, 1865. A.T. Brewer, *Sixty-First Regiment*, 133. George H. Hearne diary, April 2, 1865. *New York Herald*, April 5, 1865.

28. Crook, *Through Five Administrations*, 47. Rauscher, *Music on the March*, 226.

29. Charles Penrose (writing as "Army Officer"), "How Lincoln Received the News," *The Steuben Courier* (Bath, New York), March 6, 1885.

Chapter Ten: Sunday, April 2, 1865

"The country can never repay these men."

1. Catton, *A Stillness at Appomattox*, 198.

2. *Wisconsin State Journal*, April 15, 1865. Hazard Stevens, "The Storming of the Lines of Petersburg, *Papers of the Military Historical Society of Massachusetts*, 6:422.

3. Basler (ed.), *Collected Works*, 8:381.

4. Basler (ed.), *Collected Works*, 8:381.

5. Philadelphia *Inquirer*, April 3, 1865.

6. Trudeau, *Last Citadel*, 360.

7. Huyette, "Reminiscences of a Private," 1:98-99.

8. Stevens, "The Storming of the Lines of Petersburg," 6:423-4.

9. Greene, *Breaking the Backbone of the Rebellion*, relates this story in even more detail along with full citations, 300-301, 330-31 note 16.

10. *Philadelphia Inquirer*, April 5, 1865.

11. *OR* 46/3: 448, 449.

12. Basler (ed.), *Collected Works*, 8:282.

13. *Philadelphia Inquirer*, April 3, 1865.

14. Trudeau, *Last Citadel*, 370-375.

15. Dowdey and Manarin, *Wartime Papers of Robert E. Lee*, 924-25.

16. Rauscher, *Music on the March*, 226. Pavey, "When Admiral Porter Drove the President," *Boston Herald,* February 9, 1919.

17. *Malvern* log, April 2, 1865. Simon (ed.), *Papers of Ulysses S. Grant,* 14:319n.

Rockland (New York) *County Journal,* April 15, 1865.

18. *Washington Daily National Republican*, April 3, 1865. *New York Herald,* April 4, 1865.

19. Agassiz (ed), *Meade's Headquarters*, 334. *New York Tribune*, April 5, 1865.

20. Peck letter, April 3, 1865. *Philadelphia Inquirer*, April 5, 1865.

21. Porter, *Campaigning with Grant*, 446. *Philadelphia Inquirer*, April 5, 1865. *New York Herald,* April 5, 1865.

22. *OR* 46/3: 446.

23. Turner and Turner (eds.), *Mary Todd Lincoln*, 211.

24. Basler (ed.), *Collected Works*, 382-383.

25. Grant, *Personal Memoirs*, 2:453. Porter, *Campaigning with Grant*, 448. Simon (ed.), *Papers of Ulysses S. Grant*, 14:330.

26. *OR* 46/3:449.

27. Simon (ed.), *Papers of Ulysses S. Grant*, 14: 323.

28. Basler (ed.), *Collected Works*, 8:383.

29. Basler (ed.), *Collected Works*, 8:382-383.

30. *Philadelphia Inquirer,* April 3, 1865.

31. Basler (ed.), *Collected Works*, 8:384. Charles Penrose (writing as "Army Officer"), "How Lincoln Received the News," *The Steuben Courier* (Bath, New York), March 6, 1885.

32. *Philadelphia Inquirer,* April 3, 1865.

33. Porter, *Incidents and Anecdotes*, 292.

CHAPTER ELEVEN: MONDAY, APRIL 3, 1865

"I have had a sort of a sneaking idea for some days that
you intended to do something like this."

1. Dowdey and Manarin, *Wartime Papers of Robert E. Lee*, 926.

2. Gallagher (ed.), *Fighting for the Confederacy*, 518. Clark, *North Carolina Regiments*, 2:76.

3. Trudeau, *Last Citadel,* 403. Gallagher (ed.), *Fighting for the Confederacy,* 519.

4. Semmes, *Memoirs*, 811.

5. *Richmond Despatch*, November 24, 1895.

6. Porter, *Incidents and Anecdotes*, 293. Crook, *Through Five Administrations*, 48.

7. J.E. Henderson, "Entering Petersburg," *National Tribune*, August 10, 1911.

8. Bruce, "The Capture and Occupation of Richmond," 14:129. Lucius Mattison, "Memories of Richmond's Fall," *Oswego Palladium*, April 2, 1927. "C," *Vermont Watchman and State Journal*, April 14, 1865.

9. Bruce, "The Capture and Occupation of Richmond," 14: 135.

10. Woods, *Essays, Sketches and Stories*, 217. William T. Wixcey, "First Flag in Petersburg," *National Tribune*, July 4, 1907.

11. *OR* 46/3: 509.

12. Barnes, "With Lincoln," 744.

13. *OR* 46/3: 510.

14. *OR* 46/3: 509.

15. Porter, *Campaigning with Grant*, 449-450. Lowe (ed.), *Meade's Army*, 359.

16. Meade, *Life and Letters*, 2:269.

17. Jacob Buch, "Lincoln at City Point," *National Tribune*, October 23, 1890. [A letter from Buch containing similar content in Duke University's Perkins Library clearly describes the animal as a "lead horse."] Basler (ed.), *Collected Works*, 8:383n.

18. Cyrus Goodwin letters, April 2, 1865.

19. *Philadelphia Inquirer*, April 4, 1865.

20. Basler (ed.), *Collected Works*, 8:384.

21. *New York Herald*, April 5, 1865.

22. Plum, *The Military Telegraph during the Civil War*, 322.

23. Castine, *Sacramento Daily Union,* May 8, 1865.

24. Coffin, *Abraham Lincoln*, 498-500. Carlton does not relate this story in any of his newspaper pieces filed at this time.

25. Crook, *Through Five Administrations*, 48. Jacob Buch, "Lincoln at City Point," *National Tribune*, October 23, 1890.

26. Jacob Buch, "Lincoln at City Point," *National Tribune*, October 23, 1890.

27. Allen, *Forty-six Months with the Fourth Rhode Island,* 352.

28. *History of the Thirty-Fifth Regiment Massachusetts Volunteers,* 394.

29. Pope, Diary, U.S.Army Heritage and Education Center Collection.

30. Albert (ed.), *History of the Forty-Fifth Regiment Pennsylvania Veteran Volunteer Infantry*, 176.

31. Cushman, *History of the 58th Regiment, Massachusetts Volunteers,* 21.

32. Merrill, "Reminiscences."

33. *History of the Thirty-sixth Regiment Massachusetts Volunteers*, 293.

34. Porter, *Campaigning with Grant*, 450. Grant, *Personal Memoirs*, 2:459.

35. Grant, *Personal Memoirs,* 2:459. Simon (ed.), *Papers of Ulysses S. Grant*, 14:336.

36. Coffin, *Abraham Lincoln*, 498.

37. Carpenter, "President Lincoln in Petersburg," 306. *Wisconsin State Journal*, April 27, 1865.

38. Grant, *Personal Memoirs*, 2:460.

39. Porter, *Campaigning with Grant*, 451.

40. Porter, *Incidents and Anecdotes*, 201. Barnes, "With Lincoln," 745.

41. Porter, *Campaigning with Grant*, 451.

42. Badeau, *Military History,* 436.

43. Best, *History of the 121st New York*, 213. Vaill, *History of the Second Connecticut Volunteer Heavy Artillery*, 163. Peck, "A Recruit Before Petersburg," 42. Lewis B. Fuller, recollection in *Watertown Daily Times* (New York), February 11, 1914. Haynes, *History of the Tenth Vermont*, 378.

44. Morgan, "From City Point to Appomattox," 247.

45. Badeau, *Military History*, 436.

46. Carpenter, "President Lincoln in Petersburg," 306. Garland, *Ulysses S. Grant*, 303. "Army Correspondence," *Greenfield Gazette and Courier* (Massachusetts), April 24, 1865.

47. Charles Clark, Letter April 28 1898.

48. Porter, *Incidents and Anecdotes*, 291.

49. Porter, *Incidents and Anecdotes*, 290. *Rochester Union and Advertiser* (New York), April 18, 1865.

50. Barnes, "With Lincoln," 745.

51. Cyrus Goodwin, Letters.

52. *OR*, 46/3:509.

53. *OR*, 46/3: 509.

54. Basler (ed.,), *Collected Works* supplement, 285.

55. Simon (ed.,), *Personal Memoirs of Julia Dent Grant,* 149.

56. Crook, *Through Five Administrations*, 49.

CHAPTER TWELVE: TUESDAY, APRIL 4, 1865

"It is well to be humble."

1. *ORN* 12:98.

2. *ORN* 12:98.

3. *Philadelphia Inquirer*, April 5, 1865.

4. Barnes, "With Lincoln," 746.

5. USS *Bat* log, April 4, 1865.

6. Porter, Journal. Barnes, "With Lincoln," 747.

7. Porter, *Incidents and Anecdotes*, 294.

8. Barnes, Egotistrophy, 269.

9. *The Statesman* (Yonkers, New York), February 16, 1911. *Springfield Globe Republic,* February 6, 1885.

10. George H. Gordon, *A War Diary of Events*, 393-399.

11. Porter, *Incidents and Anecdotes*, 294.

12. Porter, Journal.

13. Porter, *Incidents and Anecdotes*, 295. Porter, Journal (Library of Congress).

14. *Boston Journal*, April 8, 1865 (April 3 letter).

15. *Boston Journal*, April 8, 1865 (April 4 letter).

16. Porter, *Naval History*, 798. Porter, Journal.

17. Dudley, "Lincoln in Richmond," *National Tribune*, October 1, 1896.

18. *Boston Journal*, April 8, 1865 (April 4 letter).

19. *Boston Journal*, April 8, 1865 (April 4 letter). Coffin, *Freedom Triumphant*, 436. Coffin, Letter to Thomas Nast, July 19, 1866.

20. Coffin, *Boys of '61*, 538. Clemens, Letter, April 4?, 1865.

21. Penrose letter, April 10, 1865, in Nicolay/Hay, *Abraham Lincoln: A History* (volume 10), 218-19. Crook, *Through Five Administrations*, 54.

22. Boston *Journal*, April 8, 1865 (April 4 letter). Coffin, Letter to Thomas Nast, July 19, 1866.

23. Barnes, Egotistigraphy, 269.

24. Coffin, *Boys of '61*, 541. Coffin, *Freedom Triumphant*, 440.

25. Shepley, "Incidents of the Capture of Richmond," 26. Barnes, Egotistigraphy, 270. Porter: *Incidents and Anecdotes*, 302. Kautz, Memoir.

26. Barnes, "With Lincoln," 748. Shepley, "Incidents of the Capture of Richmond," 27. *Richmond News Leader*, April 3, 1935. *Free-Lance Star*, September 28, 1948. Knox, Letter, April 5, 1865.

27. Porter, *Incidents and Anecdotes,* 297-98.

28. Plum, *Military Telegraph During the Civil War*, 2:324. Bates, *Lincoln in the Telegraph Office*, 357.

29. Clemens, Letter, April 4?, 1865.

30. Clemens, Letter, no date. Roberts, Letter to brother, April 16, 1865. Dudley, "Lincoln in Richmond," *National Tribune*, October 1, 1896. *Washington Daily Morning Chronicle*, April 10, 1865.

31. *New York Times*, January 28, 1885. Parker, "Recollections of President Lincoln.

32. Barnes, "With Lincoln," 749.

33. Coffin, *Boys of '61,* 541. Duff Green description: Pat Calhoun, "Admiral Porter's Romance," *Charleston News and Courier,* February 15, 1885. Basler (ed.), *Collected Works*, 8:332.

34. Green, *Facts and Suggestions*, 232.

35. Barnes, "With Lincoln," 749.

36. Kautz, Memoir. Kautz, "The Fall of Richmond," *The National Tribune*, May 10, 1888.

37. Coffin, *Freedom Triumphant*, 441. Pryor, *Reminiscences of Peace and War*, 357. Frances Anne Sutton Doswell, Diary, Virginia Historical Society.

38. Weitzel (ed. Manarin), "Richmond Occupied," 58.

39. Blackett (ed.), *Thomas Morris Chester: Black Civil War Correspondent*, 297. Porter, *Incidents and Anecdotes*, 301-302.

40. *OR* 46/3: 567.

41. Brock, Letter, n.d., *Christian Recorder*, May 6, 1865.

42. *Boston Journal*, April 8, 1865.

CHAPTER THIRTEEN: WEDNESDAY, APRIL 5, 1865

"I cannot bring myself to believe that any human being
lives who would do me any harm."

1. North Carolina slave narratives: Charity Austin. Levine, *Black Culture and Black Consciousness*, 88.

2. Porter, *Incidents and Anecdotes*, 297.

3. Batchelor, Memoir. Roberts, Letter to Son, April 5, 1865. Porter, *Incidents and Anecdotes*, 295. Blackett (ed.), *Thomas Morris Chester*, 297. *Washington Herald*, February 7, 1909.

4. Porter, *Incidents and Anecdotes*, 298. Austin, "Army Recollections," *Mexico Independent* (New York), August 19, 1937.

5. Bartlett, *History of the Twelfth Regiment New Hampshire Volunteers*, 272.

6. Porter, *Incidents and Anecdotes*, 298. Parker, "Recollections of President Lincoln, *History Magazine*, 11.

7. *Oswego* (New York) *Palladium*, April 2, 1927.

8. Ripley, "Capture and Occupation of Richmond," 25.

9. Reverend P. D. Gurley, quoted in Chapman, *Latest Light on Abraham Lincoln*, 2:500.

10. Myers, "Abraham Lincoln in Richmond," 321.

11. Campbell, "A View of the Confederacy from the Inside," 950. Myers, "Abraham Lincoln in Richmond," 321. Campbell, Letter to Horace Greeley, April 26, 1865.

12. Campbell, Letter to Horace Greeley, April 26, 1865. Campbell, *Recollections of the Evacuation of Richmond*, 12.

13. Myers, "Abraham Lincoln in Richmond," 322. Campbell, "A View of the Confederacy from the Inside," 953. OR 46/3: 593.

14. Myers, "Abraham Lincoln in Richmond," 322. Weitzel, *Richmond Occupied*, 57.

15. Logbooks for the USS *Monodnock* and USS *Casco*, April 5, 1865. Bates, *Lincoln in the Telegraph Office*, 2:358.

16. Simon (ed.), *Papers of Ulysses S. Grant*, 14:347.

17. Basler (ed.), *Collected Works*, 8:387.

18. Basler (ed.), *Collected Works*, 8:386.

19. Collis (Septima), *A Woman's War Record*, 61-70. Calkins, *The Appomattox Campaign*, 83.

20. Sparks (ed.), *Inside Lincoln's Army*, 488.

21. Basler (ed.), *Collected Works*, 8:388n. Stanton to Lincoln, sent 8:00 P.M. April 5, 1865 (Lincoln Papers/Library of Congress).

CHAPTER FOURTEEN: THURSDAY, APRIL 6, 1865

"Nothing I have done is to interfere with you in your work."

1. Stanton to Lincoln, April 5 & 6, 1865 (Lincoln Papers, Library of Congress).

2. Simon (ed.), *Papers of Ulysses S. Grant*, 14: 352.

3. Turner and Turner (eds.), *Mary Todd Lincoln*, 214.

4. Basler (ed.), *Collected Works*, 8:389.

5. Wilkinson, "History and Fiction," *New York Daily Tribune,* April 26, 1885.

6. Wilkinson, "History and Fiction," *New York Daily Tribune,* April 26, 1885.

7. Turner (eds.), *Mary Todd Lincoln*, 215.

8. *OR* 46/3: 593.

9. *OR* 46/3: 595.

10. Forsyth, *Thrilling Days in Army Life*, 175-76. Newhall, *With General Sheridan in Lee's Last Campaign*, 132-33.

11. Porter, *Campaigning with Grant*, 453.

12. Robert Stiles, *Four Years Under Marse Robert*, 333. James W. Dixon, "Recollections of the Civil War," *Flushing Daily Times* (New York), August 13, 1904.

13. Charles Coffin, "The Pursuit of Lee," *Boston Journal*, April 13, 1865. Stephen Z. Starr, *Union Cavalry in the Civil War*, 2:471. Korn, *Pursuit to Appomattox*, 125.

14. Calkins, *The Appomattox Campaign*, 116.

15. Marquis de Chambrun, "Personal Recollections of Mr. Lincoln," 27.

16. Kecky, *Behind the Scenes*, 64. Chambrun, "Personal Recollections of Mr. Lincoln," 28.

17. Taylor & Taylor (eds), *Mary Todd Lincoln*, 220. Chambrun, *Impressions of Lincoln and the Civil War*, 76.

18. Simon (ed.), *Personal memoirs of Julia Dent Grant*, 150.

19. Simon (ed.,), *Papers of Ulysses S. Grant*, 14:359-60.

CHAPTER FIFTEEN: FRIDAY, APRIL 7, 1865

"Every day brings new reason for confidence in the future."

1. Basler (ed.), *Collected Works*, 8:389.

2. *Jamestown Evening Journal* (New York), February 12, 1916. Huidekoper, *Personal Notes and Reminiscences of Lincoln*, 19-20.

3. Basler (ed.), *Collected Works*, 8:390-92.

4. *Philadelphia Inquirer*, April 8, 1865.

5. *OR* 46/3: 619.

6. Basler (ed.), *Collected Works*, 8:392.

7. Beckwith, "Lincoln's Shadow," *New York World*, April 27, 1913.

8. Chambrun, "Personal Recollections of Mr. Lincoln," 28-29.

9. Keckly, *Behind the Scenes*, 166-67.

10. *Grant's Petersburg Progress*, April 10, 1865. Pryor, *My Day: Reminiscences of a Long Life*, 257-57.

11. Chambrun, "Personal Recollections of Mr. Lincoln," 29.

12. Keckly, *Behind the Scenes*, 168.

13. *OR* 46/3: 619.

14. Fox, *History of Political Parties, National Reminiscences, AND The Tippecanoe Movement*, 218.

15. Morgan, "From City Point to Appomattox," 247. Garland, *Ulysses S. Grant: His Life and Character*, 306.

16. Grant, *Personal Memoirs*, 2: 479.

Chapter Sixteen: Saturday, April 8, 1865

"I came here to take by the hand the men who
have achieved our glorious victories."

1. *OR* 46/3: 641.

2. *OR* 46/3: 641. Grant, *Personal Memoirs*, 2:480. Porter, *Campaigning with Grant*, 461. OR 46/3: 652.

3. Fox, *History of Political Parties, National Reminiscences, AND The Tippecanoe Movement*, 218. *Cortland* (New York) *Democrat*, July 13, 1934.

4. Kennard, *Transatlantic Sketches*, 24-29.

5. Robertson, Jr. (ed.), "English Views of the Civil War," 201-212; also *Illustrated London News*, May 20, 1865.

6. Basler (ed.), *Collected Works*, 8:333, 7:32.

7. Chambrun, "Personal Recollections of Mr. Lincoln," 29-30.

8. Hancock (ed. Jaquette): *South After Gettysburg*, 179. *Franklin Repository* (Chambersburg, Pennsylvania), December 6, 1865.

9. Palmer, *Story of Aunt Becky's Army Life*, 186.

10. Livermore, *History of the Eighteenth New Hampshire*, 68.

11. Baird diary, April 8, 1865. Low letter, April 12, 1865.

12. Humphrey, "Shook Hands with Lincoln, *National Tribune*, August 26, 1915.

13. Muffly, *Story of Our Regiment*, 892.

14. "Frank," letter of April 9, 1865, in *The Soldiers' Journal,* April 19, 1865. Anderson, "Where I Saw Lincoln," *Peekskill Highland Democrat* (New York), February 20, 1909.

15. Spring, John A. "The Dying Cavalryman," *National Tribune*, April 2, 1903. *New Castle News* (Pennsylvania), December 30, 1930. Bowerman, "President Abraham Lincoln's Visit to the United States Hospital at City Point, Va.," *National Tribune*, April 11, 1907.

16. "A Visit from Lincoln," *Bluffton Chronicle* (South Carolina), May 12, 1909.

17. George Mendenhall letter to Joseph H. Barrett, May 2, 1865. *Utica Weekly Herald* (New York), July 9, 1889.

18. Fellows, *Rochester Democrat and Chronicle* (New York), May 31, 1929. Goodwin letter, April 9, 1865. *Watertown Daily Times* (New York), February 14, 1914. Albert, *History of the Forty Fifth Regiment*, 389. Tarbell, *Life of Lincoln*, 4:161.

19. Albert, *History of the Forty Fifth Regiment*, 529.

20. Livermore, *History of the Eighteenth New Hampshire Regiment*, 68-69.

21. Chambrun, "Personal Recollections of Mr. Lincoln," 31.

22. "Comrade C. Hull Grant," *Brooklyn Daily Eagle,* April 28, 1895.

23. Macomber, "Honoring Lincoln's Memory," *San Francisco Call*, May 29, 1897.

24. Fisk (ed. Rosenblatt), *Anti-Rebel*, 322.

25. Basler (ed.), *Collected Works*, 7:32. Reed (ed.), *War Papers of Frank B. Fay*, 130. Fehrenbacher and Fehrenbacher (eds.), Recollected Words of Abraham Lincoln, 396. Keckly, *Behind the Scenes*, 171.

26. Barnes, "With Lincoln," 524.

27. Simon (ed.), *Personal Memoirs of Julia Dent Grant*, 151. I believe she was referring to an aria from a popular opera of the 1840s, *The Bohemian Girl*, by Michael William Balfe.

28. Keckly, *Behind the Scenes*, 171-72. Chambrun, "Personal Recollections of Mr. Lincoln," 34.

29. Barnes, "With Lincoln," 751.

30. Chambrun, "Personal Recollections of Mr. Lincoln," 34.

31. Grant, *Personal Memoirs*, 2:483.

32. *OR* 46/3: 641.

33. Cadwallader (ed. Thomas), *Three Years with Grant*, 319.

34. Young, *Around the World with General Grant*, 2:627. Cadwallader (ed. Thomas), *Three Years with Grant*, 319.

CHAPTER SEVENTEEN: SUNDAY, APRIL 9, 1865
"I think we are near the end at last."

1. Barnes, Egotistography, 275. Barnes, "With Lincoln in 1865," 751.

2. *OR* 46/3: 664.

3. *OR* 46/3: 664.

4. Grant, *Personal Memoirs*, 2:485.

5. *OR* 46/3:665.

6. Porter, *Campaigning with Grant*, 467.

7. Chambrun, "Personal Recollections of Mr. Lincoln," 35, 33. Page, *Lincoln on the River Queen*, 11.

8. Grant, *Personal Memoirs*, 2:492.

9. Robert Lincoln to Justice Harlan, May 15, 1908, Abraham Lincoln Presidential Library.

10. Porter, *Campaigning with Grant*, 486.

11. *OR* 46/3: 663.

12. Chambrun, "Personal Recollections of Mr. Lincoln," 35.

13. *Washington Evening Star*, April 10, 1865. Crook, *Through Five Administrations*, 58.

14. Chambrun, "Personal Recollections of Mr. Lincoln," 35.

15. Frederick Seward, *Reminiscences of a War-Time Statesman and Diplomat*, 253.

16. Fanny Seward diary, April 9, 1865. Frederick Seward, *Reminiscences of a War-Time Statesman and Diplomat*, 253.

17. Thomas and Hyman, *Stanton: The Life and Times of Lincoln's Scretary of War*, 353. *OR* 46/3: 663-64. Johnson, "Lincoln and Grant," *Washington Evening Star*, February 15, 1896. Morris, *Memorial Record and the Nation's Tribute to Abraham Lincoln*, 13.

18. Luthin, *The Real Abraham Lincoln*, 604.

EPILOGUE

1. *Washington Evening Star*, April 10, 1865. *Sacramento Daily Union*, May 8, 1865. *New York Herald*, April 9, 1865. *Washington Daily Morning Chronicle*, April 12, 1865.

2. Kunhardt, *Lincoln*, 343. Welles, *Diary*, 2:287. Bringham, *James Harlan*, 338. Keckly, *Behind the Scenes*, 138. Burlingame mss. *Abraham Lincoln: A Life*, volume 2, chapter 36, 4014.

3. Pierpont, Recollections.

4. Niven (ed.), *Salmon P. Chase Papers*, 1:530. Ambler, *Francis H. Pierpont*, 256-57.

5. Welles, *Diary,* 2:279-80. *Philadelphia Press*, April 13, 1865. Welles, *Diary,* 2:281.

6. Basler (ed.), *Collected Works*, 8:393-94.

7. Brooks, *Statesmen*, 214.

8. Brooks, "Personal Reminiscences of Lincoln," 567.

9. Basler (ed.), *Collected Works*, 8:399-405.

10. Mitgang (ed.), *Lincoln As They Saw Him*, 442-445.

11. Basler (ed.), *Collected Works*, 7: 243, 8:403. Quoted in Burlingame mss. *Abraham Lincoln: A Life,* volume 2, chapter 36, 4006.

12. Basler (ed.), *Collected Works*, 8:399.

13. Basler (ed.), *Collected Works*, 8:405.

14. Moss, "Lincoln and Wilkes Booth as seen on the day of the assassination," 951.

15. Chambrun, "Personal Recollections of Mr. Lincoln," 34.

16. Keckly, *Behind the Scenes*, 137.

17. Burlingame, *Abraham Lincoln: A Life* (online manuscript version), 4016.

18. *OR* 47/3: 207-8.

19. P. Tecumseh Sherman, "General Sherman in the Last Year of the Civil War," 17-18.

20. *Saratoga Springs* (New York) *Sentinel,* February 23, 1882.

21. Young, *Around the World with General Grant*, 2:354.

22. Welles, "Lincoln and Johnson," 191. Simon (ed.), *Grant Papers,* 18:263-64.

23. Grant, *Personal Memoirs*, 2:497. Maurice (ed.), *An Aide-de-Camp of Lee,* 275.

APPENDIX ONE: SOURCES CASEBOOK

1. Barbee Papers, O'Brien letter of January 4, 1951. Washington *Post,* April 28, 1895.

2. Doug Hill, email to the author, April 17, 2012.

3. *OR* 46/3, 173.

4. Sherman, *Memoirs*, 2:325.

5. Baker, *Mary Todd Lincoln,* 240. Clinton, *Mrs. Lincoln*, 239.

6. Beckwith, "Grant's Shadow," *New York Sun*, April 27, 1913.

7. Porter, *Incidents and Anecdotes*, 316-17.

8. *New York Herald*, April 4, 1865.

9. Schurz, *Reminiscences*, 3:110. Schafer (ed.), *Intimate Letters of Carl Schurz*, 327.

10. Randall, *Mary Lincoln*, 374. Schafter (ed.), *Intimate Letters of Carl Schurz*, 327-28. Sedgwick, *Happy Profession*, 163.

11. Porter, *Incidents and Anecdotes*, 292-93.

12. *New York Herald*, April 5, 1865.

13. Sparks, *Inside Lincoln's Army*, 487.

14. Penrose, "Lincoln's Visit to Richmond," *Century Magazine*, June 1890, 307.

15. Robert Todd Lincoln to A. K. McClure, May 10, 1879, Abraham Lincoln Presidential Library.

16. Hanser, "Mr. Lincoln Visits Richmond," 48. Green, *Facts and Suggestions*, 232.

17. Pat Calhoun, "Admiral Porter's Romance," *Charleston News and Courier* (South Carolina), February 15, 1885. Woodard, "Abraham Lincoln, Duff Green, and the Mysterious Trumbell Letter," 219.

18. Porter, *Incidents and Anecdotes*, 301-302. ORN 12:176.

19. Gates (ed.), *Men of Mark in America*, 2:343-344.

20. Bullard, *Tad and his Father*, 81-82.

21. Keckly, *Behind the Scenes*, 171.

22. Abraham Lincoln Presidential Library press release, archived at http://archives.lincolndailynews.com/2008/Feb/22/News/today022208_a.shtml

23. *Washington Evening Star*, April 10, 1865.

24. *New York Sun*, April 4, 1865.

BIBLIOGRAPHY

Manuscripts

Abraham Lincoln Presidential Library
John A. Campbell papers
Logbook page from the USS *Malvern*
Robert Todd Lincoln letters

Allegheny College Special Collections
Ida Tarbell Papers: Charles Clark letter, April 28, 1898

Archives of Manitoba, Winnipeg, Manitoba, Canada
Minnie (Buck) Campbell Papers: Letters of Dr. Anson Buck

Duke University
Confederate Veteran Papers: "The Charge on Fort Stedman"
Thomas Low Papers: Letter to Brother, April 12, 1865

Fredericksburg-Spotsylvania National Battlefield Park
John Baird diary
James F. Merrill reminiscence

Georgetown University Special Collections
The David Rankin Barbee Papers

Library of Congress Manuscripts Division
David Dixon Porter Journal
Abraham Lincoln Papers

Maine Historical Society
Rebecca Usher letters

National Archives of the United States
RG24: Records of the Bureau of Naval Personnel / Logs of Ships and Stations,
1801-1946 - Logs of US Naval Ships, 1801-1915

Logbooks:
USS *Atlanta*
USS *Bat*
USS *Casco*
USS *Malvern*
USS *Monadnock*
USS *Monticello*
USS *Onondoga*
USS *Perry*

National Park Service: Ford's Theater
Oldroyd Collection: Mary Lincoln telegram, March 25, 1865

New York Historical Society
John Sanford Barnes. "The Egotistigraphy of a Rolling Stone, that gathered Moss, herein scraped off for the information and amusement of his family." (Naval History Society Collection, MS 439.) [A complete transcription was posted on line by the Barnes family, with the link at the time of this writing: https://sites.google.com/site/johnsanfordbarnes/]
Alexander Knox Letters

New York Public Library Manuscripts and Archives Division
The Century Magazine Archive:
C. C. Carpenter letter
Charles R. Penrose letter
Horace Porter letter

New York State Library Manuscript and Special Collections
Charles L. Hagar letters
Henry J. Peck letters

Petersburg National Battlefield Park
Rufus Barringer diary
George H. Hearne diary
Samuel Henry Roberts letter (to son), April 5, 1865

Private Collections
Benjamin Batchelor memoir (courtesy: Julie Houghton Durkee)
Cyrus T. Goodwin letters (courtesy: Pauline Roberts)

Renssalaer Polytechnic Institute Archives and Special Collections
    Skilton Family Papers, 1845-1903: James A. Skilton, "Two Great Republicans"

Signal Corps Association, 1860-1865
    www.civilwarsignals.org
    William W. Clemens letter, April 4?, 1865

Southern Historical Collection, University of North Carolina
    Campbell and Colston Family Papers: Letter of John A Campbell to Horace Greeley,
    April 26, 1865
    Henry Armand London. Letter, March 25, 1865

Southern Methodist University, Bridwell Library, Special Collections
    John Heyl Vincent Papers

U.S. Army Heritage and Education Center, Carlisle, Pennsylvania
    Calvin Berry diary
    Thomas Campbell diary
    Albert B. Chandler papers
    Earl M. Hess Collection: John Walraven diary
    Albert Pope diary
    August Valentine Kautz papers, 1828-1895

U.S. Military Academy Library at West Point
    William T. Sherman papers: Letter to George P.A. Healy, January 13, 1868

University of Chicago Library
    William E. Barton Collection of Lincolniana: George Mendenhall letter to Joseph H.
    Barrett, May 2, 1865

University of Michigan, Clements Library
    Schoff Civil War Collection: Letter of Charles C. Coffin to Thomas Nast, July 19,
    1866

University of Rochester Rare Books & Special Collections
    Fanny Seward diary

Virginia Historical Society
    Francis Anne Sutton Doswell diary
    John R. Hamilton letter, March 28, 1865
    Samuel Henry Roberts letter (to brother), April 16, 1865

West Virginia University Archives & Manuscripts
Francis Harrison Pierpont papers

Newspapers

Adams Sentinel (Pennsylvania)
Auburn Morning Dispatch (New York)
Bluffton Chronicle (South Carolina)
Boston Daily Globe
Boston Evening Journal
Boston Herald
Chicago Tribune
Christian Recorder (Philadelphia, Pennsylvania)
Chatham Courier (New York)
Cortland Democrat (New York)
Elyria Independent Democrat (New York)
Flushing Daily Times (New York)
Franklin Repository (Chambersburg, Pennsylvania)
Fredonia Censor (New York)
Free-Lance Star (Fredericksburg, Virginia)
Gazette & Farmer's Journal (Baldwinsville, New York)
Globe Republic (Springfield, Illinois)
Grant's Petersburg Progress (Petersburg, Virginia)
Greenfield Gazette and Courier (Massachusetts)
The Holly Standard (New York)
Illustrated London News
The Irish-American (New York)
Jamestown Evening Journal (New York)
Journal and Republican (Lowville, New York)
Louisiana Capitolian
Manufacturers and Farmers Journal (Providence, Rhode Island)
Mexico Independent (New York)
Naples Record (New York)
New Castle News (Pennsylvania)
New York Evening Express
New York Herald
New York Herald-Tribune
New York Sun
New York Times
New York World
The National Tribune (Washington, D.C.)

Northern Budget (Troy, New York)
The Oregonian
Oswego Commercial Advertiser (New York)
Oswego Palladium (New York)
Peekskill Highland Democrat (New York)
Philadelphia Daily Evening Bulletin
Philadelphia Inquirer
(Philadelphia) *Press*
Republican Advocate (Batavia, New York)
Richmond Despatch (Virginia)
Richmond News Leader (Virginia)
*Rochester Democrat and Chronicle (*New York)
Rochester Union and Democrat (New York)
Rockland County Journal (New York)
Roman Citizen (Rome, New York)
*Rome Daily Sentinel (*New York)
Sacramento Daily Union (California)
San Francisco Call (California)
Saratoga Springs Sentinel (New York)
Springfield Republican (Massachusetts)
The Statesman (Yonkers, New York)
The Soldiers' Journal (Alexandria, Virginia)
The Steuben Courier (Bath, New York)
Utica Weekly Herald (New York)
Vermont Watchman and State Journal
(Washington) *Daily Morning Chronicle*
(Washington) *Daily National Republican*
Washington Evening Star
Washington Herald
Washington Post
Watertown Daily Times (New York)
Winnipeg Free Press (Canada)
Wisconsin State Journal
The Yonkers Statesman (New York)

Official Documents

Official Records of the Union and Confederate Navies in the War of the Rebellion
(Washington, D.C.: Government Printing Office, 30 volumes), 1894-1922.

Proceedings, Findings and Opinions of the Court of Inquiry Convened by Order of the President of the United States in the Case of Gouverneur K. Warren (Washington, D.C.: Government Printing Office, 3 volumes), 1883.

The War of the Rebellion: A Compilation of the Official Records of the Union and Confederate Armies (Washington, D.C.: Government Printing Office, 127 volumes), 1880-1901.

United States House of Representatives, 38th Congress, 2d Session, Report No. 24: "Trade with Rebellious States," March, 1865.

Abraham Lincoln

Arnold, Isaac N. *The Life of Abraham Lincoln* (Chicago, Illinois: A.C. McClurg & Co.), 1909.

Basler, Roy P. (editor). *The Collected Works of Abraham Lincoln* (New Brunswick, New Jersey: Rutgers University Press, 8 volumes), 1953.

——. *The Collected Works of Abraham Lincoln: Supplement* (Westport, Connecticut: Greenwood Press), 1974.

—— and Christian O. Basler (eds.). *The Collected Works of Abraham Lincoln: Second Supplement* (New Brunswick, New Jersey: Rutgers University Press), 1990.

Brooks, Noah, "Personal Reminiscences of Lincoln," *Scribner's Magazine* (February, 1878)

——. *Statesmen (Men of Achievement)* (New York: Charles Scribner's Sons), 1893.

Browne, Francis F. *The Every-Day Life of Abraham Lincoln* (New York: N.D. Thompson Publishing Company), 1886.

Bullard, Frederic Lauriston. *Tad and his Father* (Boston, Massachusetts: Little, Brown, and Company), 1915.

Burlingame, Michael. *Abraham Lincoln: A Life* (Knox College, Illinois: Uncut Manuscript), 2008. http://www.knox.edu/academics/distinctive-programs/lincoln-studies-center/burlingame-abraham-lincoln-a-life.html.

—— (ed.). *Lincoln Observed: Civil War Dispatches of Noah Brooks* (Baltimore, Maryland: Johns Hopkins University Press), 1998.

——. *The Inner World of Abraham Lincoln* (Chicago, Illinois: University of Illinois Press), 1994.

Chapman, Ervin (ed.). *Latest Light on Abraham Lincoln* (New York: Fleming H. Revell Company, 2 volumes), 1917.

Donald, David Herbert. *Lincoln* (London, England: Jonathan Cape), 1995.

Fehrenbacher, Don E. and Virginia Fehrenbacher (eds.). *Recollected Words of Abraham Lincoln* (Stanford, California: Stanford University Press), 1996.

Foner, Eric. "If Lincoln hadn't died," *American Heritage*, volume 58, no. 6, Winter 2009.

Gates Jr., Henry Louis (ed.). *Lincoln on Race & Slavery* (Princeton, New Jersey: Princeton University Press), 2009.

Harris, William C. *Lincoln's Last Months* (Cambridge, Massachusetts: Belknap Press), 2004.

Kunhardt Jr., Philip B. and Philip B. Kunhardt III and Peter W. Kunhardt (eds.). *Lincoln: An Illustrated Biography* (New York: Alfred A. Knopf), 1992.

Luthin, Reinhard H. *The Real Abraham Lincoln* (Englewood Cliffs, New Jersey: Prentice-Hall, Inc.) 1960.

Masur, Louis P. *Lincoln's Last Speech* (New York: Oxford University Press), 2015.

Mitgang, Herbert (ed.). *Lincoln As They Saw Him* (New York: Collier Books), 1962.

Morris, Benjamin F. (compiler). *Memorial Record of the Nation's Tribute to Abraham Lincoln* (Washington, D.C.: W.H. & O.H. Morrison), 1865.

Nicolay, John G. and John Hay (eds.). *Complete Works of Abraham Lincoln* (New York: Francis D. Tandy Company, 15 volumes), 1894.

———. *Abraham Lincoln: A History* (New York: The Century Co., 10 volumes), 1909.

Oates, Stephen B. *With Malice Toward None: The Life of Abraham Lincoln* (New York: Harper & Row, Publishers), 1977.

———. *Abraham Lincoln: The Man Behind the Myths* (New York: New American Library), 1984.

Paludan, Phillip Shaw. *The Presidency of Abraham Lincoln* (Lawrence, Kansas: University Press of Kansas), 1994.

Pinsker, Matthew. *Lincoln's Sanctuary: Abraham Lincoln and the Soldiers' Home* (New York: Oxford University Press), 2003.

Tarbell, Ida M. *The Life of Abraham Lincoln* (New York: The Doubleday & McClure Co., 4 volumes), 1900.

Thomas, Benjamin P. *Abraham Lincoln: A Biography* (New York: The Modern Library), 1968.

Ulysses S. Grant

Badeau, Adam. *Military History of Ulysses S. Grant* (New York: D. Appleton and Company, 3 volumes), 1881.

———. *Grant in Peace: From Appomattox to Mount McGregor* (Hartford, Connecticut: S.S. Scranton & Co.), 1887.

Garland, Hamlin. *Ulysses S. Grant: His Life and Character* (New York: The MacMillan Company), 1920.

Grant, Jesse R. (in collaboration with Henry Francis Granger). *In the Days of My Father General Grant* (New York, Harper & Brothers Publishers), 1925.

Grant, Ulysses S. *Personal Memoirs of U. S. Grant* (New York: Charles L. Webster, 2 volumes), 1885.

McCormick, Robert R. *Ulysses S. Grant: The Great Soldier of America* (New York: D. Appleton-Century Company), 1934.

Porter, Horace. *Campaigning with Grant* (New York: The Century Company), 1897.

———. "Lincoln and Grant," *The Century Magazine*, volume 30, number 6, October 1885.

———. "Address of General Porter," *Proceedings at the Third Annual Dinner of the Republican Club of the City of New York* (New York: Mercantile Printing & Stationary Co.), 1889.

Richardson, Albert D. *A Personal History of Ulysses S. Grant* (Hartford, Connecticut: American Publishing Company), 1868.

Simon, John Y. (editor). *The Papers of Ulysses S. Grant* (Carbondale and Edwardsville: Southern Illinois University Press, 31 volumes), 1967-2009.

Simpson, Brooks D. *Ulysses S. Grant: Triumph Over Adversity, 1822-1896* (New York: Houghton Mifflin Company), 2000.

———. *Let Us Have Peace: Ulysses S. Grant and the Politics of War and Reconstruction, 1861-1868* (Chapel Hill, North Carolina: University of North Carolina Press), 1991.

Smith, Jean Edward. *Grant* (New York: Simon & Schuster), 2001.

Stoddard, William O. *Ulysses S. Grant* (New York: White, Stokes, & Allen), 1886.

Waugh, Joan. *U.S. Grant: American Hero, American Myth* (Chapel Hill, North Carolina: University of North Carolina Press), 2009.

Wister, Owen. *Ulysses S. Grant* (Boston, Massachusetts: Small, Maynard & Company), 1900.

Young, John Russell. *Around the World with General Grant* (New York: The American News Company, 2 volumes), 1879.

Autobiographies, Biographies, Diaries, Letters, Memoirs, Speeches, and Personal Narratives

Agassiz, George R. (ed.). *Meade's Headquarters 1863-1865: Letters of Colonel Theodore Lyman* (Boston, Massachusetts: The Atlantic Monthly Press), 1922.

Ambler, Charles H. *Francis H. Pierpont: Union War Governor of Virginia and Father of West Virginia* (Chapel Hill, North Carolina: University of North Carolina Press), 1937.

Backus, Clarence W. "Closing War Scenes," *The Magazine of History*, volume 20, number 6 (June, 1915), pp. 251-259.

Baker, Jean H. *Mary Todd Lincoln: A Biography* (New York: W.W. Norton & Company), 1987.

Barnes, John Sanford. "With Lincoln from Washington to Richmond in 1865," *Appleton's Magazine*, volume 9, number 5 (May, 1907), pp. 515-525; volume 9, number 6 (June, 1907), pp. 742-751.

Barrier, J. D. "Breaking Grant's Line," *Confederate Veteran*, volume 33, number 11 (November, 1925).

Barringer, Paul B. *The Natural Bent* (Chapel Hill, North Carolina: University of North Carolina Press), 1949.

Bates, David Homer. *Lincoln in the Telegraph Office* (New York: The Century Company), 1907.

Blackett, R.J.M. (ed.). *Thomas Morris Chester: Black Civil War Correspondent* (Baton Rouge, Louisiana: Louisiana State University Press), 1989.

Brett, Martin W. *Experiences of a Georgia Boy in the Army of Northern Virginia, 1861-1865* (Statesboro, Georgia: Bulloch County Historical Society), 1988.

Brigham, Johnson. *James Harlan* (Iowa City: State Historical Society of Iowa), 1913.

Bruce, George A. "The Capture and Occupation of Richmond," *Papers of the Military Historical Society of Massachusetts* (Boston, Massachusetts: The Military Historical Society of Massachusetts), 1918.

Butler, Jason T. Letter, March 27, 1865. *Lincolnian*, volume 6, number 1 (September-October 1987).

Campbell, John A. *Recollections of the Evacuation of Richmond, April 2, 1865* (Baltimore, Maryland: John Murphy & Co.), 1880.

———. *Reminiscences and Documents Relating to the Civil War during the Year 1865* (Baltimore, Maryland: John Murphy & Co.), 1887.

———. "A View of the Confederacy from the Inside," *The Century Magazine*, volume 38, number 6, October 1889.

Carpenter, C. C. "President Lincoln in Petersburg," *The Century Magazine*, volume 40, number 2, June, 1890.

Chamberlain, Joshua Lawrence. *The Passing of the Armies* (New York: G.P. Putnam's Sons), 1915.

Chambrun, Marquis de, "Personal Recollections of Mr. Lincoln," *Scribner's Magazine* (January, 1893)

———. *Impressions of Lincoln and the Civil War* (New York: Random House), 1952.

Clinton, Catherine. *Mrs. Lincoln: A Life* (New York: HarperCollins Publishers), 2009.

Coburn, Frederick W. *Moses Greeley Parker, M.D.* (Lowell, Massachusetts: privately printed), 1922.

Coffin, Charles Carleton. *The Boys of '61; or, Four Years of Fighting* (Boston, Massachusetts: Estes and Lauriat), 1886.

———. *Freedom Triumphant* (New York: Harper & Brothers), 1891.

———. *Abraham Lincoln* (New York: Harper & Brothers), 1893.

Collis, Septima M. *A Woman's War Record* (New York: G.P. Putnam's Sons), 1889.

Connor, Henry G. *John Archibald Campbell* (New York: Houghton Mifflin Company), 1920.

Cresap, Bernarr. *Appomattox Commander: The Story of General E. O. C. Ord* (New York: A.S. Barnes & Company, Inc.), 1981.

Crook, William H. (compiled and written down by Margarita Spalding Gerry). "Lincoln As I Knew Him," *Harper's Monthly Magazine*, volume 114 (December, 1906).

_____. "Lincoln's Last Day," *Harper's Monthly Magazine*, volume 115 (September, 1907).

_____. *Through Five Administrations* (New York: Harper & Brothers Publishers), 1910.

Davies, Henry E. *General Sheridan* (New York: D. Appleton and Company), 1895.

Davis, Jefferson. *The Rise and Fall of the Confederate Government* (New York: Da Capo Press, 2 volumes), 1990 – reprint of 1938 edition.

De Forest, B.S. *Random Sketches and Wandering Thoughts* (Albany, New York: Avery Herrick, Publisher), 1866.

Drayton, Percival. *Naval Letters: 1861-1865* (New York: privately published), 1906.

Emerson, Jason. *Giant in the Shadows: The Life of Robert T. Lincoln* (Carbondale and Edwardsville, Illinois: Southern Illinois Press), 2012.

Epstein, Daniel Mark. *The Lincolns: Portrait of a Marriage* (New York: Ballantine Books), 2008.

Evans, W. A. *Mrs. Abraham Lincoln: A Study of Her Personality and Her Influence on Lincoln* (New York: Alfred A. Knopf), 1932.

Farragut, Loyall. *The Life of David Glasgow Farragut* (New York: D. Appleton and Company), 1879.

Federal Writer's Project. *Slave Narratives: A Folk History of Slavery in the United States with Former Slaves* (Washington, D.C.: Library of Congress), 1936-38. Volume XI: North Carolina narratives.

Fellman, Michael. *Citizen Sherman: A Life of William Tecumseh Sherman* (New York: Random House), 1995.

Flanagan, Vincent J. *The Life of General Gouverneur Kemble Warren* (PhD. Dissertation, City University of New York), 1969.

Fleischner, Jennifer. *Mrs. Lincoln and Mrs. Keckly* (New York: Broadway Books), 2003.

Forsyth, George A. *Thrilling Days in Army Life* (New York: Harper & Brothers), 1900.

Fox, Dorus M. *History of Political Parties, National Reminiscences, AND the Tippecanoe Movement* (Des Moines, Iowa: Iowa Printing Company), 1895.

Freeman, Douglas Southall. *R.E. Lee* (New York: Charles Scribner's Sons, 4 volumes), 1934-1935.

Gallagher, Gary W. (ed.). *Fighting for the Confederacy: The Personal Recollections of General Edward Porter Alexander* (Chapel Hill, North Carolina: University of North Carolina Press), 1989.

Goff, John S. *Robert Todd Lincoln: A Man in His Own Right* (Norman, Oklahoma: University of Oklahoma Press), 1969.

Gordon, George H. *A War Diary of Events* (Boston, Massachusetts: James R. Osgood and Company), 1882.

Gordon, John B. *Reminiscences of the Civil War* (New York: Charles Scribner's Sons), 1904.

Gray, John Chipman and John Codman Ropes. *War Letters 1862-1865* (New York: Houghton Mifflin Company), 1927.

Green, Duff. *Facts and Suggestions, Biographical, Historical, Financial, and Political* (New York: C.S. Wescott & CC's Union Printing Office), 1866.

Gutmann, Joseph (ed.). *Moses Jacob Ezekiel: Memoirs from the Baths of Diocletian* (Detroit, Michigan: Wayne State University Press), 1975.

Healy, Mary. (ed.). *Life of George P.A. Healy* (privately published), n.d.

Huidekoper, H.S. *Personal Notes and Reminiscences of Lincoln* (Philadelphia, Pennsylvania: Bicking Printers), 1896.

Humphreys, Charles Alfred. *Field, Camp, Hospital and Prison in the Civil War* (Boston, Massachusetts: Press of George H. Ellis Co.), 1918.

Huyette, Miles Clayton. "Reminiscences of a Private," *National Tribune Scrap-Book* (Washington, D.C.: The National Tribune, 3 volumes), 1909.

Jaquette, Henrietta Stratton. (ed.). *South After Gettysburg: Letters of Cornelia Hancock, 1863-1868* (New York: Thomas Y. Crowell Company), 1937.

Johnson, Robert Underwood and Clarence Clough Buel (eds.). *Battles and Leaders of the Civil War* (New York: The *Century* Company, 4 volumes), 1889.

Jones, John Beauchamp. *A Rebel War Clerk's Diary* (Philadelphia, Pennsylvania: J.B. Lippincott & Co., 2 volumes), 1866.

Jones, Thomas G. "The Last Days of the Army of Northern Virginia," *Southern Historical Society Papers*, volume 21, (January-December 1893).

Keckly, Elizabeth. *Behind the Scenes, or, Thirty Years a Slave, and Four Years in the White House* (New York: G.W. Carleton & Co., Publishers), 1868.

Kennard, Edward. *Transatlantic Sketches; or, Sixty Days in America* (London, England: Sampson Low, Son & Co.), 1865.

Kilmer, George. "Gordon's Attack at Fort Stedman," In Johnson and Buell (eds.), *Battles and Leaders of the Civil War*, volume 4, 1889.

Lewis, Lloyd. *Fighting Prophet* (New York: Harcourt, Brace and Company), 1932.

Lincoln Financial Foundation Collection: *Reminiscences about Abraham Lincoln*, n.d.

Linn, George Wilds. *An Echo of the Civil War: From Richmond to Appomattox* (Lebanon, Pennsylvania: Press of Sowers Printing Co.), 1911.

Lowe, David W. (ed.). *Meade's Army: The Private Notebooks of Lt. Col. Theodore Lyman* (Kent, Ohio: The Kent State University Press), 2007.

Lewis, Paul. *Yankee Admiral: A Biography of David Dixon Porter* (New York: David McKay Company, Inc.), 1968.

Mare, Marie de. *G.P.A. Healy: American Artist* (New York: David McKay Company, Inc.), 1954.

Maurice, Frederick. (ed.). *An Aide-de-Camp of Lee, being the Papers of Colonel Charles Marshall* (Boston, Massachusetts: Little, Brown and Company), 1927.

McBride, Robert E. *In the Ranks: from the Wilderness to Appomattox Court-House* (Cincinnati, Ohio: Walden & Stowe), 1881.

Meade, George (ed.). *The Life and Letters of George Gordon Meade* (New York: Charles Scribner's Sons, 2 volumes), 1913. [The editor was Meade's son.]

Mende, Elsie Porter. *An American Soldier and Diplomat: Horace Porter* (New York: Frederick A. Stokes Company), 1927.

Merrill, James M. *William Tecumseh Sherman* (New York: Rand McNally & Company), 1973.

Morgan, M. R. "From City Point to Appomattox with General Grant," *Journal of the Military Service Institution,* September-October, 1907.

Moss, Helen Palmes. "Lincoln and Wilkes Booth as seen on the day of the assassination," *The Century Magazine,* volume 77, number 6, April 1909.

Myers, Gustavus A. "Abraham Lincoln in Richmond," *The Virginia Magazine of History and Biography,* volume 41, 1933.

Nevin, John. (ed.). *The Salmon P. Chase Papers* (Kent, Ohio: Kent State University Press, 3 volumes), 1993-94.

Newhall, Frederic Cushman. *With General Sheridan in Lee's Last Campaign* (Philadelphia: J.B. Lippincott & Co.), 1866.

_____, "With Sheridan in Lee's Last Campaign," *The Maine Bugle,* campaign 1, call 4 (October 1894).

Owens, Richard H. *Biography of General and Ambassador Horace Porter* (Lewiston, New York: Edwin Mellen Press), 2002.

Palmer, Sarah A. *The Story of Aunt Becky's Army-Life* (New York: John F. Trow & Co.), 1867.

Parker, Moses Greeley. "Recollections of President Lincoln," *Contributions of the Lowell Historical Society* (Lowell, Massachusetts: Butterfield Printing Company), 1913.

Pearce, T. H. (ed.). *Diary of Captain Henry A. Chambers* (Wendell, North Carolina: Broadfoot's Bookmark), 1983.

Pease, Theodore Calvin and James G. Randall (eds.). *The Diary of Orville Hickman Browning* (Springfield, Illinois: The Trustees of the Illinois State Historical Library, 2 volumes), 1925.

Peck, George B. "A Recruit Before Petersburg," In *Personal Narratives of Events in the War of the Rebellion, Being Papers Read Before the Rhode Island Soldiers and Sailors Historical Society* (Providence, Rhode Island: Published by the Society), 1880.

Penrose, Charles R. "Lincoln's Visit to Richmond," *The Century Magazine,* volume 40, number 2, June 1890.

_____ (writing as "Army Officer"). "How Lincoln Received the News," *The Steuben Courier* (Bath, New York), March 6, 1885.

Plum, William R. *The Military Telegraph during the Civil War in the United States* (Chicago, Illinois: Jansen, McClurg & Company, 2 volumes), 1882.

Porter, David Dixon. *Incidents and Anecdotes of the Civil War* (New York: D. Appleton and Company), 1885.

_____. *Naval History of the Civil War* (New York: The Sherman Publishing Company), 1886.

_____. "President Lincoln's Entry into Richmond after the Evacuation of that Place by the Confederates," *Belford's Magazine,* volume 5, June-November 1890.

Pryor, Sara A. *Reminiscences of Peace and War* (New York: The Macmillian Company), 1904.

Randall, Ruth Painter. *Mary Lincoln: Biography of a Marriage* (Boston, Massachusetts: Little, Brown and Company), 1953.

_____. *Lincoln's Sons* (Boston, Massachusetts: Little, Brown and Company), 1955.

Redkey, Edwin S. (ed.). *A Grand Army of Black Men* (New York: Cambridge University Press), 1992.

Reed, William Howell (ed.). *War Papers of Frank B. Fay* (privately printed), 1911.

Ripley, Edward H. *The Capture and Occupation of Richmond* (New York: G.P. Putnam's Sons), 1907.

Risley, Theodore G. "Colonel Theodore S. Bowers," *Journal of the Illinois Historical Society,* volume 12, number 3, October 1919.

Rosenblatt, Emil. (ed.). *Anti-Rebel: The Civil War Letters of Wilbur Fisk* (Croton-on-Hudson, New York: privately printed), 1983.

Sandburg, Carl and Paul M. Angle. *Mary Lincoln: Wife and Widow* (New York: Harcourt, Brace and Company), 1932.

Schafer, Joseph (ed.). *Intimate Letters of Carl Schurz 1841-1860* (Madison, Wisconsin: State Historical Society of Wisconsin), 1928.

Schneller, Robert J. (ed.). *Under the Blue Pennant or Notes of a Naval Officer (John W. Grattan)* (New York: John Wiley & Sons, Inc.), 1999.

Schurz, Carl. *Reminiscences of Carl Schurz* (New York: The McClure Company, 3 volumes), 1908.

Semmes, Raphael. *Memoirs of Service Afloat during the War Between the States* (Baltimore, Maryland: Kelly, Piet & Co.), 1869.

Seward, Frederick W. *Reminiscences of a War-Time Statesman and Diplomat, 1830-1915* (New York: G.P. Putnam's Sons), 1916.

Shepley, George F. "Incidents of the Capture of Richmond," *The Atlantic Monthly,* volume 46, issue 273, July 1880.

Sherman, Philemon Tecumseh. *General Sherman in the Last Year of the Civil War* (New York: R.G. Cooke), 1908.

Sherman, William T. *Memoirs of General William T. Sherman* (New York: D. Appleton, 2 volumes), 1886.

_____. *Address to the Eighteenth Re-Union of the Army of the Potomac, Saratoga Springs,* New York, June 22d and 23d, 1887.

_____. "Unpublished Letters of General Sherman," *The North American Review,* volume 152, issue 412, March 1891.

Sheridan, Philip H. *Personal Memoirs of P.H. Sheridan* (New York: Charles L. Webster & Company, 2 volumes), 1888.

Simon, John Y. (ed.). *The Personal Memoirs of Julia Dent Grant* (New York: G.P. Putman's Sons), 1975.

Simpson, Brooks D. and Jean V. Berlin (eds.). *Sherman's Civil War: Selected Correspondence of William T. Sherman, 1860-1865* (Chapel Hill, North Carolina: University of North Carolina Press), 1999.

Soley, James Russell. *Admiral Porter* (New York: D. Appleton and Company), 1903.

Sparks, David S. (ed.). *Inside Lincoln's Army: The Diary of Marsena Rudolph Patrick* (New York: Thomas Yoseloff), 1964.

Stahr, Walter. *Seward: Lincoln's Indispensable Man* (New York: Simon & Schuster), 2012.

Stevens, Hazard. "The Storming of the Lines of Petersburg by the Sixth Corps, April 2, 1865," *Papers of the Military Historical Society of Massachusetts* (Boston, Massachusetts: The Military Historical Society of Massachusetts), 1907.

Stiles, Robert. *Four Years Under Marse Robert* (New York, Neale Publishing Company), 1904.

Taylor, John M. *William Henry Seward: Lincoln's Right Hand* (Washington, D.C.: Brassey's), 1991.

Thomas, Benjamin P. (ed.). *Three Years with Grant: As Recalled by War Correspondent Sylvanus Cadwallader* (New York: Alfred A. Knopf), 1955.

Thomas, Benjamin P. and Harold M. Hyman. *Stanton: The Life and Times of Lincoln's Secretary of War* (New York: Alfred A. Knopf), 1962.

Tilney, Robert. *My Life in the Army* (Philadelphia, Pennsylvania: Ferris & Leach), 1912.

Tobie, Edward P. "Personal Recollections of General Sheridan," In *Personal Narratives of Events in the War of the Rebellion, Being Papers Read Before the Rhode Island Soldiers and Sailors Historical Society* (Providence, Rhode Island: Published by the Society), 1888-1890.

Turner, Justin G. and Linda Levitt Turner (eds.). *Mary Todd Lincoln: Her Life and Letters* (New York: Fromm International Publishing Corporation), 1987.

Van Deusen, Glyndon G. *William Henry Seward* (New York: Oxford University Press), 1967.

Walker, James A. "Gordon's Assault on Fort Stedman," *Southern Historical Society Papers*, volume 31, (January-December 1903).

Weitzel, Godfrey. *Richmond Occupied: Entry of the United States Forces into Richmond, Va., April 3, 1865 – Calling Together of the Virginia Legislature and Revocation of the Same* (Richmond, Virginia: Richmond Civil War Centennial Committee), 1965.

Welles, Gideon. "Lincoln and Johnson," *The Galaxy,* volume 13, issue 4, April 1872.

_____. *Diary of Gideon Welles* (New York: Houghton Mifflin Company, 3 volumes), 1911.

West Jr., Richard S. *The Second Admiral: A Life of David Dixon Porter* (New York: Coward-McCann, Inc.), 1937.

Wharff, William H., "From Chapin's Farm to Appomattox," *The Maine Bugle*, campaign 3, call 4 (October 1896).

Wilson, James Harrison. *The Life of Charles A. Dana* (New York: Harper & Brothers Publishers), 1907.

_____. *The Life of John A. Rawlins* (New York: Neale Publishing Company), 1916.

Woods, George Bryant. *Essays, Sketches, and Stories* (Boston, Massachusetts: James R. Osgood and Company), 1873.

Wright, Cathy. "Mary O'Meilia: Irish Immigrant, Confederate Housekeeper," *The Museum of the Confederacy Magazine*, Summer 2014.

Unit Histories

Albert, Allen D. (ed.). *History of the Forty-fifth Regiment Pennsylvania Veteran Volunteer Infantry* (Williamsport, Pennsylvania: Grit Publishing Company), 1912.

Allen, George H. *Forty-six Months with the Fourth R.I. Volunteers* (Providence, Rhode Island: J.A. & R.A. Reid, Printers), 1887.

Aubery, James Madison. *The Thirty-sixth Wisconsin Volunteer Infantry* (Milwaukee, Wisconsin: Evening Wisconsin Co.), 1900.

Bartlett, A. W. *History of the Twelfth Regiment New Hampshire Volunteers* (Concord, New Hampshire: Ira C. Evans, Printer), 1897.

Beach, William H. *The First New York (Lincoln) Cavalry* (Milwaukee, Wisconsin: Burdick & Allen Printers), 1902.

Beecher, Herbert W. *History of the First Light Battery Connecticut Volunteers, 1861-1865* (New York: A.T. de la Mare Printing and Publishing Company, 2 volumes), 1905.

Best, Isaac O. *History of the 121st New York State Infantry* (Chicago, Illinois: W.S. Conkey Co.), 1921.

Brewer, Abraham T. *History Sixty-first Pennsylvania Volunteers, 1861-1865* (Pittsburgh, Pennsylvania: Art Engraving and Printing Company), 1911.

Caldwell, J. F. J. *The History of a Brigade of South Carolinians* (Philadelphia, Pennsylvania: King & Baird Printers), 1866.

Clark, Walter (ed.). *Histories of the Several Regiments and Battalions from North Carolina in the Great War, 1861-'65* (Goldsboro, North Carolina: Nash Brothers, printer, 5 volumes), 1901.

Cheek, Philip. *History of the Sauk County Riflemen* (Madison, Wisconsin: Democrat Printing Co.), 1909.

Cheney, Newel. *History of the Ninth Regiment, New York Volunteer Cavalry* (Poland Center, New York: Jamestown, Martin Merz & Son), 1901.

Cunningham, John L. *Three Years with the Adirondack Regiment, 118th New York Volunteers Infantry* (Norwood, Massachusetts: The Plimpton Press), 1920.

Cushman, Frederick E. *History of the 58th Regiment Massachusetts Volunteers* (Washington, D.C.: Gibson Brothers, Printers), 1865.

Day, William Albertus. *A True History of Company I, 49th Regiment North Carolina Troops in the Great Civil War* (Newton, North Carolina: Enterprise Job Office), 1893.

Denison, Frederic. *Sabres and Spurs: The First Regiment Rhode Island Cavalry in the Civil War* (Central Falls, Rhode Island: Press of E.L Freeman & Co.), 1876.

Dowdey, Clifford and Louis H. Manarin. *The Wartime Papers of R.E. Lee* (New York: Bramhall House), 1961.

Haines, William P. *History of the Men of Co. F the 12th New Jersey Volunteers* (Camden, New Jersey: C.S. Magrath, Printer), 1897.

Haynes, Edwin M. *A History of the Tenth Regiment, Vermont Volunteers* (Lewiston, Maine: Journal Steam Press), 1870.

History of the Thirty-fifth Regiment Massachusetts Volunteers, 1862-1865 (Boston, Massachusetts: Mills, Knight & Co.), 1884.

Hopkins, William Palmer. *The Seventh Regiment Rhode Island Volunteers in the Civil War* (Providence, Rhode Island: Providence Press), 1903.

Kreutzer, William. *Notes and Observations made during four years of service with the Ninety-Eighth N.Y. Volunteers* (Philadelphia, Pennsylvania: Grant, Faires & Rodgers, Printers), 1878.

Lewis, George. *History of Battery E, First Regiment Rhode Island Light Artillery in the War of 1861 and 1865 to Preserve the Union* (Providence, Rhode Island: Snow & Farnham), 1909.

Livermore, Thomas L. *History of the Eighteenth New Hampshire Volunteers* (Boston, Massachusetts: The Fort Hill Press), 1904.

Muffly, J.W. (ed.). *The Story of Our Regiment* (Des Moines, Iowa: Kenyon Printing & Manufacturing Co.), 1904.

Mulholland, St. Clair Augustin. *Story of the 116th Regiment* (Philadelphia, Pennsylvania: F. McManus Jr. & Co.), 1899.

Rauscher, Frank. *Music on the March* (Philadelphia, Pennsylvania: Press of William Fell and Company), 1892.

Rogers, William H. *History of the One Hundred and Eighty-Ninth Regiment of New-York Volunteers* (New York: John A. Gray & Green, Printers), 1865.

The Sixty-Seventh Ohio Veteran Volunteer Infantry (Massillon, Ohio: Massillon Printing and Publishing Co.), 1922.

The Story of One Regiment, the Eleventh Maine Infantry Volunteers in the War of the Rebellion (New York: J.J. Little & Co.), 1896.

Thomas, Henry W. *History of the Doles-Cook Brigade* (Atlanta, Georgia: The Franklin Printing and Publishing Company), 1903.

Vaill, Theodore F. *History of the Second Connecticut Volunteer Heavy Artillery* (Winsted, Connecticut: Winsted Printing Co.), 1868.

Willson, Arabella M. *Disaster, Struggle, Triumph* (Albany, New York: Argus Co.), 1870.

Woodward, E. Morrison. *History of the One Hundred and Ninety-Eighth Regiment Pennsylvania Volunteers* (Trenton, New Jersey: MacCrellish & Quigley, Book and Job Printers), 1884.

Secondary Sources

Andrews, J. Cutler. *The North Reports the Civil War* (Pittsburgh, Pennsylvania: University of Pittsburgh Press), 1983.

Barrett, John G. *Sherman's March Through the Carolinas* (Chapel Hill, North Carolina: University of North Carolina Press), 1956.

Bearss, Edwin and Chris M. Calkins. *Battle of Five Forks* (Lynchburg, Virginia: H.E. Howard), 1985.

Blue and Gray Magazine, "The General's Tour"

Calkins, Chris M., "The Battle of Five Forks: Final Push for the South Side," volume 9, issue 4 (April 1992).

Greene, A. Wilson, "April 2, 1865: Day of Decision at Petersburg," volume 18, issue 3 (Winter 2001).

Wyrick, William C., "Lee's Last Offensive: The Attack on Fort Stedman March 25, 1865, volume 25, issue 1 (2008).

_____. "Bursting of the Storm: Action at Petersburg March 25, 1865," volume 28, issue 5 (2012).

Boritt, Gabor S. (ed.). *Lincoln's Generals* (New York: Oxford University Press), 1994.

Brown, J. Willard. *The Signal Corps, U.S.A. in the War of the Rebellion* (Boston, Massachusetts: U.S. Veteran Signal Corps Association), 1896.

Catton, Bruce. *A Stillness at Appomattox* (Garden City, New York: Double & Company, Inc.), 1954.

Calkins, Chris M. *The Appomattox Campaign: March 29-April 9, 1865* (Conshohocken, Pennsylvania: Combined Books), 1997.

Coski, John M. *Capital Navy: The Men, Ships, and Operations of the James River Squadron* (Campbell, California: Savas Woodbury Publishers), 1996.

Crozier, Emmet. *Yankee Reporters: 1861-65* (Westport, Connecticut: Greenwood Press), 1956.

Davis, Burke. *To Appomattox: Nine April Days, 1865* (New York: Rinehart & Company, Inc.), 1959.

Furgurson, Ernest B. *Ashes of Glory: Richmond at War* (New York: Alfred A. Knopf), 1996.

_____. *Freedom Rising: Washington in the Civil War* (New York: Alfred A. Knopf), 2004.

Gates, Merrill E. *Men of Mark in America* (Washington, D.C.: Men of Mark Publishing Company, 2 volumes), 1905-06.

Glatthaar, Joseph T. *Partners in Command: the Relationships Between Leaders in the Civil War* (New York: The Free Press), 1994.

Greene, A. Wilson. *Breaking the Backbone of the Rebellion: The Final Battles of the Petersburg Campaign* (Mason City, Iowa: Savas Publishing Company), 2000.

_____. *Civil War Petersburg: Confederate City in the Crucible of War* (Charlottesville, Virginia: University of Virginia Press), 2006.

Guelzo, Allen C. "Holland's Informants: The Construction of Josiah Holland's 'Life of Abraham Lincoln,'" *Journal of the Abraham Lincoln Association*, Winter 2002.

Hanser, Richard. "Mr. Lincoln Visits Richmond," *The Saturday Review*, February 11, 1956.

Holzer, Harold. *When Lincoln and Son came to Richmond* (Commissioned by the United States Historical Society for the National Park Service), 2002.

Hubbard, Charles M. (ed.). *Lincoln Reshapes the Presidency* (Macon, Georgia: Mercer University Press), 2003.

Johnson, Rossiter. *The Story of a Great Conflict* (New York: Bryan, Taylor & Co.), 1894.

Johnston, W.J. *Telegraphic Tales and Telegraphic History* (New York: W.J. Johnston, Publisher), 1880.

Leech, Margaret. *Reveille in Washington* (New York: Carroll & Graf Publishers, Inc.), 1969.

Knight, Dean. "Lincoln's Dramatic Confederate White House Visit Recounted," *The Museum of the Confederacy Magazine*, Winter 2009.

Korn, Jerry. *Pursuit to Appomattox* (Alexandria, Virginia: Time-Life Books), 1987.

Krick, Robert K. *Civil War Weather in Virginia* (Tuscaloosa, Alabama: University of Alabama Press), 2007.

Lang, Theodore F. *Loyal West Virginia from 1861 to 1865* (Baltimore, Maryland: The Deutsch Publishing Co.), 1895.

Lankford, Nelson. *Richmond burning: The Last Days of the Confederate Capital* (New York: Viking), 2002.

Levine, Lawrence W. *Black Culture and Black Consciousness* (New York: Oxford University Press), 1977.

Magness, Phillip W. "Benjamin Butler's Colonization Testimony Reevaluated," *The Journal of the Abraham Lincoln Association*, volume 29, no. 1, Summer 2008.

O'Connor, Thomas H. "Lincoln and the Cotton Trade," *Civil War History*, Volume 7, Number 1, March 1961.

Page, Elwin L. *Lincoln on the River Queen* (Concord, New Hampshire: By Order of the House of Representatives), 1943.

Pfanz, Donald C. *Abraham Lincoln at City Point: March 20-April 9, 1865* (Lynchburg, Virginia: H.E. Howard, Inc.), 1989.

_____. *The Depot Field Hospital at City Point,* study prepared for the National Park Service, 1988.

Robertson Jr., James I. (ed.). "English Views of the Civil War," *The Virginia Magazine of History and Biography,* volume 77, April 1969.

Scharf, J. Thomas. *History of the Confederate States Navy* (New York: Rogers & Sherwood), 1887.

Sedgwick, Ellery. *The Happy Profession* (Boston, Massachusetts: Little, Brown and Company), 1946.

Shenk, Joshua Wolf. *Lincoln's Melancholy* (New York: Houghton Mifflin Company), 2005.

Stackpole, Edouard A. "The 'River Queen,'" *Yankee Magazine,* February 1969.

Starr, Louis M. *Reporting the Civil War* (New York: Collier Books), 1962.

Starr, Stephen Z. *The Union Cavalry in the Civil War* (Baton Rouge, Louisiana: Louisiana State University Press, 3 volumes), 1981.

Temple, Wayne C. *Lincoln's Travels on the River Queen During the Last Days of His Life* (Mahomet, Illinois: Mayhaven Publishing), 2007.

_____. "Mary Todd Lincoln's Travels,'" *Lincoln Sesquicentennial Commission,* Lincoln Sesquicentennial, 1809-1959.

Trefousse, Hans L. *Andrew Johnson: A Biography* (New York: W.W. Norton & Company), 1989.

Trudeau, Noah Andre. *The Last Citadel: Petersburg, Virginia, June 1864-April 1865* (El Dorado Hills, California: Savas Beatie), 2014.

_____. *Out of the Storm: The End of the Civil War* (Boston, Massachusetts: Little, Brown and Company), 1994.

_____. *Like Men of War: Black Troops in the Civil War* (Boston, Massachusetts: Little, Brown and Company), 1998.

Woodard, David E. "Abraham Lincoln, Duff Green, and the Mysterious Trumbull Letter," *Civil War History,* volume 42, no. 3 (September 1996).

Zinnen Jr., Robert O. "City Point: The Tool That Gave General Grant Victory," *Quartermaster Professional Bulletin,* Spring 1991.

Miscellaneous Works

[WJLA-ABC (Washington, DC) Meteorologist] Doug Hill, email to the author, April 17, 2012.

Keim, B. Randolph. *A Guide to the Potomac River, Chesapeake Bay and James River* (Washington, D.C.: The Compiler), 1881.

National Archives & Records Administration: Register of Meteorological Observations, under direction of the Smithsonian Institution (RG 27 Records of the Weather Bureau).

National Park Service. *Civil War City Point: 1864-1865 Period of Significance Landscape Documentation,* July 2009.

Acknowledgments

My research for this book directed me to archives and materials not heretofore utilized in Lincoln studies. Time and again, my poking around turned a faint lead into something more tangible, and led me to individuals at archives, libraries, and reference centers, whose assistance was critical in locating an item and making it available. I did my best to keep a running log, but my apologies to anyone not on this list who should be:

Abraham Lincoln Presidential Library: James M. Cornelius, Lincoln Collection Curator.

Archives of Manitoba: M. Christopher Kotecki.

Berea College, Hutchins Library, Special Collections & Archives: Jaime Marie Bradley.

The Huntington Library, Norris Foundation Curator of American Historical Manuscripts: Olga Tsapina.

Maine Historical Society: Jamie Kingman Rice.

Marine Corps Archives, History Division and Gray Research Center: J. Michael Miller.

National Archives and Records Administration: Mark C. Mollan, Archivist Old Navy/Maritime Reference

National Park Service: Roger Powell (Washington, D.C.: Ford's Theater), Robert E. L. Krick and Mike Gorman (Richmond National Battlefield), and James Blankenship and Chris Bryce (Petersburg National Battlefield).

Naval Surface Warfare Center (Carderock Division): Dana Wegner, Curator of Ship Models.

New York State Library, Manuscripts and Special Collections: Victor DesRosiers.

Sailor's Creek Battlefield (Virginia State Parks): Chris M. Calkins, Park Manager and Historian.

Senate House State Historic Site (Kingston, New York): Deana Preston.

University of Rochester Rare Books & Special Collections: Lori Birrell.

Thanks and tips of the hat to Pauline Roberts, who shared fine transcriptions of letters from her ancestor, Civil War soldier Cyrus T. Goodwin; and to Bermuda Hundred Campaign Historian and Preservationist George L. Fickett Jr., for a memorable tour of Point of Rocks. A special thanks to the descendents of John Sanford Barnes for alerting me to the existence of the *Egotistigraphy*, also providing an unpublished image of the man, as well as their interest and efforts to locate his wartime letters to his wife, a campaign that has yet to be crowned with success. I am grateful to the Lincoln scholar, Dr. Wayne C. Temple, for his advice and encouragement.

I would be remiss if I did not express my awe for the work of Tom Tryniski. His website (www.fultonhistory.com) is an unparalleled free archive of (mostly) New York state historic newspapers, all accessible via a reasonably efficient search engine, and which provided a rich trove of Lincoln witnesses. As one example, it led me to the 1885 letter from Hanson Risley (an upstate New York favorite son) confirming my supposition that he met with Lincoln and Grant at City Point in March 1865.

There are thanks due to Roy Feinson who skillfully revived several images that existed only in mediocre copies. And to Kee Malesky, who copy edited the manuscript and got me in tune (mostly) with the *Chicago Manual of Style*. Finally, my deep personal thanks to Theodore P. Savas, of Savas Beatie, for his belief in the book, and his willingness to publish the manuscript.

And in the last but certainly not the least category, applause applause for Donald C. Pfanz, whose groundbreaking investigation of Lincoln's visit opened my mind to the possibilities and whose support has been unstinting.

Index

Fox, Gustavus V., coordinates Lincoln's City Point visit, 8-10
"Frank," 235
Gilson, Helen L., 238-239
Givin, William J., 199
Goodwin, Cyrus T., 165, 177, 237
Gordon, John B., 24, 26-34, 146-147; plans Fort Stedman attack, 16-18
Gould, Charles G., 148
Grant, C. Hull, 239
Grant, Clara, 4
Grant, Julia, 3-4, 37, 77-78, 93, 240; accompanies Mary Lincoln March 26: 55-56, 59-60; accompanies Mary Lincoln March 27: 69-70; lobbies for Lincoln visit, 6-7; meets Mary Lincoln March 24: 22; refuses to join Lincolns at Ford's Theater, 258; visits Richmond April 6: 218-219; image, xiv
Grant, Jesse, 37, 58-59; image, xiv
Grant, Ulysses S., 4-7, 31, 36, 93; accompanies Lincoln March 25: 37-45; decision to pre-approve Warren's relief, 132-133; departs City Point for spring offensive, 92-95; invites Lincoln to visit, 7; invites Lincoln to visit front April 2: 156; leadership, 98, 108, 112-113, 114, 126-127, 144, 152-154, 155-156, 163, 164, 172-173, 206, 210-211, 219; plans Petersburg spring offensive, 20, 23, 61, 62, 64-65, 87; post surrender meeting with Lee, 261; presidency influenced by Lincoln, 260-261; relationship with Lincoln, 6, 61, 98, 260; relationship with Sheridan, 5-6, 48-50, 87, 112-113; relationship with Sherman, 5, 74-79, 81; River Queen conference with Lincoln, Sherman, Porter, March 28: 82-86; surrender exchanges with Lee, 225, 226, 227, 242-243, 245-246, 247; surrender meeting with Lee April 9: 248-250; visits Lincoln with Leggett and Patrick March 27: 72; visits Lincoln with Sherman March 27: 76-77; images, xiv; 49, 83, 171
Gravelly Run, 97
Graveyard Reach, 181
Green, Duff, 195-196

Gregory, Edgar M., 100
Griffin, Charles, 115
Halleck, Henry W., 87
Hampton Roads Peace Conference, 23
Hancock Station (USMRR), 165; image, 94
Harlan, Ann, 217
Harlan, James, 217, 252
Harlan, Mary, 217
Harrison, William Henry, 48
Hartsuff, George L., 77, 224
Hatcher's Run, 89, 95
Hendrick, Leonard A., 43
Halifax Road, 43
Harris, Clara, 10
Healy, George, 82
Hill, Ambrose Powell, 150
Holloway, John B., 235
Houghton, Charles H., 238
Huidekoper, Henry S. 220-221
Humphreys Station (USMRR), 98
Ingalls, Rufus, 78, 112
James, William L., 19
James River, 3, 8, 15, 20, 52, 53, 96, 159, 177, 179, 225; 230, 241; military obstacles, 182
Jeff Davis (horse), 38
Jerusalem Plank Road, 90, 144, 146, 153, 154, 164, 168, 170
Johnson, Bushrod, 95, 97
Johnston, Joseph E., 15, 87
Kautz, August V., 38, 192, 196-197
Keckly, Elizabeth, 217-218, 228, 240, 252; visits Petersburg April 7, 222-225
Kennard, Thomas W., 228, 230
Kimball, Jamain, 108
Kettles, William E., 166-167
Lee, Agnes, 86, 95
Lee, Fitzhugh, 15
Lee, Robert E., 15, 33-34, 40, 45, 86, 132; April 2 actions, 150-151; countermoves to Grant's spring offensive, 95, 109; post-surrender meeting with Grant April 10: 261; strategic options March 1865, 15-18, 23; surrender meeting with Grant April 9: 248-250
Leggett, Mortimer D., 87; visits Lincoln March 27: 72

Robert Malesky

About the Author

Noah Andre Trudeau is a history graduate of the State University of New York at Albany. His first book, *Bloody Roads South*, won the Civil War Round Table of New York's prestigious Fletcher Pratt Award, and enjoyed a cameo appearance in the hit web television series *House of Cards*. His fourth book, *Like Men of War*, a combat history of black troops in the Civil War, was honored with the Grady McWhiney Research Foundation's Jerry Coffey Memorial Book Prize. His other books include a best-selling history of the Battle of Gettysburg, Sherman's "March to the Sea," a compact biography of Robert E. Lee, and a revised and expanded 150th Anniversary edition of *The Last Citadel: Petersburg, June 1864 — April 1865* (Savas Beatie, 2014).